European Disability Pension Policies

Public Policy and Social Welfare
A Series Edited by Bernd Marin

**European Centre Vienna**

Volume 26

Christopher Prinz (Ed.)

European Disability Pension Policies

11 Country Trends 1970-2002

With an Introduction by Bernd Marin

LONDON AND NEW YORK

First published 2003 by Ashgate Publishing

Reissued 2018 by Routledge
2 Park Square, Milton Park, Abingdon, Oxon OX14 4RN
711 Third Avenue, New York, NY 10017, USA

Routledge is an imprint of the Taylor & Francis Group, an informa business

Copyright © European Centre Vienna, 2003

All rights reserved. No part of this book may be reprinted or reproduced or utilised in any form or by any electronic, mechanical, or other means, now known or hereafter invented, including photocopying and recording, or in any information storage or retrieval system, without permission in writing from the publishers.

Notice:
Product or corporate names may be trademarks or registered trademarks, and are used only for identification and explanation without intent to infringe.

Publisher's Note
The publisher has gone to great lengths to ensure the quality of this reprint but points out that some imperfections in the original copies may be apparent.

Disclaimer
The publisher has made every effort to trace copyright holders and welcomes correspondence from those they have been unable to contact.

Copy-editing and DTP: Willem Stamatiou

A Library of Congress record exists under LC control number: 2003545090

ISBN 13: 978-1-138-72658-1 (hbk)
ISBN 13: 978-1-138-72653-6 (pbk)
ISBN 13: 978-1-315-19131-7 (ebk)

Contents

List of Figures and Tables   7

Preface: Recent European Centre Disability
Welfare Studies and the OECD Report 2003   13
Bernd Marin

PART A: INTRODUCTION AND THEORETICAL OVERVIEW   21

Chapter 1
Transforming Disability Welfare Policy.
Completing A Paradigm Shift   23
Bernd Marin

Chapter 2
Disability and Disability Insurance   77
Philip R. de Jong

PART B: COUNTRY TRENDS   107

Chapter 3
Disability Pensions in Austria   109
Karl Wörister

Chapter 4
Disability Pensions: Trends and Policies in Denmark   139
Per H. Jensen

Chapter 5
Disability Pensions in Finland   165
Raija Gould

Chapter 6
Disability Pensions in Germany 197
Holger Viebrok

Chapter 7
Disability Pensions in Italy: The Law and the Numbers 225
Emanuele Baldacci / Gustavo De Santis

Chapter 8
The Dutch Disability Experience 253
Leo Aarts / Philip R. de Jong

Chapter 9
Disability Pensions and Social Security in Norway 277
Svenn-Åge Dahl / Hans-Tore Hansen

Chapter 10
Invalidity Pensions: Trends and Policies in Poland 317
Stanislawa Golinowska / Katarzyna Pietka

Chapter 11
Invalidity Pensions: The Case of Slovenia 345
Cveto Ursic / Tine Stanovnik

Chapter 12
Social Security and Disability in Sweden 369
Agneta Kruse

Chapter 13
The Particularities of Swiss Invalidity Insurance 393
Christopher Prinz / Bruno Nydegger Lory

List of Contributors 425

List of Figures and Tables

List of Figures

Chapter 2: Disability and Disability Insurance

Scheme 1:	Etiology of work disability	81
Scheme 2:	Social versus private insurance	88

Chapter 3: Disability Pensions in Austria

Figure 1:	All early retirement pensions and unemployed	129
Figure 2:	Disability rates, 1970-2000	129
Figure 3:	Disability pensions: per cent of all first-time pensioners	132

Chapter 5: Disability Pensions in Finland

Figure 1:	New disability pensions under the private sector earnings-related pension scheme, 1970-2001	180
Figure 2:	Incidence of new recipients of earnings-related pensions in the private sector, 55-64 years of age	186
Figure 3:	Incidence of ordinary disability pensions by disease category under the private earnings-related scheme, 1990-2001 (age-standardized)	190
Figure 4:	Rejection rate for new earnings-related disability pensions in the private sector and unemployment rate 1970-2001	192

Chapter 6: Disability Pensions in Germany

Figure 1: Share of occupational disability pensions in all new disability pensions 1960-1999 — 205

Figure 2: Pensions because of incapacity to work: average pension by age at the beginning of the pension (new pensions 1999) — 210

Figure 3: Effect of the 2000 reform on the disability pension level — 219

Figure 4: Pensions because of incapacity to work: frequency of new pensions in Germany per age group of the population in 1999 by age at beginning of the pension — 220

Chapter 7: Disability Pensions in Italy: The Law and the Numbers

Figure 1: How to access a disability benefit in Italy — 226

Figure 2: Beneficiaries (aged 15-64) of Social Security disability pensions in Italy, 1975-1998 — 240

Figure 3: New beneficiaries (aged 15-64) of Social Security disability pensions in Italy, 1975-1998 — 241

Figure 4: Percentage disabled by sex and age group, Italy 1995 — 243

Chapter 12: Social Security and Disability in Sweden

Figure 1: Sick leave incidence by age and socio-economic group in 1998-1999 — 382

List of Tables

Chapter 2: Disability and Disability Insurance

Table 1: Self-reported disability and disability beneficiaries as a percentage of the 20-64 population, 1999 — 82

Chapter 3: Disability Pensions in Austria

Table 1: Net pension in per cent of most recent net income — 113

Table 2:	Working age recipients of welfare benefits 1999	128
Table 3:	Frequency of sickness and disability risk 1995	132
Table 4:	Causes of disability by age, 1999	134

Chapter 4: Disability Pensions: Trends and Policies in Denmark

| Table 1: | Rates of disability pensions (January 1999) | 148 |
| Table 2: | Numbers of reported and recognised accidents at work in 1999 distributed by age | 153 |

Chapter 5: Disability Pensions in Finland

Table 1:	Recipients of disability pension under different pension schemes in 2001	168
Table 2:	Earnings-related disability pensions in the private sector in 2001	171
Table 3:	Rejection rate for new earnings-related disability pensions in the private sector in 2001 (in %)	191

Chapter 6: Disability Pensions in Germany

Table 1:	Minimum requirements for pensions from the statutory pension scheme (excluding miners' association), as of 2001	206
Table 2:	Raising the retirement age in Germany (as of December 2000)	209
Table 3:	Earnings limits as a function of the share of the occupational disability pension being drawn (until the end of 2000)	211
Table 4:	Duration of unemployment benefits according to length of service and age	213

Chapter 7: Disability Pensions in Italy: The Law and the Numbers

| Table 1: | Pension benefits provided to disabled people (or their survivors) in Italy in year 2000: a general overview | 228 |
| Table 2: | Ratios of disability allowance to unemployment benefits | 234 |

Table 3:	Labour force and disability pensioners in Italy, by gender (age: 15-64)	241
Table 4:	Incidence of disability and unemployment in Italy, by geographical area (age: 15-64)	244

Chapter 9: Disability Pensions and Social Security in Norway

Table 1:	Number of new early retirees aged 60-66 years by early retirement regime, 1993-1997	292

Chapter 10: Invalidity Pensions: Trends and Policies in Poland

Table 1:	Structure of assigned invalidity pensions by the degree of incapacity for work	318
Table 2:	Comparison: disability assessment institutions and the object of assessment	322
Table 3:	Farming and working disability pension	328
Table 4:	Development of unemployment and disabled levels	331
Table 5:	Balance of changes in population on the labour market – increases/decreases compared to previous year	334

Chapter 11: Invalidity Pensions: The Case of Slovenia

Table 1:	Ratio of net old-age pension and disability pension to net average wage (in %), Slovenia, 1991-1999	347
Table 2:	Pension beneficiaries (by type of pension) and contributors (active insurers), Slovenia, 1990-1999	348
Table 3:	The outlays of the Institute for Pension and Disability Insurance as percentage of GDP, Slovenia, 1991-1999	348
Table 4:	The number of recipients of disability pensions, disability benefits and other disability-related compensations, Slovenia, 1970-1999	362
Table 5:	The structure of outlays of the Institute for Pension and Disability Insurance of Slovenia, 1980-1999	365

List of Figures and Tables

Chapter 12: Social Security and Disability in Sweden

Table 1:	Public expenditure on disability pensions, number of disability pensioners and newly granted disability pensioners	370
Table 2:	Housing supplements to disability pensions	374
Table 3:	Partial pensions. Number in 1000s	377
Table 4:	Disability pensioners by sex and age	378
Table 5:	Newly-granted disability pensions by sex and age per 1000 insured excluding disability pensioners	379
Table 6:	Gender differences in newly-granted disability pensions, 1996	380
Table 7:	Newly-granted disability pensions in a sample of regions, per 1000 insured excluding those with a disability pension	381
Table 8:	Number of disability pensioners by citizenship. Percentage of the population aged 16-64. Age-standardized, 1994	383
Table 9:	Newly-granted disability pensions by sex. Total number in hundreds and per cent receiving a full pension	384
Table 10:	Sick leave incidence rate by sex and age, 1987-1999	387

Chapter 13: The Particularities of Swiss Invalidity Insurance

Table 1:	Supplements to pensionable earnings in per cent, by age at onset of the disability	399
Table 2:	Expenditure by the public invalidity insurance 1965-1999	405
Table 3:	Development of the number of disability benefit recipients, 1986-2000	407
Table 4:	Disability benefit recipients by degree of disability, 1990 and 1998	408
Table 5:	Disability benefit recipients by cause of disability, 1982-1997	408
Table 6:	Disability prevalence rates by age and gender 1986-2000	410
Table 7:	Disability incidence rates by age and gender in 1999, and estimates from stock data for the years 1985 and 1995	411

Table 8:	Disability benefit recipients per 1000 employed in 1995, and increase in the number of disability benefit recipients 1982-98, by canton	412
Table 9:	Ratio between recipients of rehabilitation measures and recipients of disability pensions 1991 and 1997, and annual percentage growth in the number of recipients of rehabilitation measures between 1991 and 1997, by canton	414

Preface: Recent European Centre Disability Welfare Studies and the OECD Report 2003

Bernd Marin

European Centre Work on Disability Welfare

Since many years, the European Centre has been actively involved in studying disability issues and suggesting ideas as how to improve living conditions of people with impairments as well as effectiveness of policies towards persons with handicaps. Recently, its programme on "Ageing, Care Policies, and Social Services" has contributed to the comparative study "Definitions of Disability in Europe: A Comparative Analysis", financed by the Commission of the European Communities, DGV, and coordinated by Brunel University, United Kingdom (Giedenbacher/Strümpel, 2001). Another most recent study on "Labour Market Policies in Favour of Disabled People, Migrant Workers and Women in Nine Countries", carried out for the University of Leuven (for submission to the Government of Flanders) was completed in early 2003.

In the second half of the 1990s, the *Autonome Provinz Bozen / Provincia Autonoma di Bolzano, Regione Trentino – Alto Adige* commissioned the establishment of a new care allowance scheme, which should combine the best practices of the Austrian, German and the Luxembourg institutions, to the European Centre: the Centre designed a new *Pflegeversicherung / La copertura previdenziale per non autosufficienti* institutionally, prepared a care allowance / disability classification scheme, accompanied its implementation scientifically, and evaluated the first steps of this institutional innovation in the years

2000 to 2002 (Leichsenring/Prinz, 1997; Leichsenring, 2001a, b). With respect to its interest in and competence regarding care allowance regulations in a comparative European perspective, the European Centre has already been active in the early 1990s in contributing to prepare the establishment of a *Pflegegeldgesetz* in the Host Country (Evers/Leichsenring/Pruckner, 1992; Evers/Pijl/Ungerson, 1994).

Another study on "Social Public Services: Quality of Working Life and Quality of Services", commissioned by the European Foundation for the Improvement of Living and Working Conditions, Dublin, has been completed in 1999. In the mid-1990s, employment policies for people with disabilities, questions of mandatory employment or equal opportunities (Leichsenring/Strümpel, 1995), of vocational integration of persons with disabilities (Leichsenring/Strümpel, 1997), the working and housing conditions of persons with disabilities, in particular alternatives to nursing homes (Leichsenring/Strümpel/Groupe Saumon, 1998), better care for dependent people living at home (Evers/van der Zanden, 1993), organizational responses to HIV and AIDS-management (Kenis/Marin, 1997), client's rights (Evers/Leichsenring/Strümpel, 1995) and developing quality in personal social services (Evers et al., 1997), as well as new housing and living experiments of persons with mental disabilities have been investigated, both on the level of single provinces as well as in a European comparative perspective (Leichsenring/Strümpel/Groupe Saumon, 1998).

Currently, within the framework of the European Union LEONARDO-programme, a project on "Stakeholders' Views of Supported Employment Initiatives – Quality Criteria and Development" is under way: case studies of suppliers of supported employment programmes in five European (European Union, accession, and non-EU-OECD) countries, namely the United Kingdom, Austria, Norway, the Czech Republic and Hungary are carried-out in order to test which quality criteria are most relevant for which of the stakeholders such as labour force participants with disabilities, employees of service providers, employers, and financial supporters. The mix of countries chosen allowed for cross-national comparisons of and an interesting exchange of experiences between countries with highly divergent philosophies and institutions of supported employment programmes, as has been demonstrated by the final concluding conference in October 2002 in Budapest (Strümpel et al., 2002).

Towards the end of 1998, after successfully bidding for a tender by the Swiss Federal Office of Social Insurance (*Bundesamt für Sozialversicherung,*

Bern) on *"Invalidenversicherung: Europäische Entwicklungstendenzen zur Invalidität im Erwerbsalter"*, the European Centre's programme on "Social Policy Modelling" has started to look into developments in disability pension policies throughout Europe (Prinz, 1999). Originally, seven countries have been covered; in a second round by extending the original investigation towards a broader domain, four more countries have been additionally included so that the following countries are now being taken into account in analysing disability pensions in Europe: Austria, Denmark, Finland, Germany, Italy, Netherlands, Norway, Poland, Slovenia, Sweden, and Switzerland.

The resulting series of 11 country case studies prepared by national experts on the basis of a unified framework are assembled in this collected volume. With respect to comparative lessons to be drawn, a few insights are systematically reviewed in a theoretical chapter in this book (Chapter by Philip R. de Jong), where a conceptual framework on disability insurance is developed and illustrated if not tested by empirical evidence from the country studies. A more comprehensive view on disability welfare policy achievements and failures and more systematic comparative analysis – thereby drawing extensively on material published recently by the OECD (see below) – is presented in the introduction to this book (Chapter by Bernd Marin). Some findings to be generalized and some wider policy conclusions to be derived from, yet smaller, comparative empirical material were already to be found in another book published earlier (Prinz, 1999a).

The OECD Report "Transforming Disability into Ability"

The full wealth of geographical domain covered, data generated, analytical dimensions included, evidence reviewed, alternative hypotheses tested and policy conclusions corroborated or rejected is to be looked up in a companion volume to this book. This publication is based on another study managed by the editor of this volume. It is in many ways an extension and follow-up to the present study, published simultaneously with this book – the new OECD report on *Transforming Disability into Ability. Polices to Promote Work and Income Security for Disabled People* (OECD, 2003). What about these two efforts and how do they relate to each other?

Work on disability pensions carried out at the European Centre in 1999 coincided with efforts by the OECD, Social Policy Division of the Directorate for Employment, Labour and Social Affairs, in Paris to launch a project on "Policies to Support and Integrate Working Age People with Disabilities". In this process, Christopher Prinz as the author of this study at the European Centre has been hired temporarily to coordinate also the OECD project and to draft the resulting report available in autumn 2002 and released in February 2003. This project extended the focus from disability pension policies to employment and rehabilitation policies for disabled people, thereby moving much closer to some of the work undertaken earlier and still by the European Centre's programme on "Ageing, Care Policies, and Social Services" (Leichsenring/Strümpel, 1995; Giedenbacher/Strümpel, 2001).

"Transforming Disability into Ability" summarises findings and policy conclusions of the OECD project, which was launched in April 2000 and covered 20 OECD Member Countries – and thus a significantly broader country domain than the present volume: while it covered almost all countries taken into account in this book (with the exception of Finland and Slovenia), it additionally included an interesting diversity of other countries such as Belgium, Canada, France, Portugal, Spain, Turkey, the United Kingdom and the United States, as well as three Non-UN-European countries. In sum, the empirical base for this follow-up and partly overlapping study has been quite impressive: 17 UN-European countries (Austria, Belgium, Canada, Denmark, France, Germany, Italy, the Netherlands, Norway, Poland, Portugal, Spain, Sweden, Switzerland, Turkey, the United Kingdom and the United States), and three Non-UN-European countries (Australia, Korea and Mexico).

The OECD project built on the findings of a more comprehensive and systematic data collection on more countries, but also on the results of the case studies assembled in this book, while it went beyond disability benefit trends: it aimed at investigating the relationship between and coherence of compensatory disability policies for the working-age population on the one hand, and activation or employment-oriented policies on the other. In both projects and books, working age is defined as the 20-64 age range, irrespective of diverging legal retirement ages. Disability is defined in a very broad sense as a "self-reported limitation in relation to activities of daily living"; thus, a person would have to report a long-term health condition *and* a limitation in daily activities resulting from this health problem. Covering severely disabled people as well as people with chronic conditions such as back pain, on the basis of this definition typically about 14% of the working age population in OECD countries are classified as disabled, around a third of them as severely disabled.

The success of labour market integration policies for people with disabilities cannot be tested or benchmarked without careful consideration of compensatory benefit systems; and vice versa.

The OECD study looked at combinations of and trade-offs between activation measures on the one hand and income replacement policies on the other. A typology developed in order to classify disability policies according to their orientation along these two dimensions is used to explain varying disability benefit recipiency rates as well as the highly divergent employment rates of people with disabilities compared with the population at large. While the study started on the assumption that policy matters and that variation in outcomes may be sufficiently well explained by decision-making and policy parameters, only a few simple and robust relations between outcomes and different policies could be established. Hence, whereas bad practices could quite easily be recognized in several dimensions, and good practices could be found in a number of fields in a number of countries, *best practices* or more precisely: *best overall disability policy packages* are so far *simply not to be identified*.

Bernd Marin

Selected European Centre Publications on Disability Welfare

Evers, A./ Leichsenring, K./Pruckner, B.(1992) *Pflegegeld in Europa*. Wien: Bundesministerium für Arbeit und Soziales.
Evers, A./van der Zanden, G.H. (Eds.) (1993) *Better Care for Dependent People Living at Home. Meeting the New Agenda in Services for the Elderly*. Bunnik: Netherlands Institute of Gerontology.
Evers, A./Pijl, M./Ungerson, S. (Eds.) (1994) *Payments for Care: A Comparative Overview*. Aldershot: Ashgate.
Evers, A./ Leichsenring, K./Strümpel, C. (1995) *Klientenrechte: Sozialpolitische Steuerung der Qualität von Hilfe und Pflege im Alter*. Wien: Bundesministerium für Arbeit und Soziales.
Evers, A./Haverinen, R./Leichsenring, K./Wistow, G. (Eds.) (1997) *Developing Quality in Personal Social Services. Concepts, Cases and Comments*. Aldershot: Ashgate.
Giedenbacher, Y./Strümpel, C. (2001) Definitions of Disability – Austrian Contribution to the EU Study: "Definitions of Disability in Europe: A Comparative Analysis". Vienna: European Centre.
Giedenbacher, Y./Stadler-Vida, M./Strümpel, Ch. (2002) *Stakeholders' Perspective of Quality in Supported Employment. An Evaluation Manual*. Vienna: European Centre.
Kenis, P./Marin, B. (Eds.) (1997) *Managing AIDS. Organizational Responses in Six European Countries*. Aldershot: Ashgate.
Kraan, R./ Leichsenring, K. (Eds.) (1995) *Managing Care and Welfare – Governmental and Non-Governmental Initiatives in Central European Countries*. Eurosocial Report No. 58. Vienna: European Centre.
Leichsenring, K. (1994) 'Dare all'utente la possibilità di decidere: i servizi di consulenza a sostegno delle strategie per una maggiore partecipazione in Austria', pp. 281-296 in: Ministero dell'Interno/Centro Europeo di Ricerca sulle Politiche Sociali (a cura di), *Innovazione e partecipazione nell'assistenza agli anziani: L'Italia incontra l'Europa*. Roma: Ministero dell'Interno (Studi ricerche e documentazioni).
Leichsenring, K. (1997) 'New Developments in Care and Welfare Policies in Europe', *Journal for Mental Changes. Perspectives of Economic, Political and Social Integration* 3 (2): 23-30.
Leichsenring, K. (Hg.) (1998) *Alternativen zum Heim / Alternatives to Nursing Homes*. Die "Groupe Saumon" und Innovative Projekte aus Europa / The "Salmon Group" and Innovative Projects from Europe. Wien: Bundesministerium für Arbeit und Soziales.
Leichsenring, K. (1999) 'El sistemo austriaco de protecciòn social para las personas necesitadas de cuidados', pp. 119-146 in: Observatorio de Personas Mayores (Ed.), *Vejez y protección social a la dependencia en Europa*. Madrid: Ministerio de Trabajo y Asuntos Sociales/IMSERSO.
Leichsenring, K. (2000) 'Internationale Trends der Privatisierung sozialer Dienste – Hintergründe und Entwicklungslinien am Beispiel der Reformen in Delft und Stockholm', S. 95-115 in: Boessenecker, K.-H./Trube, A./Wohlfahrt, N. (Hg.), *Privatisierung im Sozialsektor. Rahmenbedingungen, Verlaufsformen und Probleme der Ausgliederung sozialer Dienste*. Münster: Votum Verlag.
Leichsenring, K. (with Gerhard Majce and Sabine Pleschberger) (2001) 'Solidarity and Care in Austria', in: ter Meulen, R./Arts, W./Muffels, R. (Eds.), *Solidarity in Health and Social Care in Europe*. Dordrecht/Boston/London: Kluwer Academic Publishers.

Leichsenring, K. (2001a) Die Reform sozialer Pflege in Südtirol. Endbericht der wissenschaftlichen Begleitung im Auftrag der Autonomen Provinz Bozen – Assessorat für Personal-, Gesundheits- und Sozialwesen. Wien: Europäisches Zentrum.

Leichsenring, K. (2001b) Erhebung der individuellen Pflegebedürftigkeit. Test des adaptierten deutschen Einstufungsverfahren und dessen Konsequenzen in Südtirol. Endbericht im Auftrag der Autonomen Provinz Bozen – Assessorat für Personal-, Gesundheits- und Sozialwesen. Wien: Europäisches Zentrum.

Leichsenring, K./Prinz, Ch. (1997) Ausgewählte Aspekte der vorliegenden Optionen zur Pflegeversicherung in der Region Trentino–Alto Adige. Gutachten im Auftrag der Autonomen Provinz Bozen-Südtirol. Wien: Europäisches Zentrum.

Leichsenring, K./Strümpel, C. (1995) *Mandatory Employment or Equal Opportunities? Employment Policies for People with Disabilities in the UN-European Region*. Eurosocial Report No. 55. Vienna: European Centre.

Leichsenring, K./Strümpel, C. (1997) *Berufliche Integration behinderter Menschen: Innovative Projektbeispiele aus Europa*. Wien: Bundesministerium für Arbeit und Soziales.

Leichsenring, K./Stadler, M. (1998) Purchaser-Provider Relationships and Quality Assurance in the Area of Personal Social Services in Vienna. Austrian report in the framework of the EU project 'Qualification for Development' supported by the European Commission (DG XXIII). Vienna: European Centre.

Leichsenring, K./Stadler-Vida, M. (1999) Personal Social Services: Quality of Service and Quality of Working Conditions. Austrian Report as part of an international study for the European Foundation for the Improvement of Living and Working Conditions. Vienna: European Centre.

Leichsenring, K./Bahr, C./Strümpel, C. (1999) 'Political Participation of Older Citizens in Austria', pp. 65-82 in: Walker, A./Naegele, G. (Eds.), *The Politics of Old Age in Europe*. Buckingham: Open University Press.

Leichsenring, K./Strümpel, C./Groupe Saumon (1998) *L'accueil des personnes souffrant de démence en petites unites de vie*. Eurosocial Report No. 65. Vienna: European Centre.

Marin, B./Prinz, Ch. (2003) *Facts and Figures on Disability Welfare. A Pictographic Portrait of an OECD Report*. Vienna: European Centre.

Melvyn, P. (1993) *Social Integration and Vocational Rehabilitation for Persons with Mental Disabilities / L'Insertion Sociale et la Réadaptation Professionnelle des Personnes avec un Handicap Mental*, International Expert Meeting, Velm, Austria, 6-11 December 1991, Conference Report. Eurosocial Report No. 44. Vienna: European Centre.

Münz, A./Stadler-Vida, M./Strümpel, C./Kinds, H. (2001) Building Bridges for New Social Partnerships. Final Report. Vienna: Kinds Community Partnerships/European Centre.

OECD (2003, forthcoming) *Von Behinderung zu Beteiligung. Beschäftigung bei sicheren Einkommen*. Mit einer Einführung von Bernd Marin. Frankfurt/New York: Campus.

Prinz, C. (1999) *Invalidenversicherung: Europäische Entwicklungstendenzen zur Invalidität im Erwerbsalter*, Band 1, Forschungsbericht Nr.7/99. Bern: Bundesamt für Sozialversicherung.

Prinz, C. (1999a) 'Invaliditätspension als *die* Frühpension? Österreichische Entwicklungen im europäischen Vergleich', S. 417-483 in: Prinz, Ch./Marin, B. (Hg.), *Pensionsreformen. Nachhaltiger Sozialumbau am Beispiel Österreichs*. Frankfurt/New York: Campus.

Stadler-Vida, M./Strümpel, C. (2000) 'Austria – National Report', pp. 28-35 in: Kinds, H./Münz, A./Horn, L., *Volunteering into Participation. A Strategy for Social Inclusion*, KCP Final Report. Amsterdam: Community Partnership Consultants.

Strümpel, Ch./Stadler-Vida, M./Giedenbacher, Y. (Eds.) (2002) *Quality in Practice. Stakeholders' View of Supported Employment*. Final Report. Vienna: European Centre.

Part A:

Introduction and Theoretical Overview

CHAPTER 1

Transforming Disability Welfare Policy.
Completing A Paradigm Shift

Bernd Marin

I What does disability mean?

Before we address the mainstreaming of disability from sort to self-determination as well as the salience, success and failure of modern disability welfare policies, some thoughts about what disability actually means are at place: How can this most complex phenomenon be defined and measured – and how can people, their needs, hardships and behaviour, their restricted employment opportunities, life chances and their compensation requirements be classified accordingly? What are the problems that these definitions, measurements and classifications involve, and how do these problems impact on disability entitlements?

Problems of definition, classification, measurement – and entitlement

Medical complaints, sickness, illness, chronic disease, impairment, functional limitations, disability, and incapacity to work are ill-defined and complex phenomena. Disability in particular is a slippery and potentially expansive category: it is inherently subjective, ambiguous, fuzzy, elusive and inevitably problematic to define and measure. Disability cannot be observed directly but must be inferred from presumed causes (impairments) with distinct consequences, namely a restriction or incapacity to perform normal work roles. Health impairments causing work disability must be certified medically, though clinical certification of impairment is necessary but not sufficient for work disability or eligibility for disability benefits.

Assessing disability requires, in addition, a judgement on the severity, curability or irreversibility / permanence of this health condition as well as its limiting consequences for occupational task performance. Assessments are difficult and painful for the claimants concerned and unavoidably subjective: Conceptions of disability – and adequate responses to it and their affordability – change over time, and clinical judgements on which eligibility is based are (apart from highly different individual tastes and social values of the examiners) notoriously unreliable. "Deborah Stone (1985: 133) shows how unreliable clinical judgements are. She cites comprehensive research on the accuracy and consistency of disability determinations in the United States: In one study clinical teams and agency teams independently came to opposite conclusions on more than one-third of a sample of 1,500 cases. In another study comparing different state agencies using the same criteria there was complete agreement on disposition in only 22% of the cases. The limits of diagnostic procedures combined with the biases of doctors, administrators, courts, public opinion, and the uneven political pressures of applicants themselves assure very limited reliability and equity of decisions regarding disability benefits."[1]

Impairment may result from disease, accident traumatisms, congenital deformities or prolonged disuse of organs, muscles, senses, and brain functions. The origin of one and the same symptom of incapacity matters a lot when attributed a causation and irrevocability: whether e.g. a failure to concentrate or "learning disability" stems from temporary grief or permanent depression or somatic pathologies can be relevant for invalidity awards. However, it is not only the causal origin and permanence presumed, but also the impact on the work situation which may make the very same impairment or limitation a work disability in one workplace not in another: a flatfoot is likely to disable a postman (if he does not do marathon running in his leisure time) but not a scientist in her laboratory, a seeing limitation a waiter more than a radio reporter or a disc jockey, an even minor hearing problem a member of an orchestra more than the mailman.

Yet, with changing welfare regimes, fiscal resources or labour market conditions, unemployed persons may all the sudden be reclassified as invalid and early retirees without a chance to flexible retirement may find themselves labelled as incapacitated (e.g. in order to prevent actuarial deductions from their pension benefits). Categories identifying persons as "disabled", "unemployed" or "pre-retired" are frequently hard to distinguish; still, as the value and the accessibility of benefits usually differ significantly by status categories, membership to the "disability" group often is more attractive than being unemployed or simply in early retirement.

In addition to this generally growing generosity not easily found in other fields of welfare policy and a corresponding magnetic effect of invalidity, an ever-growing share of disability benefits is awarded for mental conditions as well as for musculoskeletal disorders such as lower back pain. These are ailments most difficult to diagnose and objectify in terms of pain, suffering, and work disability – and most difficult to cure. Consequently, we find almost everywhere trends towards inclusion of ever-broader limitations as constituting disability to work; and ever-shrinking probability to get-off the rolls once an invalidity status has been granted. As the average age of first-time claimants is down to 42 years of age in countries like the Netherlands and further life expectancy and survival rates continue to increase strongly in all age cohorts, the duration and permanence of work incapacity continues to grow. Finally, all this expansionary dynamics is further reinforced by another tendency at broadening "disability" categories, namely to take into account labour market conditions and the availability of jobs suited for persons handicapped in one way or another to find jobs at all. With labour slack and mass unemployment, employers, works councils and unions frequently colluded to adopt disability labels available in order to shift costs for dismissals and downsizing to social security.[2]

Governments usually tend to respond favourably to the claims of the organized aged as their interest associations are frequently very powerful indeed. But even if the old are not well organized, the sheer electoral weight of constituencies nearing in many OECD countries a median voter's age of 50 or above during this decade makes politicians disproportionately open to demands from so-called older workers and the elderly; as well as to demands from disabled people at all ages – here rather for reasons of higher legitimacy than those of electoral weight. But abusing pre-fabricated tailor-made "invalidity" categories in order to dismiss people into early retirement in their late 40s at public expense as described in Note 2 was overdoing a widely tolerated fiddling with "disability" labels by provocative fraud. Abuse became intolerable only when it was publicly disclosed and documented by the Court of Accounts and not a hidden practice any longer. But even under normal circumstances of regular and legal behaviour, disability assessments frequently are collections of oddities and quite queer decisions.

On the one hand, complex regulations of occupational protection may lead to decisions most difficult to understand: a learned, certified knife sharpener with a completed apprenticeship, for instance, who is unable to carry out one single particular turn necessary for his professional performance is entitled to an invalidity pension in Austria, if he has worked in his profession for more than six months; i.e. he is awarded a lifelong work incapacity benefit even in his early 20s on grounds of *Berufsschutz*, apart from the fact that he may perform many other occupational activities – and he is actually allowed to continue in any other than the learned or *Verweisungsberuf* fulltime with a full salary in addition to his lifelong invalidity rent. Would the knife sharpener be either semi-skilled or unskilled a worker *(angelernter Arbeiter oder Hilfsarbeiter)* only or a self-employed craftsman *(selbständiger Gewerbetreibender)* he would not be entitled to such an invalidity pension on the same grounds – even after decades of practice, social security contributions and at an advanced age at which he may objectively be difficult to retrain for another job.

To dismiss such coherent inconsistencies only as unique remnants of on old, corporatist system of professional protection would, however, miss the point. Looking at the most developed, strictly medical or "scientific" attempts at objectifying "abnormalities or losses", that is impairments causing work incapacity, so-called Baremas, we find an even stranger and more arbitrary variation in assessing particular levels of invalidity. Here too, assessed incapacity varies strongly between countries, within the same countries over time and between different, mostly occupational groups of insured persons for the very same losses or impairments. Such curiosities are less surprising than one would expect; they may understandably be experienced as "unjust", of which frequent appeals to widespread denials are an indicator, but they are not necessarily or even intentionally unfair, given the complexities involved.

As we have already indicated, chronic illness or disability must not lead to work incapacity, as, the other way round, invalidity benefit award does not have to coincide with self-perceived disability. This incongruence between disability and disability benefits corresponds to the difference between health status and health demand: people may be sick without voicing medical complaints, and medical complaints may vary drastically across comparable prevalence rates between countries;[3] chronic disease may or may not cause impairment, impairment may or may not cause functional limitations, functional limitations may or may not cause disability in terms of incapacity to work.

In short: between health and illness, between the need of medical care or no such need there are fuzzy boundaries; objective health conditions and care requirements on the one hand and subjective health awareness, desire of treatment and take-up of medical services on the other are only very loosely related. Demand for medical care services varies enormously between and within societies; with health status as just one among many determinants of effective health care demand. Effective demand for medical services, thus, only marginally reflects the objective incidence of morbidity within a society – health demand has little to do with health conditions.

Chronic illness of whatever sort may or may not lead to *functional limitations* in seeing, hearing, speaking, walking, lifting, climbing stairs; and functional limitations may or may not lead to dependence on others in *activities of daily living* (ADLs) such as eating, getting in or out of bed, dressing and undressing, bathing, using the toilet; and dependence on others in activities of daily living may or may not lead to dependence in *instrumental activities of daily living* (IADLs) such as household work, laundry, preparing meals, shopping, managing money, using a telephone, etc.

Depending on whom one asks and how, highly different answers and corresponding highly different rates of illness, functional limitations and disabilities will be measured. So far, different disability measures are not at all reconciled with each other. Very little is known so far about their interrelationships. As an unsurprising outcome of this we find that disability measures over time are extremely unreliable, with great statistically unexplainable ("noise") variations from one period to the next despite very large samples in health statistics; and we find, for instance, 18% of the US population suffering from functional limitations; 10% with a work disability; and 4% of the working age population with a disability benefit (SSDI or SSI).

In addition, things change significantly over time: what used to be a severe impairment that incapacitated for work and full participation in social life a few years ago may have become a minor trivial problem today – severe arthritis, grave depression, strong hearing impairments, heart diseases or hip or knee impairments as cases in point of chronic conditions the better treatment of which has made them of much less concern than a generation ago. Today, technical health aids, assisting devices and adaptations of workplace, housing, and public buildings allow to live independently and without any or comparable limitations with the very same physical condition than years ago – eyeglasses, canes, walkers, electric wheelchairs, walk-in showers, support rails and handicapped access facilities, special taxi transportation services for disabled people, pre-prepared meals, meals on wheels, home delivery and home help services, all these aids and/or environmental improvements and/or social support systems facilitate life for impaired persons independently from improvements in underlying health conditions or not. High-tech joint replacement of hips and knees, intensive heart surgery, anti-inflammatory drugs for arthritis treatment and other pharmaceutical quick fixes which may help to cope with depression and other mental problems in a way that makes self-perception and general outlook less pessimistic and negative have become frequent applications of medical innovations.

Thus, changes in health conditions or chronic illness rates may stem from true changes in illness prevalence; they may also reflect changes in health behaviour; they may mirror changes in diagnostic practice and capacity detecting illnesses previously undiagnosed or under-diagnosed; they may also result from better medical treatment and longer life with chronic illness so that more people are surviving to report having encountered a specific illness they may not have had a chance to encounter at earlier stages in life; they may also come from changing stigmas, taboos or "fashions" in illnesses (e.g. allergies may be, haemorrhoids or contagious mycosis or cognitive conditions may not be a health status symbol one brags about; blood pressure, certain mental disorders or venereal diseases may have highly different images in different subcultures – thinking of a young writer who felt "not sick enough to be a poet"; alcohol and drug addiction may be rejected quite differently in different milieus) so that different people grossly over- and under-report certain illnesses and health conditions.

Finally, a disease may change in severity, or rather the management and medical control of an unchanged health condition may totally change the objective life expectancy and self-perception of persons, for instance, with hepatitis C or HIV infection where residual life expectancy in all stages has increased significantly over the last decade. Last but not least, class differences and disparities in disability and healthy life expectancy are still very strong, varying from around six years in Nordic countries up to 20 years of differential life expectancy between different socio-economic status groups in the United States; disability risks in OECD countries are roughly doubling with lower educational attainment, lower social status and lower income.

II   Mainstreaming disability:
From sort to self-determination?
And from "bone-rates" of "abnormality" to normalcy?

The paradigm shift regarding disability that took place during the last few decades changed public perception and policy responses to impairment most significantly. Social protest and successful political mobilization of people with impairments led to an unprecedented degree of organized self-help, campaigning and lobbying, formation of interest associations and NGOs, pressure group activities on governments, legislators and administrators and a resulting new public concern for persons with disabilities. The United Nations acted as a lead agency, declaring 1981 the International Year of Disabled People, proclaiming 1983-1992 as the Decade of Disabled Persons, and setting global standards (the famous 22 Standard Rules on the Equalization of Opportunities for Persons with Disabilities, adopted by the UN General Assembly in its 48th session), including determining the preconditions of equal participation and the target areas, implementation measures and monitoring mechanism. The European Union followed only lately by nominating 2003 "The European Year of People with Disabilities".

Most important, the World Health Organization (WHO) as the specialized UN-agency dealing with disability, has complemented its *International Classification of Disease* (WHO 1976) by a new *International Classification of Impairments, Disabilities and Handicaps (ICIDH)* (WHO, 1981), with a scheme detailing the consequences of disease. WHO distinguished between *impairment* as loss or abnormality of anatomical, physiological, psychological structure or function, i.e. parts or systems of the body not working properly; *disability* as any restriction or lack (resulting from an impairment) of ability to perform an activity in the manner or within the range considered normal, i.e. things that people cannot do, primarily basic skills of daily living; and *handicap* as disadvantage resulting from an impairment or disability that limits or prevents the fulfilment of a (culturally variable) role. The most recent system adopted by the World Health Organization is called *International Classification of Functioning, Disability and Health (ICF*, http://www3.who.int/icf/icftemplate.cfm). Before this broader, more complex and dynamic view was adopted, assessment of disability was reduced to measuring impairments in a pseudo-scientific way through so-called Baremas.

Bernd Marin

Assessing "abnormality or loss":
The strange world of "bone-rates" or Baremas

Originally, abnormality or loss was restricted to persons who were blind or deaf or paralysed, or without an organ or a leg. These were the heydays of the so-called *Baremas*, scales for compensating injuries dating back to mediaeval ages: Germanic law related money sums for the loss of body parts to the *"wergeld"* or *"manngeld"* to be paid as a compensation for killing a free man. Later, the French mathematician François Bareme transposed such scales to percentages, labeled "Baremas", or (more dramatically in German) *"Knochentaxe"* (bone-rate). Then, doctors created the equivalent of such a limb-rate *("Gliedertaxe")* also for mental and psychological or "neuropyschiatric disorders", with even greater fuzziness. A glance at European Baremas and their variation among (even neighbouring, e.g. Scandinavian) countries shows a strange and quite arbitrary codex of particular levels of incapacity, varying a lot between countries – and over time within the same countries, and within the same countries between different, mostly occupational, groups of insured persons, i.e. corporatist distinctions which have nothing to do with residual work capacities or risk structures – for the very same losses or impairments, allowing for a lot of variation and discretionary decision within the same categories of harms, and for strange comparisons across injuries and between corporatist special interest groups.

In the UK in the 1960s, for instance, the loss of fingers and a leg amputated below the knee constituted a 50% disability, while the loss of three fingers and the amputation of a foot or the loss of an eye translated into a 30% incapacity rating; today, the very same lost foot rates for 100% disability in the same country, whereas the amputation of one foot counts for only 30% in Germany, 50% in Belgium as against 100% in England, but both feet only 70% in Italy. Today, an amputation of a lower limb at hip level constitutes 35% incapacity in Iceland, but 90% in England and Belgium, the amputation at ankle level 30% in Denmark but only 9% in Sweden. Within the same country, for instance Austria, the very same physical loss of a limb amputated below the knee counts for 50% degree of the reduction of capacity for remunerative work *(Grad der Minderung der Erwerbsfähigkeit)* if it happened to somebody during the war, whereas the very same impairment counts for 40% if it happens to a farmer today, but only 30% if it affects either a white collar employee or a blue-collar worker. An infarct or a coronary heart disease makes for a 100% impairment in Italy, but for only between 30 to 60%

in Belgium. Fractures of the vertebral column with neurological consequences rate between 20% (and 25%) and 100% within the same countries Denmark, Norway and Sweden; inflammatory and degenerative phenomena of the vertebral column may vary between 5% and 100% in Belgium, leaving all discretion to medical doctors. Unstable insulin-dependent diabetes mellitus counts for 50-75% in France, 60-100% in Belgium, 30-100% in Lithuania, 51-60% in Italy, 50-80% in Estonia, 75-100% in Ireland, but only up to 40% in Iceland, and a 50% minimum in Germany. A total loss of vision of both eyes makes for 100% impairment in Germany, Denmark, Norway, 95% France, but for only 68% in Sweden. "Severe facial disfigurement" rates as 100% impairment in England, 80-100% in Italy (wolf-mouth, Binder's syndrome), whereas "visually repulsive" disfigurement counts only 50% in Germany, and between 10 to 100% in Belgium – leaving all the room for discretionary judgements on "ugliness" and the corresponding disability benefits to bureaucrats. France, on the other hand, does not know such repulsive facial disfigurement at all but operationalizes "major impairment" by "disorders seriously hindering or preventing feeding, head carriage, and saliva retention" (50-70%), with dependence on a third party 80%.

Over time, in an international comparison, as well as when comparing injuries with each other, this mechanistic approach of attributing single summary figures for benefits based on Baremas demonstrates its arbitrary and strange character: "*The Set Points*: how do you compare a fractured leg with schizophrenia ... *The Paired Organs Problem*: what do you do about the one-eyed man loosing his remaining eye; *The Whole Body Proble*m: if loss of a finger is 10%, and back pain is 20%, and depression is 40%, what is the total award for an individual with all three conditions; *The Threshold Problem*: if benefit is awarded at a threshold (such as 30% for a partial disability pension, and 80% for a full one), how do you decide whether someone falls at 29%, 30% or 31%?".[4]

Sometimes, national Baremas simply reflect long-standing stigmatization or prejudices, if they are shared by the medical profession. In Austria, for instance, around 60,000 persons with schizophrenia are totally excluded from work due to the stigma attached to their health condition, still widely seen, also by medical experts in assessment committees, as equivalent to psychosis (*"psychoseadäquat"*) and as a mental illness (*"Geisteskrankheit"*). As first incidence of illness occurs around the age of 20 for men (who, on average, have little if any occupational record at that age), and around the age of 30 for women, most people diagnosed with schizophrenia will be on a lifelong invalidity pension for about half a century – despite the fact that 70% of them are both able and willing to work.[5] Even if the lifetime incidence of schizophrenia of 1% is significantly lower than that of other psychiatric illnesses – who's share in overall disability benefits is rapidly increasing everywhere in Europe – it is the sort (and exclusion from work and life) of several million Europeans which is at stake with this one mental health condition only; and it will concern dozens of millions of Europeans of all ages when it comes to alcoholism, panic attacks and social phobias, or depression, including very severe ones.

Despite these severe problems with Baremas, they are still widely used for awards of compensation of injuries. This widest possible use of the most problematic and most widely criticized assessment method should be less surprising as it may be at a first glance: it is a very old, well-established system, dating back to centuries; it has an institutional first-mover advantage in that it was established in the early days of disability welfare system evolution; it seems difficult to apply, requiring "scientific" tests and examinations known to professionals only; by assigning numbers to highly complex, multidimensional phenomena, it gives a flair of objectivity (at least to lay persons, while it may be ridiculed as misplaced over-precision by other professionals), comparability and, thus, of social fairness; it is to be used very flexibly for awarding benefits both for impairments and for disabilities arising from impairments, so that either injuries themselves or only disablement resulting from injuries may become compensated, leaving ample room for lawmakers as well as for social administrators to shape and re-shape practices according to changing public moods, fiscal constraints, and political requirements; and the professional autonomy and discretion of both medical doctors and bureaucrats remains extremely high, given the latitude inherent in impairment-based Baremas, so that they keep a monopoly of deciding about the working status of people with disabilities, income, in-kind benefits and service entitlements, in short: a far-reaching control about people's lives.

Alternative methods of assessing disabilities and handicaps

None of the *alternative methods* of assessing the legitimacy of a person's claims to disability benefits does erode the core role of the medical profession. But all of them somewhat undermine its monopoly by creating multidisciplinary teams in order to integrate a strictly medical examination by a physician into a broader assessment combined with knowledge from vocational rehabilitation, occupational therapy, work organization, labour market, social work, psychology and physiotherapy etc. More complex and widely practiced alternatives to the Baremas include, for instance, the method of *assessing care needs* (e.g. for home nursing in assessing general attendance allowances), where the amount of the attendance allowance granted varies with the average extent of need for support and care, for instance defining seven levels of disability by qualitative and quantified care requirements between 50 and 180 hours monthly; or *functional capacity assessments* through individual *"ability profiles"*, which should allow to identify, compare and match abilities with templates of actual job requirements, in order to facilitate employment opportunities for persons with disabilities (whereas the previous concentration on deficiencies and disabilities instead of abilities will inevitably lead to greater social exclusion). Finally, there is the method of *calculating economic loss*, referring either to existing or previously held jobs or jobs in general, or anything in between. This method combines a medical examination of impairments and incapacities with a vocational investigation of relevant work opportunities in order to determine the nature of the handicap – and its compensation.

With these broader and more sophisticated perspectives and assessment tools, professional domination of the process is not broken, but even further extended. The former obsessive fixation on anatomical or other "abnormalities" is not fully abandoned but significantly softened: severe injuries such as blindness may or may not fully incapacitate for a given workplace, and formerly often ignored (or rigidly categorized) chronic illness which may interfere with physiological or psychological processes in multiple ways such as arthritis, epilepsy and schizophrenia have been included into a broader definition of impairments leading to disability. In surveys using such a wider scheme, the severity of disability was measured by functional limitations in reaching and stretching, dexterity, seeing, hearing, personal care, continence, communication, locomotion, behaviour and intellectual functioning, and a much larger share of populations was found disabled – about one in seven of the (UK) population, and a third of the more than six million disabled resident population was found in the two least severe disability categories (1-2), about one third in the three middle categories (3-5) and around one third in the five more to most severe categories (6-10).[6]

As a consequence of the authoritative WHO-led broadening of official disability definitions and of practised assessment procedures, as well as of the aforementioned political and intergovernmental activities, a fundamental shift of perspectives came about. Impairment was less and less seen as a personal tragedy of passive "victims" condemned to a life of individual isolation, dependency and assistance from family members and kinship network. Instead, views moved towards those of a more self-determined life assisted by welfare benefits and services tailored for persons with disabilities. Disability was not longer seen as a personal problem above all in need of individual, medical treatment by professional experts who care about a "poor" person with difficulties to adjust to a given environment; but rather as a social problem affecting persons with impairment oppressed by an environment indifferent or even structurally hostile to their specific needs, thereby depriving them of equal opportunities in work and social life. Instead of relying primarily on professional treatment and external expertise, persons with impairments would need to rely on their own experience and to act-up collectively into self-help and political interest organization.

But, paradoxically, in order to strengthen their political position as an interest group, people with impairments had to get disability recognized by professional experts as an issue affecting significant and much higher proportions of the population than previously expected – in the late 1980s, early 1990s, between more than 14.2% (6,2 million UK citizens) and 19.4% (48.9 million US citizens) were reported as persons with impairments in national surveys conducted at both sides of the Atlantic. At this point of the development, the sheer numbers of persons and the shares of the population affected as recognized by professional expertise made for a normalization or mainstreaming of disability.

III The ambiguity of modern disability welfare: Success story or political fiasco?

At first glance, as well as after various in-depth investigations from different perspectives, modern disability policy presents itself quite ambiguous. First, underlying trends with respect to foreseeable problem loads are extremely contradictory and highly puzzling: Is overall disability likely to further increase or decrease? And how come that disability in older age (+65 years) and very old age is declining significantly whereas it increases in working age (20-64 years) (and maybe even for children), despite the uncontested fact that the risk of invalidity rises with age?

Apart from such contradictory developments regarding case-loads, the last decades can be seen both as a remarkable and most obvious success story as well as a kind of certain political *fiasco* or disaster. The following sections will indicate both undeniable, major achievements on the one hand and equally irrefutable main failures of modern disability welfare policies on the other. But the most plausible, reassuring metaphor from the glass half full or half empty fully misses the point: it is not an intermediate level of success or failure, but the simultaneity of a great and indisputable success in reframing the mind-sets and world views concerning disability, thereby advancing the social rights of people with impairments on the one hand, and an evident failure on the other to consequently pursue and complete this paradigm shift, which started to redefine invalidity from a sinful impairment or stigmatized crippling condition over a tragic individual sort to a disabling environment generating avoidable deprivation and social exclusion.

More specifically, the failure of modern disability policies is not at all accidental but an inevitable and incontestable by-product, an unintended but inescapable consequence of a purposeful and successful social compensation policy. Compensation produces income security for persons with assumed earnings restrictions without a corresponding level of integration offers and activation demands. But as even comprehensive and ambitious integration policies do not matter much, if at all, with regard to employment levels of persons with disabilities, as will be seen, realistic chances to overcome this dilemma may actually be modest, indeed.

Modern disability welfare salience

Success or failure of modern disability welfare is in many ways crucial for the future of welfare states or welfare societies. Above all, it is an important component of social expenditures and, thus, of fiscal pressures on and *financial sustainability of the welfare state*.

A structural feature of modern European welfare states is that the *main determinants of public spending are not revenue but entitlements to welfare benefits*, for instance to transfers for old-age pensions or pre-retirement, invalidity pensions and disability benefits, unemployment and other social security or social assistance programmes, the provision of health and education, etc. Spending on welfare entitlements cannot be changed according to short-term cyclical fluctuations in the economy and is not even easily adapted over mid-term periods, but is rather driven by long-term population developments, structural and socio-cultural changes: the great expansion of (higher) education beginning in the 1960s responded to the post-war baby boom; increasing expenditures for pensions, medical and care services for the elderly react to population ageing. Both spending developed dynamically and irrespective of the state of the economy. And unemployment expenditures, which *are* caused by business cycles and the state of the economy and less by demographic factors, were exploding just at the times when job search benefits were most needed while contributions were much weaker, thus reinforcing budgetary crises.

But what do significant increases in invalidity pensions and disability benefits for the working age population reflect under conditions of improved health and more disability-free life expectancy, compression and postponement of morbidity? What does a steep rise in incapacity recipiency rates simultaneously with a reduction of chronic and occupational diseases, accidents and work injuries actually signal? Without a convincing answer to explain these *puzzling paradoxes*, disability welfare as a kind of garbage can social welfare category will rather continue to contribute to aggravating fiscal pressures than to maintain or restore stability and long-term sustainable welfare.

While overall social policy spending has roughly doubled between 1960 and 1980 and further increased since by more than a fifth, all cuts in order to reduce deficits or taxes have remained soft in terms of slowing down the rate of expenditure expansion and have never been absolute cuts; and they seem to have affected disability benefits less than any other social expenditure so far. Extension of programmes, number of beneficiaries, and amount of expenditures for disability have steadily increased since the late 1960s even if one controls for the changing age structure of societies. Periodic efforts at retrenchment (mid-1970s, 1990s) have succeeded in slowing down recipiency growth rates, but never growth of beneficiaries as such; both the stock of benefit recipients remained high and the inflow rates much higher than outflow. As a consequence, even incapacity benefit expenditures have begun to show reduced inflow rates, i.e. *continuing, though slowed-down expansion dynamics* so that overall cost containment will be a core challenge in the years to come.

Because disability benefits are generally welcome once the insured risk has occurred (or can be evoked), *incapacity as a potentially catastrophic risk* is much feared and almost every other risk is preferred over impairment, chronic illness, disease and invalidity – except for *death*. Nowadays, everybody seems "to want to die young – but as late in life as possible", that is dying not prematurely but in longevity and disability-free; though most people most of the time will prefer disability over death, except maybe very young people. But the risk of death is, in the long run by definition, greater than that of invalidity – except for younger people (in wealthy and healthy societies) who rather have incapacitating accidents than die.

Inasmuch as the risk to become incapacitated at all significantly grows with rising age and will become higher (in a non-linear, later almost exponential fashion), the older one is, *invalidity is greater a risk than death, the younger one is*. The risk of invalidity is also *much riskier a risk, the younger one is*: it is much riskier a risk in terms of injuries occurring, the younger one is; it is much riskier a risk in terms of current and future income lost, the younger one is; and it is much riskier a risk in terms of obstacles to benefits eligibility and disability entitlements, the younger one is – for instance, with respect to pre-employment record, necessary waiting periods, capped earnings replacement rates, works and earnings tests, etc. In some countries such as the US in the postwar period, young people, even with previous work records and insurance contributions, were completely excluded from cash disability benefits, as incapacity had not only to be medically examined as leading to death or indefinite duration, but was restricted to workers over age 50 only.

Thus, disability policies are also relevant for those without disabilities today (without that they may know this, though) as much as they are relevant for currently disabled people. They are relevant for non-disabled and young people because, firstly, they may one day in the future become disabled themselves, and secondly, as their own labour market behaviour (more than they may ever realize) is influenced by regulations applying to persons with disabilities and social rights and benefits attached to the status of (partial) incapacity. As "the status of 'disabled' typically brings privileges beyond cash and special medical assistance: draft exemption, special education and training, easier access to housing subsidies, a moratorium on debts or extensions of credit"[7] and is generally considered morally worthy and deserving more than other categories of social support, it may attract self-selection into the category more than other welfare benefits. *Disability poli-*

cies are, therefore, policies *relevant for both disabled and non-disabled people;* and they are relevant for *all age cohorts* in society, though quite differently.

In some developed societies with high non-employment rates, disability welfare plays a *major role in depressing labour force participation.* Low activity rates imply a low number of persons producing goods and services, and a correspondingly high load to working people of supporting large numbers of persons kept unproductive. Low employment also requires high taxes / social security contribution rates on productive people, which, in turn, discourage these productive strata to work as hard as they otherwise would and rather set incentives for eventually leaving the labour force (temporarily or part-time) for better paid moonlighting, off-the-books businesses and other informal earnings, or even for unpaid activities, leisure, etc. As a consequence, labour market participation drops further and taxes / contributions rise higher, and so forth, so that economies supporting large numbers of people on disability benefits out of work are ever more prone to entrapment in a high taxes and social security contributions / low activity and employment rates *trap of socio-economic underperformance*, i.e. loss of economic competitiveness and social welfare decay.

This *vicious low activity / high tax circle* may be caused by any other social policy spending as well, but is particularly likely to be *more devastating* in case of pay-as-you-go old-age pensions and even more so *in case of disability benefits*. Both types of benefits lend themselves easier to the temptation of political rent-seeking and manipulation, to using pre-retirement and invalidity pensions schemes for facilitating industrial restructuring or for hiding unemployment, for getting votes instead of making welfare schemes compatible with standards of fairness, competitive requirements and long-term affordability. As with pensions, disability benefits allow for trading short-term political popularity for long-term sustainability. Easier access to early retirement, broader coverage, more generous replacement income, more relaxed screening of eligibility and assessment of claims buy immediate satisfaction of interest groups and voters, whereas fiscal burdens of non-funded liabilities are shifted to later generations of working populations, without easily discernible relationships with the goodies distributed in earlier periods.

But in contrast to political leniency with respect to regular old-age pensions, thoughtless generosity regarding disability benefits instead of giving wisely changes the behaviour not only of current invalidity beneficiaries and that of potential claimants, but that of non-disabled employees, their employers and that of social administrators and all other interest groups as well. As with sickness and health insurance, *moral hazard in disability welfare may become contagious*, spreading over to others, *demoralizing* previously innocent bystanders watching what they may consider malingering at their own expense by free-riding recipients – and possibly give-in to the temptation to use incapacity schemes that are easier and cheaper a way to deploy surplus workforce than regular dismissals.

Thus, enterprises frequently find themselves in the paradoxical situation to complain about a rise of non-wage labour costs which they themselves have previously produced by abusing pre-retirement and invalidity pensions schemes to offload large proportions of middle-aged workers at public expense. In a situation where up to half of all social spending is spent for pensions, where up to 90% of new retirement is pre-retirement before the legal retirement age, and where invalidity often is the single most important determinant of pre-retirement, nothing less than a full *turnaround* will be *indispensable*. Sticking to the mind-blowing political double-bind message that both work and early retirement are intrinsically desirable, and to the hypocrisy or self-delusion that disability is a soft and painless way-out of labour market problems for redundant middle-aged workers cannot be upheld any longer. But it is still open how a new, reformed disability welfare would look like.

For without *compassion, compensation and solidarity*, the burden of incapacity would have to be shouldered exclusively by persons with impairments themselves, their family, kinship, partners, friends, and potential charitable sponsors. Loss of earning following loss of health and work capacity; additional expenses for medical care or mobility not fully covered by social security; additional costs of care attendance for household members or relatives and their necessary adjustments, even in terms of working time and corresponding employment opportunities and income foregone; all these and other *external effects of incapacity* would be most harmful to the people concerned and could be destructive for society at large without solidarity and compensation. They help to re-internalize some of these extra costs of widespread individual suffering by collective pooling and absorption of individually devastating or catastrophic risks.

But are there no other, better solutions of *risk insurance for disability* than traditional social security arrangements? Truly *alternative options*, apart from hybrid forms frequently found, are either *free private insurance market* solutions or *judicial liability* assignments and procedures. But generally they are held as being *too costly alternatives to public disability welfare*, either in terms of health, welfare, fairness and social cohesion foregone in case of free market disability insurance; or in terms of tort costs, i.e. of potentially endless costs of legal litigation in case of legal liability judicature.

Juridification of disability programmes is most advanced in the United States. This does not protect US disability development from a trend towards broadening definitions of disability, looser eligibility criteria, rising recipiency rates, and from corresponding cost expansion as more advanced and generous welfare states. To the contrary, an interaction of growing interest organization of disabled people, media populism, and the self-interests and eigendynamics of professional groups and the judiciary through its District Court rulings, which ever more reversed benefit denials ever more appealed to by rejected claimants, together these forces led to constraining all attempts at cost containment and retrenchment. Efforts to improve management of disability programmes and to speed-up adjudication procedures actually increased generosity of awards, as it made judges more inclined to approve of claims and to grant awards in case of doubt in order to improve their records towards less appeals.

As a consequence, the social security administration operating the Social Security Disability programme ran "the largest system of administrative adjudication in the world"[8] with *excessive tort costs*: already at the time of President Reagan's massive efforts of rollback of disability benefits and beneficiaries, year by year 1,250,000 disability claims plus 250,000 previously denied applications were reviewed by 5,600 examiners, and around 150,000 subsequent appeals to denial decisions were adjudicated by 625 administrative law judges at the state and ultimately at the federal level. As a consequence, the intended reduction in rolls of disability recipients failed, whereas the unintended and undesired mobilization of political and judicial action against administrative decisions flourished. Countervailing pressure group dynamics, the juridification of claims, a system open to media populism and legal litigation in a battlefield of medical and legal disability specialists, liberal judicial rulings, this mix of American exceptionality actually produced similar outcomes and overall tendencies of bureaucratization and expansion as classical state welfarism – at somewhat lower direct overall costs but much harsher conditions for the handicapped.

Unregulated market insurance against loss of earnings caused by disability would inevitably leave large groups without affordable insurance, as necessary risk-rating would automatically exclude "bad risks" and poor people by disabling them from even purchasing a private disability insurance; it could not cover pre-existing disabilities, thus excluding for instance people with congenital impairments or already workless due to a previous accident; and it is inevitably extremely costly in terms of assessments and monitoring pre-onset behaviour of insured and post-onset behaviour of beneficiaries. Not even regulation of private insurance markets by, for instance, mandatory insurance through legally fixed standard contracts can solve the problem of social exclusion; it would still require public intervention and compensatory arrangements.

In view of this *market failure for disability insurance*, most countries have, therefore, organized *disability insurance through social security* – as mandatory, public monopolies, with universal coverage, uniform conditions, solidary premium rating (flat-rate or earnings-related instead of risk-rated contributions), and pay-as-you-go financing mechanisms. Risks are pooled and shared collectively, though the degree of risk-pooling and interest aggregation may vary from the level of economic sectors to society as a whole; and all other parameters of disability insurance, from eligibility requirements to benefit calculation rules, are regulated by law. Despite these common traits, public disability welfare schemes differ a lot with respect to how they organize their functioning as an insurance, i.e. managing claims, assessing eligibility, calculating fees and benefits, organizing collection of contributions and payment of transfers, instituting prevention, rehabilitation and curative efforts. Monitoring of behaviour of the insured and of beneficiaries and controlling potential moral hazard, however, plays much less of a role than in private insurances.

Consequently, no or little moral hazard makes *social insurance* arrangements significantly *less costly* than private insurance market products: Contracts are uniformly standardized, obligatory, and covering everybody, no competition does not require marketing, and largest possible numbers of insured make for maximum economies of scale. But if moral hazard arises under these circumstances, there are little to no incentives – and mechanisms compatible with social insurance – to contain harmful opportunistic behaviour, i.e. social insurance may actually loose its comparative cost advantage and become *more costly* than private market insurance. Thus, *whether the potential comparative cost advantage of social insurance systems can actually be realized or not depends largely on their capacity to contain moral hazard or abuse of benefit arrangements.*

Whereas *experience rating* may still be an option at the level of economic sectors or even large firms, it could not be applied on lower levels of aggregation. *Risk-rating*, bonus/malus schemes rewarding careful behaviour by lowering premiums, *cost-sharing* schemes shifting part of the losses incurred to the patient or the disabled person, or *exclusion clauses* excluding certain claims based on subjective complaints which cannot easily or at all be checked medically from insurance coverage, all these control instruments of private insurers may be used within a social security system either not at all, or with utmost prudence only. Thus, in a system of *socialized disability welfare not only individually unbearable risks, but abuse, fraud and waste also tend to be socialized* – making for rising costs (and contribution requirements) of the overall system. This expansion dynamics can only be contained by benchmarking and overall cost/benefit comparisons and controls.

Modern disability welfare is most salient a social policy for a number of *other unique features* as well, such as, for instance: Above all, it "is the most difficult social program to administer. And it is the most resistant to cost containment. Medical or clinical judgements on which eligibility is based are notoriously unreliable." (Wilensky, a.a.O.). There are most tricky problems of defining, classifying, and measuring disability, of assessing severity, curability or irreversibility of health conditions and of their occupational impact and social consequences not found in any other classical field of social welfare such as labour market policy and unemployment benefits, social assistance, family or pensions policy. Discretionary decisions make room for almost unavoidable unequal treatment by programme administrators. Fuzzy risks allow for influencing the actual probability of incurring a harm and its degree of disability by the patient's own subjective perception, his/her willingness to work, motivation to succeed in rehabilitation etc. It is also torn between archaic legacies in (subliminal) perception or cultural codes and hypermodernity of some of the diagnostic and treatments methods, and between moral values, moralizing postures and amoral self-seeking interests. It contains elements of incomparable institutional and technical complexity, cross-sectoral inter-penetration, and ethical dilemmas. In short, modern disability welfare is a kind of laboratory for all modern welfare problems and failures – from variability of incidence to mismatches of service supply and demand, from overclaim to social exclusion problems and unrecognized non-take-up; from paradoxes of targeting or anti-discrimination policies over perverse incentives to long-term welfare dependency; from discrepancies between health and health demand to those between disability prevalence as a medical condition, disability as a labour market prospect, and disability as benefit recipiency.

Modern disability welfare success

In several most advanced countries, disability policies have been a remarkable success during the last decades of the twentieth century. It may be summarized as a, probably irreversible, process of *emancipation* of people with disabilities, as a *trend towards integration and normalization, to independence and self-determination*. Traditional segregation of persons with disabilities into homes, special schools or sheltered employment sites has been partly overcome through *integrated schooling* and *assisted employment* which allows even severely impaired persons to work together with non-disabled people in the regular labour market; and *new forms of housing* have helped to move away from nursing homes to smaller housing units or single apartments with ambulant care services.

Together with integration and normalization grew the awareness that persons with disabilities are not pitiable creatures to be patronized by well-intended professionals, but that they are able to speak and act for themselves. Thus, it has become accepted that persons with disabilities including mentally disabled persons may take care of themselves, live autonomous lives, represent their own interests and may co-determine or help in designing the service at their disposal. For this purpose, a number of new instruments have been developed during the last decades: *care attendance allowances*, personal assistance, particularly widespread in Scandinavian countries, which allow even most severely impaired persons to live autonomously, *interest group associations* such as the "Centers for Independent Living" or the *"Selbstbestimmt Leben Bewegung"*, disabled persons organizing themselves and not, as traditionally, through their parents; umbrella or peak associations such as "Save Our Security", organizing grass-root organizations; or specialized lawyers associations such as the US National Association of Disability Claims Representatives. Social services are ever more set up for *user involvement* which allows people with disabilities to influence the services established to support them and to end their previous forced infantilization.

Furthermore, the impact of human-built environmental factors that often incapacitate persons with or without impairments (preschool children, young mothers with small children, frail elderly as much as wheelchair users) has been recognized and thus the (co-)causation and not just the *social construction of disability*. While disability was previously seen as a static feature of persons with impairments which must be accepted and can not, in principle, be changed significantly, *the social definition of handicap* allows for identifying the social and physical barriers which limit the opportunities of full participation in society for those with illness and impairments and trying to shape these contextual barriers. Mobile early *childhood developmental support*, *measures to adapt workplaces, communication facilitators* such as general availability of sign language or large type, screen magnifiers and voice synthesizers built into the basic design of computers and other widespread technologies, as well as legal regulations to guarantee equal access to public buildings (such as the Americans with a Disability Act) are cases in point of this new approach.

Non-discrimination and mobility support outside the home by *equal accessibility of public buildings* may be a most visible example of a disability welfare policy success, though it has been achieved only partly so far. Once the principle of general and equal – and equally easy – accessibility of buildings, shops, transports and communications will have been generally accepted and ramps, lifts, moving staircases will be safely useable for every human and animal companion including Seeing Eye dogs, automatic doors, adaptable buses, trains, plane gangways, tramways and underground metros have been introduced, not only persons with impairments such as wheelchair users, but everybody more or less fragile without impairments – from small children to young mothers with strollers or little children to frail elderly persons to healthy middle-aged people with buggies, trolleys or heavy luggage or cyclists or roller-skaters – everybody benefits from the fact that *design features of equality of access and comfort have become a pure public good*. To the extent that the full range of abilities of potential users is taken into account, no – potentially discriminating and stigmatizing – selection and identification of those with disabilities for special treatment in distinction from able-bodied others is necessary any longer.

Equal and easy public accessibility is a *best-practice case in point* of success of a modern disability policy. While its non-identification or anonymity as well as the non-rivalry in consumption features even avoid to set some people apart by classifying those users as "disabled", these ideal qualities do not extend to all measures established in support of persons with impairments: paradoxically, a child with mental retardation or an adult with physical impairments must first be identified (and even be certified) as such before measures necessary to guarantee his/her support and non-discrimination could effectively be taken; and any measure taken in more traditional social policies such as health and medical care, education, personal care and social services will rival in consumption with other claims for uses of public funds (whereas accessible buildings, once built, are useful investments not consuming further scarce funds depending on their actual usage, rather the opposite: the more frequently they are used, the more useful the outlet proves to be).

Anti-discrimination has become an *indispensable key feature of modern disability policy*. But the less persons with impairments are automatically viewed as handicapped or disabled and in need of compensation, but just in need of equal access and equal opportunities and non-discrimination, the less they can count on automatic support, affirmative action or reversed discrimination – as an effective anti-discrimination policy and positive discrimination measures require selective identification (as against full anonymity). It is one thing to systematically take stock of discriminatory measures – such as the prohibition of blind persons to act as witnesses to a marriage only recently eliminated in an advanced welfare EU-country – in order to eliminate them and another to think that effective anti-discrimination and equalizing personalized services can be provided without selective delivery.

The widely unacknowledged *core paradox of non-discriminatory anti-discrimination and equal opportunity disability policy* is, of course, that strictly universalistic public policies are attractively anonymous and non-discriminatory, but cannot guarantee effective non-discrimination, as they must disregard individual needs and personal circumstances of people discriminated against structurally. In addition, they may actually even lead to a reduction of resources available to persons with disabilities. Social compensation policies of an affirmative action kind for impaired persons in order to make up for barriers encountered by them, on the other hand, may improve their resource endowment and lead to a reversed, positive discrimination, but at the expense of more "discrimination", i.e. more intrusive, "policing" investigations and bureaucratic and medical professional assessments of disadvantages resulting from these impairments – or even the gravity and credibility of the impairments themselves. But even if an inevitable discrimination for the purpose of positive discrimination may be unobtrusive and not stigmatizing, a predominance if not monopoly of medical professionals in assessing people as disabled will prevail in order to allow for most legitimate ("objective") classifications and easy administration of benefit provision and to protect programme administrators as well as claimants against charges of malingering.

Disability right campaigners object to this medicalizing and individualizing approach, without being able to say how identification of beneficiaries could credibly be done without professional dominance, either of medical doctors or of discretionary social case workers. Obviously, the dilemma between the values of integrity, privacy, anonymity and non-discrimination on the one hand and well-targeted help on the other is not easily balanced out. But there are far more troublesome problems of modern disability welfare than some inherent inconsistencies of underlying values and paradoxes in implementing these guiding principles.

Modern disability welfare failure

The very expansion of disability welfare may not be a sign of more overall welfare and well-being of disabled people, but of an administrative incapacity to provide welfare and cater it well enough to the persons with impairments in need. In short: *disability welfare expansion as a potential welfare failure, rather than an unquestionable welfare increase and success of social policies.* As with spending on unemployment, hospitals, prisons, pharmaceuticals etc., more spending on sickness, accidents, work injuries and disabilities may signal less welfare for each disabled person and for society at large.

Indeed, the very expansion of pension dependency of persons in working age and the (partly very steep) increase in disability expenditures over the last decades – apart from a puzzling misallocation of disability benefits – contrast sharply to a series of generally favourable social and health conditions. Most *puzzling queries* arise: How is it to be explained that disability recipiency rates for working age populations and costs expand in spite of improved health and increased life expectancy?

.... despite declining disability of population groups at higher disability risk such as the elderly beyond working age 65?
.... despite a simultaneous compression rather than extension of morbidity?
.... despite the reduction and postponement of morbidity at ever-later age beyond working age?

.... despite the growing concentration of between a third and half of all health costs over the life cycle to the ever-later last 12 months in life?
.... despite a significant reduction of incapacitating chronic diseases?
.... despite much fewer work injuries?
.... despite less traffic and other accidents?
.... despite less exposure to infectious and contagious diseases (some of which have virtually disappeared or have been strictly contained such as rheumatic fever, typhoid fever, syphilis) and to hazardous substances such as asbestos and other carcinogens, dust, etc.?
.... despite the fact that they should actually fall proportionately to the extent that all populations are becoming more educated, as chronic illness and disability rates are highly correlated with low education (they roughly double with lower education)?
.... and despite the remarkable progress in medical treatment and health care institutions?

How is it, at the level of single welfare societies, to be explained that without any evidence of health deterioration, government spending for sickness and disability has, in the UK for instance, quadrupled over the past two decades, and 40% of working-age recipients of state benefits now claim sickness and disability compensation? How can small countries like Austria or the Netherlands, despite most advanced medical and health care systems, nevertheless face hundreds of thousands up to a million persons of working age on disability (pension) benefits, with an overall increase of invalidity pension recipiency rates up to 86% between 1980 and 1997 and of up to 555% for age cohorts 55/56 years within a few years only?[9] How can disability pensions expand sharply exactly in those middle years of working age where up to 90% of workers quit work prematurely but permanently, but where overall disability-related care attendance requirements are on average about half, and median to severe care requirements only around 27% to 17% of the overall population care requirements and only 3 to 7% of disability care requirements of elderly persons above 80 to 85 years of age?[10] And how is it possible that in small neighbouring countries of similar population size and economic structure Switzerland, for instance, has 10% to 12% the number of invalidity pensioners in the middle-aged cohorts from 55 to 65 years than Austria? (Despite or because of the fact that the latter country accepts full invalidity pensions [with more than 50% inability to participate in remunerative work] only, whereas Switzerland has quite a differentiated – and generally generous – IV system of awarding a quarter benefit for less than 40% income loss, half a benefit for minus 50% and a full benefit for minus 66% income loss after injury?)

Modern disability policies are based on a so-called *"social model" of disability*: socio-environmental *handicaps* are seen as incapacitating people with (anatomical, physiological, psychological) *impairments* into a *disability* of performing "normal" activities or fulfilling conventional societal roles properly. While such an interactionist, dynamic perspective makes much sense and certainly more sense than an individualistic, strictly medical conceptualization of disability, it also makes by its very nature for *fuzzy and ever shifting boundaries between disabled and non-disabled persons*. As an inevitable consequence, it lends itself to systematic overclaims and waste, and even invites chronic overuse, abuse, opportunistic behaviour and moral hazard as well as inclusion and exclusion errors in assessment.

Thus, the deficiency of modern disability welfare is a *triple failure*:

- Firstly, the failure to *contain the case load*, the *inclusionary auto-dynamics* and the corresponding fiscal burdens at "reasonable" and that may just be traditional, previous levels of disability prevalence and disability costs or at benchmarked levels of comparable, advanced welfare societies – overall disability-related programme expenditures as a percentage of GDP, or of total public social spending, or *aggregate contribution rates to disability insurance* as the only *prices signalling overdose*, waste and abuse;
- Secondly, the failure to deliver the kind of benefits most needed by needy disabled persons, be they in-kind assistance or service offers, be they monetary transfers to substitute for income losses or earnings restrictions due to disability-related employment constraints, without constraining present or future employment and income opportunities; and
- Thirdly, the failure to focus and target disability benefits on those disabled people most in need of support, in particular severely disabled people, instead of wasting them on either non-deserving persons often neither poor nor needy or on persons in need but deserving and being better helped by other than disability benefits.

Quite obviously but surprisingly, disability policy does reach none of the main goals and objectives of disability welfare. Yet *the failure*, so the hypothesis, *of modern disability policies is not at all accidental but an inevitable by-product, an unintended but unavoidable consequence of a purposeful and successful social compensation policy*. Compensation produces income security for persons with assumed earnings restrictions *without a corresponding level of integration offers and activation demands.*

While the *generous support and compensation policies* now in place in the majority of countries investigated have not only helped disadvantaged people to live decent lives despite disabilities as far as income maintenance is concerned, it has also frequently contributed to their *social exclusion* from the labour market. But without gainful employment persons of working age in job-holding societies are also excluded from full participation in social life. They have, on the other hand, generated a *proliferation of beneficiaries* of disability transfers, many of whom are not only considered able-bodied and perfectly capable of work by their environment but many of whom do consider themselves being "not disabled" at all. The OECD study *Transforming Disability into Ability* reports that *on average one in three (between one in six and one in two) disability benefit recipients do not classify themselves as disabled.*[11] Millions of Europeans, self-declared not disabled, are using the *disability track as the easiest or most attractive exit-path from the labour market* under conditions of chronic stress, dissatisfaction at work, job insecurity, threatening structural unemployment – or, ever more so, under *revealed preferences for lasting leisure* among mature, middle-aged and more or less healthy employees not yet qualifying for regular or early retirement without (actuarial) deductions from pension entitlements.

The conspicuous gap between successful income compensation and failed employment integration, together with an impressive inflow of successful new claimants to invalidity entitlements, has, on balance, generated an *uncontrollable expansion* (and in some cases an explosion) *of disability benefits and costs* over the last decades. Social expenditures on disability are totalling now *several times the social costs of unemployment*, even under adverse conditions of very high unemployment rates: in 19 out of 20 OECD countries investigated (with the exception of Belgium), disability costs were significantly higher than the costs for unemployment, on average more than double the costs (2.17 times), up to 11.9 times the unemployment costs in Norway (*a.a.O.*: Tab. 2.1). *European underemployment malaise seems to have shifted from mass unemployment to a massive non-employment*, of which widespread invalidity has become a major current.

Above the age of 50, in particular, the relationship between unemployed and economically inactive persons, many of them on disability benefits, is now 1:8. The average male is outside the labour force for more than 10 years during working age, the average woman for 22 years, of which the average person is likely to be unemployed or on job search for not more than two years – unemployment (while still quite high) becoming a minor problem as against overall non-employment. Whereas one-in-five adult men of working age is now outside the labour force and another one-in-ten-to-twelve is not working because of unemployment, male unemployed are less than a third of the male non-employed in Europe today ... the proportion of women outside the labour force is six times greater than the proportion unemployed.[12]

Obviously, invalidity accounts for only one faction, though an important and growing one, of overall growing non-employment of adult Europeans of working age. And labour market hypotheses for explaining the rise of disability welfare and related non-employment are all the more plausible, as *no demographic explanations* could be accepted as a possible alternative (they play no role for the working age population, as could be seen already in the first paragraph); and as all medical experts agree that there is no increase in invalidity prevalence and, therefore, *no medical or epidemiological explanation* for this steep increase in invalidity pensions and invalidity expenditures. Aarts and De Jong,[13] in a quantitative study of determinants of change in disability recipiency shares in the Netherlands in the 1980s concluded that only a third of the variance in inflow into disability status is explained by medical factors, two thirds by non-medical determinants, above all benefit generosity and unemployment rates.

At the same time and despite boosting incapacity benefit expenses, not just a few handicapped persons but an unbelievable *majority of those severely disabled* and most in need of support (despite the fact that some of them may actually work) may have been *deprived of the necessary support* (OECD, 2003: Chart 3.8, Tab. 3.7). One could, expressed somewhat sloppy, speak of the forgotten many, the disabled majority of people with (severe) impairments. Current invalidity policies, thus, not only tend to overspend scarce public funds but to divert generous disability funds towards recipients either not in need at all or in need of other re-integration measures than incapacity benefits, while leaving many of those in need of protection without social protection. And it seems to be the very expansion of disability welfare and its inclusionary auto-dynamics that feeds this *widespread misallocation* of benefits awarded frequently at the expense of excluding most of the needy. But are all these millions of invalidity beneficiaries who declare themselves as being not disabled, and these millions of invalidity beneficiaries who receive awards despite their ability to work, do they both also constitute *so many million non-deserving invalidity benefit recipients?*

Certainly not, *inclusion problems* are *much more complicated* than that. By no means, for instance, is the lack of a full overlap or identity between those who are disabled to work (or not), and those who receive disability welfare benefits (or not), caused mainly by either bureaucratic ignorance or cruelty of programme administrators, or by malingering of claimants of disability awards. Manifold are the reasons to explain this most *crucial mismatch*. Though disabled persons are mostly treated as if they were unable to work, the opposite assumption would be more realistic, sound and productive. But even today, with an incapacitating compensation philosophy still widespread, *many welfare recipients are able and interested to continue to work despite a partial incapacity*. More precisely, *one in three recipients of a disability benefit works*, ranging from 10% in Australia to 68% in Sweden (*a.a.O.*: Chart 3.7); and it may just be the income supplement which allows them to integrate not just into the labour market but economically as well on a level of equal consumption opportunities as people without constraining incapacities. Thus, their benefit recipiency is well-targeted and fully effective. Others who declare that they are not disabled and still receive disability benefits may be among those particularly brave and unusually painless and tough people who state their health status as either good, or bad but good enough of not being "moderately or severely hampered in ... daily activities by (this) chronic physical or mental health problem, illness or disability" (so the disability definition of the OECD study), thus simply *understating their handicaps*.

Institutional factors rather than personal toughness may also explain why disability benefits must not have been unjustly awarded to persons declaring themselves as not disabled, for instance when benefits are given to persons with a temporary condition extending beyond the mandatory waiting period (an earnings "sacrifice" asked for as a kind of proof of serious disability before long-term or permanent incapacity to work benefits are granted) before claims are adjudicated. And *wrong inclusion assessment* may also be due to overly lenient, patronizing attitudes or misguided social or labour market considerations of decision-making bodies and not to misrepresentation of the health condition by claimants.

Inversely, many denial decisions may only correctly identify hypochondriac persons who tend to overstate their condition of impairment and disability, thus justly excluding unjustified claims. The significantly *high denial rates* – of an OECD average of 39%, and up to 69% in several countries – as well as the relatively *small share of successful appeals* among rejected applicants of an OECD average of only 16% in 1999 (*a.a.O.*: Tab. 4.13) somewhat corroborates this hypothesis of *widespread overclaims* (if one dismisses the alternative assumption of an overly and well-synchronized, orchestrated strictness by administrators, medical examiners, and independent judges alike). But overclaim (or careless risk behaviour) would be less of a problem – apart from ever rising assessment costs and tort costs, the costs of legal litigation – could it effectively be contained through improved assessment procedures and mechanisms constraining moral hazard (such as, for instance, co-insurance and close monitoring of care-taking behaviour). *Erroneous admission* or false inclusion, on the other hand, if it occurs, is more typical for a public disability scheme and very costly, but less damaging for the persons concerned than the opposite screening error of erroneous denials or unjustified exclusion.

While *unjust exclusion* is expected to happen more systematically within private insurance schemes, its occurrence *in public disability welfare systems*, reputated for maximizing inclusion, but minimizing exclusion errors of unjustified benefit denial, would seriously undermine their legitimacy in an unexpected way. But empirical evidence of *widespread exclusion and misallocation errors* in disability determinations are all too strong to be easily ignored or interpreted away: If between 53.3% and 56% of people who state their illness conditions and sufferance such that they feel "*severely disabled*" do nevertheless *not* receive any disability-related benefit (*a.a.O.*: Tab. 3.7); and if, in addition, 35% of those disabled *and* therefore also non-employed do not receive any disability benefit income at all (*a.a.O.*: Chart 3.8, Panel B); and if of those disabled and non-employed who *do* receive some welfare benefit less than 54% receive a genuine disability benefit while others are dependent on unemployment, social assistance, retirement pension or some other type of differently targeted benefit (*a.a.O.*: Tab. 3.8); then the assumption of frequent award exclusion errors and, therefore, of millions of disabled people either unjustly denied compensation or so discouraged that they have given up even to apply for it any longer, will be difficult to falsify and dismiss. And if erroneous exclusion from benefit recipiency is so widely claimed, even unjustly, then there *is* a real problem of misallocation of awards – or of lack of legitimacy, at least – for an inherently subjective state of affairs such as health, medical and other care needs.

In short: it is the inherently subjective, ambiguous, fuzzy, elusive nature of disability which makes for *almost inevitable shares of non-disabled persons with benefits* on the one hand *and of disabled people without benefits* on the other; but it is *the very size of both these shares* which determines the quality scale or failure rate, i.e. the *overall performance of the disability welfare system*. And the recent OECD report (OECD, 2003) shows quite impressively that, according to whatever standards one would refer to, the mismatch is nothing less than shocking, when a clear majority of severely disabled people is not awarded an incapacity benefit whereas more than 40% of disability recipients are self-declared non-disabled.

In sum, *modern disability policies have been so successful that they have become self-negating and self-destructive:* They attract literarily millions of seemingly non-deserving beneficiaries while depriving neediest disabled non-recipients from disability benefits. They allow for a conspicuous gap between successful income compensation (*a.a.O.*: Chart 3.2) and failed employment integration (*a.a.O.*: Chart 3.6). They allow work wither away for people with disabilities and to make it pay less for them than for people without impairments, despite the fact that work through gainful employment only guarantees a full and equal participation in social life in job-holding societies. They award many more people permanent pensions than they place in rehabilitation (*a.a.O.*: Chart 5.1) or employment programmes (*a.a.O.*: Chart 5.2). They are not able to effectively create employment through activating programmes. Everywhere, they exclude exactly those persons most in need for occupational re-insertion, i.e. above 45 years of age where inflow rates are highest, most systematically from return to work programmes (*a.a.O.*: Table 5.5) – the great age-mismatch between disability inflow and vocational rehabilitation offer (*a.a.O.*: Table 5.6). Thus, they are completely writing-off broad middle-aged cohorts of persons with partial impairments and whole generations of so-called elderly workers having gone through longer spells of unemployment. They invite massive claims for invalidity pensions and illness-related pre-retirement for ever-younger cohorts and frequently even grant early retirement under false disability labels. They have resigned that invalidity expenditures and non-employment costs for disabled people within generally more healthy populations have become many times the unemployment expenditures. They have accepted widespread paid non-employment of employable persons with (partial) disabilities. They take it for granted that extremely low outflow rates for even partial disability tend to make invalidity benefits, once granted, a lifelong welfare dependency. They even tend to channel social problems of long-term unemployment, social assistance and non-employment through the invalidity track, thus making disability a major entrapment for surplus labour populations. They thereby not just misallocate resources at a grand scale but misdirect and reduce energies and work capacities at large. They demoralize and misguide – to the extent these mismatches become widely visible and publicly debated – disabled and non-disabled citizens alike, corrupt norms of solidarity and reciprocity by inviting opportunistic behaviour and widespread abuse of social rights, and threaten to undermine the legitimacy of welfare entitlements and welfare state arrangements altogether.

Though disability welfare policies obviously have done much good, they certainly could do much better in terms of welfare value for programme money spent, both from the point of view of persons with disabilities, in particular those with severe impairments, and from the perspective of society at large.

IV Towards an employment-oriented equal opportunity model: A second or a completed paradigm shift?

As a consequence, the radically ambiguous paradigm shift which has occurred during the last decades must be followed-up by a *shift towards a more coherent employment-oriented equal opportunity model*. Whether this is to be seen either as an evolutionary development, as a consequent continuity and completion of the social model or rather as another radical break, another paradigm shift – away from a system which is becoming unsustainable both in terms of fiscal affordability as well as in terms of social effectiveness, fairness and legitimacy – towards a new synthesis is a minor question of interpretation. *What is crucial is that the normalization and mainstreaming of disability inherent in the social model finally moves away from modelling disability benefits primarily according to a lifelong retirement pension scheme without return option, and moves instead more towards job search, job return and other (re-)start programmes.*

The philosophy underlying these re-insertion and re-integration programmes will value economic independence and full social integration of persons with impairments. It will make all efforts for providing regular employment opportunities for disabled people, and, above all, to make them as equal as possible. As a consequence, today's large numbers and population shares of disability income benefit recipients (in working age!) will simply not be tolerated and seen as a collective welfare failure to be remedied – a failure of public health care and prevention, of social services, of accident prevention, of labour market and of disability policies – and not as a sign of welfare success.

This applies even more so to the (on average) *two thirds majority of persons receiving (partial) disability benefits* who are *excluded from the world of work*: with the exception of Sweden, Mexico and Korea, a majority of welfare beneficiaries in 20 countries investigated does not work, and whereas more than two thirds of disability recipients are active in Sweden, an opposite two thirds is inactive or unemployed in the other OECD countries. The currently *very low* (38% less) *employment* (a.a.O.: Chart 3.6. and Table 3.3.) and *extremely high* (81% higher) *unemployment* rates (a.a.O.: Table 3.5) of persons with health impairments compared to non-disabled persons would have to become totally unacceptable: less than minor differences, measured by the relative (un)employment rate of disabled over non-disabled, at least for those moderately disabled, could just not be taken for granted any longer.

Two groups currently out of work could be *targeted for new employment opportunities* in particular: people with a partial disability or a disability not preventing them from doing any productive work at all, but whose impairment prevents them from finding work at the prevailing wages and working conditions; and those people able to find gainful employment at given income and work environment, but who opt for being defined as disabled since preferring to receive replacement income through incapacity benefits and lasting leisure – or possibly significantly higher overall income through additional undeclared income in the informal sector – over accepting available jobs may be by far the most rational choice from an individual point of view.

Here, *re-designing incentive structures* will be indispensable: for instance, by *de-coupling disability and benefit awards*, recognizing impairment as a condition independent from eligibility for or actual receipt of benefits or employment status (OECD, 2003). Other than today, invalidity recipients could then take the "risk" of taking up a job without knowing whether they will turn out to be fully fit for work in general or that work in particular, without loosing both the return-to-non-work and replacement income option, and without being taxed away all extra income from gainful employment in a confiscatory way (at a 100% marginal tax rate). Furthermore, one would have to ensure people of all disability-related services available according to personal needs and health requirements and irrespective of work status, insurance, and benefit receipt.

As with care attendance allowance, disability benefits should rather compensate for additional expenses due to the impairment, such as extra costs for medical treatment, personal care services, mobility, or education and training. *Tax allowances plus in-kind services plus in-work benefits* may produce better conditions for people with disabilities than the current cash benefits, which are most frequently awarded to substitute for work income, instead of supplementing (restricted or even unconstrained) income from work. *Benefits* for disabled persons will not end (or fall drastically) with taking-up work or gaining income from work, thus being *neither conditional upon non-work, nor on low income irrespective of work (means-tested), nor on no or low income from work*, i.e. being taxed away for reasons of work.

Specific measures which could be meaningful in principle such as, for instance, the *Disability Working Allowance (DWA)* introduced in 1992 in the UK and which since has been replaced by the *Disabled Workers Tax Credit (DWTC)* programme, would have to be radically re-designed in order to make them more effective. This bonus for finding a job was denied to 90% of all 20,000 claimants asking for it within half a year of its introduction because of means-testing results or because the job was not yet in hand. The lesson to be drawn from this failure is obvious: Paradoxically, restricting the number of eligible recipients for return-to-work support policies too much implies to continue the trend to expand the number of incapacity beneficiaries and claimants instead of reducing them. Narrow time limits (of six months) and strict low-income limits, unrelated to the size of the disability benefits, undermine the efficiency of employment vouchers. But for getting people on disability benefits (back) into work, the size of employment vouchers would have to depend exclusively on that of the incapacity benefits awarded, so that the more money is currently spent on maintaining incapacitated persons out of work, the more incentive it offers the disabled person to become employed. Only a generous, uncapped, positive relationship between the value of employment vouchers and disability benefits will make vouchers "buy" incapacitated people into regular employment, whereas an all too stingy flat-rate conception ceiling-off their exchange value will not do the job of getting most persons with disabilities constraining their employability on the job. But employment vouchers will have to remain in place and disabled persons will continue to qualify for them even after they have found employment, though not necessarily for the original employer. This innovative employment-oriented approach towards getting disability beneficiaries into employment suggests to give the recipients of incapacity benefits the – voluntary! – option to use a portion of these benefits to provide employment vouchers for employers that hire them. It is to be found in a recent paper by Orszag and Snower.[14]

The aforementioned and other prerequisites of a successful *Incapacity Benefit Transfer Programme* (IBTP) are modelled after the Unemployment and Training Accounts (UTAs) and the Benefit Transfer Programmes (BTPs)[15] and represent a new approach to employment initiatives, tailor-made for disability benefit recipients. It claims that (under specified premises) "it is *always* possible to stimulate employment through self-financing employment vouchers" and that "for plausible values of the autonomous separation rate and the rate of displacement – they constitute a large fraction of the existing incapacity benefits" (a.a.O.: 4). The positive-sum quality of the IBTP game consists in raising "the take-home pay of the newly recruited (previously incapacitated) workers, while at the same time reducing their cost to the employers. The difference between what the employees receive and what the employers pay is the fraction of the incapacity benefit that has been transferred to employment vouchers. When people draw incapacity benefits, the government bears the cost of supporting them single-handedly. But when they transfer their incapacity benefits to employment vouchers, the government shares this cost with the firms that hire them. Since the amount that the government spends on the employment vouchers is set so as not to exceed what would have been spent anyway on incapacity benefits, the reduction in incapacity and consequent increase in employment can be achieved at no extra budgetary costs." (a.a.O.: 3). In addition, the absence of relevant deadweight for disability beneficiaries allows designing self-financing employment vouchers for incapacitated persons more generous than other employment subsidies for non-employed people.

Creative thinking to create new and better employment opportunities for people with disabilities starts on the premise that it is just *not good enough a disability welfare practice and outcome* if the relative average income of disabled over non-disabled persons or households with a disabled person does not fall back behind too much (OECD, 2003: Chart 3.2). It is much more important that comparable income stems from work, as, once disabled people *do* find work, the income from gainful employment already today is little different from that of non-disabled members of the labour force (*a.a.O.*: Chart 3.4). In short: *work pays and non-work burdens* both disabled *and* non-disabled persons – though (and that is a core policy design problem) *not quite alike*: the relative average personal income of those not working over those working is almost everywhere (with the exception of Belgium, Italy and Norway) significantly better for disabled as against non-disabled persons, this *comparative income protection advantage of disabled people paradoxically making work pay relatively much better for non-disabled persons* over disabled people (*a.a.O.*: Chart 3.5). The big variation in income according to working status is even bigger for non-disabled persons and, therefore, rewards them significantly higher for working efforts than people with impairments.

In the end, *societies will always get more of what they pay more for collectively*. Where unemployment benefits last long, unemployment lasts long, and long-term unemployment may even prevail over short spells of involuntary job turnover.[16] When paying disabled persons an income compensation largely apart from work efforts and not as in-work benefits in order to compensate earnings restrictions through income supplements, social security will produce the expectable though undesired result, namely much more disabled persons out of work than both the people concerned and the society at large may wish for. The effects of disability benefits on the labour market may be similar to those of unemployment benefits, which may actually reinforce the very problem the consequences of which they are intended to mitigate: they may prolong or even fully discourage job search, or taking a job when offered in order not to loose transfers and other, transfer-related entitlements to necessary services; they put upward pressures on wages and induce both workers and employers to opportunistic behaviour such as taking greater risks of dismissals, etc. If you pay for inactivity, that is what you get; if you pay for incapacity, that is what you get.

If you pay for inactivity caused by incapacity or impairment / disability conditioning non-employment, that is what you get. The empirical *correlation between compensation generosity and beneficiary numbers* supports this assumption and basic political wisdom: the more generous (and broader in terms of coverage) the disability entitlements, the higher not only the welfare recipiency stock, but also the new beneficiary inflow rates (OECD, 2003: Charts 6.4-6.6). And certain restrictions of welfare benefits during the last decade have been accompanied by an overall decline in the total number of new disability recipients, i.e. in inflow rates 1999 over those 1995 as against those in 1990 (a.a.O.: Table 4.5). Thus, cutting back on welfare generosity – not in terms of pay granted but in terms of strings attached to grants awarded! – may, quasi automatically, also cut back the numbers of new disability recipients. It may also – in the longer term, once that new policy orientation has become generally known if not accepted – reduce the number of new claimants of entitlements. But studies also show a discouragingly long time lag for institutional changes to trickle down to the persons affected – legislative changes normally take five years before the population at large and not just a few people most concerned take note of the new situation.

Given the alternative of *long-term if not life-long non-employment invalidity entrapment, conditioning benefit payment on increasing employability* is actually without serious alternative. As with long-term unemployment, all measures preventing it, as well as measures improving skills and thereby employability, are preferable at almost any cost, as the costs of failure are inevitably even higher. In principle, persons with disabilities must be made attractive to employers, be it through active help with motivation and job-finding, be it through specific skill formation, be it through a flexible system of wage differentials and either income supplements or employment vouchers for persons with earnings restrictions due to impairment.

If society gets too much inactivity caused by incapacity because that is what it pays for, there are two alternative solutions: either cutting off disability benefit payments, or continue to keep paying them, but after a period of non-employment payment only for activity rather than inactivity. This will eliminate long-term or life-long disability welfare dependency – the more serious the more long-life societies will become. Long-term incapacity dependence is as terrible a waste and social ill as long-term unemployment, as, after a while, long-term non-employed persons become practically unemployable and long-term non-employment prevents employment from rising which in turn causes ever long non-employment. The answer, therefore, is to prevent disabled people entering long-term non-employment in the first place, a policy priority that has been formulated in the EU guidelines adopted at the Luxembourg Summit in 1997 with respect to effectively combating long-term unemployment.

Generosity of disability benefits *per se* will not only not *undo* non-employment of persons with impairments, but rather co-produce it. The crucial factor is how society treats people with disabilities: whomever it allows to be discriminated against, discrimination will effectively take place against these vulnerable groups; and whatever it subsidizes, it gets more of it, both inactivity and activity. In order to prevent long-term if not life-long inactivity of people with disabilities, a better use of the benefit money is – to subsidize jobs. If there is anything which can be done to reduce non-employment and unemployment of persons with incapacity, it is offers of work, or training, retraining, work practice, vocational rehabilitation or other measures of creating employability for the non-employed disabled persons at the earliest possible stage in order to break a pattern of life in a culture of dependence.

Long-term non-employment, thus, more than unemployment is an *invalidity trap* of first order with next to no return opportunities: the longer someone is out of work, the lower the chances of re-entry into the labour market. As with unemployment, its long-term (over one year) duration becomes the single most important determinant of continued unemployment – so-called *hysteresis* – and a stigma in itself. Employers having a choice will always prefer people with short spells of job search as against long-term unemployed however better their qualifications may be. Long-term joblessness is even more stigmatizing and makes people even more *unemployable* in employers' perception if the persons concerned may be attributed other comparative disadvantages such as disability or having stayed not only out of specific jobs or work but out of the workforce altogether by even given-up job search and labour market availability at all. Publicly *subsidizing non-employment of* previously and potentially *employable persons with handicaps* – instead of subsidizing all efforts at job maintenance or rapid re-insertion and upgrading their employability – is a *core entrapment* of many disability welfare policies.

Consequently, *timing of preventive action* and *sequencing of return-to-work and activation measures* is crucial. This requires occupational health and safety investment to reduce occupational hazards and risks of work injuries; early intervention to prevent pathological conditions from illness or accidents turning into impairments; rapid and sound medical rehabilitation to correct impairments by medical treatment, aids or appliances in order to prevent them from becoming chronic or even leading to functional limitations; and vocational rehabilitation, or workplace accommodation, and work assistance for strengthening offsetting capacities in order to prevent functional limitations turning into prolonged or irreversible work disability. Everything will have to be done to *prevent exit from work in working age* in general and to *block the disability exit-path* – often after long-term unemployment or social assistance or long-term sickness – in particular.

While everybody will agree in principle with this focus on early intervention in order to prevent long-term benefit dependency from arising at all, much *time* is *lost* in practice *by inadequate timing* of activation. In many countries vocational rehabilitation, for instance, if it exists at all or not just formally (such as, e.g. in the United Kingdom where until recently – till about the year 2000 – rehabilitation efforts were virtually nil and the Employment Rehabilitation Service was meant to be privatized), starts only when a person is potentially entitled to or even already paid a disability benefit (OECD, 2003). By this practice, the long and critical period of sickness absence is irrevocably lost for re-integration – and the potential and initial motivation to return to work may be withered away after one year or more out of work with up to the full previous income. As a counter-intentional result of these perverse practices widely prevailing, it is less the very nature of the initial health condition, or the impairment stemming from it, or the objective severity of functional limitations, but the permanency of the work-disabling condition of a prolonged stay out of work artificially produced by delayed re-insertion measures which transforms unused abilities into disability and dependence.

The crucial difference and strategic institutional deficiency at stake, thus, is *not income but job discrimination* and *adverse self-selection into non-employment*. And it is this, partly politically induced, option for non-employment and the, partly politically accepted, job discrimination of employers that will have to be overcome. The same applies for overall *absenteeism due to health conditions* which is not monitored systematically and comparatively so far: anything more than a few percentage segments in every working age population which are so acutely sick or ill or injured or incapacitated that work is actually completely impossible, could be critically screened, surveyed and regularly reviewed for its causes and assessed against comparative benchmarks. The fact that overall absenteeism rates, sickness and disability benefits and costs vary that strongly not just between countries of different socio-economic development – and probably very different underlying health conditions of the population and health care capacities – but vary also equally strongly between similarly advanced, similarly wealthy and similarly healthy populations shows impressively that *institutions and policies* do *matter*, and matter a lot. Differences in health and disability welfare institutions, as well as differences in labour markets and social policies, make for far more difference in disability prevalence socially accepted as work-disabling than the differences in subjectively perceived and "objective" health status.

Absenteeism from work is a good case in point of how institutional arrangements may or may not first invite moral hazard and, after its occurrence or not, require policy change in order to contain opportunistic behaviour – or not. Some of the most advanced welfare states such as Sweden or Germany by the very generosity of their sickness benefit conditions first invited widespread abuse of sickness insurance and then introduced harsh measures in order to cut down on sickness pay – by reduced income replacement rates, waiting periods (*"Karenztage"*), differential replacement rates by lowering substitute income for the first two or three months of absence, increased employer's cost-sharing for sickness payments, etc. Sweden, after taking recourse to waiting periods punishing short-term absence from work and illness by income losses, succeeded to cut absenteeism from an average of about 27 workdays annually by almost half; it then found itself at the same level of illness-related absence from work as Austria without any such punitive action and with the same level of generosity of benefits as Sweden before. Welfare generosity obviously requires a collective containment of moral hazard.

By the very nature of sickness, work-related accidents, occupational diseases or other forms of disability, moderate and therefore *partial disablement* would be expected to prevail over *total work disability*, and *temporary incapacity* should prevail over *lifelong and irreversible* one. But empirically, the opposite is true: *outflow rates from disability benefits*, even for partial disability, *are extremely low*, i.e. around 1% (!) in 80% of the countries investigated (*a.a.O.*: Chart 4.1), so that *benefits once awarded are an almost irreversible way into long-term welfare dependency*, regardless of the underlying health conditions. Those countries investigated that offer partial benefits (a quarter of them even partial disability at several gradations), also happen to be among the countries with the highest recipiency rates. The existence and availability of partial benefits seems not only not constraining but rather expanding overall disability recipiency, demonstrating that preventing partial benefits creeping into full or permanent dependency is a major challenge in offsetting disability welfare spread. Currently, even in countries providing partial benefits, only one in three awards is for partial disability, whereas the great majority of benefits is for full incapacity.

Furthermore, in contemporary welfare systems *more people are awarded a disability benefit than receive vocational rehabilitation services* (a.a.O.: Chart 5.1) and *ten times more people are on benefits than in special employment programmes for disabled people* (a.a.O.: Tab. Chart 5.2). Despite the fact that the *employment value for active programme money* seems to be quite *doubtful*, given the weak correlation between employment rate and expenditure on active employment-related programmes for disabled persons (a.a.O.: Chart 5.4), it certainly is an indication of societies which have not got their priorities right, namely towards return to work measures.

In a paper for the European Centre,[17] the editor of this book and main author of the OECD report summarizes the – rather disenchanting – *relationship between "policy and employment outcome"* such: "Differences in employment population ratios are apparently not explained by differences in countries' employment and rehabilitation policies ... The relationship between the two variables is virtually zero. One could argue that this result is a consequence of the fact that current employment outcome is determined by yesterday's rather than today's policy... However, correlating late 1990s employment rates with pre-1990 activation policies does not affect the conclusion. High employment rates are found in countries with strong as well as weak employment and rehabilitation policies, and vice versa. To be more precise, none of the ten integration policy sub-components is correlated with employment outcome. These results hold for absolute employment levels as well as for employment rates of disabled people relative to those of their non-disabled peers. Hence, the general employment level – as an indicator of social and economic status – does not explain this non-relationship between employment rates and the integration component either." (a.a.O.: 11; for the integration policy sub-components see OECD, 2003: Table A2.2).

Still, *prioritizing re-insertion implies complementing strictly medical rehabilitation by vocational rehabilitation*. Quite obviously, crunches and wheelchairs, artificial limbs or artificial hips may be necessary for restoring body functioning sufficiently in order to be able to move or walk again without too much impairment; but they are far from sufficient in guaranteeing full work capacity again, except in a few well-practiced routine cases. If around one million artificial hips for an annual cost of about 20 billion Euro are implanted each year worldwide with the purpose of letting a million persons not become disabled but enable them again to walk normally, the social value added of these medical expenditures is far from obvious and different welfare philosophies and health practices prevail. Whereas in the United States, for example, patients spend five days in hospital under the premise "a good surgical intervention does not need any follow-up treatment" and are then left to themselves for a privately covered reconvalescence period, the very same hip implantation will take six weeks in Austria; 21 days of hospital treatment plus another 21 days of nursing care and rehabilitation under the premise that "the patient will leave after six weeks of comprehensive care completely healthy and capable to work".

Nevertheless, encompassing comparative cost-benefit analysis of different rehabilitation strategies – such as covering the 5 : 42 difference in days of supported invalidity after an artificial hip implantation surgery described in the paragraph above – are greatly lacking. Furthermore, in his theoretical introduction to this volume Philip R. de Jong points at a number *of "problems surround(ing) rehabilitation policy"*, namely the inherent complexity of assessing the rehabilitative potential ("as complex as screening for partial disability is"), the set-up of an adequate individualized rehabilitation programme, and the unclear character of their efficacy. And all experts from all disciplines stress *the crucial role of subjective motivation,* as if the faith in one's own recovery could actually remove mountains of physical impairment, whereas giving up hope and confidence in successful rehabilitation is as good as its programmed failure. This demonstrates vividly how in cases of medically defined risks and disabilities the insured patient himself – and other parties with interests of their own – may influence the occurrence as well as the degree of invalidity.

In sum, an *employment-oriented equal opportunity disability policy model* would emphasize activation, customized early intervention, tailor-made work assistance, seasoning, vocational training and occupational rehabilitation, removal of disincentives to work and employment; it would develop schooling, training, job placement and assistance services, subsidize or otherwise compensate employers for competitive disadvantages eventually stemming from disabled members of the workforce, and support disabled people working by in-work benefits and a rights-based approach of effective anti-discrimination legislation. It would try to develop a *culture of mutuality*. Within this *new social contract* between society, people with disabilities and their employers, *every party will have more rights a n d more obligations* at the same time, as the OECD report claims as well. Recipient's obligations will match their rights as beneficiaries; and employers will be more obliged than they currently are to accommodate the workplaces for persons with disabilities. Disabled persons will be entitled to a tailor-made, personalized assistance for re-integration into work – and income supplements to the extent of their failure only – and not above all to replacement income benefits. And employers in an employment-oriented disability policy will be mandated to accommodate workers with disabilities, take and retain them and be compensated for that, instead of massively using or abusing disability entitlements to discharge surplus workforce at public expense and contributing to widespread, costly, and absolutely unnecessary non-employment of the overwhelming majority of non-employed people with disabilities, as is currently the case.

Thus, *employers* too will have new rights and new obligations under this *new deal*. Above all, external costs generated by using disability benefit schemes as a workforce management tool will have to be re-internalized by some form of experience rating – employers producing more accidents, occupational diseases, work injuries, sickness, disability and pre-retirement will on some intermediate level of risk pooling (enterprise, sector, region) be held responsible for their decisions. They will have to become actively involved in prevention, rehabilitation and re-integration – and to be publicly supported in sharing and carrying-out public functions and compensated for *"undue hardship"* undermining their competitive edge. If, for instance, employment quotas for persons with handicaps are used as a policy instrument, non-compliance with legal obligations and free-riding at the expense of competing enterprises will have to be prevented by cost-sharing arrangements and fines reflecting realistic costs. But more than guaranteeing fairness in burden-sharing, public authorities will have to make sure that companies willing to retain or recruit persons with disabilities will be technically assisted to actually do so: workplace and job adjustments usually are not expensive financially, but complex and demanding socially throughout the process of problem assessment over developing an intervention strategy to evaluating outcomes of the accommodation process.

Public authorities too will have to re-direct their policies, for reasons both of social cohesion impact and effectiveness of disability welfare as well as its cost-efficiency. In an employment-oriented equal opportunity disability policy model, a much greater share of overall expenditures on disability welfare will have to go to active programmes instead of passive benefit transfers. *Activation* is not only promising in terms of long-term sustainability of funds allocated, both vocational rehabilitation and training programmes are actually less expensive than benefit transfers without return option. Sheltered employment, in contrast, is not only frequently inappropriate and most problematic for its ghettoizing segregation effects and its permanence, it is also much more expensive not only than activation programmes but even than passive disability benefits themselves. It is the more surprising that sheltered employment mostly remains as important as ever before and that its replacement by supported employment initiatives in the regular labour market does not advance as one could rationally expect it to do.

But without individualized participation offers, work re-integration packages, personal job coaches and help in work-related and extra-occupational activities, normalization and integration of people with disabilities into regular labour markets and work opportunities is doomed to fail. Worst of all, the *striking age-mismatch between disability inflow and vocational rehabilitation offer* will have to be ended: currently, there is almost no participation in active programmes of those most in need, namely above age 45, whereas younger people have an attendance far above their disability prevalence requirements (*a.a.O.*: Chart 5.6). And, as was shown repeatedly throughout this chapter, disability benefits will have to be re-designed by public authorities, policy-makers, legislators and programme administrators in such a way that incentives, including strong financial incentives for both firms and their handicapped employees, will be reoriented towards return-to-work incentives instead of their current out-of-work bias.

Cautionary Postscript as an Appendix: Forever beyond the Dark Ages of sin, stereotypes, stigma, sanitizing – and much worse?

Normalization or mainstreaming of disability do not imply that rationality, fairness and equality in treating people with disabilities exist. Rather, collective compassion is distributed quite unevenly and arbitrarily, though not accidentally – but with serious consequences for the categories of handicapped persons concerned. This *graded or unequal compassion for various types of disability* has been observed by scholars like Wilensky and tried to explain as *"a hierarchy of sympathy"*: "a blind colleague briefed me on the amazing array of benefits the state supplied to the blind, even the partially blind. I then inquired into state benefits for the deaf, for paraplegics, and other groups. They were nowhere near what had already been achieved by organizations of and for the blind, with the possible exception of polio victims, whose plight had been dramatized by FDR and the immensely successful National Polio Foundation ... One would be hard put to say that a partially blind person is worse off than a paraplegic. A psycho-political explanation for the differences in state largesse might go like this: A well-dressed blind person with a tapping cane and a handsome guide dog is as appealing on the street as the picture of the smiling child on crutches in the Polio Foundation posters. But a paraplegic in a wheel chair is less mobile. If she appears in public, she makes the passer-by uneasy. And unlike the blind, the paraplegic cannot readily make her way up the Capitol steps or the state capitol offices to lobby for her particular group as the blind person and his dog can. All this began to change in the 1960s as other groups became more militant and better organized ..., began to coordinate political action across types of disability, and acquired better technology and support."[18]

Furthermore, normalization or mainstreaming of disability do not mean that earlier attitudes of indifference and rejection, that even hostility and discrimination are completely overcome and do not persist. But underlying currents can neither prevail overtly, nor are stigma and stereotypes and unequal access and opportunity any longer politically tolerable. This is important enough to notice against the background not just of the ultimate horrors of systematic mass killing of *"life unworthy of living"* (*lebensunwertes Leben*), often simply ill people who could not be healed and had no prospect of recovery within a regime which saw itself as a healing movement, or people of "inferior races", by the Nazis.[19] It seems absolutely unimaginable today that only somewhat over half a century ago, two to three decades ago before the recent paradigm shift towards mainstreaming and integration of people with impairments occurred, it was still considered a *"volksschädliche"* disability worthy of *forced internment* in special asylum institutions, against the will of the persons concerned and that of their parents, when children were stigmatized as *"asozial"* in their behaviour, or used to be even only *bed-wetting* or *nail-biting*. This may be less surprising in view of the fact that people were even killed for "crimes" such as "disobedience", not denouncing a hidden Jewish friend, carrying felt boots, not respecting the law prescribing shop closing hours, the possession of carrier pigeons and the illegal slaugther of animals, owning radios in some occupied territories and the unauthorized hearing of BBC, or occasional black labour or black market trading of say, cigarettes.[20]

It may have been this *ultimate insanity of Nazi sanitarianism*, the ultimate cruelty and grotesqueness of the obsession with *sanitizing society*, biopolitically conceptualized as a *Volkskörper* in need of eliminating everything defined as "insane", of coercive health, trimming, fitness, rejuvenation, cleaning and purification which should have once for ever discredited the discrimination of people with impairments and disabilities. Sanitarianism made great efforts at controlling all public health-relevant action and population development – from sexuality, generative behaviour over lifestyle, dietary practices, drinking etc. to low-cost dying. It aggressively propagated, for instance, breast-feeding, cancer prevention and nutrition therapies, wholemeal bread and soja bean, raw diet, vegetarianism, clean air, and crusaded against cancer, asbestos, food colouring and conservation matter, pesticides, alcohol and nicotine (including a ban on sports-related and erotic marketing of tobacco), against "decadent" make-up, marketing of baby food stuff, obesity, abortion, homosexuality, vivisection, etc.[21]

Though attacks on impaired people or their overt discrimination may never again be tolerated, contemporary societies, unfortunately, have by no means finally overcome all other biopolitical and eugenic temptations. They range from grounding politics not in socio-economic interests, but in inherited, "natural" identities; over perfecting the human race through genetic screening to eugenic manipulations; to policing, sanctioning, finally eradicating "unhealthy" behaviour of all sorts, stigmatized as contagious or only dangerous for oneself, but irresponsible and costly to society. The Nazi Hitler youth movement propagated *"Du hast die Pflicht, gesund zu sein!" – you are obliged to be healthy;* or *"Ernährung ist keine Privatsache" – nutrition is not a private matter*. But *biopolitics* and *eugenics* have not only preceded but also survived Nazism and have, as does *euthanasia*, recently had a surprising revival in modernized and humane form in several Western societies.[22]

Mid twentieth-century Nazism has peaked in the utmost possible perverse way a long history of cruelty or ruthlessness towards persons with disabilities. Whether intolerance of deviance and diversity (difficult to cope with and challenging otherwise not challenged persons), what Jacques de Goff called "the inner demons" of European history will have been finally overcome once and forever is still to be seen. History, anthropology and ethnology teach us an incredible diversity of *what constituted "impairment" and "disability" across time and space – and what did not do so*; and what behaviour was socially accepted or not, what was disapproved or even stigmatized and what norms and obligations towards persons with disabilities – and by them – were prevailing.

Cultural diversity is actually striking: Many societies fully integrated people with what today is perceived as a severe physical impairment or a grave mental disorder, or as social deviance or deprivation, such as being insane and/or being homeless, being unable to hold down a job or unable to read and write, being dirty and unkempt, or simply being obese and still appear in public; while other societies strongly stigmatized traits (or behaviour) considered normal or fully acceptable in our societies such as being infirm or ugly or infertile, living alone unmarried, or having no children, or having children with congenital impairment, or drinking alcohol, or being HIV positive; with "ugliness" as an impairment starting with a crooked nose, excessive freckles, or flabby or small buttocks.

Judeo-Christianity oscillated between interpreting impairments as warranting healing, charity for the sick and support on the one hand and as signs of wrongdoing, justifying the separation of people supposedly unclean and ungodly on the other. In the Old Testament, it was the incapacity to pray in the community of others and not that to work which constituted disability: people with crooked noses, sores, missing limbs, leprosy, skin diseases and crushed testicles displayed human impairments precluding them from participation in religious rituals. Throughout the Middle Ages, truly Dark Ages of stigma for persons with disabilities, the Church and some of its Saints such as St. Augustine continued to interpret *impairment as punishment for sin* and people with impairments as living proof of Satan's existence and power over ordinary mortals. Disordered minds, in particular, were attributed to demonic forces. An impaired infant was seen as a "changeling", the Devil's substitute for a human child or the product of the mother's involvement with sorcery and witchcraft. Birth of an impaired child was a proof of parents' involvement with witchcraft, sinful practices or wickedness, impairment was a *shameful stigma* provoking fear, ridicule and mockery, if not isolation, ostracism and even persecution. In normal periods of everyday life, in contrast, people with impairments and mental disorders were tolerated and integrated into families and into domestic and agricultural labour, before capitalist industrialization pushed ever growing numbers of "the aged and the infirm", "the sick", "the insane" and "the defectives" and others unable to meet the pace of factory production into segregation in workhouses, asylums, and later into residential homes or sheltered employment institutions.[23]

History, anthropology and ethnology also teach us that it always was and is less the physical or psychic impairment as such but the *meaning* of disability within the social order and production process that determines societal reactions to incapacity. If a congenital impairment, for instance, is seen as caused by nature or God, individuals cannot be blamed for it – as they often are, more or less openly, in modern Western societies. In several contemporary Central African cultures, in contrast, *impairment is not at all stigmatized, while ugliness or childlessness are*. Physically impaired persons may work and marry, become parents and participate in community life to the best of their abilities, whereas *"faults" of "ugliness"* such as "excessive freckles, protruding navel, absentmindedness, and flabby or small buttocks" may make it difficult if not impossible to marry.[24]

It is easy to think of functionally equivalent forms of "ugliness" stigmatized in modern and post-modern societies, with different "faults" actually disapproved, ranging from disadvantageous to acutely disabling in occupational and private life, acting as barriers to careers at professional work, to marriage and conviviality, though in a much more hidden, inauthentic, self-denying – and therefore also more difficult to combat and to overcome – manner. In contrast to *handicaps caused by physical impairment*, *incapacities resulting from social deprivation* such as being poor, looking poor, being low-skilled, clumsy, extremely timid, speech deficient, functionally illiterate, having ticks or ridiculous habits, being homeless, unable to hold down a job, unwashed and unkempt in public, or having social phobias or panics (at least as long as they are not recognized in medical terms as a health condition or mental illness) and their consequences frequently lead to joblessness and social isolation, but with (almost) no entitlements to income or other benefits.

Generally, it is less a physical impairment as such which defines disability but its interpretation. In traditional societies, it is less the ability or disability to perform certain tasks, but the place of a person in cosmology and thus its personhood which defines disability; then, the primary focus is less on improving the situation of an impaired person, but on interpreting the fault. The fault is best interpreted such that divine intervention – or sort in modern, secularized societies – plays more of a role than any kind of failure, failure of parents to respect food or sex taboos, bad family relationships leading to sorcery, lack of respect for ancestors – or unhealthy, even risky lifestyle in our societies. Traditionalism stigmatizes *childlessness* and even denies personhood to persons without children: "In many traditional societies.... The key 'disabling' condition is failure to have children: parenthood is the key to adult status. Those without children of their own ... are sometimes given children by other members of their family, so that they can acquire full personhood ..." (a.a.O.: 15).

The WHO study on "Disability and Culture. Universalism and Diversity"[25] demonstrates impressively that archaic conceptions are not restricted to traditional tribes such as the Masai, Punan Bah, Songye or Tuareg. Rather, intolerance against deviance from mainstream patterns of behaviour and moralizing of unhealthy lifestyles as harmful if exercised by disapproved marginal groups prevails in many contemporary post-industrial societies: "someone who is dirty and unkempt"..."should not appear in public and tried to be stopped", even less so than "someone with a chronic mental disorder who 'acts out' ". Even infertility is assigned a minor "disabling effect" of health conditions (a.a.O.: 270). Childlessness may continue to meet disapproval in important segments of many so-called modern Western societies, as traditionalist groups are trying to establish childlessness as the result of a kind of sinful, egotistical, irresponsible, and that is sanctionable and stigmatized behaviour. Superficially, declining birth rates and corresponding population shrinking and its consequences are taken as reasons for increasing the salience of this issue and to politicize it. But the scapegoating of childless persons as embodiment of a collectively disabling and harmful condition is even more puzzling in view of the facts: first, the share of women without children in today's Western societies of around 15 to 20% is significantly below, often around only a half of that of the times of their grandmothers at the early twentieth century when childlessness was above 30% of the female population; and secondly, not only has childlessness fallen and not increased in a secular perspective, it also contributes much less to declining birth rates than the falling fertility of women who *do* have children, but on average significantly less than at times before demographic maturity.

Furthermore, *blaming the victim for congenital impairment* in particular is far from being overcome in folklore and broad popular sentiments and resentments. Intolerance against deviance and less calculable behaviour is still deep-rooted though rarely expressed openly nowadays. Thus, even obviously "innocent" outsiders such as physically impaired persons, brain-damaged children, mentally ill or infirm old people may not just be discriminated against by avoiding contact but may see themselves being prejudiced through moralizing attribution of self-infliction and culpable behaviour. A study reporting opinion poll survey results in Germany in the late 1960s demonstrated as supposedly "most important causes of physical impairments: medicament abuse by parents (73%), alcohol- and nicotine abuse (62%), hereditary transmission (55%), attempts at abortion (42%), venereal diseases (37%)". Crippling of the child was attributed to a culpable behaviour of its parents.

Underlying such a pitiless stigmatization of disabled people may be a hidden since forbidden desire of annihilation. Another study in the mid-1970s analysing anonymous protest calls to the Austrian Broadcasting Corporation ORF found many anonymous protests to complain about the "*disgusting*" *appearance of severely impaired children* in public TV, some of which even asked for an "elimination" of such "burdening" creatures.[26] But hostility which stops short of demands for physical elimination and asks for displacement and segregation of disabled people "only" frequently does not even hide behind anonymity: Law suits have been filed – and rejected – for "spoiled vacation pleasures" of "having to see" greater numbers of guests with severe disabilities in tourist recreation sites; and local communities mobilized against the establishment of sheltered workshops and residential housing for disabled children and youth in their neighbourhood.

Apart from the fact that the "hereditary disease" these persons actually suffered from may have been the remnants of their or their ancestors' Nazi-past and its *Herrenrassen* ideology, it also proofs how easily political correctness of speech codes and norms of decency may wither away under conditions of "permission" through either unsanctioned anonymity of expression or through socially approved instigation to hatred or contempt or political mobilization – or self-righteous moralizing. Then, hidden and suppressed wishes of strongly prejudiced persons at destruction of provoking diversity which makes feeling insecure will become the more open, the weaker and more helpless the secretly detested and disdained objects of prejudice actually are.

It is not difficult to imagine, how little it would take in order to again stigmatize people with (congenital or acquired) impairments, or their parents, could it be proved scientifically (or only credibly be asserted) that some extremely dangerous or contagious or costly or repellent or publicly rejected diseases were caused by a behaviour to be blamed for its occurrence or spread, such as, for instance, drug or alcohol or nicotine abuse, unconventional sexual practices or promiscuity, unhealthy lifestyle, non-compliance with compulsory vaccination requirements risky for public health, costly negligence of medical treatment prescriptions or (in the future maybe) the non-take-up of genetic screening facilities, whether voluntary or not.

Under these circumstances, even objectively harmless but cumbersome disruptions of public order (such as a frequent occurrence of incontinence or vomiting of drug dependent persons in public places or spaces) or widespread small "survival" delinquency by ill and destitute "junkies" may evoke deeply hostile popular reactions. The popular stigmatization of HIV infection in the early period of the pandemic, which was most skilfully contained in later stages, shows, nevertheless, the potentially explosive dangers of blaming the victim for self-inflicted disease, disability, and transmission of risk. And even after the successful medicalization and normalization of HIV/AIDS, heavy social disapproval or stigma against persons infected persists in almost all countries[27] – despite the astonishing fact that HIV infection was found to be the most variable health condition in the study, being ranked from the most disabling of all health conditions in Egypt and Tunisia to the third-least disabling condition in Luxembourg (a.a.O.: 271) but with almost identical disapproval ranking in these countries. Thus, it is not just the infectiousness and danger of a potentially deadly disease which arouses stigma but the moral indignation and social disapproval as such – alcoholism and drug addiction were most strongly stigmatized almost everywhere despite their being less dangerous for public health.

Notes

1. Wilensky, H.L. (2002) *Rich Democracies. Political Economy, Public Policy, and Performance*. Berkely et al.: University of California Press, p. 550, Fn 1, see also Stone, D.A. (1985) *The Disabled State*. London: Macmillan.

2. Occcasionally, this strategy went as far as in a number of large semi-public enterprises in the course of their privatization in Austria. Between 1998 and 2002, post, telecom, public bus and public railways dismissed thousands of their employees into early retirement via disability pensions. Obvious irregularities and conspicuous regularities generated a suspicion of abusive patterns and led to an investigation by a special commission of the Federal Office on Crime *(Bundeskriminalamt)*. After screening the first third of the files documenting the early retirement practices, inquiries confirmed not only the suspicion of widespread abuse but detected refined forms of exploiting a legal situation where regular early retirement would be at the expense of companies whereas incapacity-related pre-retirement must fully be covered by public schemes: if an equivalent job to the one somebody is unable to carry out is not available, pre-retirement is foreseen at public expense by the law regulating civil service. In searching systematically for reasons given for invalidity with the help of computer programmes, investigators found out that early retirees (of an age 45 and lower) always displayed exactly those illnesses and impairments which made them unable to work exactly but only at the position they were holding before: most chauffeurs retired because of back pain not allowing for prolonged sitting; postmen mostly had a prolapsed disc incapacitating them from lifting or carrying heavy things; employees working on computers had almost always seeing impairments preventing them to continue working on screens; office workers were most frequently diagnosed with mental and psychological problems which did not allow them to concentrate on their work that, therefore, had to be given up. Thus, whereas practically none of the around 4,500 diagnosed "invalids" sent into pre-retirement up to more than two decades before legal retirement age was attested a general disability to work, all of them were finally defined as disabled to work – as they were diagnosed as unable to work at their previous workplaces and seen able to work in all those other areas where no work was available. Each enterprise and each category of disability to work had a special group of medical examiners issuing the medical assessments. The Chamber of Physicians *(Ärztekammer)*, a mandatory corporatist interest representation of medical doctors, which had previously complained with some of the companies that several of their members were put under pressure to hand-out benevolent clinical expertises refused to help the criminal investigations and to collaborate with the judicial authorities in order to protect those of its members which had collaborated with business companies in falsely diagnosing tailor-made "disabilities to work" (status as of early Fall 2002).

3. Wolff, M. et al. (1995) *Where We Stand*, pp. 122, 123, documenting the Number of Medical Complaints per 1,000 People over a Three-Year Period found, for instance, that Germans seek 23 times more often treatment against back pain than US-Americans and 2.5 times so often than French; they consult physicians 10 times more frequently than Americans and 3 to 4 times more often than French regarding heart problems; when it comes to bronchitis, Germans see doctors 15 times more often than Americans and 5 times the French; whereas French people seek treatment of depressions around 15 times more often than Americans; nervousness gets the French 4 times more frequent to the doctor than Americans and twice as often as Germans; insomnia makes French clients seeking help

239 times more often than Americans and 4 times the neighbouring Germans, while Germans complain 11 times more frequent about skin problems than US citizens and 4 to 5 more often than the French.

4   Council of Europe (2002) *Assessing Disability in Europe – Similarities and Differences*. Strasbourg: Council of Europe, p. 16.
5   Soukup, W. (2000) 'Psychiatrisch-neurologische Erkrankungen', p. 14 in: BMSG, *Fachtagung "Invalidität" der Kommission zur langfristigen Sicherung des Pensionssystems*, 30-31 October. Wien: Bundesministerium für Soziale Sicherheit und Generationen.
6   Martin, J./Meltzer, H./Elliot, D. (1988) *OPCS Surveys of Disability in Great Britain*, 4 Vols. London: HMSO, Tab 3.6.
7   Wilensky, op. cit., p. 550.
8   Mashaw, J.L. (1983) *Bureaucratic Justice: Managing Social Security Disability Claims*. New Haven, CT: Yale University Press, p. 18.
9   Prinz, C. (1999) 'Invaliditätspension als *die* Frühpension? Österreichische Entwicklungen im europäischen Vergleich', pp. 417-483 in: Prinz, C./Marin, B. (1999), *Pensionsreformen. Nachhaltiger Sozialumbau am Beispiel Österreichs*. Frankfurt/New York: Campus.
10 Badelt, Ch./Holzmann-Jenkins, A./Matul, Ch./Österle, A. (1997) *Analyse der Auswirkungen des Pflegevorsorgesystems*, Forschungsbericht im Auftrag des Bundesministeriums für Arbeit, Gesundheit und Soziales, Wien, p. 44, Tab. 9.3.
11 OECD (2003) *Transforming Disability into Ability. Policies to Promote Work and Income Security for Disabled People*. Paris: OECD, Chart 3.9.
12 Rose, R. (2000) 'Demographic Shifts, Fiscal Pressures and Long-term Employment Opportunities', p. 385f. in: Marin, B./Meulders, D./Snower, D.J. (Eds.), *Innovative Employment Initiatives*, and Marin, B., 'Introducing Innovative Employment Initiatives', op. cit. p. 75.
13 1992, 1993, see also Aarts, L./Burkhauser, R./de Jong, P. (1996) *Curing the Dutch Disease. An International Perspective on Disability Policy Reform*. Aldershot: Avebury.
14 Orszag, J./Snower, D.J. (2002) Incapacity Benefits and Employment Policy, Discussion Paper No. 529. Bonn: IZA.
15 See Snower, D.J. (1994) 'Converting Unemployment Benefits into Employment Subsidies', *American Economic Review* 84 (2): 65-70; and Snower, D.J. (2000) 'Creating Employment Incentives', pp. 317-346 in: Marin, B./Meulders, D./Snower, D J. (Eds.), op. cit.
16 Layard, R. (2000) 'Clues to Overcoming Unemployment', p. 257 f. in: Marin, B./Meulders, D./Snower, D J. (Eds.), op. cit.
17 Prinz, C. (2001) Disability Policies for the Working Age Population across Europe and Beyond, Working Paper. Vienna: European Centre.
18 Wilensky, H.L. (2002), op. cit., p. 551, Fn 3.
19 Lifton, R.J. (1986) *The Nazi Doctors. Medical Killing and the Psychology of Genocide*. New York: Basic Books.
20 Mende, S. (1999) *Die Wiener Heil- und Pflegeanstalt Am Steinhof im Nationalsozialismus*. Frankfurt et al.: Peter Lang; Gross, J. (2000) *Spiegelgrund. Leben in NS-Erziehungsanstalten*. Überreuter Verlag; Hubenstorf, M. (2000) 'Anatomical Science in Vienna 1938-1945', *Lancet*, 355: 1385f.; and the novel by Kusnezow, A. (2002) *Babij Jar*. Munich: Matthes & Seitz.
21 Proctor, R.N. (1999) *The Nazi War on Cancer*. Princeton/New York: Princeton University Press.
22 Feher, F./Heller, A. (1994) *Biopolitics*. Aldershot: Ashgate; and Heller, A./Puntscher-Riekmann, S. (1996) *Biopolitics. The Politics of the Body, Race and Nature*. Aldershot: Ashgate.

23 Barnes, C./Mercer, G./Shakespeare, T. *Exploring Disability*. Cambridge: The Polity Press, pp. 17-18.
24 Ingstad, B./Whyte, S.R. (Eds.) (1995) *Disability and Culture*. Berkeley: University of California Press, p. 6.
25 WHO – Üstün et al. (2001) *Disability and Culture. Universalism and Diversity*, p. 270.
26 Marin, B. (2000) 'Sozialer Friede und Aggression im Alltag', in: Marin, B., *Antisemitismus ohne Antisemiten. Autoritäre Vorurteile und Feindbilder*. Frankfurt/New York: Campus, pp. 803, 804, 809.
27 See WHO – Üstün et al. (2001), op. cit., p 276.

CHAPTER 2

Disability and Disability Insurance

Philip R. de Jong

1 Introduction

Disability policies seek to increase the welfare of the disabled population by promoting economic self-sufficiency and social integration. Some countries have a large number of people that receive disability income transfers and low employment rates among disabled people. Other countries spend less on disability benefits, and focus on the types of interventions that enable individuals to remain at work, return to work, or enter the workforce for the first time, despite having chronic health conditions or impairments.

The latter approach is generally preferred over the first. Most people would agree that a life of productive employment is far more desirable for individuals with disabilities, for their families, and for society at large than relying on cash benefits as a substitute of wages. Moreover, even when persons with disabilities cannot be fully self-supporting, there may be major gains in family economic welfare and substantial contribution to aggregate productivity when impairments can be accommodated to permit some paid work (Mashaw and Reno, 1996). And, finally, generous and accessible disability benefit programmes have proved to be fiscally and socially unsustainable, as exemplified by the cases of Poland and the Netherlands (Andrews and Hoopengardner, 1999; Aarts et al., 1996).

For younger people the risk of disability is far greater than the risk of death. Disability policy, therefore, also addresses the needs of those that are without disabilities today but may become disabled at some point in the future. Their welfare is increased by offering insurance against loss of earnings due to a medically determined reduction of productivity. Public provision or, at a minimum, public regulation of such insurance is necessary because – as we will argue in Section 3.2 – unregulated, competitive markets fail to provide coverage against disability risks in a form and at a level that is socially adequate.

Social disability insurance primarily offers cash earnings replacement but it may also offer services such as vocational rehabilitation and job mediation, and tangible provisions in kind. The design and operation of a disability benefit scheme reflect the orientation of disability policy at large. If a country's disability policy aims at making employment opportunities of disabled people as equal as possible to those without disabilities access to permanent disability benefits will be restricted. Such an employment-oriented policy stresses prevention and vocational rehabilitation. It may contain legislation that prohibits discrimination of disabled people, mandates employers to accommodate jobs to the limitations of their employees, imposes an employment quota, or mandates benefit recipients to join a vocational rehabilitation programme improving the chances to return to paid work.

While formation and restoration of the earning capacity of the disabled population of working age is the prime goal of disability policy, in every society there is a group of people who are so severely disabled that they are permanently left without productive capacity. As they have no employment opportunities, the welfare of totally and permanently disabled people can be improved by income transfers and in-kind benefits that support their social inclusion. The size of this group depends on medical and rehabilitative technology, but also on the willingness of society to spend money on reducing their social exclusion.

This book offers a comparison of disability policies in eleven European countries, and the policy reforms they have witnessed. These countries range from very prosperous welfare states (Switzerland and Norway) to East European transition states (Poland and Slovenia). Apart from their current economic prosperity they differ in many other respects – e.g. their political and economic history – that have an impact on the shape and outcomes of their social policies. Each country chapter, therefore, not only dwells on the design, amendment and operation of disability transfer programmes but also on the broader set of employment and income policies that attempt to correct or ameliorate the consequences of job loss, unemployment, and reduced employability. Moreover, by putting disability policy in a broader social policy framework the various incentives affecting labour force, or transfer programme participation can be discussed more comprehensively.

Emphasizing incentives means calling attention for benefit size, eligibility standards, assessment procedures, rehabilitation mandates, and employers' obligations. In this Chapter we discuss these aspects of disability benefit programmes in general terms and show how they interact. The next two Sections give a conceptual basis for analysing disability and disability insurance policy. In the following Section we elaborate the concept of disability. Section 3 deals with the problems related to unregulated market provision of disability insurance, and the pros and cons of public insurance. Section 4 discusses the parameters of general disability schemes using the variation in legally established disability insurance contracts defining coverage, eligibility, and entitlements as examples. First, the dimensions of the legal framework of disability insurance schemes are discussed. Then some aspects of administering the rules are dealt with. In the last section disability schemes are put in a broader framework that may help explain the different outcomes among the eleven countries studied.

2   The concept and prevalence of disability

2.1   *The disability concept*

Disability is an ill-defined and complex phenomenon. It is not directly observable but must be inferred from its presumed causes and consequences. The World Health Organization (1980) defines disability as any restriction or lack (resulting from impairment) to perform an activity in the manner or within the range considered normal. Disability is limited to incapacity caused by one or more distinct impairments because otherwise being timid, clumsy or illiterate could also be considered as disabilities.

Assessment of impairments and their limiting consequences involves difficult and painful judgements by the individual afflicted and equally cumbersome verifications by the members of the individual's social setting. The inevitable subjectivity of these judgements makes individual tastes, social values, and financial evaluations part of the perception of disability. Disability, therefore, is also a behavioural phenomenon.

In the definition of disability, health impairments are causally linked with reduced task performance. The presence of impairment is necessary but not sufficient. Some types of impairment have no incapacitating effects at all; others prevent performance but their adverse consequences may be eliminated by training, medicine, aids, or appliances; still others imply total and irrevocable incapacity. Impairment is defined as an anatomical or psychological loss or other abnormality (Nagi, 1969). These losses and abnormalities may stem from diseases, traumatic injuries, congenital deformities, or prolonged disuse of muscles or organs. They remain after the stage of active pathology has passed. The nature and severity of the underlying pathology determine the extent and permanency of impairment.

Impairments become manifest through the limitations in function or capacity they effect. Functional limitations are evident at the level of the person and represent a restriction or lack of ability to perform particular tasks or activities. Evidently, limitations at the level of activities may result from diverse combinations of lower level limitations. For example, the inability to concentrate may be due to emotional factors, may have somatic origins, or both. And the inability to lift a heavy weight may be caused by energetic or locomotive limitations.

The obvious advantage of defining limitations at the level of activities is that they relate to the demands of task performance. Concerning work disability, only those limitations are relevant which interfere with job demands. Thus, two people with exactly the same limitations may suffer different degrees of work disability. A hearing limitation is likely to affect a violinist more than a labourer, whilst a foot injury would affect the labourer more than the violinist. Impaired workers that are unable to meet the requirements of their current job may create alternatives to enrolment in disability benefit programmes through rehabilitation. They may acquire new skills and/or find a new job commensurate to their limitations.

Scheme 1 summarizes the causal chain leading from pathology to disability. According to this scheme, work disability can be defined as the inability to meet the demands of gainful activity, due to functional limitations, caused by impairment. It takes a medical-vocational point of view that corresponds with the definition of disability under a disability insurance scheme. Two dimensions along which the elements of this causal chain can be further conceptualized are severity and permanency. Other dimensions relate to the nature of the impairment, limitation, or disability (e.g. physical versus mental), or refer to their cause (e.g. whether they are work-related or not). Most countries have three separate programmes covering work disability that differ according to cause and permanency. Two programmes usually cover earnings loss due to general, i.e. non-work related disabilities: a sick pay scheme for short-term sickness and a disability insurance scheme covering long-term risks. The third is a separate scheme for work-related injuries and diseases.

Scheme 1: Etiology of work disability

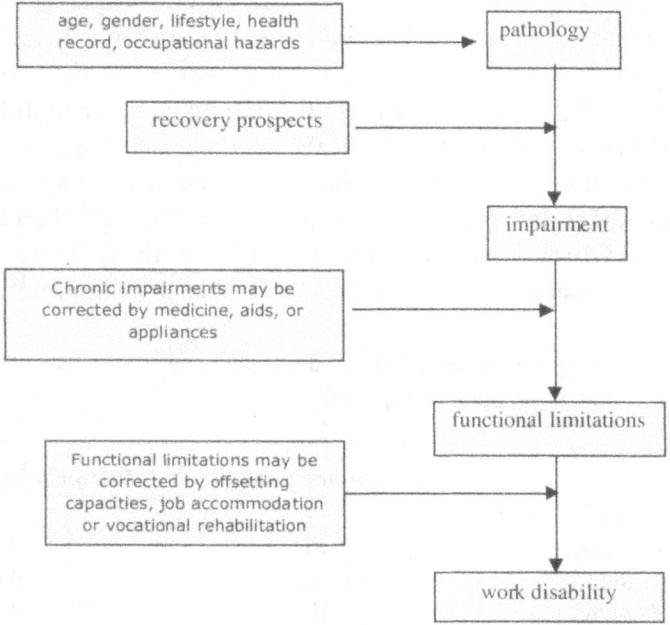

From a medical-sociological perspective one can discern four elements that interact to result in the inability to perform what sociologists call "the work role" (Mashaw and Reno, 1996: 31):
1) a person's chronic health condition or impairment;
2) the tasks that constitute work the person can do;
3) the person's offsetting capacities or compounding limitations in performing those tasks; and
4) the environment in which the person is expected to live and work.

This approach stresses the importance of a person's capacities and limitations that existed before impairment in determining post-impairment work role performance. The importance of compensating capacities is illustrated by the negative correlation between schooling and disability risks.

2.2 Cross-country disability and disability benefit recipiency

Being disabled and being a disability benefit recipient are two contingencies that do not fully overlap. The sizes of the non-overlapping parts – disabled without benefits and non-disabled with benefits – are an indication of the targeting performance of a disability insurance system. Due to the elusiveness of disability these non-overlapping parts will never be empty.

As an illustration of the complexity of the concept of disability Table 1 shows prevalence rates of self-perceived disability and disability benefit recipients as a percentage of the working-age population in 1999. The countries in the table are those that are studied in detail in the following Chapters. Disability is measured by using survey data and counting those that report having a lasting (chronic) health problem resulting in severe or moderate limitations in performing normal activities. In terms of Scheme 1 this definition is closer to the notion of functional limitation than that of work disability, which is the concept underlying benefit eligibility. The relative number of disability beneficiaries is derived from programme statistics.

Table 1: Self-reported disability and disability beneficiaries as a percentage of the 20-64 population, 1999

	Self-reported disability	Disability beneficiaries
Austria	13	4
Denmark	19	8
Finland	(a)	9
Germany	18	4
Italy	7	6
Netherlands	19	9
Norway	17	9
Poland	15	12
Slovenia	(a)	8
Sweden	21	8
Switzerland	15	6
OECD-19[b]	14	7[c]

Notes: (a) No data available.
(b) Includes the countries in this book, except Finland and Slovenia, *plus* Australia, Belgium, Canada, France, Korea, Mexico, Portugal, Spain, United Kingdom, United States.
(c) Includes the countries listed in note (b), except Korea and Mexico.

Sources: OECD (2003), chapters on Finland and Slovenia in this book.

In each of the eleven countries the relative number of people with disabilities is larger than the relative number of disability beneficiaries.[1] Apart from that, there is hardly any relationship between the number of self-reported disabled people and the number of disability beneficiaries.

Disability beneficiary rates appear to vary widely across countries, even among similarly prosperous and healthy populations (compare, for instance, Netherlands and Germany). The basic assumption in this paper is that such variation is largely due to the rules of disability and other transfer programmes and the incentive structures these rules induce.

3 Private versus social disability insurance

3.1 Introduction

Social disability insurance is designed to reduce the risk of earnings' loss due to impairments to function in gainful activity. The full private and social costs of disability exceed the losses related to reductions in productivity alone. They also include medical care expenses and the losses in social and psychological well-being suffered by impaired persons. A person's impairment may also affect the well-being of others. Family members and friends may have to make practical, financial, and psychological adjustments to accommodate people with handicaps. Society at large may also suffer some loss of well-being simply by knowing of, or observing, the economic consequences of another's impairment. Such external effects are denoted as "collective compassion costs". They introduce feelings of solidarity as motives for the creation of private charities or collective government programmes.

In the absence of any form of compensation, impairment costs would fall fully on people with disabilities, their relatives, friends, and other individual members of society. Social welfare, as conceived by economists to be the aggregate of the personal welfare of all individuals, would probably be lower than in societies that have some form of compensatory system to internalize collective compassion cost. Hence, even from the narrow economic efficiency perspective, a collective system can be justified by its contributions to increasing social welfare.

Compensation means transferring income from one party (disability programme contributors) to another (disability benefit recipients). Social insurance is just one way to organize these income transfers. Private insurance and judicial liability assignments are conceivable alternatives to public arrangements. In practice, total compensation is often a combination of government benefits supplemented by private arrangements. Such public-private mixtures are very common, although their relative importance may vary widely across countries depending on the size of their public schemes.

3.2 Unregulated market supply of disability insurance

In principle, private markets are able to provide disability insurance to a given population through the interaction of risk-averse consumers and profit-seeking private insurance providers. Efficient contracts can be drafted such that policy-holders maximize their expected well-being subject to the constraint that the insurers make normal profits. Such contracts provide partial or full coverage against income loss – the present value of foregone earnings during the period of disability. Each individual is charged a premium depending on his or her expected loss. Premiums, then, differ according to probabilities of disability, as indicated by age, health, and occupation. Per euro covered, workers with high disability probabilities are confronted with correspondingly high insurance premiums, and pre-existing disabilities are excluded from coverage.

Rating according to risk ('risk rating'), or according to previous claiming behaviour ('experience rating') is an inescapable consequence of unregulated competition. An insurance firm that would calculate an average premium rate so that low-risk groups would subsidize high-risk groups would run a loss because their low-risk clients would be offered lower rates by competitors that charge rates equivalent to risk, and leave.

3.2.1 The market for insurance

Risk-averse individuals are willing to pay an insurance premium that exceeds their expected losses. How much value they place on certainty depends on the depth of their risk aversion and on the size of expected loss. Using standard (expected utility) theory the value (V), or welfare surplus, derived from being covered can be expressed in money terms.

On the supply side, insurance policies are offered only if the premium is high enough to cover the carrier's cost. Apart from transfers to policy-holders who suffer losses the premium should also cover the transaction costs (T) involved in running the insurance business, such as the costs associated with the distribution of policies and the management of claims. Private insurance carriers are willing to sell insurance policies if the insurance premium at least covers the expected loss plus the transaction costs per policy.

An individual exposed to risk and an insurer will engage in an insurance contract if the transaction cost is less than the money value of certainty induced by that contract (see Barr, 1998: 120), or

$$T \leq V \tag{1}$$

Put differently, the social welfare gain from establishing an insurance contract equals V–T. The higher an individual's aversion towards risk, or the lower an insurer's transaction cost, the larger the welfare gain obtained from buying insurance.

The welfare gain from insurance may be reduced when the covered risk contains fuzzy elements. Such elements are inevitably present in any medically defined risk, whether the risk is health care expenses or wage-loss due to (short-term) sickness or (long-term) disability. The claim of having a health problem is sometimes difficult to certify, and even if its presence is easy to assess its severity, permanency, curability, and vocational consequences leave patients, physicians, and the gatekeepers of benefit programmes room for discretion. When compensating health contingencies the insured and other interest parties may influence both the occurrence and the extent of loss.

3.2.2 Lack of information: adverse selection and moral hazard

Fuzzy elements allow for behavioural reactions that may be difficult to predict. Consequently, those who provide disability insurance may lack reliable information on which to estimate individual risks and corresponding premiums and base grouping of the insured population into risk categories. If private insurance premiums do not closely reflect differences in expected losses, *adverse selection* can be a significant problem. Low-risk people will tend not to buy insurance, unless they are extremely risk-averse, whereas high-risk individuals will only buy insurance as long as they can afford it.

The resulting high average risk among those who buy insurance will compel a correspondingly high premium, and participation in the insurance will further decline. Eventually the market may disappear unless insurers (are allowed to) invest in medical checks and exclude existing disabilities. Hence, if insurers suspect adverse self-selection among their clients, unregulated market supply of disability coverage will at best be incomplete.

Due to its fuzziness the extent of disability risk may be influenced by one's willingness to work. By choosing the level of care taken to prevent or contain damages an individual can affect both the probability of incurring a loss and the amount of loss. This is the problem of *moral hazard*. Moral hazard emerges if, upon full coverage, the insured act as if damages would not involve costs and the returns to taking care were zero. This is again a problem of missing information on the part of insurers, as they cannot predict the behavioural change induced by insurance coverage. As insurers are unable to monitor the care-taking effort of the insured, they cannot calculate the appropriate (efficient) premium rate. The presence of moral hazard, therefore, reduces the welfare gain from insurance coverage. The size of the moral hazard component (MHC) under an insurance arrangement that covers income loss depends on the income elasticity of the demand for leisure. If leisure is a normal good higher benefits imply a stronger demand for leisure and, hence, a higher MHC. The net welfare gain of insurance in the presence of moral hazard can simply be written as[2]

$$V - T - MHC \qquad (2)$$

The solution to correct careless risk behaviour is to confront the insured with the cost of carelessness. Since risk rating is a necessary condition to survive in a competitive setting, market provision of disability insurance will help containing moral hazard as it rewards careful behaviour through lower premium rates.

Another way to contain moral hazard is through co-insurance. Co-insurance means offering less than full coverage or, in the case of insurance against income loss, offering replacement rates that are less than 100%. The degree of coinsurance – the part of the loss that is left uncovered – is a matter of choice. "The degree to which it is desirable to reduce coverage and subject the insured to risk would depend on the incentive thereby created to exercise care, and such an incentive would in turn depend on the cost of taking care" (Shavell, 1979: 541). The optimal level of coverage is obtained when, for a given extent of risk aversion, the marginal cost of taking care equals the marginal benefit from reducing expected losses.

And, finally, using strict eligibility rules and closely monitoring the caretaking behaviour of the insured may contain moral hazard. The insurer may exclude claims based on complaints (low back pain, stress) that cannot be substantiated by medical checks. After having excluded subjective complaints the severity of impairment, its incapacitating effect, the likelihood of cure, and the rehabilitative potential of those with lasting functional limitations need to be assessed. Assessment costs, and other costs related to damage control, such as prescribing and monitoring preventive efforts of the insured, and rehabilitative efforts of benefit recipients, are all part of the operational cost term T.

Expression (2), then, allows to illustrate the trade-off implied by two of the instruments to contain moral hazard – co-insurance, and monitoring the risk behaviour of the insured. Co-insurance means a reduction both of the welfare gain a risk-averse individual enjoys by buying certainty (V) and the moral hazard component (MHC). On balance, a gain remains as long as the reduction in moral hazard is larger than the loss of certainty. Similarly, monitoring increases T and reduces MHC.

To summarize, unregulated market supply of insurance against wage-loss due to disability is possible but leaves large groups uncovered. Pre-existing impairments cannot be covered, and risk rating makes the purchase of insurance for low-income and high-risk groups difficult. The financial accessibility to private insurance is further jeopardized by inevitably high costs related to claims' assessment and monitoring.

On the other hand, a private insurance company can only survive in a competitive setting if it rates premiums according to risk, and if it monitors the pre-onset behaviour of its insured and the post-onset behaviour of its beneficiaries. Risk rating and monitoring both contribute to reducing moral hazard. Moreover, a private market respects the sovereignty of consumers: they are free to choose if, and how, they cover their risks.

3.3 The case for government intervention

When the market fails to provide adequate (universal, affordable) coverage of risks which have pervasive and drastic consequences people turn to government. At a minimum, government may respond by regulating the private insurance market, for example, by mandating purchase of a legally fixed standard insurance contract. However, as argued before, provision of social (mandatory) insurance by private competitors means risk rating and exclusion of people with existing disabilities. Additional programmes, solidarity funds, or efficiency-reducing forms of price regulation, then, have to take care of vulnerable groups that the market is unable to cover at affordable rates.

As an alternative a public monopoly that calculates pay-as-you-go contribution rates may offer base (first pillar) disability insurance covering every resident. This solution to the exclusion problem is found in almost all countries that have public disability insurance. Moreover, in transition countries capital and insurance markets may still be deficient and may find it difficult to cover disability risks through a competitive market. In that case, there is no other alternative than public monopoly disability insurance. However, as we will argue below, public administration of a pay-as-you-go fund may exacerbate the moral hazard problem (Lindbeck, 1994). This, then, poses the basic dilemma in the design of social disability insurance: how to combine efficiency with adequacy?

Scheme 2: Social versus private insurance

	Social	Private
Participation	Mandatory	Voluntary
Policy conditions	Uniform	Negotiable
Premium rates	Solidaristic	Risk-dependent
Financing method	Pay-as-you-go	Funding
Insurance provider	Public monopoly	Private competitors
Claims' management	Public monopoly	Private competitors

Scheme 2 lists some distinguishing characteristics of public and private insurance. The distinction between these two types of insurance is to some extent arbitrary. One could argue that private insurance turns into a social one when a specified group (e.g. employees) is legally mandated to buy a statutory insurance package. Coercive consumption of a legally established insurance contract can be seen as the prime characteristic of social insurance. Coercive consumption solves the adverse selection and exclusion problems that are natural consequences of competitive supply because no member of the covered group is allowed to opt out.

If social (mandatory) disability insurance is supplied through a competitive market private insurance companies have to accept every member of the legally defined group of insured. However, mandatory insurance implies that private insurers have to accept all the legally insured, without exclusions. Under mandatory acceptance private insurers can only prevent losses if they can charge rates that vary by individual risk. But then high-risk persons face forbiddingly high premium rates. Therefore, mandatory insurance always requires some form of pooling through which low-risk groups (are forced to) subsidize high-risk groups. In mandatory health insurance arrangements this problem is sometimes solved through rate regulation. For instance, by setting a floor and a ceiling between which rates may vary. Insurers, then, run losses on high-risk groups that they can compensate through the profits they make on low risk people. A problem with such a regime is that insurers get a return on investment in risk selection (creaming) because they can increase their profits by focussing on low-risk groups.

A second crucial characteristic of social insurance, therefore, is risk sharing. The way in which premium rates are differentiated among the insured population reflects the degree of (risk) solidarity under an insurance contract. In the case of disability insurance, degrees of risk sharing run from taxing earnings at a nationally uniform rate, via rates that differ by sector, to rates which vary by firm or by individual. As argued above an individual rating regime is only possible through rate regulation.

The first three characteristics in Scheme 2 are the basic conditions that make an insurance arrangement a social one. Besides mandatory consumption and risk-sharing, policy conditions like the definition of the insured population, eligibility requirements, and benefit calculation rules are laid down in law. Under social insurance the legislator also establishes who takes care of the different elements of the "insurance function". These elements are (1) claims' management (eligibility assessment, medical and vocational rehabilitation); (2) funding (calculation and collection of premiums); (3) calculation and payment of benefits; and (4) prevention. Privatization of social insurance, then, means having a social insurance contract, i.e. mandatory provision of a standard policy at regulated prices, provided by private competitors. Under privatized social insurance the insurance function (the last three entries in Scheme 2) is taken care of by private agencies.

While the establishment and operation of a commercial insurance company is based on private business decisions a social insurance scheme is the outcome of a legal-political decision process, irrespective of the degree of involvement of private parties in its operation. The traditional design of a social (disability) insurance arrangement is a combination of all features listed under the heading "social" in Scheme 2. In fact, most of the eleven countries in this book fit classic social insurance model as regards general disability insurance (except Switzerland and the Netherlands). Under such a classic arrangement disability risks are pooled nationally, and financed by pay-as-you-go.

Pay-as-you-go financing can only be used to cover large financial liabilities – such as long-term payment of disability benefits – if the insurance has a broad base, and the covered population cannot choose between competing insurance funds. In other words, pay-as-you-go is only feasible if a public monopoly fund acts as the social insurer and participation is mandatory.

3.4 Government failure

In the absence of moral hazard the unit cost of providing social insurance through a public monopoly is potentially considerably lower than market production. The product is a non-negotiable standard contract, purchase is mandatory which eliminates marketing expenses, and there are large economies of scale. In the presence of moral hazard, however, the problem with pooling is that the higher the level of risk sharing the smaller the returns to avoiding, or limiting, damages. When a disability programme is financed by nationally uniform pay-as-you-go rates the cost of inappropriate use is shifted to a national fund. Micro-economic incentives to control losses, then, are eliminated, and the only price that signals abuse is the aggregate contribution rate.

The political process that determines the initial design and later amendments of a social disability insurance programme may exacerbate this incentive (moral hazard) problem. Experience learns that disability benefit schemes have been used to facilitate structural change in, for instance, transition countries and to reduce open unemployment in established market economies. Moreover, lenient eligibility conditions may reflect a political urge to earn votes rather than design a balanced and sustainable scheme.

Satisfying political needs by manipulation of the parameters of a disability benefit programme is more easily achieved in a traditional social insurance setting – with public monopoly administration and pay-as-you-go funding – than in a competitive market environment. The political risk looks similar to the one that pay-as-you-go pension schemes may run, but could well be larger. Disability coverage can be extended, benefits can be raised, and the gates of the programme can be swung open more widely by easing eligibility or by allowing gatekeepers to relax their eligibility screenings. In the short run such policies yield political popularity at low cost because the financial consequences of unfunded liabilities only become clear after many years.

One of the reasons why the impact of such practices may be larger for disability insurance than for pensions is that increases in generosity and leniency do not only change the behaviour of covered employees, but also that of their employers and the programme gatekeepers. As with health insurance the incentive (moral hazard) problem may extend to other interest groups. Just as health care providers may exploit the insurance coverage of their patients to increase their income, employers can use disability insurance as an instrument of employment policy if the disability route is cheaper and administratively less burdensome than openly terminating an employment contract. Likewise, programme gatekeepers who operate in a public monopoly setting may be inclined to pursue a conflict-avoiding strategy towards claimants, both to reduce their workload and the psychological burden of being strict. Such attitudes lead to lenient interpretation of eligibility rules, even when they look stringent on paper.

The issue of careful application of eligibility rules points to a crucial role of those responsible for claims' management in limiting the moral hazard problem. One of the core problems of public management of pay-as-you-go disability insurance programmes is the lack of cost consciousness among those who screen eligibility conditions as they are not confronted with the financial consequences of their adjudicative practices.

3.5 Conclusion

To summarize, public monopoly provision of disability insurance, which is the standard in most countries, has its pros and cons. By mandatory participation of a politically defined group of citizens in a legally established disability insurance package the state can offer universal, and affordable, coverage. This is a major advantage, but it comes at a price. Usually, disability insurance is provided by a public monopoly and financed by uniform pay-as-you-go contribution rates, or by taxes. First, pooling risks at levels higher than those where they can directly be influenced by covered employees and their employers makes the returns to controlling benefit expenditures smaller. This increases the moral hazard problem and may induce wasteful spending. Second, a state-run disability benefit scheme is subject to political risks that may further aggravate the moral hazard problem, and increases the productivity losses of locking people up in benefit programmes.

4 General disability insurance

4.1 Introduction

Except the Netherlands and Slovenia all countries reviewed here have four separate programmes covering the disability risk, each with its own legal base, funding, and administration:

1) A *sickness benefit scheme* covering short spells of (total) disablement of employees. Often, these benefits are wage-related and of limited duration with a maximum of one year. After lapse of entitlement to sick pay one may apply for a general disability benefit.
2) A *work injury programme* covering work-related accidents and occupational diseases suffered by employees. Usually such a programme covers both transitional and permanent disabilities. It distinguishes partial from total disablement and offers wage-related benefits.
3) A *general disability contributory (social insurance) programme* covering non-work related incapacity of employees, or the population at large, including the self-employed, and those who are handicapped from birth or before they enter the labour market. A contributory programme is funded by earmarked (pay-as-you-go) premium rates. Some general disability programmes distinguish partial from full disablement. In some schemes entitlement only starts after a mandatory waiting period, and in most schemes it runs out at pension age. Only in Slovenia and the Netherlands the general contributory programme also covers work-related injuries and occupational diseases.
4) A *general disability non-contributory programme* which either covers those that have no insurance status or the entire population. Non-contributory programmes provide flat transfers which are means-tested and financed through general revenue. Italy and as of mid-2003 also Germany are examples of countries that offer means-tested disability benefits to those not (fully) covered by disability insurance. Denmark is the only country that only has non-contributory social transfers, except for its work injury scheme.

Usually this set of programmes has a historical background. But it may also serve to make the coverage of disability risks more manageable. Risks associated with short-term and work-related contingencies are easier to calculate than the broad set of general disability contingencies. Sick pay coverage often has limited entitlement duration, whereas work injury risks are defined narrowly. Several work injury programmes use well-developed point systems to scale the limiting effects of injuries and a list of covered occupational diseases. Such restrictions help to contain claims.

The fact that some countries have sick pay and work injury liabilities covered by private insurance, or by mandating employers to pay for these benefits, illustrates the fact that these risks are more calculable. Examples are sick pay in the Netherlands, and work injury schemes in Denmark and Finland. Treating these more calculable risks separately allows policy-makers to focus on the programme that is the more difficult to manage – the general disability insurance scheme. With very few exceptions (general) disability benefits are provided by a public monopoly.[3]

4.2 Factors influencing benefit recipiency rates

In Table 1 we showed rates of disability benefit recipients as a percentage of the working-age population in the eleven countries under scrutiny. Benefit recipiency varies widely across these countries. Differences in underlying health status may partly explain the cross-country variation. A population's health status is determined by a host of factors, such as the availability and quality of health care, demography, work conditions, economic prosperity, crime rates, and domestic and international conflicts. The numbers in Table 1, however, also vary strongly among similarly prosperous, peaceful, and healthy populations. This suggests that differences in disability policy design are at least as important as differences in health status.

A broader assessment of a country's disability policy primarily calls for identification of its goals. Generally, disability programmes – both benefit schemes and rehabilitation provisions – aim at supporting the livelihood of those that have irreversible health-related limitations to such an extent that they are unable to earn enough money to reach an accepted minimum standard of living. But disability programmes also aim at promoting self-sufficiency of those that have sufficient residual capacity to earn. Whether policies are successful in reaching these conflicting goals can be assessed by inspection of the employment status of persons with disabilities, their economic well-being and that of the households in which they live, and the composition of individual and household (equivalent) incomes, relative to the non-disabled population. By relating these performance measures to policy indicators, such as strictness of the benefit programme, extent of private insurers' involvement, and spending on vocational rehabilitation, the success of differential policies can be judged.[4]

The variety in disability beneficiary volumes across countries (Table 1) can be partly attributed to the position chosen in reaching the conflicting aims of adequacy (protecting the livelihood of the disabled) and efficiency (reducing productivity losses). This position is best described by the parameters of the programmes that cover disability risks. In the remainder of this section we elaborate two of these parameters for a general disability scheme. The first is the legal framework: the rules that determine coverage, eligibility, entitlements, and return to work measures. The second is administrative structure, i.e. the way in which this framework is put into operation.

4.3 The legal framework

As we saw in Scheme 2 the basic features of social insurance are (1) mandatory consumption of (2) a legally established insurance contract. Mandatory participation in an insurance arrangement solves the adverse selection problem because low risks cannot opt out. It also solves the freerider problem, although contribution evasion may be a serious problem in societies with low tax morale.

4.3.1 Coverage

When a country seeks to protect its citizens against the financial consequences of disablement the coverage conditions should be broadly defined. Depending on political preferences, and a country's prosperity, coverage may include all citizens, the full labour force, or only those in wage employment. For instance, broad and prosperous welfare states such as Norway, Sweden, and Switzerland, have one national (first pillar) programme that covers the entire working-age population in so far as they meet certain residence requirements. Intermediate cases are countries like Germany and Italy, which cover the workforce but have only means-tested programmes for those without a sufficient employment record. Other OECD countries, such as the Netherlands, have wage-related programmes for employees, and separate (flat benefit) programmes for other specific groups, such as the self-employed and those handicapped before age 18. Another instance is Poland with its special programme for farmers.

Often, full coverage is only obtained after a certain number of "insurance years". With few exceptions, coverage ends at the age of entrance into the old-age pension system. Those who do not meet the requirements for coverage may apply for a non-contributory, means-tested disability welfare provision. Italy, for instance, has a dual system, where those who do not meet the coverage requirements of the wage-related insurance programme may apply for a flat, means-tested disability welfare transfer.[5]

Coverage not only refers to the insured population but also refers to the part of earnings that is covered by statutory social insurance. Almost every public disability insurance programme has an income ceiling above which earnings are not covered. These ceilings are usually between one and two times the average wage. Those with earnings beyond the ceiling may buy additional coverage from the private insurance market, or participate in an occupational arrangement. The same applies to groups, such as the self-employed, that are entitled to flat benefits only. These supplements are often stimulated by tax breaks.

A final dimension is coverage for in-kind provisions. Apart from cash benefits disability, or other, programmes may also cover in-kind provisions, services, subsidies for caretakers, or subsidies for employers. Some of these benefits have an ameliorative function – to improve daily living conditions, others serve a rehabilitative purpose.

4.3.2 Eligibility

Waiting periods Because disability insurance programmes aim at those with a long-term, or permanent, inability to work, eligibility sometimes only starts after a mandatory waiting-period during which claimants must have been without earnings as proof of the permanency of their disability. Some programmes have a fixed mandatory waiting period. In Poland this period is six months, in Switzerland and the Netherlands it is 12 months. Most other countries in this book have no fixed waiting period but will only consider a benefit claim after a completed vocational rehabilitation plan has not led to reinsertion in paid work (Austria, Denmark, Finland, Germany, Norway, Sweden). Entitlement to Sickness Benefits precedes disability benefit eligibility.

Ending point Usually, eligibility for disability benefits ends when eligibility for national pensions starts. Only in very few countries – Poland is an example – people can choose between a disability benefit or an old-age pension. Since for many people in Poland disability benefits are higher than social security pensions the number of disability beneficiaries includes a sizeable number of pensioners (but those over age 65 are excluded in the data in Table 1).

Earnings test The logic of an insurance against wage loss due to disablement should imply that benefits are earnings-tested at a 100% implicit tax rate: for every euro earned the benefit is reduced by the same amount. Most disability benefit schemes, however, are less refined and let eligibility end as soon as one resumes work at an earnings level that surpasses a certain threshold amount. Poland offers an extreme case as disability beneficiaries may earn 70% of the average wage without any reduction in their disability benefits (Andrews and Hoopengardner, 1999: 18). In systems that reward partial disability, partial benefits can be combined with decreased post-disability earnings, and in some countries, such as Austria and Germany, this combination may yield a higher income than pre-disability wages.

Definition of disability Given the elusiveness of disability, and the ensuing moral hazard problems, countries that define the disability risk in stricter, less ambiguous, terms have programmes that are more manageable. In line with Scheme 1, risk definitions run from a medical assessment of impairment, or functional limitations, to a measure of loss of work capacity, or earning capacity, which involves a confrontation of limitations with job demands. Work capacity definitions add difficult-to-measure vocational aspects to the, already cumbersome, determination of functional limitation.

The Dutch and Swiss disability insurance schemes are examples of an elaborate definition that further complicate the adjudicative process. These schemes measure the extent of disablement by considering the residual earning capacity. Capacity is defined by the earnings flowing from jobs commensurate with one's residual capacity as a percentage of pre-disability (covered) earnings. The degree of disablement, then, is the complement of residual earning capacity. From such a definition earnings loss can be measured on a continuous scale, allowing for several classes of partial disability (seven in the Netherlands, and three in Switzerland). In 1984, Italy moved from an earnings capacity definition to the stricter medical notion of reduced work capacity, and significantly reduced the number of beneficiaries.

Instead of an earnings capacity definition most countries use loss of work capacity as the risk covered under disability insurance. Such a definition confronts functional limitations with activities that are normally required in paid work. The extent to which activity performance of an impaired worker is below what is normally required defines the reduction in work capacity. These assessments include vocational consequences of impairment but stay short of measuring the effect of reduced capacity on earnings. As the examples of Sweden and Norway show, work capacity ratings do not preclude partial disability categories. Sweden has four disability classes (starting from 25% disablement). Another instance is Germany that introduced a new scheme in 2001, establishing that someone who, due to medical reasons, can work three hours a day at most is considered fully disabled, whereas those who can work no more than six hours are considered partially disabled. To assess capacity any job may be considered.

Two more aspects may further complicate disability definitions. First, schemes differ in the type of jobs they consider suitable if one loses the capacity to perform one's current, or usual, line of work. Suitable jobs are those that are compatible with one's training and work experience. Under such ruling a worker is considered fully disabled if he is unable to do suitable work. Germany, Austria and Switzerland are countries that have a suitable work stipulation. The Netherlands abolished it in 1993, to curtail eligibility, as did Norway in 1991.

Second, some systems that recognize partial disablement award full benefits to those partially disabled who are unable to find a job that is commensurate with their residual capacity. Sweden, Norway and Germany have such stipulations. Until 1987, the Netherlands explicitly recognized the barriers partially disabled workers may encounter when looking for work. This rule was applied so leniently that almost 90% of new awards were based on full disablement irrespective of the extent of the underlying medical disability. Hence, it was abolished.

Consideration of labour market opportunities blurs the distinction between disability and unemployment and aggravates the moral hazard problem considerably. Swiss rules, therefore, explicitly refer to a balanced labour market in considering employment opportunities. They ignore the fact that employment opportunities of disabled persons worsen when a labour market is slack but they may take account of smaller opportunities for the disabled in general. It is unclear how such a complicated rule is applied in practice, and whether it reduces or increases leniency.

4.3.3 Entitlements

Disability insurance entitles primarily to cash benefits. Some programmes also include benefits in kind, such as vocational rehabilitation, wage subsidies for employers, and subsidies for work place adaptation. Often, rehabilitation measures are covered by a separate programme, or by health insurance, or are non-existent.

Cash benefits   Generally speaking there are two types of cash benefit systems for general, long-term or permanent, disability. The first consists of two tiers. Sweden and Switzerland are examples of such a system. Each working-age resident that meets the eligibility criteria is entitled to a flat benefit. Disabled employees are entitled to a second tier benefit under the same eligibility standards. This second tier benefit supplements the base benefit up to a percentage of covered earnings.

The second type of benefit system has no universal base benefits but awards earnings-related benefits to employees, and may have separate schemes for special groups, like the self-employed and those handicapped from birth or in youth, awarding these groups a flat benefit. This model is mostly found in countries like Germany and Austria where disability insurance is part of the public pay-as-you-go pension scheme. In such schemes the benefit amount depends on the contribution record.

Wage-related benefits replace only part of earnings lost, even when fully disabled. In many countries (Switzerland, Germany, Netherlands) statutory replacement rates depend on contribution years, or age. Minimum income guarantees usually protect disabled workers and their households from destitution. Income floors imply that low-income groups have higher replacement rates than those with higher incomes. Wage-related benefits are capped because insurable earnings have a maximum, which further reduces the replacement rate at higher wage rates. In several countries statutory benefits are supplemented by collectively bargained supplements, leading to higher effective replacement rates, and correspondingly weaker work incentives.

Partial benefits   Programmes that recognize partial disability, and assign persons with residual capacity to disability classes according to their degree of disablement, award partial benefits correspondingly. Partial benefits serve a dual purpose. First, they provide an indemnity for lost earnings capacity. Second, they intend to work as a wage subsidy by allowing handicapped workers to offer themselves at a reduced price in order to compensate employers for their lower productivity. In other words, as long as a person with a partial benefit is unemployed the benefit serves as an indemnity (sometimes supplemented by a partial unemployment insurance benefit). As soon as the partially disabled person returns to work the benefit functions as a wage subsidy.

In actual practice, however, disability benefit adjudicators often find it difficult to make assessments within the discrete disability categories that are laid down in law, and tend to award full, or no benefits to those partially disabled. In the first case they widen the gates to disability benefits and are a disincentive instead of an incentive to return to work. In countries where benefit levels are closely linked to the degree of disability most awards are based on full disablement. In 2000, the share of full benefits among new beneficiaries was 63% in the Netherlands, 66% in Switzerland and Norway, and 68% in Sweden. From these figures one could conclude that partial benefits increase the accessibility of benefit schemes, and the related problem of moral hazard. But these percentages were higher in the past. As a result of increased stringency the share of partial benefits has grown.

The relative frequencies of partial versus full benefits induce two questions. The first was asked before: Do more disability categories make a benefit scheme weaker? Because of the inherent complexities of determining who is disabled full disablement is already difficult to assess. Assigning people to a refined set of disability categories is all the more difficult. As a consequence programme gatekeepers may have an easier job assuming that claimants either are not disabled or fully disabled. They may be inclined to ignore partial capacity, unless a claimant has already partially resumed his old, or other, work. The second question therefore is whether "(...) *partial disability (is) conceptually distinguishable from a host of other factors that may make a person more or less successful in labour markets*" (Graetz and Mashaw, 1999: 218).

In kind benefits   As part of a disability scheme, or, under a separate programme, independent from their eligibility for cash benefits, handicapped persons may be entitled to services and provisions in kind to ameliorate their living conditions, to improve their productivity and to prevent social exclusion. Subsidies may be awarded to facilitate mobility and daily activities in and around one's home. Productivity-enhancing measures are usually part of rehabilitation and will be discussed as part of return-to-work provisions in Section 4.3.5.

4.3.4 Prevention

To prevent workers with disabilities from leaving employment some countries submit employers to a quota-levy regulation. In Austria, Germany, Italy and Poland firms are obliged to have around 5% of their workplaces occupied by handicapped workers. They have to pay a levy (penalty) for each month they stay short of their quota obligation. Usually the levies are paid to a prevention and rehabilitation fund from which subsidies are granted that support the employment of workers with disabilities.

The status of handicapped worker offers a number of perquisites, such as more holidays and less work hours, or dismissal protection. Moreover, employers may get wage subsidies or subsidies toward work place accommodation. These subsidies differ from partial benefits in that they compensate employers, instead of impaired workers, for their lower productivity. They have a major advantage: while partial benefits can only be awarded upon entry onto the disability rolls, in-work allowances can be obtained without leaving the job.

4.3.5 Return to work measures

Vocational rehabilitation programmes contain a variety of measures, all directed at helping disabled persons to stay in or return to paid work. They include schooling, training, job mediation, subsidies for work place accommodation, and wage subsidies for employers who offer jobs to disabled persons. To this list one may add quota-levy systems and anti-discrimination legislation. All of these measures mandate employers to accommodate workers with disabilities. They should be distinguished from medical rehabilitation provisions (wheelchairs, seeing-eye dogs, artificial limbs, and other aids and appliances) that focus on reducing the incapacitating effects of impairment.

Most of the countries reviewed in this book have public funds that offer rehabilitation services. In several of these countries (Denmark, Norway, Sweden, Germany, Switzerland, and Austria) rehabilitation is mandatory before a benefit claim can be filed. Only after rehabilitation has failed eligibility for cash benefits is assessed.

Three problems surround rehabilitation policy. First, to assess rehabilitative potential is as complex as screening for partial disability is. Second, to set up an effective rehabilitation programme in each individual case may be even more difficult. And, third, the efficacy of rehabilitation measures is unclear. Fixed quota or subsidies for employers are potentially inefficient as they deny the variation in accommodation costs among companies. Likewise, vocational measures such as schooling and training have unclear effects. Motivation is an important factor, and can be promoted by a combination of mandatory rehabilitation and benefits of limited duration. Nevertheless, many of the countries reviewed here spend considerable amounts of money on medical and vocational rehabilitation. These expenses should be weighed against the benefits saved by resumption, or continuation of employment.

Rehabilitation measures that aim at getting disability beneficiaries back to work are more successful the larger the residual capacity of those on the disability rolls. Rehabilitation, therefore, is more relevant in schemes that recognize temporary and partial disability. Programmes that only accept workers that are permanently and severely disabled, as Italy's and Austria's disability insurance do, naturally have low work resumption rates among beneficiaries. Most disability schemes, however, have more than one disability category, or recognize the temporary status of disability by awarding a specific rehabilitation benefit during (mandatory) rehabilitation. In those cases, vocational rehabilitation is an important tool both to restore productivity and to contain unnecessary programme expenditures.

Comparison of the disability benefit recipiency rates of Germany, Austria and Switzerland with those in Sweden and Norway suggests that rehabilitation policies in the former countries are more successful in containing the beneficiary volume than those in Scandinavia (Table 1, see also Aarts et al., 1996).

4.4 Administration: gatekeepers' incentives

4.4.1 Medical and socio-economic disability

The basic problem of disability insurance is verifying the occurrence of the insured risk. To the extent that social adequacy requires coverage of all members of a specified population (employees, self-employed, or the working-age population) against the whole gamut of medical contingencies, it introduces a potentially sizeable amount of screening error into disability determinations (see Diamond and Sheshinski, 1995; Parsons, 1991). Two types of error can be distinguished: erroneous denials (or exclusion error) and erroneous admissions (or inclusion error). Because of competitive pressure private insurance is likely to give a priority to minimizing inclusion error. Public monopoly insurance, on the other hand, has a record of minimizing exclusion error. A balanced disability benefit scheme, however, should minimize the sum of these two, mutually exclusive, types of error.

Irrespective of its definition in specific benefit schemes disability is influenced by the business cycle. While the cyclical influence on disability awards is stronger if eligibility standards take account of actual labour market conditions, disability benefit incidence and the unemployment rate are also found to correlate under stricter regimes. In a slack labour market more people with disabilities will try to seek shelter under a disability benefit programme. Among a larger pool of applicants more people will be found eligible. Conversely, under favourable labour market conditions the number of people who are eligible for disability benefits but still work is larger than otherwise (see, e.g. Rupp and Stapleton, 1995). This finding stresses that the decision to apply for benefits is often a matter of choice.

Programme gatekeepers, on the other hand, often find it difficult to carefully distinguish between the (medically based) inability to work and the (economically) based inability to *find* work that is commensurate with one's limitations. A major issue in disability benefit administration is to design and operate assessment procedures that distinguish between medical and labour market factors. This administrative difficulty is aggravated by pressures – from politicians, labour unions, or individual claimants – to ignore this distinction and use disability schemes as an unemployment or early retirement programme. Hiding part of a country's unemployment problem under the disability label may look attractive to politicians because lower official unemployment rates give a prettier picture of economic performance. For redundant workers being unemployed under the disability label may be both financially and psychologically more attractive in so far as disability insurance schemes pay higher or longer running benefits and are less stigmatizing.

Administrative practices by which the distinction between medical and economic disability is blurred pose a major risk to the sustainability of social arrangements. Jobless workers that are recognized as disabled have an incentive to protect their livelihood by clinging to their disabilities and stay on disability as long as they can. They lose their professional skills or their taste for formal employment. Being recognized as permanently disabled also means that workers are considered as, sometimes very early, pensioners who are not supposed to go back to work. Such practices induce benefit liabilities that are larger and longer running than those for the regularly unemployed. Hiding cyclical, or structural, unemployment under disability creates long-term social and financial problems that are more difficult to redress than the ones one seeks to solve in the short run.

4.4.2 Assessment procedures[6]

Assessment of disability claims involves medical expertise. In most countries specialized (insurance) doctors employed by the social insurance agency, or external medical commissions decide on the nature and degree of disability. The ultimate benefit decision is usually taken by a single insurance officer or (in Italy, Netherlands and Switzerland) by an – often interdisciplinary – team of experts at the insurance body. But often the information on which these experts base their decision comes from the claimants themselves and their treating physicians because budgetary and institutional restrictions do not allow for independent examinations.

On the other hand, the increasing subjectivity of health complaints and the related complexity of medical assessment call for independent assessment using methods that allow measuring mental strength and the disabling effects of psychosomatic problems. Whether it is possible to design assessment protocols that warrant uniform treatment of claimants with complex complaints is still an unresolved issue.

Given their focus on full recovery, and commitment to their patients, treating doctors may not always be the best examiners of work capacity, especially when health complaints are not objectively testable. They may lack knowledge of the legal disability criteria, the work conditions at the current job and the wider labour market opportunities of the claimant. They sometimes seem to adhere to the notion that illness precludes work, which in many cases is untrue.

4.5 Disability benefits as part of social welfare policy

Disability policy is part of a broader set of employment and income policies that attempt to correct or ameliorate the consequences of job loss, unemployment, and reduced employability. Each of the following country chapters, therefore, dwells on the alternative options that workers with disabilities face.

Based on a framework developed by Aarts et al. (1996), one may analyse cross-country differences in disability beneficiary rates by distinguishing five different "paths" that workers may take following the onset of a disability. These paths are:

- the "work" path encompassing measures intended to integrate, retain or reintegrate a worker in the labour market, such as rehabilitation, sheltered employment, job protection legislation, quota and anti-discrimination laws;
- the "disability" path which refers to disability schemes, including work injury compensation, providing benefits for disabled persons who have never entered the labour market, short-term sickness pay for disabled workers, long-term disability cash benefits and, in most countries, health care for disabled people;
- the "unemployment" path consisting of unemployment insurance benefits which are usually provided at a higher short-term and a lower long-term replacement rate;
- the "early retirement" path which is frequently used to exit older disabled workers from the labour force;
- the "welfare" path consisting of means-tested programmes for those workers without earnings who are not eligible for disability or unemployment insurance.

The incentives for employees and employers to choose the disability path depend on its attractiveness relative to the other options. At the onset of disability, for example, employees' willingness to continue working is influenced by the rewards connected to each path, but also by the incentives for companies to assist continued employment. Firms may prefer a specific exit option because it is relatively cheap and easy to administrate.

Across programmes the subjectivity of the insured risk defines the role and degree of autonomy of the programme gatekeepers. Given its elusiveness the gates of programmes that cover the disability risk are more difficult to control than those that cover unemployment or early retirement. Likewise, disability programme administrators have a larger discretion to deny or award benefits than the gatekeepers of other transfer programmes. As a consequence, administrative incentives may be used to steer gatekeeper behaviour. This is an issue that is largely unexplored in general, and is only incidentally touched upon in the following country chapters. But the design and operation of alternative benefit programmes certainly play a role in how workers with disabilities, and their employers, weigh their options.

Notes

1. According to OECD (2003) an average of 35% of non-employed disabled persons is excluded from disability benefits whereas 33% of disability beneficiaries report being without disabilities.
2. See Aarts and De Jong (1998).
3. In Switzerland second-tier benefits are provided by a heavily regulated private insurance market and in the Netherlands firms may opt out of the public scheme and carry the risk of the first five years of disability benefit payment themselves.
4. See Burkhauser and Daly (1998). The OECD has recently completed a project on policies to support and integrate disabled people of working-age which uses – among other indicators – the relative employment and income status of disabled persons to make cross-country comparisons of disability policies. Twenty out of the thirty OECD countries participated in this project. See OECD (2003).
5. Having worked (and paid premiums) for at least five years, at least three of which in the last five years.
6. This section is based on OECD (2003).

References

Aarts, Leo/de Jong, Philip (1998) 'Privatization of Social Insurance and Welfare State Efficiency: Evidence from the Netherlands and the United States', in: Flora, Peter et al., *The State of Social Welfare 1997*. Aldershot U.K.: Ashgate.

Aarts, Leo/Burkhauser, Richard/de Jong, Philip (1996) *Curing the Dutch Disease. An International Perspective on Disability Policy Reform*. Aldershot U.K.: Avebury.

Aarts, Leo/Burkhauser, Richard/de Jong, Philip (1998) 'Convergence: A Comparison of European and United States Disability Policy', pp. 299-388 in: Thomason, Terry/Burton, Jr., John F./Hyatt, Douglas E., *New Approaches to Disability in the Workplace*. Madison, WI.: Industrial Relations Association Series, University of Wisconsin – Madison.

Andrews, Emily S./Hoopengardner, T. (1999) 'Disability and Work in Poland', Draft Discussion Note. Washington, D.C.: World Bank.

Barr, Nicholas (1998) *The Economics of Welfare State*, 3d Edition. London: Weidenfeld & Nicholson.

Burkhauser, Richard V./Daly, Mary C. (1998) 'Disability and Work: The Experiences of American and German Men', *Federal Reserve Bank of San Francisco Economic Review* 2: 17-29.

Diamond, Peter/Sheshinski, Eytan (1995) 'Economic Aspects of Optimal Disability Benefits', *Journal of Public Economics*: 1-23.

Graetz, Michael J./Mashaw, Jerry L. (1999) *True Security: Rethinking American Social Insurance.* New Haven: Yale University Press.

Lindbeck, Assar (1994) 'Uncertainty under the Welfare State: Policy-induced Risk', OCFEB Research Memorandum 9403. Rotterdam: Erasmus University Rotterdam.

Mashaw, Jerry L./Reno, Virginia P. (1996) 'Overview', in: Mashaw, John L. et al. (eds.), *Disability, Work and Cash Benefits.* Kalamazoo, Michigan: W.E. Upjohn Institute for Employment Research.

Nagi, Saad Z. (1969) *Disability and Rehabilitation: Legal, Clinical, and Self-Concepts and Measurements.* Ohio: Ohio State University Press.

OECD (2003) *Transforming Disability into Ability. Policies to Promote Work and Income Security for Disabled People.* Paris: Organisation for Economic Cooperation and Development.

Parsons, Donald O. (1991) 'Self-Screening in Targeted Public Transfer Programs', *Journal of Political Economy*: 859-876.

Rupp, Kalman/Stapleton, David (1995) 'Determinants of the Growth in Social Security Administration's Disability Programs – an Overview', *Social Security Bulletin*: 43-70.

Shavell, Steven (1979) 'On Moral Hazard and Insurance', *Quarterly Journal of Economics*: 541-562.

World Health Organization (1980) *International Classification of Impairments, Disabilities and Handicaps.* Geneva: WHO.

Part B:

Country Trends

CHAPTER 3

Disability Pensions in Austria

Karl Wörister

1   Survey of the Austrian pension system

In the Austrian social security system, provision for persons with permanently reduced earning capacity is an essential task of the pension system. The public system consists of two parts, pension insurance and civil service pensions.

At present, 87% of public pensions come under the pension insurance scheme. The remaining pensions come from various civil service pension schemes (including federal and provincial officials, railways and post office). As very little information is available about civil service pensions, they will only be dealt with in passing. The following contribution is restricted mainly to pension insurance.

Persons covered

With the exception of public officials, practically all persons earning an income have pension insurance.[1] Some low-income jobs are exempt from pension contributions (monthly income of less than EUR 296 in 2001). Since January 1998 it has been possible to 'opt in' and make voluntary contributions. At present around two-thirds of low-income earners are covered by pension insurance.

Non-earners can also make voluntary contributions, but this option is little used (currently less than 0.5% of the insured).

Organization

There are seven pension insurance institutions, classified by professional group (blue-collar workers, white-collar workers, tradesmen, farmers, non-tenured railway workers, miners and notaries). They are all members of an umbrella organization (Hauptverband der österreichischen Sozialversicherungsträger), to which health and accident insurers (work accidents, vocational illnesses) also belong.

These groups are covered by five federal laws. Except for the small group of notaries, the provisions are the same for all. The differences are in the regulations governing contributions and the definition of disability, which is adapted to the particular situation in each of the groups.

The central law covering social insurance for the non-self-employed (health, accident and pension insurance) is the *General Social Insurance Act (ASVG)*, established in 1955.

Types of pensions

Apart from disability pensions, the Austrian pension system has two other types of early pension as well as a sliding pension. While the regular pensionable age since the ASVG entered into force has been 65 for men and 60 for women, applicants could, until September 2000, take early retirement five years earlier (women 55, men 60). By the end of 2002 these age limits will be gradually raised by 1.5 years. They also apply to sliding pensions.

The various types of pensions are described below.

a) *Normal old-age pension* (regular retirement age). Prerequisite for this pension is normally 15 years of contributions.[2] In fact, this pension is not 'normal' since in 2000, for example, only 20% of new pensions were of this type (women 34%, men 9%).

The lower retirement age for women (60) is due to be raised to that of men (65) between 2024 and 2032.[3]

b) *Early retirement for long-term contributors* was possible until 1996 if the applicant had 35 years of contributions and had not yet reached the corresponding age limit (55/60). By the year 2000 this minimum period had been raised to 37.5 years. In that year, 37% of new pensions were of this type (men 40%, women 33%).

c) *Early retirement because of unemployment* can be applied for after one year's unemployment, if the applicant has 20 years of contributions;[4]

until 1996 15 years was sufficient. Five per cent of new pensions were of this type in 2000 (women 8%, men 2%).
d) It has been possible since 1993 to apply for a sliding pension. The same age limits as for early retirement apply. This sliding pension is barely used, however (2000: 0.3% of new pensions). It is intended for white-collar workers, who account for 90% of the claimants.

Between 1993 and 2000 there was also *early retirement on account of reduced work capacity*. This pension corresponded to a special ruling within the disability pension scheme for persons over 55 who were restricted in their ability to work. In 1996 the age limit for men was raised to 57. In May the European Court of Justice abolished the different age limits for men and women. The Government took this decision as an opportunity to do away with this pension at once as part of its consolidation policy. (This aspect is discussed in greater detail in the next section.)

The following section considers first of all the individual legal provisions. It is followed by a description of legal developments, especially since 1980. Then there will be a discussion of the court decisions defining the criteria for distinguishing between disability and non-disability. The final section will look at the results of studies that have been carried out.

2 Survey of legal provisions

Unlike most legal provisions in social insurance, the term disability is defined differently for the different professional groups. Among non-self-employed persons alone there are three different groups (blue-collar workers, white-collar workers and miners). Public officials have their own regulations and among the self-employed there are different provisions for farmers and tradesmen.

A distinction is made in the legal provisions between
- the term 'disability' and its definition,
- the qualifying period (= minimum period of contributions) required for a pension,
- special regulations for calculating the pension, and
- provisions for short-term disability pensions.

The following section does not deal with the concept of disability, which will be discussed in detail in the final section.

2.1 Entitlement to disability pension

The required length of contributions depends above all on the age of the person concerned. For young invalids the period of contributions is lower than it is for older persons:

- Persons who are disabled before the age of 27 require only six months of contributions.
- Up to the age of 50, five years (60 months) of contributions are required and must have been made within the previous 10 years.
- For persons aged 50 to 60, the contribution period is 15 years (disability after the age of 60). For example, a person aged 54 who applies for a disability pension must have nine years of contributions over an 18-year period (between the age of 36 and 54).[5]
- Persons who have 15 years of contributions (i.e. without replacement periods) at the time of disability, satisfy the conditions irrespective of their age.
- Special provisions applied for *early retirement on account of reduced work capacity* (1993-2000). Until 1996, ten years of contributions were required, the requirement being raised thereafter to 15 years.
- If the disability was the result of a work accident or recognized vocational disease, no specific amount of contributions is required.
- Before 1985, the entitlement provisions were even more generous.

2.2 Calculation of pension

The amount of the disability pension is calculated like the old-age pension and therefore depends on the number of years of contributions and the income in the calculation period.

For young disabled persons, however, there is a special ruling. Until 30 June 1993, the following supplement applied: if the disability pension became due before the claimant had attained the age of 50, the incremental amount,[6] based on the number of years of contribution, was increased to a maximum of 50%, the increment for each year up to the age of 50 being 1.9%.

Following the pension reform in 1993, both the maximum incremental amount and the age limit were raised and an additional limit included. The provisions of the reform were as follows:

- Periods without contributions up to the age of 56 are taken into account.
- The maximum resulting incremental amount is 60%.

The assessment base has been modified several times since (1996, 1997 and 2000). The current ruling is as follows:
- For old-age and disability pensions, the pension amount increases by 2% of the assessment base (average income for the 15 'best' years of contribution) for every year of contribution.[7]
- If a pension becomes due before the claimant reaches pensionable age (60 for women, 65 for men), the incremental amount is decreased by 3% per year of contributions.[8] The maximum amount that can be deducted is 10.5% or 15% of the original incremental amount.[9]
- If disability occurs before the claimant is 56.5 years old, the missing contribution periods until then are taken into account provided that the total incremental amount is not more than 60% (after allowance for the deduction). Transitional rulings apply until 2004.
- The pension calculated in this way remains unchanged even after the claimant reaches the regular pensionable age.
- The pension system guarantees a minimum income, with further income being taken into account. The amount in 2001 is EUR 613 per month for single persons and EUR 875 for married couples.
- Pensions in Austria are paid out 14 times a year.

As a result of the rules in force, a claimant receiving a disability pension can expect to receive less than an old-age pensioner. This is confirmed by data from the Hauptverband and the Federal Ministry of Labour and Social Security.

Table 1: Net pension in per cent of most recent net income (new claimants 1998, non-self-employed) (averages):

	old-age pensions*	disability pensions**
men	84%	76.5%
women	76%	68%

Notes: *) including early retirement pensions on account of reduced work capacity

**) excluding early retirement pensions on account of reduced work capacity

In 1999 the average new disability pension (median) for previously non-self-employed men was EUR 948 per month (gross) and hence 38% lower than the corresponding old-age pension (EUR 1,536). For women the new mean disability pension was EUR 570, 22% lower than the mean old-age pension (EUR 733).

This calculation method could well discriminate against disabled persons.[10] It should also be borne in mind that persons who were disabled when young had no possibility of earning income, a fact that is reflected in the assessment base and hence in the pension itself.

2.3 Time limit for disability pensions

Since 1996, disability pensions have been limited by law to a maximum of 24 months, unless "permanent disability is to be assumed on account of the physical or mental state". If the disability continues, the pension is paid if an application for continued payment is made within three months. In 1999, 77% of the new disability pensions granted by the pension insurance scheme were time-limited.

Apart from pensions granted with a time limit from the outset, permanent disability pensions can be revoked if the conditions are no longer satisfied. If the pension is revoked because the recipient has recovered his/her mental or physical capacities, the pension is stopped at the end of the month in which the decision is served. According to the court interpretation, a 'significant' improvement must have taken place (Teschner/Widlar, 1974: 580f.). In 1999, 400 disability pensions were revoked by the pension insurance funds (social law statistics of the Hauptverband der österreichischen Sozialversicherungsträger).

2.4 Legal recourse

As with all other decisions by social insurance funds, refusals and revocations can be contested by the person concerned. An objection can be filed with the competent labour or social court within three months of service of the decision. This suspends the decision (or that part of it that is objected to).[11] Further instances are the Oberlandesgericht (appeal) and Oberstes Gerichtshof (appeal on points of law).

In 1999, the pension insurance funds recognized 16,000 disability pension claims and rejected 24,000. This means that four out of ten applications were accepted. As in previous years, one in two of the rejections was taken to the next instance (social court), but only one in four appellants was successful.

The situation was a little easier for persons who had applied for an *early retirement pension on account of reduced work capacity*, where three-quarters of the applications were accepted (14,400 compared with 4,500 rejections). Those who took their case to the social court were also more successful (six out of ten).[12]

3 Development of legal regulations

There were two reforms in the early 1960s that had an important effect on the development of disability pensions:

- The introduction of *early retirement pension for long-term contributors* in 1961 was designed as a remedy to the large number of disability pensions (particularly among blue-collar workers). Persons who had 35 years of contributions and were still in employment could retire five years before the regular retirement age (60 for women, 65 for men).[13] Although there was no change in the legal provisions for disability pensions, this decision was based on the gross assumption that a long working life would inevitably have a wearing effect on the health.[14]
- In 1962 'job protection' was introduced for skilled (and semi-skilled) workers, which meant that they could no longer be assigned to unskilled work. This decision brought the regulations for blue-collar workers into line with a similar disability pension provision for white-collar workers.

Work protection for older workers from 1981

The next significant change in the law came in 1980 (effective from 1981) for persons over the age of 55. This reform also created a type of protection for unskilled workers who had been doing the same or similar work for 15 years. If the health requirements were fulfilled they could no longer be assigned to a different job. This also took account of the deteriorating employment situation for older workers.[15]

A condition for this special work protection was insurance contributions for 180 months (counting towards the assessment base[16]), making it stricter than other disability pensions, where five to eight years of contributions were required. From 1985 the qualifying period was gradually raised to ten years (for 55-year-olds) or 15 (for 60-year-olds) (see below for further details).

The ruling applied originally only to unskilled workers, but was extended to skilled and semi-skilled workers in 1984.

The 1993 pension reform transferred this provision for elderly disabled to a special old-age pension for persons aged 55+ (*early retirement on account of reduced work capacity*). Unlike the earlier ruling, this pension was not applicable if the claimant earned income above the minimum level. For this pension, only 10 years of contributions (within a period of 20 years) were required. In 1996 the age limit for men was raised to 57, resulting in a considerable reduction in new pensions, particularly among male workers.

In 2000 this type of pension was abolished and replaced by a special regulation within the existing disability pension system for men and women over the age of 57. It will be up to the courts in future to define disability for this age group, since the formulation in the law is not very clear: "A disabled person is an insured person aged 57 or over who is incapable on account of an illness or other infirmity or reduction in his physical or mental capacities to carry out work that he/she has performed continuously for at least 120 calendar months of the previous 180 calendar months before the qualifying date[17]. Reasonable changes in this work are to be taken into account." This revision is stricter than the previous law, since the person now has to have performed the same or similar work for two-thirds of the time (the last 15 years), with other 'reasonable' work being taken into account.

Change in entitlement provisions

Until 1984, five years of contributions within the previous ten years were required for a pension entitlement, provided that the contributions had started before the age of 50, otherwise eight years were required.

As a result of this provision, older persons with a relatively short contribution period could acquire a pension entitlement of their own. This was of particular benefit to women (working in agriculture after taking over the business from their husband, for example) and certain groups of workers (such as tenured railway workers after retirement, usually at the age of 53[18]).

These provisions were tightened in 1984 and now the same contribution period is required at the age of 60 as for an old-age pension (15 years).

From 1 April 1991: no pension entitlement while still working

Under the Welfare Law Modification Act of 1991 (BGBl 157/91), pensions will not be granted as long as the applicant is still making compulsory contributions. Earlier, a disability pension was attainable even if the applicant was still working (at least while he/she was sick). Under the new provision, a pension is not payable until the employment has been terminated. If the person worked again afterwards, however, the pension is not forfeited.

4 Definition of disability

Apart from the qualifying period, the distinction between disability and non-disability is a decisive criterion when granting a pension.

As mentioned earlier, the legal definition of disability is different for the individual insured groups. The definitions specify only rough criteria to be taken into account in decisions. The precise definition of disability has played an important role, however, in court decisions.

The reason for this is that the legal formulations have been extensively overtaken by reality. The main distinguishing criterion in the ASVG is whether work capacity has been reduced "as a result of a physical or mental condition to less than half of that of a physically and mentally healthy insured person" (s. 255 ss. 1, provision for skilled and semi-skilled workers)[19]. For unskilled workers the earnings are more important: "... is considered disabled if as a result of his mental and physical state he is no longer able to perform an activity recognized as employment and reasonable for him to perform with due consideration of the activities performed by him, that would allow him regularly to earn at least half of the income that a physically and mentally healthy insured person regularly earned through such an activity" (s. 255 ss. 3).[20]

These provisions were taken over from the Reich Insurance Decree and date from the end of the nineteenth century. At that time income was not completely controlled by collective bargaining agreements (or legal minimum wages, etc). According to the current welfare legislation, social insurance contributions must be paid for wages at the collectively agreed level at least (s. 44 and s. 49 ASVG). According to labour law, other arrangements on the basis of individual agreements are not valid (Berger, 1993: 38).

A health-related reduction in employment cannot therefore result in income below the collectively agreed level. To this extent, the provisions mentioned above are to all intents and purposes 'dead'.

The courts have determined a number of individual criteria for defining disability, the main ones being:
- determination of reduced earnings capacity (expert opinions),
- health aspects,
- health restrictions and their acceptability for employers,
- significance of the labour market,
- employee's mobility,
- restrictions regarding the acceptability of specific employment (including job protection),
- part-time work and assignability.

a) Determination of reduced earnings capacity

After the pension application has been submitted to the competent pension fund, the applicant is summoned for examination. Private medical reports that the applicant brings are treated only as guides for the pension fund's medical staff. The decision as to the applicant's capacity lies exclusively with the fund's own experts. The medical examinations are usually fairly thorough.[21]

If an objection is made to the rejection of an application, new examinations are carried out by a sworn expert appointed by the court. Here, too, private medical opinions are not acceptable as proof.

Surveys by the *Kammer für Arbeiter und Angestellte* [Chamber for Blue- and White-Collar Workers] in Vienna on medical opinions at the court of arbitration (1985) and the labour and social court in Vienna (1990, 1995) have shown that the quality of the expert opinions is very uneven and that the result of the medical examination depends to a large extent on the examining physician. The doctors differ in:
- the nature of capacity restrictions typically used,
- the number of categories of reduced capacity,
- the frequency with which specific capacity reductions are determined,
- the estimation of the extent of specific capacity reductions (e.g. weights in the case of acceptable lifting and carrying work).[22]

In isolated cases, applicants are admitted to hospital for additional tests.

b) Health aspects

Apart from specific capacity restrictions, the assessment of general questions is also of importance.

In determining capacity, it is necessary to decide how much work is possible seated, standing or walking, the dexterity of the applicant, and whether work in exposed places (on ladders, dangerous machines, etc.), under time pressure or while bending is possible.

Clarification of these questions can have a bearing on the decision as to whether someone can perform certain tasks within a potentially assignable occupation.

The following determinations by higher courts are also of relevance. They have decided that a person is disable if:
- he can carry out an occupation only at the risk of deterioration of his health,
- he can carry out an occupation only with pain or special effort,
- he can repeatedly walk a distance of 100 m only after resting for 10 to 15 minutes or can only walk a maximum of 200 m four times in one day,
- he is no longer able to keep regular working hours and is therefore forced to take longer breaks than normal,
- he is not able to keep up a diet prescribed for the condition,
- sickness leave of more than six weeks in a year is likely,
- more than one or two epileptic fits in a month are likely.

Alcoholism at the level of an uncontrollable addiction must also be taken into account.

Personal circumstances are not taken into account. These might be:
- incompatibility of work and household obligations,
- language difficulties (foreign workers),
- the fact that the insured person has or does not have a car.

Sometimes work capacity can be restored through operations or treatment. The degree to which such treatment is acceptable depends on the associated risks, pain, prospects for success, seriousness of the intervention and its consequences. This must be decided on a case-by-case basis.

c) Health restrictions and their acceptability for employers

From the above survey it can be seen that court decisions also include limits as to what is acceptable or unacceptable for employers, such as the likely length of sick leave, the number of anticipated epileptic fits, certain capacity restrictions (that might not be relevant to specific occupations but restrict the worker's availability). In fact, these considerations are a fairly realistic reflection of the actual obstacles to hiring that would be encountered on the labour market.

No particular concessions on the part of employers are basically expected. Thus, a person may be regarded as disabled if he can perform his work only because the employer chooses to ignore certain normal requirements for the job.

This is indicative of an economic order in which social responsibility is not bindingly expected of employers. This also means that a number of disability pensioners could work if the employer (and colleagues and friends) were willing to make certain concessions.

As will be seen, however, the requirements expected of persons with reduced work capacity who seek a job are much greater.

d) Labour market and disability

One of the central problems encountered by many disability pension applicants is that they cannot find a position commensurate with their work capacity. Most of these cases involve older persons, whose job prospects are known to be particularly poor. Prejudices on the part of employers and the usually limited availability of the persons concerned turn job-hunting into a nightmare.

The courts have always distinguished clearly between 'unemployment' and 'disability'. In principle, the chance of finding a job is not a criterion for awarding a disability pension. Since there is a close connection in reality between reduced work capacity and unemployment, however, the court decisions must be regarded as 'abstract'. The correlates to this abstract treatment are two different social security institutions: unemployment insurance and pension insurance (employment office and pension fund).

The courts also take into account some concrete aspects. If, for example, someone can only pursue an occupation for which too few vacancies are available in Austria, he will not be assigned to this job and will therefore be regarded as disabled. The limit is set at around 100 available jobs. If there are many more than 100 jobs available (regardless of whether they are taken or not) and this occupation is acceptable from a health point of view, the person is no longer regarded as disabled.

Many occupations are reserved for one sex, in which case a person of the other sex cannot be assigned to them. Here, too, if there are more than 100 people of the applicant's sex working in this occupation, he or she may be assigned to it.[23]

e) Mobility expected of workers with reduced work capacity

As can be seen, an applicant can be assigned anywhere in Austria. The criterion is whether the person with a defined capacity and with account taken of job or work protection could theoretically perform a job for which there are enough vacancies on the Austrian labour market.

The central problems for the persons concerned are the housing costs if a change of accommodation is required or the costs of a second apartment and restrictions to family life. Even married persons with dependants to look after are expected to look for work in other provinces.

This is particularly serious when one considers that the length of occupation cannot normally be foreseen in advance but that considerable costs for changing accommodation are nevertheless incurred.

In unemployment insurance some of these persons are classed as 'difficult to place' and provided with additional benefits. (Once the entitlement to unemployment benefit has expired, these benefits are granted in needy cases only.) In 1998 on average, some 40,000 unemployed persons were classed as difficult to place on account of a physical or mental handicap (just under one in five unemployed).

f) Acceptability of specific occupations (including job protection)

One aim of Austrian pension law is to secure the standard of living. This includes protection from a drop in social standing. A person who cannot continue to work in his former occupation because of his health is regarded as disabled if further employment in another occupation would be associated with a drop in social standing. This is covered by the following provisions.

SKILLED AND SEMI-SKILLED WORKERS may not be assigned to another profession. A person who cannot work in his profession – or in the subcategories within the profession – because of his health is regarded as disabled. With semi-skilled workers it must first be ascertained that they have acquired all the essential skills that a skilled worker needs for his profession. If this condition is not fulfilled, the person is regarded as an unskilled worker.

WHITE-COLLAR WORKERS may be assigned only to positions one grade below their current one.[24] Unlike blue-collar workers, the comparison is not based on the occupation they have performed in the last 15 years, but on the most recent occupation. For white-collar workers who have had positions as blue-collar workers (blue-collar workers with white-collar worker employment contracts) the disability definition for blue-collar workers is used.

DISABILITY AND WORK INCAPACITY OF MINERS: Miners whose health prevents them from performing the jobs they have had hitherto (or a similar job) or which would force them to accept a drop in income of more than 20% as a result are regarded as having a work incapacity or partial disability. Until they are eligible for a *miners old-age pension* these persons are entitled to a *miners pension*. In most cases they take another job or obtain unemployment benefit. Otherwise the disability definitions for blue-collar workers apply.

PERSONS AGED OVER 57 (1981-1996: 55)[25]
a) Special arrangement before June 2000: Persons who had worked in the same or similar occupation for the previous 15 years and had completed the corresponding qualifying period could no longer be assigned to another occupation. The same or similar occupation is one with similar mental or physical requirements in terms of skill, intelligence and knowledge of the work, precautions, responsibility, posture, stamina, difficulty and concentration. Since 1988 the courts have emphasized that the similarity must apply to the core aspects; differences in peripheral activities are insignificant if they are not typically connected with an occupation.
This arrangement was established because of labour market considerations. It was based on a similar arrangement for self-employed persons over 55, which had already been in existence for some time.
b) The current arrangement has already been discussed. It will be up to the courts to define disability more precisely.

UNSKILLED WORKERS: Unskilled workers under the age of 57 (formerly 55) and those who do not meet the special conditions for older workers do not have any job protection. If they are healthy enough to carry out any occupation on the labour market, they are not entitled to claim a disability pension.

DISABILITY FOLLOWING REHABILITATION MEASURES: A claim to a disability pension remains intact even if the claimant has acquired the ability to pursue a new occupation as a result of rehabilitation measures by the pension or accident insurance fund. Only if a significant improvement occurs to enable the recipient to pursue his/her old occupation is the pension entitlement revoked. Since 1 July 1993 (amendment to ASVG) the pension entitlement is revoked in the new occupation if:
a) the resultant income is twice the assessment base and
b) the income is higher than the maximum assessment base; if the income drops below these limits, the entitlement is validated again on application.

This relatively generous arrangement following successful rehabilitation is designed to help the persons concerned to re-integrate into the labour market.

g) Part-time work and assignability

According to the courts, a person in full-time occupation can be assigned to part-time work provided that the job pays half of the amount "that a healthy insured person would receive for such an occupation."[26] In practice, this court decision is not likely to be significant.

h) Closing remarks

Apart from the insurance provisions, the granting of a disability pension depends on a number of other criteria that have been established by the higher courts. One feature of these decisions is that they are abstract in nature.

The first abstraction relates the person with reduced earning capacity to the labour market. The residual capacity according to the courts is generally set higher than the social reality. The second abstraction relates to the possibility of finding (secondary) accommodation at a reasonable cost. The courts assume a mobility that is often far in excess of the person's real capabilities (unless they want to put themselves completely into debt).[27] For the court decisions to become realistic, the courts would have to change their attitude to disabled persons and to the other aspects of the housing market and childcare facilities.

It is also interesting to note that protection from reduction in social standing is based on simple schematic criteria and it is questionable whether these criteria are sufficiently in line with current realities. It would be useful, for example, if more account were taken of the role of income as an indicator of social status rather than its correlation to a specific professional group.

5   Demarcation from other aspects of the social insurance system

Pay during sickness

- Payment by employer

Until the year 2000, blue-collar workers were paid in full by their employers for four to ten weeks; white-collar workers received full pay for six to twelve weeks, the number of weeks in both cases depending on the length of service with the employer. Salaried workers had a further four-week entitlement to half pay and half sickness benefit. From January 2001, the situation of blue-collar workers was generally brought into line with that of white-collar workers.

- Sickness benefit (usually after continued payment of wages/salary)

This is available for a maximum of 18 months (12 months according to statutory provisions and a further six months depending on the local regulations).

The amount of sickness benefit depends on the health insurance scheme. A couple of years ago I calculated the net rate for Vienna to be between 80 and 94% (increasing in direct proportion to the amount of income).

- Since 1996, the prerequisite for payment of a disability pension has been a prior work incapacity of 20 weeks; this does not mean, however, that sickness benefit must have been paid during that time. Unemployment also counts (confirmation of work incapacity by doctor).

There are no regulations providing for the possibility of a pension following a defined period of sick leave. There are cases in which a pension disability has been refused after the sick benefit entitlement has expired, even though the claimant was unable to work.

Payments from accident insurance

Usually, only a partial pension (mostly for a limited period) is recognized. This is in fact only a supplement to other income (wages, pension, unemployment benefit).

With severe disability, a disability pension from the pension insurance scheme can also be granted. In 1999, 570 persons in the entire pension insurance scheme were granted pensions on account of work accidents (including accidents on the way to/from work); in December 1999, around 10,000 persons were receiving pensions for that reason (all age groups). Most of the persons concerned also obtained an incapacity pension [*Versehrtenrente*] from the accident insurance scheme. Because of the comparatively low disability pensions, cases of 'over-pay' are probably rare.

The incapacity pensions from accident insurance are currently EUR 257 per month on average (beginning of 2001). Only around 2% were 'full pensions' with a 100% disability (2,000 out of 89,000); the full pension amounts on average to EUR 1,291.

The two payments – incapacity and disability pension – can be received together without any reductions.

The annual outlay for disability pensions in 1998 was EUR 3.2 billion, compared with EUR 160 million for incapacity pensions (both for persons up to the age of 60).

Unemployment benefit

Unemployment benefit is paid for 30 to 52 weeks, depending on age and years of work. The net rate for an average income of EUR 1,600 (14 times a year) is 55%. It is a little higher (max. 60%) for claimants with very low income and lower for claimants with higher income. The benefit can be supplemented by a family allowance, resulting in a higher rate. The maximum unemployment benefit (excluding family allowance) is currently around EUR 1,100; in 1999 half of the payments were less than EUR 660 per month (net, 12 times a year).

Unemployment Assistance (UA) can be paid, in principle for an unlimited period, after the expiry of the unemployment benefit entitlement. This is 92 to 95% of the unemployment benefit (+ family allowance). Since the partner's income is also taken into account, however, it is often reduced or not paid at all. For older persons (2 stages: 50+/55+), higher exempt amounts are applicable when calculating income. For younger persons, maximum UA have been in force for some time (minimum required for survival). In 1999, the mean UA was EUR 545 per month (median).

AMENDMENTS TO THE LAWS IN THE LAST FEW YEARS

There haven't been any appreciable changes. The changes regarding the unemployment benefit entitlement period for older persons is worth mentioning, however. Between 1988 and 1993, persons aged 50+ with long service careers in certain regions ("crisis regions") were entitled to up to four years unemployment benefit plus one year additional benefit.

This unemployment benefit based on age was replaced by larger exempt amounts of UA (see above).

Social Assistance (SA)

In cases of need, persons incapable of earning an income who were not entitled to payments from social insurance receive SA. The arrangements here vary from province to province. Because of the restrictive arrangements and its discriminatory character, SA is relatively insignificant. No data is available, unfortunately, on how many persons receive SA on account of reduced earnings capacity.

In some provinces, persons incapable of earning an income are entitled to a minimum payment equivalent to that awarded by the pension insurance. This also means, however, that income from dependants is taken into account, with the result that the persons concerned often have no entitlement.

Survivor pension on account of work incapacity

An entitlement to a widows' or orphans' pension often exists only if the person is incapable of working. This particularly affects young widows and orphans over the age of 18 (or after they have completed vocational training). The number of orphans' pensions is significant: around 15,000 adults (some of them until they are very old) are entitled to such a pension on account of work incapacity exclusively.[28]

Rehabilitation

There is no insistence on rehabilitation as this would not be useful. Medical measures, however, are regarded as part of the regular medical treatment.

In 2000, pension insurance funds spent EUR 240 million on 'rehabilitation and health care', while health insurance funds spent EUR 170 million on 'medical rehabilitation' measures.

Vocational rehabilitation measures are of relatively small significance. In the *Pensionsversicherungsanstalt der Arbeit* [Blue-Collar Workers Pension Institution] in 1999, 9,200 disability pensions (without prior old-age pension) were granted, compared with 1,700 training measures. In the *Pensionsversicherungsanstalt der Angestellten* [White-Collar Workers Pension Institution] there were 214 training measures out of 4,500 pension awards. Altogether, these two funds spent EUR 11 million on vocational rehabilitation in 1999 (including expenditure for tools and equipment and supplements for employers). The *Arbeitsmarktservice* [employment office] also provided resources for the integration of disabled persons as part of its active labour market policy.

Both institutions considerably stepped up their job integration efforts in the second half of the 1990s.

Unemployed, sick or disabled?

In many cases it is not clear whether a pension applicant is unemployed, sick or disabled under the law. Many legal proceedings are instigated to clear up this very point.

6 Disability pension figures

Most small and larger-scale studies were carried out or contributed to by the author as part of his work for the Arbeiterkammer.[29]

Disability pensions are of relatively large significance as a social welfare benefit in Austria, as can be seen from the following data:

Table 2: Working age* recipients of welfare benefits 1999

	Number
Disability pension**	226,000
Unemployment benefits	205,000
Early old-age pension	151,000
Incapacity pension	51,000
Widows pension	80,000
Orphans pension***	12,000
Maternity and post-maternity benefits	104,000

Notes: *) women up to 59, men up to 64; **) excluding civil service pensions; ***) aged 28 and over
Source: Hauptverband der österreichischen Sozialversicherungsträger, Arbeitsmarktservice

Claimants of working age receiving disability pensions are the largest group of welfare benefit recipients. If civil service pensions are included, the total amounts to around 260,000.[30] Together with orphans' pensions, which are granted in this age group only in the event of disability, the total increases by at least 12,000.

Among early-retirement pensioners, disability pensions in recent decades have accounted for 60% (= ratio of disability pensions to own pensions in working-age recipients). This proportion is particularly high among male blue-collar workers (1999: 81%).

The number of disability pensioners has increased in recent decades in a similar fashion to the number of unemployed and early-retirement pension recipients. This development is due to two factors in particular.

- Growing unemployment has led to greater use of existing claims than earlier. This is understandable in view of the relatively low benefits paid out to the unemployed. Unemployment benefits provide support for short periods of unemployment, but long-term beneficiaries would be practically at the poverty line. What is more, many unemployed persons also have health problems.

    While the average net replacement rate for disability pensions in 1998 was around 77%, the equivalent rate for unemployment benefits is less than 60%. For recipients of unemployment assistance (second phase of unemployment) the rate is even lower; in many cases there is no entitlement whatsoever because of the overall family income.

- For social reasons, access criteria for early-retirement pensions have been eased, particularly for older persons.

Between 1975 and 2000, the number of disability pensions rose from 83,000 to 232,000.

Figure 1: All early retirement pensions and unemployed, 1975-2000

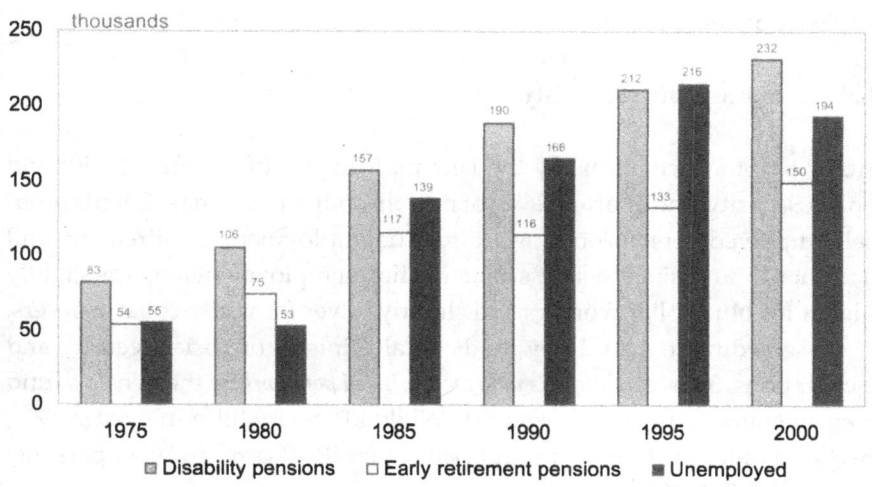

Source: Hauptverband der österr. Sozialversicherungsträger, Arbeitsmarktservice Österreich, own calculations

Figure 2: Disability rates, 1970-2000

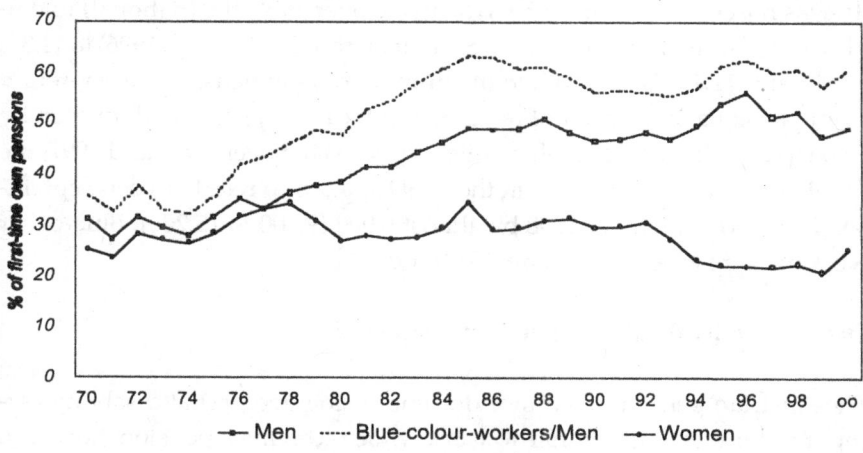

This development can also be seen in the proportion of disability pensions among new pensions. In the early 1970s, three out of ten new pensions for men were disability pensions, whereas since the mid-1980s one man in two retires with a disability pension. This development is not seen in women as they increasingly meet the criteria for an early-retirement pension (from 55 years); the disability rate has fluctuated in the last 30 years between 20% and 34% of new pensions.

Labour market and disability

According to calculations by the Federal Ministry of Labour, Health and Social Security, one quarter (26%) of new disability pension recipients (non-self-employed persons only) went from unemployment to retirement, and a further 25% obtained sickness benefit. The unemployment rate was slightly higher for blue-collar workers and slightly lower for white-collar workers.

According to a study by the Federal Ministry of Social Security and Generations, 30% of *applicants who were refused pensions* by the pension fund were unemployed and 15% were sick. While 40% were still employed in 1991, two years later the figure had dropped to just 17% (same group of persons) (Finder, 1995: 118f.).

These figures also show that the chances that this group (rejected applicants) will find a job are very slender.

The effects that restrictions in disability pensions can have on the labour market can be seen from the developments in 1996 and 1997. After the age limit for early retirement pensions on account of reduced work capacity was raised for men from 55 to 57 in October 1996, the (national) unemployment rate in the 55-59 age group for men rose from 10.4% (1996) to 11.3% (1997) and 12.7% (1998). While the number of new pensions (early-retirement pensions on account of reduced work capacity) dropped for men by 6,600 (particularly among blue-collar workers) between 1996 and 1997, the number of unemployed men in the 55-99 age group rose between September 1996 and September 1998 by almost 6,000 (9,500 to 15,200). Blue-collar workers were most affected by this trend.

Occupation by disability pension recipients

The Austrian pension insurance does not recognize partial disability (except for miners). It is possible to work while receiving a pension, however, as a part-time worker in an occupation that is not 'protected', for example. In reality, the numbers are very small. At the end of 1999, according to the Hauptverband der österreichischen Sozialversicherungsträger and my own calculations on the basis of this data, around 3,500 of the 144,000 disability pension recipients of working age had jobs (discounting insignificant income), equivalent to 2.4% of the recipients. It is interesting to note that practically half (1,600) of these were self-employed.

Since 1 January 2001 new provisions have applied to working pensioners. If the income is higher than the minimum level, the disability pension is regarded as a partial pension. The pension is not reduced, however, until the monthly income (pension + work income) exceeds EUR 872. Income beyond this amount is counted against the pension (30% reduction for income up to EUR 1,308, 40% for EUR 1,308 to EUR 1,744 and 50% for income above EUR 1,744). This arrangement is equivalent to a progressive tax rate of 30% to 50%. The 50% deduction may not, however, exceed 50% of the pension or the job income.

Disability risk

The figures show that the risk of disability differs considerably between the individual groups. Apart from the fact that older persons become disabled with particular frequency, blue-collar workers, agricultural workers and persons in particularly stressful occupations are above-averagely susceptible to disability.

Of all the new pensions in 2000, 61% of male blue-collar workers but only 34% of male white-collar workers received a disability pension (26% of female blue-collar workers and 17% of female white-collar workers).

The differences between men and women are mainly attributable to the different pensionable ages. A comparison of the disability risk by age groups (new disabled in percentage of employed persons in an age group) produces a picture similar to that for sickness statistics: female white-collar workers are more often sick and disabled than their male colleagues, while the opposite applies for blue-collar workers. This different risk is shown in the following table for the 40-49 age group in 1995 (Table 3).

Figure 3: Disability pensions: per cent of all first-time pensioners, 2000

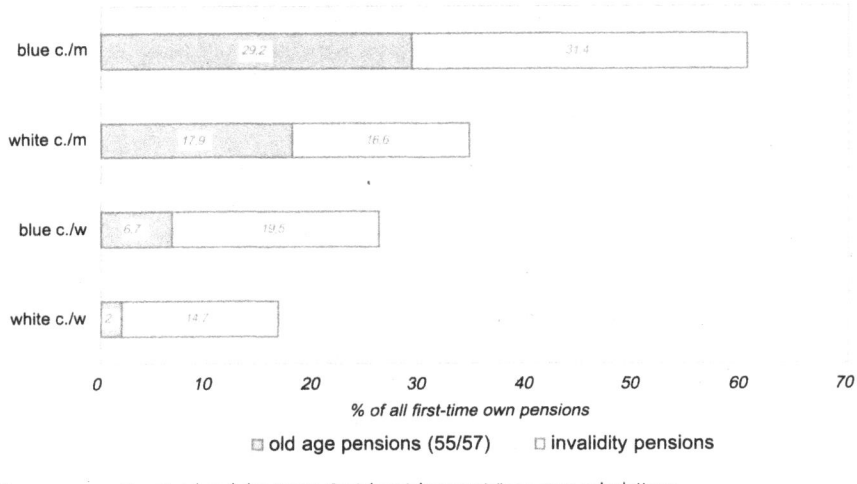

□ old age pensions (55/57)   □ invalidity pensions

Sources: Hauptverband der österr. Sozialversicherungsträger, own calculations

Table 3: Frequency of sickness and disability risk 1995 (45-49 year olds)

	blue collar/M	blue collar/F	white collar/M	white collar/F
Sick days per employee	23.7	22.7	10.2	13.8
New disabled per 10,000 employees	127	111	44	58

Note: The author has made similar calculations for earlier years and found the relationship between the two groups to be essentially unchanged.

Source: Hauptverband der österreichischen Sozialversicherungsträger, own calculations

Information from the *Pensionsversicherungsanstalt der Arbeiter* shows that the proportion of disability pensions for the individual occupation groups differs. In 1999, for example, over 70% of male blue-collar workers from some groups retired with disability pensions (glassmaking and stone, clay and glass processing, chemicals, transport and communications).[31]

Figures from 1992 also show large regional differences. While 43% of blue-collar workers in Lower Austria and 47% in Burgenland, both eastern provinces, retired with disability pensions, the figures for the tourism-oriented provinces of Carinthia (75%), Salzburg (73%), Vorarlberg (70%) and

Tyrol (68%) were much higher (own calculations based on data from the *Pensionsversicherungsanstalt der Arbeiter*).

Causes of disability

In 1999, 71% of new disability pensions in the pension insurance fund for employees were given for three sets of diseases:
- 39% for musculoskeletal diseases,
- 19% for psychiatric diseases,
- 12% for cardiovascular diseases.

These are the figures for new pensions in all age groups for the entire pension insurance fund.

The structure in the different age groups varies considerably, however. The medical grounds in the different age groups can be derived from the detailed annual reports by the two major pension insurance funds (see Table 4). In 1999, for example 40% of pensions in the under-29 age group were for psychiatric disorders and 20% for accidents; in all age groups put together, however, only 19% of pensions were awarded for psychiatric disorders and 4% for accidents. In the over-55 age groups, to whom more than half of the disability pensions were granted, 57% of pensions were for musculoskeletal diseases, 13% for cardiovascular diseases, 9% for psychiatric disorders, and 3% for accidents.

In the ten age groups, psychiatric disorders were the most frequent causes in the under-50 age groups (both blue- and white-collar workers). In the 40-49 age group, almost a third of the new disability pensions (31%) were for this group of diseases.

Long-term figures are available for the pension fund for employees. The figures show that between 1975 and 1995 the proportion of musculoskeletal diseases rose from 16% to 44%. The increase was particularly marked between 1980 and 1985 (+17 percentage points). One of the main reasons for this development was the fact that from 1981 the access criteria for older persons (55+) were particularly easy and the percentage in this age group among the new pensions therefore increased considerably. Because of the high age limit (57 for men from autumn 1996), for whom these special criteria apply, the proportion of this sickness group sank to 40% in 1997.

In the 20 years under consideration, the percentage of cardiovascular diseases, the group that had formerly dominated, more than halved – from 31 to 14% – as did the neurological disease group (9 to 3%). This does not mean that the probability of becoming disabled on account of these diseases dropped to the same extent, however. It should be remembered that the number of disability pensions increased considerably[32] and, even with the same probability of disability in these two groups, the proportion was bound to drop.

It is nevertheless interesting to note that the proportion of psychiatric disorders in the 20 years rose from 6 to 12%. The continuing steep rise until 1999 (19%) must also be seen in relation to the drop in musculoskeletal diseases on account of amendments to the pension law.

Table 4:   Causes of disability by age, 1999

Of 100 new pensions, the individual groups accounted for the following:

Sickness group	Age groups				
	-29	30-39	40-49	50-54	55-
musculoskeletal	4	9	16	25	57
psychiatric	40	45	31	14	13
cardiovascular	2	5	10	14	13
cancer	5	7	12	11	4
respiratory	1	1	3	4	4
endocrinopathy	1	3	3	3	2
work accidents	7	4	3	2	2
digestive	3	2	3	2	1
leisure accidents	13	4	2	2	1
other	23	20	17	13	6
total	100	100	100	100	100
total new pensions on account of reduced work capacity + early retirement on account of reduced work capacity	500	1,300	3,300	4,500	15,000

Excluding disability pensions for widows with four children (aged 55+; s. 254 ss. 4 ASVG)

Note: Railway workers and miners accounted for 2% of new disability pensions.
Source: Own calculations based on annual reports of blue- and white-collar pension insurance funds, 1999.

7   Outlook

Disability pensions have taken considerable strain off the labour market in recent decades. Reductions in pensions designed as a sanction for the early retirement have barely made any difference to this group.

In the last few years there have been considerable efforts at greater integration into the labour market of persons with health problems. With problems in financing pension insurance and the improved employment situation, they are encouraged today to retrain in new occupations.

The new Government formed a working group in 2000 under the leadership of Professor Theodor Tomandl (University of Vienna) to propose reforms of the disability pension system. In an expert opinion (discussion basis for the working group) Professor Tomandl suggested a number of reforms, including a partial pension system, as practised in other European countries, and also partial sickness and unemployment benefit. Instead of job protection, disability should be determined on the basis of income comparisons (achievable income in comparison with earlier income); the job protection system could be retained, if at all, for older persons.

He also suggests that incapacity pensions from accident insurance be replaced by a supplement to disability pensions. Disability insurance should be separated from pension insurance and merged with health insurance.

It is not possible at present to determine the direction that the reforms will take.

Notes

1   With public officials the pension is a direct payment by the employer. Insurance is therefore unnecessary.
2   These complex regulations will not be discussed in further detail here.
3   This transition period was decided in 1992 as part of an 'equal treatment' package. There are calls for the raising of the retirement age to be brought forward.
4   This subject is not dealt with in detail here.
5   As with old-age pensions, these periods can be extended by the 'dead times', e.g. periods of unemployment without unemployment benefit.
6   1.9% of the assessment base per year of contribution for the first 30 years.
7   The period for calculation will be gradually increased between 2003 and 2020 to the best 18 years for early retirements (including disability pensions).
8   Does not apply in this form until October 2002.

9   Example: A women retires at age 56.5 and has 30 years of contributions (early retirement on account of unemployment, for example). This makes an incremental amount of 30 times 2 = 60%. For each year up to the regular retirement age (3.5 years) 3.5 times 3 percentage points, i.e. 10.5 points, are deducted. As this deduction would represent a reduction of 17.5% but the limit is 15%, the original incremental amount (60%) is reduced by only 15%. The pension in this case is 51% of the assessment base. This special regulation was designed above all as a concession to persons with a short period of contributions (mostly women).

10 Tàlos/Wörister, 1994: 159ff.

11 One problem with the procedure is the lack of information in the decisions by the pension insurance funds, which contain next to no details of the reason for rejection. As a result, the case has to be looked at again in detail when it is taken to the labour or social court. Apart from consideration of the legal aspects, medical examinations are also repeated. This would be superfluous in many cases if the unsuccessful claimant had been informed of the reason for non-recognition of the reduced work capacity.

12 Wörister, 2000.

13 There were other conditions that will not be looked at in detail here.

14 "This new old-age pension was designed to enable claimants with long-term and continuous contributions to retire before the age of 65 (or 60) without a medical examination. " (Teschner/Widlar, op. cit.: 1279).

15 A year earlier, generalized special support had been created, allowing early retirement at the age of 54 for women and 59 for men, provided that certain conditions were fulfilled. This type of early retirement has now been extensively abolished.

16 Some of the replacement periods count towards the qualifying period but not towards the amount of the pension.

17 Normally the first day of the month after the pension application.

18 In this way they could claim an ASVG pension on top of their railway pension while still working a little.

19 A similar provision exists for white-collar workers (s. 273 ss. 1 ASVG).

20 For self-employed persons the definition of work incapacity is as follows: "An insured person is deemed to be incapable of employment if as a result of illness or other infirmity or reduction in his/her physical or mental capacities, he/she is permanently incapable of regular employment."

21 Applicants are not usually informed of the *noticed* restrictions. This is probably one of the reasons for the large number of unsuccessful appeals and the length of the procedure (all examinations are repeated although some of the issues might not be in contention).

22 Wörister (1986), Marischka (1992) and Wörister/Marischka (1995). Demands arising from this are: standardization of opinions (checklist); training in industrial medicine and improved training for experts; inclusion of treating physician's opinion.

23 OGH decision of 12 March 1991, 10 Ob S66/91

24 In the collective agreements for white-collar workers, occupations are divided into six classes based on income and social status.

25 55 years for women until June 2000.

26 Landesgericht Feldkirch 23 January 1996, 33 Cgs 112/95.

27 This court decision takes account of the health situation (when changing locations) but not of the financial situation.

28 Estimate on the basis of pension age statistics of the Hauptverband der österreichischen Sozialversicherungsträger.

29 E.g. Wörister (1982), Wörister (1986), Finder (1995), Tomandl/Mazal (1997), Obermayr et al. (1991), Bundesarbeitskammer (1993), Wörister/Marischka (1997).
30 Precise data on the number of disability pensions among civil servants is not available. The difference between them and pensions from the pension insurance has been roughly estimated on the basis of data from the Hauptverband der österreichischen Sozialversicherungsträger.
31 Annual Report of the Pensionsversicherungsanstalt der Arbeiter 1999, own calculations from it.
32 Between 1975 and 1995 the number of new disability pensions rose from 20,000 to 35,500.

References

Berger, J. (1993) *Einführung in das österreichische Arbeits- und Sozialrecht*. Vienna.
Bundesarbeitskammer (1993) *Die Lage der Arbeitnehmer 1993*.
Bundesarbeitskammer (1999) Wirtschafts- und sozialstatistisches Taschenbuch.
Bundesarbeitskammer (1998) *Statistische Informationen, November 1998* (Arbeits- und Sozialrechtsverfahren 1970-1997; Karl Wörister).
Finder, R. (1995) 'Entwicklung der Invaliditätspensionen', pp. 101-122 in: *Bericht über die soziale Lage 1994*. Vienna: Federal Ministry for Health and Social Welfare. (Study with author's collaboration)
Marischka, Chr. (1992) 'Ergebnisse einer Analyse von medizinischen Gutachten im sozialgerichtlichen Verfahren', *Das Recht der Arbeit* 42: 161-164.
Obermayr, U. et al. (also the author) (1991) 'Fakten und Trends zur Invaliditätspension', *Soziale Sicherheit* 44: 296-316.
Tàlos, E./Wörister, K. (1994) *Soziale Sicherung im Sozialstaat Österreich*. Baden-Baden.
Teschner, H./Widlar, P. (1974) *Allgemeines Sozialversicherungsgesetz (Kommentar)*. Vienna (looseleaf collection)
Tomandl, Th./Mazal, W. (1997) *Das Invaliditätsproblem*. Vienna. (Study with author's collaboration)
Wörister, K. (1982) 'Soziologische Betrachtungen zum Schiedsgerichtsverfahren', *Das Recht der Arbeit* 32: 397-403.
Wörister, K. (1986) 'Ergebnisse einer Analyse von medizinischen Gutachten im Schiedsgerichtsverfahren', *Das Recht der Arbeit* 36: 452-456.
Wörister, K. (1995) 'Die freiwilligen Versicherungen in der österreichischen Sozialversicherung', *Ausgewählte Probleme des österreichischen Sozialversicherungsrechts*, volume 1; published by Flemmich, G. Vienna.
Wörister, K./Marischka, Chr. (1997) 'Sozialgerichtsverfahren: Aktuelle Daten und Entwicklungen', *Soziale Sicherheit* 50: 248-260.
Wörister, K. (2000) *Sozialrechtsverfahren 1999*, Soziale Sicherheit 11: 922-926.

CHAPTER 4

Disability Pensions: Trends and Policies in Denmark

Per H. Jensen[1]

1 The social disability pension and related social security schemes

1.1 The social disability pension scheme

The Danish disability system is based on a single disability benefit regulated by the Social Pension Act of 1984.[2] Before 1984 the disability benefit was referred to as invalidity benefit. The terminology[3] was changed in order to neutralize the stigmatizing effects of the term invalidity.[4] Since 1984 the Social Pension Act has been adapted and modernized several times, most recently in July 1998, when a set of laws took effect comprising the Active Social Policy Act, Social Services Act and Legal Rights and Administration in Social Services Act. In the following discussion of the Danish system, reference will be made to the existing rules for awarding disability pensions. However, in December 2000 the major political parties in Parliament agreed to reform disability pensions. The purpose of the reform, which has yet not passed in Parliament, is to ensure that persons capable of working are given serious opportunities to use their potential in the labour market. The reform stresses active efforts to integrate this group of people into the labour market rather than supporting them passively. The aim is for disability pensions to be awarded only if it is impossible for the person in question to remain in or re-enter the labour market in normal conditions or in subsidized employment. The new protocol will take effect on 1 January 2003. The discussion therefore considers if and how the existing rules will be changed after 2003.

1.1.1 Definition of disability, coverage and eligibility

All Danish citizens between 18 and 67 with permanent residence in Denmark are eligible for a disability pension if their employability is reduced partly or fully due to illness, impairment, social and/or other reasons. Furthermore, people between 50 and 67 are eligible for disability pension solely on account of social conditions, i.e. for this group there is no reduced employability requirement. Disability pensions can thus be awarded either due to reduced employability or for primarily social reasons. In consequence, different types of disability pension exist targeted at different groups of people:
- *highest* disability pensions are awarded to persons between 18 and 60 years who are considered to be only minimally employable due to permanent physical or mental disablement;
- *medium* disability pensions are awarded to persons between 18 and 67 years whose employability is perceived to be permanently reduced to about two thirds, and to persons between 61 and 66 years with no or insignificant employability;
- *normal* disability pensions are divided into three types:
    1) Purely health-related pensions awarded persons between 18 and 67 years whose employability is reduced by at least 50% for health reasons.
    2) Pensions based on a 'mixture' of health and needs awarded to persons between 18 and 67 years whose employability is reduced by at least 50% without the disablement being solely caused by health.
    3) Pensions based on needs awarded to persons between 50 and 67 years for social or health reasons. This type of pension does not require reduced employability.

In general, the awarding of disability pension depends on the loss of employability.[5] In the new reform, however, the criterion 'working capacity' replaces the criterion 'loss of employability'. The underlying idea is that by focusing on working capacity, the law will be directed towards the resources and development potential of citizens rather than toward their problems and limitations. Even today, pensions are not awarded until the possibility of activation, rehabilitation, treatment or other measures for improving employability have been tested and/or rejected. The disability pension is a permanent benefit.

The majority of people awarded disability pensions had been living on sickness benefit hitherto: in 1999, 44% received sickness benefit, 27% received social assistance, 12% were wage-earners, 12% had other income, and 5% received unemployment benefit, early retirement benefit or rehabilitation benefit (Den Sociale Ankestyrelse, 2000: 13). Disability pensions were primarily awarded for mental ill health (29%) and illnesses of the motor apparatus (28%). Only 3% were awarded disability pension solely on social indications. In 1999 the authorities processed 16 091 applications for disability pensions. Of these, they rejected 3 116 (about 19%), awarded highest disability pensions to 1 806 persons, medium disability pensions to 5 140, and normal disability pensions to 6 029.

1.1.2 Organization of the disability system

In Denmark, the 275 municipalities are responsible for awarding disability pensions. They process all types of applications for disability pension apart from appeals that the National Social Appeals Board decides on.

Before 1 July 1998, any citizen could turn to his or her municipality and apply for a disability pension and the municipality was under an obligation to process the application. This is no longer the case. Today, it is not possible to apply specifically for a disability pension, but solely for social benefits according to the social legislation. This is because the municipalities must decide from a holistic perspective which of a number of means is most appropriate for helping the individual in question.[6] Options include temporary activation, temporary rehabilitation or disability pensions. Similarly, the municipality can bring up the matter of awarding a person a disability pension even though the person in question has not himself or herself applied for one.

The municipalities possess high autonomy in treating applications. For example, it is left to them to determine which administrative level decides on disability pensions. However, the high degree of municipal autonomy carries the risk that citizens might not be treated equally.[7] In practice, it is up to the National Social Appeals Board to ensure equality of treatment of all applications. The municipalities remain autonomous, among other things, because they have to bear a major part of the costs of the disability system, since the State only reimburses 35% of the costs of newly-awarded disability pensions.

When deciding whether to award a disability pension or not, the local authorities draw on medical expertise. Medical consultants advise social workers on whether or not applications are sufficiently informed from a medical point of view.[8] If this is not the case, it may be necessary to obtain medical statements from hospitals, specialists, etc. Further examination by specialists, psychologists or in a hospital may also be required. Medical consultants are responsible for obtaining and summarizing medical information and for submitting reports on the health of applicants and for assessing whether the given case involves reduced employability. In practice, however, the awarding of disability pensions depends to a large extent on the diagnosis, in that applicants suffering from serious diseases tend to be awarded higher pensions than those suffering from less serious diseases, even if the reduction in employability is identical in both cases (Damsø and Simonsen, 1998: 68).

Citizens applying to the municipality for social benefits are under an obligation to disclose all information necessary for determining which type of benefit they will be entitled to. Consequently, applicants must cooperate in undergoing examinations that the local authorities deem necessary in consultation with mèdical advisors.

From 2003, citizens will be involved much more actively in the process and their skills, desires and needs will be taken into consideration to a much greater degree. Thus, applicants will be more involved in defining and solving their individual problems *vis-à-vis* the labour market. In this sense, the reform reflects the general tendency towards reducing the role and authority of welfare employees in favour of a more service-oriented role with greater participation by the beneficiaries. In 2001, municipal staff will therefore be undergoing intensive training to prepare them for the disability pension reform, especially with a view to furnishing them with the competence to assess the working capacity and potential of the individual person rather than focusing on the degree of loss of employability.

In the present and future disability pension systems, the decisions on disability must be communicated in writing and must always be justified with reference to the provisions of the laws on which they are based. If the decision contains judgements, the justification must also include the relevant factors influencing the decision. Other facts that may have influenced the decision must also be stated. If the decision does not fully comply with the applicant's request, it must include detailed guidelines for how to lodge an appeal.

1.1.3 Types of services offered and details on rehabilitation

Since the mid-1970s, the awarding of disability pensions has been decentralized, and consequently the municipalities and counties have come to play a decisive role in all aspects of invalidity and disability. Local authorities have extensive means at their disposal for counteracting, relieving and compensating for disability. They are based on a set of laws that took effect on 1 July 1998. The purpose of the legislation was to create an all-inclusive labour market,[9] among other things to ensure that people with reduced employability remain in the labour market (Regeringen, 2000). The measures employed are rehabilitation, sheltered employment, 'flexi-jobs' and 'soft jobs'.

REHABILITATION

The purpose of rehabilitation is to help the individual regain loss of working capacity due to physical, mental or social circumstances – in other words to prevent the individual becoming a permanent recipient of disability benefits. In order to qualify for rehabilitation measures, the individual must have reasonable prospects for becoming partly or fully self-supporting. The attempt to regain working capacity can either take place within the individual's previous job or in a new one.

The municipality offers rehabilitation and works out a job plan in collaboration with the rehabilitee after having clarified what kind of job she or he will be capable of undertaking. Rehabilitation can comprise one or several of the following activities:
- testing of working capacity,
- preparatory or clarifying occupational activities (preliminary rehabilitation),
- education (rehabilitees are eligible for qualifying education at all levels),
- assistance in establishing an independent business.

During the rehabilitation period, the rehabilitee receives a monthly benefit of DKr 11 900. If the person is under 25 years the amount is DKr 5 825.

In an attempt to foster business-oriented initiatives, a new concept, 'business rehabilitation', was introduced on 1 January 1999 to encourage municipalities to develop and increase efforts at business rehabilitation. Business rehabilitation is aimed at persons above the general age of education, persons who have worked at an earlier date, or persons who are obliged to support a spouse and/or children. It consists of training in a company and is designed to reach a broader target group that might otherwise be difficult to rehabilitate. The rehabilitee receives at least the minimum wage for the given occupation. The municipality fully or partly reimburses the employer while the rehabilitee is undergoing training or education. The municipal subsidy depends on the work performed by the rehabilitee and in certain cases covers the full wage. The company can receive a maximum of DKr 730 000 over three years.

The purpose of rehabilitation is, as mentioned, to prevent individuals being excluded from the labour market. Attempts in recent years have, however, aimed increasingly at reintegrating people who have already been excluded from the labour market. This means that recipients of disability pensions are also eligible for rehabilitation so as to enable them to use their remaining working capacities.

In 1998 there were 80,000 rehabilitees, of whom 20 700 had started a rehabilitation programme. A large proportion of rehabilitees are young, and 72% are in fact under 39 years of age. In 1997 64% of rehabilitees received social assistance prior to starting on rehabilitation programmes; 43% of rehabilitees concluded rehabilitation projects with a qualification; and 83% of all rehabilitees became employed within five years of completing rehabilitation programmes (DA, 1999: 122).

Sheltered employment

The counties supplement municipal rehabilitation efforts by offering specialized counselling and rehabilitation. One or several counties can establish and operate rehabilitation institutions, sheltered workshops, etc., or they can be run by municipalities or private foundations that have entered into an agreement with the county. The county and the municipality each pay 50% of the costs of running rehabilitation institutions and sheltered workshops.

However, it is important to distinguish between rehabilitation institutions and sheltered employment. The latter is not actually a rehabilitation or labour market measure, but rather offers activity to people under 67 years who, due to significantly reduced physical and mental abilities or specific social problems, are unable to get or maintain employment on normal conditions. This segment includes recipients of disability pensions and people incapable of gaining foothold in the labour market by way of 'flexi-jobs' or 'soft jobs'. Sheltered employment is remunerated according to performance and may include reward, reimbursement of transportation costs, and actual time wages.

In 1996, county rehabilitation institutions and sheltered workshops harboured 15 728 people (Socialministeriet, 1997). It should be noted that the meaning of sheltered employment was changed in 1998. Earlier, sheltered employment had consisted of (1) individual sheltered employment with a private or public employer, and (2) sheltered employment in workshops, rehabilitation institutions and re-establishment centres. In 1998 individual sheltered employment was changed to 'flexi-jobs' and 'soft jobs'.

'FLEXI-JOBS' AND 'SOFT JOBS'
'Flexi-jobs' and 'soft jobs' were introduced in 1998 to facilitate the employment of persons with permanently reduced working capacities and to help them lead an active life.

People with permanently reduced working capacities are eligible for 'flexi-jobs'. Every person meeting the criteria for disability pension must be offered a flexi-job, but current recipients of disability pensions are not entitled to be offered them. A flexi-job can be with a private or public employer and must, to the extent possible, be a full-time job, since people in flexi-jobs are not eligible for additional social benefits. Basically, wages and working conditions are similar to those in existing agreements within the given industry. The employer pays the wages, and the municipality reimburses the employer one third, half or two thirds of the minimum wages according to the collective agreement in that municipal subvention is graduated according to the reduced working capacity of the given person. The majority of flexi-jobs (90%) carry a 50% subsidy (Socialministeriet, 1999). In case of unmerited unemployment between two flexi-jobs, the person is eligible for unemployment benefit. By May 1999 5 800 flexi-jobs existed (Arbejdsministeriet, 1999: 51). Of this population, 38% received sickness benefits and 17% social assistance in 1998. Approximately one third of those working in flexi-jobs in 1999 received no public benefits replacing income in 1998.

Soft jobs are reserved for people receiving disability pensions. In most cases these jobs are part-time jobs and the earned income is supplemented by a disability pension. Municipalities and counties offer employment in subsidized soft jobs with private or public employers. Wages and working conditions are agreed between the employer and the employee in collaboration with the relevant union. The wages must be at least one third of the starting pay within the occupation in question. The employer pays the wages and the municipality reimburses 50% to a maximum of one sixth of the minimum wage specified in the collective agreement pertaining to the occupation in question. By May 1999 5 500 soft jobs existed (Arbejdsministeriet, 1999: 53).

In order to keep people in the labour market, the Ministry of Social Affairs launched a campaign in 1994 entitled 'It concerns all of us – an initiative on the social responsibility of companies'. The aim was to reduce exclusion from the labour market (Ebsen et al., 1998) by encouraging the two sides of industry to include 'social chapters' in the collective agreements covering both the private and public sector. In addition to flexi-jobs and soft jobs, an increasing number of collective agreements have, since 1995, contained these 'social chapters' with provisions on wages and working conditions for people with reduced working capacity, which facilitate the local creation of new types of jobs. About 4% of private and public employers have established jobs in line with the 'social chapters'. In total 3 700 jobs have been created, and of these 1 100 are located in the public sector (Arbejdsministeriet, 1999: 54).

Post-2003

In the future, disability pensions will be granted to persons unable to support themselves by means of non-subsidized or subsidized employment, i.e. employment under normal conditions, social chapters or flexi-jobs. It will therefore be necessary to give higher priority to rehabilitation in order to strengthen the social policies directed towards the labour market and hence the development of an all-inclusive labour market. The new reform specifically emphasizes that working capacity must be permanently reduced prior to the application for flexi-jobs. In consequence, the impossibility of finding non-subsidized employment, including employment under social chapters, must be confirmed before people can be offered flexi-jobs. In order to emphasize that flexi-jobs must function as the last resort before awarding disability pensions, wage subsidies will be granted only to persons who have lost 50% and 75% of their working capacity, i.e. employers employing people who have lost only 25% of their working capacity will not receive wage subsidies in the future.

Finally, from 2003 onwards, a network of job centres will be established specializing in finding and arranging jobs for persons with reduced working capacities. The job centres are expected to collaborate closely with the municipalities responsible for approving flexi-jobs and soft jobs.

1.1.4 Types of social disability benefits

The various disability pensions (high, medium, and normal) refer to the extent of employability and consequently carry different levels of benefits. There are four levels of disability pension: highest, medium, increased normal, and normal. Whether a person is awarded an increased normal or a normal disability pension depends solely on his/her age at the time of application. Persons between 18 and 59 years are usually awarded increased normal disability pensions, while persons between 60 and 66 years receive normal disability pensions.

The rates are also dependent on marital status. The law distinguishes between singles, married/cohabiting couples both receiving a disability pension, and married couples of whom only one receives a disability pension.

The pension is combined with a series of different benefits. Every disability pensioner receives an annual basic amount of DKr 48 024.[10] In addition, every disability pensioner receives a supplementary pension of DKr 47 616 annually (singles) and DKr 21 468 (married). Persons awarded highest and medium disability pension receive a disablement benefit of DKr 23 364. This amount is, however, reduced to DKr 19 896 if the pensioner is married to/cohabiting with someone who also receives the highest or medium disability pension. Persons awarded the highest disability pension receive an annual incapacity to work benefit of DKr 32 244, which is reduced to DKr 23 687 if the spouse/cohabitee receives the highest disability pension. Persons awarded an increased normal pension receive an annual amount of DKr 12 204. Table 1 summarizes the rates of disability pensions.

In addition, disability recipients may receive supplementary benefits. These include benefits such as a 'support settlement', which may be granted if the recipient needs help from others for personal affairs; and a 'care supplement', which may be granted if the recipient is in need of nursing, supervision, etc.

Disability pensions are taxed like ordinary income and other welfare benefits, except for the disability benefit, which is exempt from tax and granted with the highest and medium disability pension. Furthermore, the logic of benefits reflecting working capacity is that disability pensioners are expected to supplement pensions with earned income. But if the recipient has a soft job or other types of wage work, the basic amount and supplementary pension is reduced.

Table 1: Rates of disability pensions (January 1999)

	Singles	Married to a disability pensioner	Married
Highest			
Basic amount	48 024	48 024	48 024
Supplementary pension	47 616	21 468	21 468
Disablement benefit	23 364	19 896	23 364
Incapacity for work	32 244	23 687	32 244
Total	151 248	113 075	125 100
Medium			
Basic amount	48 024	48 024	48 024
Supplementary pension	47 616	21 468	21 468
Disablement benefit	23 364	19 896	23 364
Total	119 004	89 388	92 856
Increased normal			
Basic amount	48 024	48 024	48 024
Supplementary pension	47 616	21 468	21 468
Benefit if < 60 years	12 204	12 204	12 204
Total	107 844	81 696	81 696
Normal			
Basic amount	48 024	48 024	48 024
Supplementary pension	47 616	21 468	21 468
Total	96 640	69 492	69 492

Source: Den Sociale Ankestyrelse (2000: 25).

If income exceeds DKr 176 100, the basic amount is reduced by 60% of the excess amount. For example, if the income is DKr 210 000, the basic amount is reduced by (210 000-176 100)60/100 DKr 20 340. Similarly, the supplementary pension is reduced by 30% (singles) and 15% (couples) of the income exceeding DKr 43 900 (singles) and DKr 88 000 (couples) in 1998. In other words, if a single earns DKr 90 000, his or her supplementary pension is reduced by DKr (90 000-43 900)15/100= 6 915. In 1998 pensions amounting to less than DKr 1 170 annually were not payable (Damsø and Simonsen, 1998). However, there is a special in-work disablement benefit payable to persons who would have been entitled to highest or medium disability pension had they not been working. The disablement benefit is meant to cover extra transportation and household expenses.

From 2003, the benefit structure will be simplified via grossing and the abolition of special benefits. In the future, disability pensioners will be on equal footing with other social beneficiaries, and the benefit for a single disability pensioner will equal that of unemployment benefit (DKr 152 880 annually), and for the married/cohabiting disability pensioner 85% of the unemployment benefit (DKr 129 948 annually). The effect of work income has still not been fully clarified. As an example, however, it may be noted that the unemployment benefit paid to full-time insured members working shorter hours was reduced by DKr 139.46 per working hour in 2000. In other words, a full-time insured person working shorter hours did not receive supplementary unemployment benefits if working more than 21 hours per week.

In Denmark, old age pension is a universal benefit, i.e. all citizens above 67 years of age are entitled to it. Since the late 1960s, large segments of wage-earners have supplemented their old age pensions by means of collectively bargained occupational pensions or State-subsidized private savings. Similarly, from 2003 a savings scheme will be introduced as a supplement to the ordinary old-age pension for disability pensioners. The purpose is to secure disability pensioners better conditions when they reach the pensionable age.

1.2 Related social security schemes

1.2.1 Disability and unemployment

In principle, the amount of disability pension is invariable over time unless changes in physical, mental or social situations speak in favour of changing the amount. In 1999, 16% of 27 281 appeals settled by the National Social Appeals Board concerned the raising of pensions (Den Sociale Ankestyrelse, 2000: 32).

Similarly, the amount of unemployment benefit is invariable during the period of unemployment and was fixed in 1999 at 90% of the income prior to unemployment or a maximum DKr 143 520 annually. The vast majority of recipients of unemployment benefits receive the maximum amount. The relationship between maximum unemployment benefits and disability benefits varies depending on the type of disability benefit and the household income of the recipient. In 1999, for a married person whose husband/wife did not receive a disability pension, the relationship between unemployment benefit/disability benefit was 87% for highest, 65% for medium, 57% for increased normal, and 48% for normal disability benefit.

Recipients are entitled to unemployment benefit for four years, divided into two periods: one year of unemployment benefit followed by an activation period of three years during which the person has the right and obligation to be activated. Disability and unemployment benefits cannot be combined.

1.2.2 Disability and early retirement

During the period 1980-1997 the effective retirement age dropped from 62.4 to 60.6 years (Det Seniorpolitiske Initiativudvalg, 1999: 16), and in 1999 Parliament lowered the retirement age from 67 to 65 years as of 2004.[11] There are three regular retirement pathways, but it should be noted that disability and early retirement benefits cannot be combined.

- *The early retirement scheme*: By 1 July 1999 the early retirement scheme has been subject to major changes aimed at making more people in their early sixties stay in the labour market. People between 60 years of age and official pension age can make use of the early retirement scheme, which is optional but requires membership of an unemployment fund for 25 out of the previous 30 years (in Denmark unemployment insurance is optional[12]). In addition to the general unemployment contribution, the member must pay an early retirement contribution if s/he wants to be covered by the early retirement scheme. This latter contribution is thus optional, and about 12% of all members of unemployment insurance funds have chosen to opt out. The contribution amounts to DKr 184 a month, and is expected to rise to DKr 322 in the years to come. There are considerable economic advantages by postponing early retirement from the age of 60. First, the early retiree will generally receive 91% of unemployment benefits, but if the person postpones early retirement to the age of 62, early retirement benefits will be raised to equal unemployment benefits. Second, a person who postpones early retirement until the age of 62 will be entitled to a tax exemption of DKr 8 600 for each 481 hours worked. In other words, people who do not use their right to early retirement will receive a tax exemption of DKr 103 200 when they reach the pension age.[13] Third, for people who retire between the age of 60 and 62 and have additional income from individual savings, etc., 60% of their additional income will be deducted from the early retirement benefit. However, if retirement is postponed (to between 62 and 65), only certain types of personal income are deducted from the retirement benefits. Finally, the individual can decide on a day-to-day basis how much s/he wants to work, which makes the combination of work and retirement extremely flexible. A deduction in retirement benefits is made for each hour worked. If, for instance, the individual works for half a week, the deduction equals half a week's benefits. Early retirees working for more than 29.6 hours a week receive no early retirement benefits.

- *The part-time pension scheme*: The part-time pension scheme was introduced in 1987 as a new form of early retirement for employees and self-employed persons aged between 60 and 62 who were not eligible for early retirement benefits. The Ministry of Social Affairs administers this scheme, while the Ministry of Labour runs the early retirement scheme. Minor changes were made in the part-time pension scheme in 1999 in order to adapt it to the changes in the early retirement scheme. With these adjustments, the scheme is structured as follows. The eligibility criteria are: (1) between 60 and 64 years and not entitled to early retirement benefits; (2) in the labour market for at least 20 years; (3) worked for at least nine months within the last twelve months;[14] (4) working hours reduced by 25% and at least seven hours a week, and (5) works between 12 and 30 hours a week. The benefits are calculated on the basis of an annual basic amount which is 82% of sickness benefits (in 2000 the maximum sickness benefit was DKr 2 846 a week). The annual benefit amounts to 1/37 of the basic amount for each hour the working week is reduced, and benefits are reduced according to other types of pension benefits (private savings, etc.) along the same lines as those applying to early retirement benefits.

- *The senior benefit scheme*: The senior benefit was introduced in 1997 and is linked with the formation of flexi-jobs. The intention of this new scheme was to offer an early retirement-like opportunity to people in flexi-jobs who had been in the 'ordinary' labour market until the age of 50. The scheme was targeted at people who had been contributing substantially to the early retirement scheme. Therefore at the age of 50 they justifiably expected to be able to take out the early retirement benefit from the age of 60, but unfortunately lost this opportunity due to a reduction in their working capacity between the age of 50 and 59.

The senior benefit is 82% of unemployment benefits. The eligibility criteria are: (1) must be at least 60 years of age, (2) was eligible for unemployment benefits at the age of 50, and (3) has been a member of an unemployment insurance fund for 20 of the previous 25 years.

1.2.3 Disability and work injury

The law concerning protection against the effects of industrial injury covers all Danish wage-earners; the insurance scheme is financed by employers and the State. Industrial injury comprises (1) accidents related to the performance of work and to working conditions; (2) impairment for a maximum five days as a result of work or the conditions under which it is performed; (3) injuries caused by lifting; and (4) occupational diseases. Regarding the effects of an industrial injury, a distinction is made between (a) loss of working capacity, and (b) permanent ill effects. If the industrial injury causes more than a 15% reduction in working capacity, the injured person receives a staggered benefit which, for total loss of working capacity, amounts to four fifths of his/her previous annual income. The payment for loss of working capacity expires when the person reaches pensionable age. If the injury causes permanent ill effects of more than 5% the injured person is entitle to remuneration. The degree of damage depends on the nature and extent of the impairment. The remuneration is a lump sum, which for permanent 100% ill effects amounts to DKr 340 000.

If the industrial injury is assessed to have caused more than 50% loss in working capacity, the injured person can be awarded a disability benefit. However, the benefits paid as a result of loss of working capacity as well as the lump sum paid for permanent ill effects are deducted from the basic amount and supplementary pension, as only disablement benefit, incapacity to work, and benefit if over 60 years of age are granted independently of other income.

The table below outlines the number and age structure of reported and recognized work accidents and occupational diseases.

Even if an accident is recognized, this does not necessarily mean that compensation will automatically be granted. For instance, an incident may be recognized as an accident at work, while the working capacity is classified as being reduced by only 10%. In 1999, of 19 802 reported work accidents, only 5 049 were granted compensation, and of 13 242 reported occupational diseases, only 1 627 were granted compensation.

Table 2: Numbers of reported and recognised accidents at work in 1999 distributed by age

Age	Accidents and damaged glasses (numbers)		Occupational diseases and sudden lifting injuries (numbers)	
	Reported	Recognized	Reported	Recognized
Below 20 years	793	575	189	55
20 – 24 years	1 982	1 382	776	180
25 – 29 years	2 195	1 521	1 121	200
30 – 34 years	2 580	1 738	1 561	221
35 – 39 years	2 677	1 785	1 841	219
40 – 44 years	2 603	1 810	1 971	232
45 – 49 years	2 501	1 700	2 155	260
50 – 54 years	5 519	1 849	2 384	297
55 – 59 years	1 759	1 313	1 608	269
60 – 64 years	434	334	667	162
65+ years	142	122	788	145
Total	20 187	14 129	15 061	2 240

Source: www.ask.dk/

2 Major reforms of the system

2.1 Reforms of the social disability pension scheme

Disability pension legislation can be traced back to the Disablement Insurance Act of 1921. The legislation allowed for people below the pensionable age to be awarded a disability pension for health reasons. Since the law was introduced, the category of people eligible for disability pensions has gradually been expanded, especially since World War II. Before 1984 the system comprised a wide range of schemes aimed at different groups of people:
– *Widow's pension* for widows over 55 years of age and widows over 45 who had to maintain at least two children below 18 years, and widow's pension for single women over 50 in the event of failing health and other special circumstances.

- *Early old age pension* for single women over 62, persons over 60 in the event of failing health and other special circumstances, and persons aged 55 to 59 in the event of special social circumstances or conditions pertaining to the labour market.
- *Invalidity pension* for people aged 15 to 66 with at least 50% permanently reduced working capacity caused by physical and/or mental disablement.

Benefits related to widow's and early old-age pensions much resembled the amount of national retirement pension, whereas there were three categories of disability pension: highest, medium, and lowest. The latter could be awarded only if the working capacity was reduced by 50%.

The above pension forms were abolished as part of a major reform in 1984. Men and women were now treated equally, in that the former early retirement pension was replaced by the current rules for disability pension. The reform was the outcome of a general trend. Since the mid-1960s the awarding of disability pensions for social reasons had been increasingly facilitated. One of the objectives of the 1984 reform was to transfer people permanently on welfare to disability pensions (Socialministeriet, 1992: 4). In effect, the group of disability pensioners became younger. In 1984 almost 75% of all normal disability pensioners were over 60. In 1991 the percentage had dropped to 55% (Socialministeriet, 1992: 8). The youngest 25% of disability pensioners have become significantly younger, i.e. in the fourth quartile the average age fell from 47 to 41 between 1987/88 and 1994. The tendency for disability pensioners to become increasingly younger is strongest among women. From the age of 42 there is a significant difference between men and women. The proportion of female disability pensioners increases, while the proportion of male disability pensioners increases only slightly up to the age of 50 years. After the age of 50, an increasing number of both men and women are awarded disability pensions, but the proportion of female disability pensioners increases more dramatically. This increase in female disability pensioners continues till the statutory retirement age. In the early 1990s, 40% of the total population of women aged 66 were disability pensioners (Socialministeriet, 1992: 9 cont.), though fewer older women were awarded disability pensions in 1995 than in 1985. The gender imbalance can be explained by the fact that more women than men may have had interrupted working lives. This disqualified them for early retirement benefits because they had not worked long enough. The drop in the proportion of disability pensioners among the oldest women during the period 1985 to

1995 may thus be due to women becoming increasingly integrated into the labour market.

With the 1984 reform the benefit was raised. Prior to 1984 it had not been impossible to live solely on the normal disability benefit (i.e. the lowest invalidity pension). The increase in benefits has had an independent impact on the number of applicants for/recipients of disability pension. During the period 1984 to 1995 the number of disability pensioners increased by 19%.

In the 1980s the State reimbursed the municipalities 50% of the welfare costs, 75% of the sickness benefit costs, and 100% of the disability pension costs. This system encouraged municipalities to award disability pensions rather than rehabilitation, and to transfer welfare recipients to the disability system. But in the late 1980s, the reimbursement percentage was changed and today the State reimburses the municipalities only 35% of their disability pension costs and 50% of social assistance and sickness benefit costs. Simultaneously, the responsibility for awarding disability pensions was decentralized and shifted to the municipalities in an attempt to evoke economic responsibility when awarding pensions and thus to keep the costs under control. In consequence, the municipalities were required to balance the costs of disability pension against local taxes. The changes in State reimbursement have encouraged local authorities not to grant disability pensions.

The drop in the number of disability pensions awarded is particularly notable with regard to normal and increased normal disability pensions, while the drop in highest and medium disability pensions has been less pronounced. In 1992, 8 000 persons were awarded socially-related disability pensions against 1 900 in 1999 (Den Sociale Ankestyrelse, 2000: 11). This trend is, however, also caused by a drastic fall in unemployment in the period since 1994, which, *ceteris paribus*, has eased the pressure on the disability system.

Another factor that may explain the decrease in the number of disability pensioners is that more efforts have been devoted to activating people rather than letting them stay passively on welfare. Disability pensions have thus been replaced by offers of work, education or other activities.

Attempts to integrate disabled persons into the labour market date back to the Disablement Insurance Act of 1921. The law has been amended several times, most recently in 1998 when flexi-jobs replaced '50/50' jobs, and soft jobs replaced the 'one third' system. Under the 50/50 system, people whose health did not make them eligible for a disability pension could be awarded a wage subsidy of 50% of the minimum wage within the relevant occupation paid jointly by the municipality and the county. The 'one third' system was aimed at persons who had been awarded normal and medium disability pensions, in that these pensions presuppose a maximum working capacity of one third. The pensioner was thus expected to perform one third of the normal work, and the public authorities reimbursed one third of the minimum wage for the occupation in question. In effect, it did not cost the employer anything to employ this type of labour.

In recent years efforts at rehabilitation, such as business rehabilitation introduced in 1998, have also been intensified, no doubt as a result of the growing employment possibilities. Historically, rehabilitation has been strongly conditioned by the state of the labour market. When unemployment began to fall significantly and the boom started, the Government passed the Rehabilitation Act in 1960 (Plovsing, 2000), which facilitated the rehabilitation of the physically, mentally and socially disabled (Ebsen et al., 1998). In 1976, the municipalities were made responsible for rehabilitation (assisted by the counties) and the criteria for awarding rehabilitation were widened. Rehabilitation could be arranged in as much as rehabilitation could pave the way for a person's ability to support himself or herself and his or her family in the future. This person is awarded aid for education or vocational training or retraining to the extent that no other public benefits are granted. The rehabilitation rules were altered again in 1989 with the introduction of the 'gross rehabilitation' benefit, implying (1) a fixed benefit regardless of the husband/wife's income and assets; (2) time limit for the benefit of five years; (3) establishment of a career plan. Furthermore, the groups eligible for rehabilitation are defined as: (a) persons with mental or physical impairments; (b) single parents; (c) young poorly-educated persons; (d) young people who have not started further education or have not yet got a job; (e) long-term unemployed welfare recipients; (f) recipients of sickness benefits who are not immediately assumed to be able to return to their previous jobs; (g) immigrants and refugees; and (h) drug addicts and/or criminals. In 1991, it was made less attractive for the municipalities to award disability pensions because the State reimbursement rates for the municipal costs of rehabilitation, sickness benefit and disability pension were harmonized. Rehabilitation had earlier been more expensive than disability pensions and the law was introduced in expectation of a growing number of rehabilitees. The rationale was that successful rehabilitation would reduce costs in the long run (Ebsen et al., 1998). Finally, rehabilitation was made part of the Active Social Policy Act in 1998.

2.2 Relevant reforms in other social security schemes

As mentioned, the number of pensions awarded dropped in the late 1990s. In 1998/1999 alone there was a 32% decrease, from 19 696 in 1998 to 13 435 in 1999. This trend cannot have been caused by changes in administrative practices, since the number of disability pension applications also dropped from 38 849 to 27 291 in the same period (Den Sociale Ankestyrelse, 2000). The trend can probably be explained by the dramatic fall in unemployment in the same period. The fact that the largest proportion of disability pensions is awarded in financially weak regions and that it has become more difficult to obtain other welfare state benefits, such as cash payments and unemployment, early retirement or sickness benefits seem to confirm this hypothesis.

The number of years that a person can receive sickness benefit was reduced to two years in 1983 (in connection with the disability pension reform in 1984), and the period was further reduced to one year in 1990, which must be assumed to have had an impact on the number of disability pensioners (see Socialministeriet, 1992: 5 cont.). To be eligible for sickness benefit from the employer, the employee must have been employed with the given employer for the previous eight weeks prior to falling ill and in that period must have worked for at least 74 hours. In 2000 the amount of sickness benefit was DKr 2 846 per week. It should be noted that a large share of the Danish labour force is covered by collective agreements and receives full wages during illness. Payment of sickness benefit ceases when the person has received sickness benefit or wages during illness for more than 52 weeks within the preceding 18 months, unless (1) rehabilitation is expected to start soon after this period; (2) the person is waiting for medical treatment that is likely to restore his or her working capacity; (3) proceedings for compensation for industrial injury have been instituted; (4) the application for a disability pension is being processed.

The early retirement scheme was introduced 1 January 1979 because of the high unemployment in the 1970s and, in effect, the number of disability pensions awarded stagnated. The early retirement scheme probably relieved pressure on the disability system. It had been reformed by July 1999, however. The reform included measures that will make it more profitable for people to postpone early retirement till the age of 62; measures that make the transition from employment to retirement more flexible; and stricter eligibility criteria that make it more difficult to take out early retirement.

Still, persons fulfilling the requirements for early retirement but forced to leave the labour market due to illness can choose between disability pension and early retirement. Unlike disability pensions, there is no stigma attached to early retirement.

In 1978 the 'job offer scheme' was introduced. It gave long-term unemployed about to lose their entitlement to unemployment benefits a job offer for seven to nine months, which requalified them for unemployment benefit. In principle, the unemployed person could receive unemployment benefit for two and a half years, then participate in the job offer scheme for seven to nine months, and then receive unemployment benefit for a further two and a half years, etc. In 1985 the scheme was supplemented by the possibility of receiving aid to become self-employed and by education allowances, and in the late 1980s the number of job offers that the same individual could receive was reduced to two. In 1994, the maximum duration of unemployment benefit was fixed at seven years, which was reduced to five years in 1995. From 2001 the period of unemployment benefit will be further reduced to four years. Since 1994 the unemployment benefit period has been divided into two minor periods. In the first period the unemployed is entitled to activation for a period of one year. In the second period, s/he has both the right and the obligation to be activated. Activation usually entails a combination of short-term instruction, education and job training aimed at improving qualifications and prospects. The activation activities do not entitle the individual to unemployment benefit.

Until the end of the 1980s, persons unable to support themselves or their families received cash benefits (i.e. social assistance). They were composed of a basic allowance, housing allowance (covering rent, water, heat, gas, etc.) and family allowance. The basic allowance varied according to marital status and age. To be eligible for a cash benefit, the applicant had to prove that s/he was trying to use his or her working capabilities and was registered with the job centre as job-seeking. The system distinguished between temporary and permanent cash benefits, the former being limited to nine months. The amount of permanent cash benefit was 88% of the temporary benefit. The authorities awarded permanent cash benefits if the person was judged unable to manage by himself or herself, for example if s/he was a drug addict. In other words, cash benefits could function as a permanent source of support.

Even though legislation in the 1980s included the possibility of activating recipients of social assistance, activation of cash benefit recipients became much more common at the start of the 1990s. In 1990, a new policy was introduced for young recipients of public assistance. Under this new scheme, young people (18 to 19) on social assistance were obliged to participate in either education or job training after three months of unemployment. The age limit was subsequently increased to 24 in 1993, and in early 1997 all recipients of public assistance under 30 were obliged to accept activation after having received public assistance for 13 weeks. Since 1998, people over 30 have also had the right and been under an obligation to activation after 12 months of unemployment. The goals of the activation must be outlined in an activity plan, and the client must be offered the possibility of choosing among various means and options. The municipal policy instruments include subsidized employment, individual job training, special practical courses and educational activities, voluntary activities. If employment or education is unrealistic, the aim of activation must be to stabilize and improve the general life situation of the individual. Formerly, the amount of cash benefit allowance was estimated, but the basis for determining the amount changed during the early 1990s and was given a legal basis. In 2000 persons over 25 with children received monthly DKr 9 317, other persons over 25 DKr 6 998, persons under 25 not living at home DKr 4 489, and persons under 25 living at home DKr 2 195. From 1996 to 1999 the number of cash benefit recipients dropped from 105 344 to 93 490, while the number of activated persons increased from 33 340 to 39 689.

3   Conclusion

In Denmark, employment protection legislation has traditionally been very low (OECD, 1999: Ch. 2). In practice, some segments of blue-collar workers can be dismissed from one hour to the other, or with a notice of a few days. From the point of view of the wage-earner, high job insecurity has been compensated for by extensive welfare benefits (high benefit levels and long duration). Generous social security benefits in case of unemployment have helped trade unions and workers to accept a high frequency in the hiring and firing practices of employers. Thus, in Denmark we find a very strong numerical flexibility (OECD, 1997). In 1994-95, for instance, of the total labour force of 2.9 million, about 775 000 persons were affected by unemployment. Most, however, only suffered short-term unemployment, since more than 50% of the 775 000 persons were unemployed for less than 15-16 weeks (Finansministeriet, 1995: 291).

Due to the liberal hiring and firing practices, however, the least productive parts of the workforce have suffered disproportionately from unemployment, that is, if they ever got the opportunity to enter the labour market. Consequently, the number of disability pensioners has increased steadily since the late 1960s, i.e. from 226 207 to 279 330 between 1985-1998, despite the fact that new pathways out of the labour market were established during the 1970s and 1980s. In total, between 1960-1998 the number of early exited/retired between 15 and 66 years of age has increased from 100 000 to 451 000, and in 1998 the number of early exited/retired made up 12.4% of the total population between 15 and 66.

During the 1990s, Denmark has experienced major changes in the employment patterns. Between 1993-2000 the OECD standardized unemployment rate has decreased from 10.1% to 4.7%. Simultaneously, in Denmark the major implication of the ageing of the population has been perceived to be a decrease in the overall supply of labour. Against the background of these developments, which may lead to an overall shortage of labour, a new strategy seems to emerge in Denmark, i.e. a strategy aimed at creating an all-inclusive labour market in order to ensure that people who have not totally lost their employability remain in the labour market, rather than ending up as passive welfare state clients.

The aim of including rather than excluding disabled workers from the labour market is to be achieved by a multipicity of instruments. Thus, during the 1990s a series of new instruments have been introduced. First, State reimbursements of the costs to disability pensions have been reduced to 35%, which functions as an incentive for the municipalities to award rehabilitation, sheltered employment etc. rather than to award disability pension. Second, 'social chapters' have been included in the collective agreements in order to keep disabled people in the labour market. Third, new measures such as 'flexi-jobs' and 'soft-jobs' have been introduced in order to make it possible for disabled people to remain in or re-enter the labour market in subsidized employment. First and foremost, however, a totally new approach in the treatment of disabled persons will be introduced from 2003. A new criterion, i.e. 'working capacity', will replace the old criterion, i.e. 'loss of employability', in approaching the problems of disabled persons. It is expected that by focusing on working capacity, the attention will be directed towards the resources and development potentials of citizens rather than towards their problems and limitations, which will eventually make possible that disabled persons make use of their potential in the labour market. In addition, disabled persons will much more actively be involved in defining and solving their individual problems, because the integration into paid employment must take the skills, desires and needs of disabled persons as its point of departure. The outcome of the new strategy, of course, will depend on the implementation of the new welfare programmes. Therefore, it has been planned that municipal staff will be undergoing re-education in order to furnish them with the competence to assess the working capacity and potentials of the individual rather than focusing on the degree of loss of employability. In sum, there is clear evidence that Denmark is in a transition from supporting disabled people passively to integrate this group of people into the labour market.

Notes

1   I wish to thank Christian Lindholst for helping me to collect data for this chapter.
2   Prior to the introduction of the 1984 reform, the Danish National Institute of Social Research conducted a sociological study of disability pensioners. From 1975 to 1980 the Danish National Institute of Social Research published seven reports from the Disability Pensioner Study (Hübbe, 1976; Due, 1976; Hübbe and Westergård, 1978; Hübbe, 1978; Hübbe, 1979; Martini, 1980; Koch-Nielsen, 1980). The study is in two parts: volumes 1-5 analyse the groups of persons applying for disability pensions, and volumes 6-7 analyse the groups that were awarded disability pensions.
    Volumes 1-5 analyse the background and living conditions of disability pension applicants, i.e. their health and social condition, housing, income and labour market conditions. Furthermore, the study maps out the practice for awarding disability pensions by evaluating the effect of the physician's statement on the decision, etc. Focusing on people who had been awarded disability pension, volumes 6-7 analyse the causes and effects of being awarded a disability pension, family and occupational background, and whether health and economic conditions have improved or worsened after receipt of a disability pension. The study also analyses the social relations of disability pensioners, i.e. contact with friends, family, political parties and invalid organizations.
3   The Danish word for disability pension is *foertidspension*, which literally translated means 'early retirement pension'. In this article, however, we will use the term 'disability pension', since a special early retirement scheme for people aged between 60 and 66 was introduced in 1979.
4   Results from studies in the early 1980s showed that 18% of disability pensioners felt that other people's attitudes toward them had changed negatively after they had retired on disability pensions (Martini, 1980: 177), despite the fact that many had been forced to accept a disability pension. In 1991, 78.4% stated that the disability pension was involuntary (Socialkommissionen, 1993a: Table III.9). The most frequent reason for having to

accept a disability pension is poor health (Socialkommissionen, 1993: 79 cont.; Finansministeriet, 1995: 14). About 73% of persons leaving the labour market involuntarily (disability pension and early retirement) report poor health as the reason for retirement (Nørregaard, 1996: 27, Table 5.1). Health problems among disability pensioners are particularly significant among unskilled workers and occupational groups that have been exposed to physically and mentally demanding working conditions, such as noise, draught or heavy labour (Zeuner and Nørregaard, 1991: 84 cont.; Nørregaard et al., 1995: 15). In this perspective, poor health and disability pensions are the effects of poor working conditions. Disability pensions are thus a measure by which the company can externalize the costs of wearing down labour.

5 Disability pensioners represent an extremely heterogeneous group. Some are severely disabled, while others have retained some working capacity. Some are born disabled, while others have gradually been run down or suddenly fallen ill due to industrial injury. Other factors, such as economy, family affairs and social relations also reflect great variations among disability pensioners. The introduction of the 1984 pension reform, which made it possible to award disability pension based on social criteria, made the picture even more varied.

6 From 2003 individuals will again be able to ask the social services department to consider an application for a disability pension only. In principle this is a fundamental break with the idea underlying the Danish social legislation that activation must be given priority over passive support. The new rules were introduced as a political compromise. To support the 2003 reform the Socialist People's Party made it a condition that the individual be entitled to demand a disability assessment on the existing basis. It is not clear why the Socialist People's Party made this a condition during negotiations.

7 Some studies have analysed whether the decentralization of competence for awarding disability pensions in the early 1990s has caused regional differences in who is granted such a pension (Gregersen, 1995). The authorities realize that the municipalities apply different criteria for awarding disability pension. Therefore, the National Social Appeals Board attempts to coordinate practice by way of random sampling. Based on these samplings, the National Social Appeals Board informs the municipalities of possible problems in their administrative practices.

8 All applications for disability pension start with the family doctor, typically after the applicant has been ill for a shorter or longer period. The doctor informs the potential disability pensioner about how to apply for disability pension and will often get actively involved in the case.

9 Studies in the 1990s (Bengtsson, 1991; Juul, 1992) have focused on younger disability pensioners, i.e. persons under 50 years of age. They have analysed the causes of the increasing number of young disability pensioners and their life quality. They conclude that activation and rehabilitation are preferable to awarding disability pensions and that it is too easy for social workers to award disability pensions (Bengtsson, 1989)

10 The following account is based on rates as of 1 January 1999.

11 The main purpose was to adapt the pension age to the actual retirement age. Furthermore, a long series of incentives was introduced to encourage people to remain in the labour market until the pensionable age. A person wishing to retire at the age of 64, for instance, would benefit from remaining in the labour market for one more year. All things being equal, this might help to postpone the decision to retire until the age of 65. Under the old rules, there were no incentives to postpone retirement, and a person at the age of 64 wishing to retire may have found it too daunting to remain in the labour market for a further three years.

12   If a person without voluntary unemployment insurance becomes unemployed, he/she will apply for social assistance.
13   This is only true for those who have voluntarily chosen to contribute to an early retirement option.
14   From 2003 new rules will come into force according to which the applicant must have worked for 30 hours a week on average within the previous 24 months.

References

Arbejdsministeriet (1999) *Udviklingstendenser på det offentlige arbejdsmarked.* København.
Bengtsson, Steen (1989) *Førtidspension eller ...?* København: Socialforskningsinstituttets Rapport 89:11.
Bengtsson, Steen (1991) *Førtidspension til unge - i socialpolitisk beslysning.* København: Socialforskningsinsituttets Rapport 91:11.
Bengtsson, Steen/Henius, Charlotte Meyer (1995) *Arbejde trods handicap.* København: Socialforskningsinstituttet, Arbejdsnotat 1995:2.
DA (1999) *Socialpolitikken & arbejdsmarkedet.* København.
Damsø, Mogens/Simonsen, Flemming (1998) *Førtidspension - en praktisk vejledning.* København: Frydenlund Grafisk.
Den Sociale Ankestyrelse (2000) *Førtidspensioner - Årsstatistik 1999.* København: Den sociale Ankestyrelse.
Det Seniorpolitiske Initiativudvalg (1999) *Seniorerne & arbejdsmarkedet - nu og i fremtiden.* København.
Due, Johannes (1976) *En forundersøgelse af invalidepensionsansøgeres sociale forhold.* København: Socialforskningsinstituttet.
Ebsen, Frank/Guldager, Jens/Kristiansen, Bitten (1998) *Hvordan står det til med revalidering i krydsfeltet mellem aktivering og arbejdsfastholdelse?* København: Center for Forskning i Socialt Arbejde.
Finansministeriet (1995) *Finansredegørelse 95.* København.
Gregersen, Ole (1995) *Kommunernes pensionspraksis.* København: Socialforskningsinstituttet.
Hübbe, Per (1976) Invaliditetsbegreb og invalidepension. København: Socialforskningsinstituttet.
Hübbe, Per (1978) *Ansøgere til invalidepension.* København: Socialforskningsinstituttet.
Hübbe, Per (1979) *Forhold efter første ansøgning.* København: Socialforskningsinstituttet.
Hübbe, Per/Westergård, Poul (1978) *Materiale og metoder.* København: Socialforskningsinstituttet.
Juul, Søren (1992) *Yngre førtidspensionister.* København: Socialforskningsinstituttets Rapport 92:17.
Koch-Nielsen, Inger (1980) *Opvækstvilkår og erhvervsbaggrund.* København: Socialforskningsinstituttet.
Martini, Sten (1980) *Invalidepensionisternes levevilkår.* København: Socialforskningsinstituttet.
Nørregaard, Carl (1996) *Arbejde og tilbagetrækning i 90'erne - og fremtidens pensionister.* København: Socialforskningsinstituttet.
Nørregaard, Carl et al. (1995) *Fagbevægelsens seniorer og pensionister.* København: Socialforskningsinstittet.
OECD (1997) *Employment Outlook.* Paris: OECD.

OECD (1999) *Employment Outlook*. Paris: OECD.
Plovsing, Jan (2000) *Socialpolitik*. København: Munksgaard.
Regeringen (2000) *Regeringens debatoplæg om det rummelige arbejdsmarked*. København: Finansministeriet.
Socialkommissionen (1993a) *Analyser vedrørende ældre*. København.
Socialkommissionen (1993b) *De ældre - en belysning af ældregenerationens forsørgelse*. København.
Socialministeriet (1992) *Aktivering, Beskæftigelse, Førtidspension, Myndighedsstruktur - Bilag 1*. København.
Socialministeriet (1996) *Førtidspension. Tilkendelsesregler og forenkling - Bilag 2*. Førtidspensionsudvalg II, 2nd rapport. København.
Socialministeriet (1997) *Hvad, Hvor og Hvorfor om den sociale opgavefordeling*. København.
Socialministeriet (1998) *Rapport om undersøgelse i 30 kommuner af revalideringsindsatsen*. København.
Socialministeriet (1999) *Sociale Tendenser*. København.
Zeuner, Lilli/Nørregaard, Carl (1991) *Fortjent otium*. København: Socialforskningsinstituttet.

CHAPTER 5

Disability Pensions in Finland

Raija Gould

1 Introduction

The basis of the current disability pension programme is the statutory earnings-related pension scheme founded in 1962. Before the inception of this scheme only civil servants and seamen were included in a statutory pension scheme. Other employees and self-employed people were covered only through flat-rate and means-tested national pensions, employment accident insurance and some voluntary arrangements. Initially, the pension benefits of the statutory earnings-related scheme included only old-age and disability pensions. Since then, pension benefits have become more diversified, for instance with the introduction of various early retirement benefits.

The earnings-related scheme was established in cooperation with labour market organizations, and over the years these organizations have also taken an active part in the development of the scheme. The recent agreements between the social partners on the development of the statutory earnings-related pensions, reached in November 2001 and September 2002, will be the largest reforms in the 40-year history of the scheme. The main elements of these reforms will take effect in 2005.

During the last 30 years disability pensions have become an integral part of the Finnish welfare state. In 2001, expenditure on disability programmes amounted to 2.1% and total social security expenditure to 25.5% of the gross national product.

Everyone resident in Finland is insured against the risk of losing their work capacity. Along with unemployment insurance, disability pensions are the most important social security benefits for the working-age population, both in terms of money and the number of beneficiaries. In 2001, disability pensions provided a living for 7% of the population aged 16 to 64.

The large number of disability pensioners has caused growing public debate over the years about the financial and moral effects of the programme. Nevertheless, the disability programme was gradually extended until the late 1980s, and only at the start of the 1990s was there a decided change in disability policy, restricting pension rights and promoting rehabilitation. The new reforms of the statutory earnings-related pensions will further intensify this development.

The first part of this paper, section 2, describes the Finnish disability pension programme and other related social security schemes. The next section discusses the development of the disability scheme during the periods of its rapid expansion in the 1970s and 1980s. Finally, section 4 looks at the disability policy of the 1990s and the new millennium, focusing on amendments to pension acts, the effects of high unemployment and the rejection rate of pension applications.

2 Disability pensions and related social security schemes[*]

2.1 Public pensions in Finland: national pensions and earnings-related pensions

The Finnish statutory pension programme comprises a *national pension scheme* and an *earnings-related pension scheme*. The purpose of the residence-based national pension is to guarantee an adequate minimum pension income, and the earnings-related scheme is intended to maintain the level of consumption attained by employees and self-employed. The earnings-related scheme is further divided into public and private sector schemes.

The statutory earnings-related pension scheme covers all public and private sector employees as well as self-employed persons and farmers. Every employment contract and all periods of self-employment increase the individual's pension entitlement. The accrued pension right remains intact even if there is a change of employer or the person in question stops work-

---

[*] This section is based mainly on the following texts: Työkyvyttömyyseläkkeet, 1997; The Finnish Statutory Earnings-Related Pension Scheme, 1999; Tuomisto, 1999; Hilkamo, 2000.

ing altogether. Since full-time employment has been common for both men and women in recent decades, most disability pensioners are entitled to an earnings-related pension. The national pension used to be a universal basic pension, but from 1996 it was redefined as a benefit guaranteeing a minimum pension level. The national pension is now benefit-tested: once the statutory earnings-related pension reaches a certain limit, no national pension is paid at all. Persons who have been disabled since their youth or who for some other reason have never been gainfully employed, may receive only the national disability pension.

The national and earnings-related pension schemes are administered separately. The Social Insurance Institution, supervised by the Finnish parliament, administers national pensions. The organization of the statutory earnings-related pension scheme is decentralized. All employers and self-employed persons are obliged by law to take out pension insurance, but they can choose between several pension institutions. When introduced in the early 1960s, the decentralized administration was considered appropriate, since the existing institutions handling voluntary pension plans could smoothly take on the provision of statutory earnings-related pensions as well. The pension institutions in the private sector include private pension insurance companies and industry-wide or single-employer pension funds. The State, municipalities and some other public sector organizations have their own pension institutions. The labour market organizations are represented on the administrative bodies of the earnings-related pension institutions and the Central Pension Security Institute. This Institute is the central body of the earnings-related scheme, maintaining, for example, the central registers of employment contracts and accrued pensions of the insured. The Ministry of Social Affairs and Health and the Insurance Supervision Authority supervise the earnings-related pension institutions. Despite the decentralized administrative system, the earnings-related pension from different employment and self-employment periods constitutes an integrated whole.

National pensions are financed out of earmarked tax revenue on the basis of the pay-as-you-go system. The financing of earnings-related pension insurance is based on wage-related contributions paid by both the employers and the employees. In 2002, the contribution paid by the employee is 4.4% of the gross wage and the employer's share of the contribution is 16.7% on average. The method of financing is a combination of pay-as-you-go and direct funding. All pensions are taxable income, although if the pensioner has no income other than the full national pension, he or she is exempt from taxation.

Disability pensions are payable under both the national pension scheme and the statutory earnings-related pension scheme. Many disability pensioners receive both national and earnings-related pensions (Table 1). However, owing to the above-mentioned benefit-testing of national pension in regard to the earnings-related pension, which started in 1996, the proportion of disability pensioners receiving only an earnings-related pension is increasing.

Table 1: Recipients of disability pension under different pension schemes in 2001

National pension	Earnings-related pension			Both national and earnings-related pension	All
	All	Private sector	Public sector		
150 100	218 100	198 200	79 400	100 400	267 900

It is also possible to combine a disability pension from one scheme with a different benefit from another scheme. For example, in the 60-64 age group, recipients of a national disability pension often also receive an old-age pension from the earnings-related scheme, because even though the existing retirement age is normally 65, in the public sector and in some private companies lower earnings-related retirement ages are still applied to older employees.

2.2 Two types of disability pension

In both the national pension scheme and the statutory earnings-related pension scheme there are two types of disability pension: *the ordinary disability pension* and *the individual early retirement pension*. In accordance with the new pension reforms, the latter will be abolished in the near future.

Ordinary disability pension

Under the national pension legislation the ordinary disability pension is payable to persons between the ages of 16 and 64 who have been declared unfit for work. According to the earnings-related pension laws, an ordinary disability pension may be awarded to an employee who *has lost at least two fifths of his work capacity through illness, defect or injury and whose incapacity is estimated to last for at least one year including the time already passed*. In the private sector, account is also taken of the employee's ability to earn an income from work that is available and that he is assumed to be capable of, *considering his education, age, previous work experience, etc*. In the public sector, incapacity for one's own office or job by reason of illness, defect or injury is a sufficient eligibility criterion for an ordinary disability pension. Thus, in the public sector the eligibility criteria for an ordinary disability pension are occupational, while in the private sector the definition of disability is more general, although it also includes occupational elements.

In the earnings-related scheme a disability pension is either full or partial. A full disability pension is paid if at least three fifths of work capacity is lost, and a partial disability pension when between two fifths and three fifths is lost. Earnings capacity along with health-related factors determine whether the loss of work capacity entitles the worker to a full or partial disability pension. The partial disability pension amounts to half of the full disability pension. In the national pension scheme there is no partial disability pension. However, some beneficiaries of a partial earnings-related disability pension receive a full disability pension from the national scheme.

The ordinary disability pension can be paid either without a time limit or temporarily in the form of a *cash rehabilitation benefit*. A cash rehabilitation benefit is awarded if it is likely that the person may completely or partly recover the ability to work through medical treatment or rehabilitation measures. To receive the benefit, a treatment or rehabilitation plan must have been drawn up for the applicant. The cash rehabilitation benefit can be either full or partial, and the amount corresponds to the permanent disability pension.

The pension recipient is obliged to inform the pension institution of changes that affect work capacity. The pension institution may also require such information from the beneficiary, and it may use other sources of information, such as the central register of employment contracts, as an instrument of supervision. An ordinary disability pension or a cash rehabilitation benefit may be discontinued, or a full pension may be reduced to a partial pension, or vice versa, if the work capacity of the beneficiary changes. However, for those who have been awarded a disability pension without a time limit there is no automatic retesting of the disability status. Thus, for the great majority of recipients the disability status is permanent. This also holds true for many pensioners who have been granted a temporary cash rehabilitation benefit. Quite frequently, the time limit of a cash rehabilitation benefit is extended by a new decision, and after some extensions, it is often granted as a normal disability pension without a time limit. When reaching the pensionable age, which at present is normally 65, a disability pension automatically becomes an old-age pension. According to the pension reform, in 2005 the retirement age will become flexible, allowing a person to retire on an old age pension – with reduction – at age 62 and without reduction between ages 63 and 68. In line with the reforms, from 2005 the disability pension will change to the old age pension at age 63.

Individual early retirement pension

The individual early retirement pension is a special form of disability pension designed for elderly employees or self-employed persons who have experienced a permanent reduction in work capacity but who are not sick enough to qualify for the ordinary disability pension. The individual early retirement pension can be awarded to persons between 60 and 64 years of age with a long working career, provided that *their work capacity has been permanently reduced to such an extent that they cannot be expected to continue in the same place of work in their present job or occupation*. When assessing the work capacity of the employee, account is taken of health status, factors associated with ageing that affect work performance, physical or mental strain of the job, and working conditions. When considering the working conditions, in some public sector occupations special attention is paid to the safety factors.

In both the public and private sectors the definition of disability for the individual early retirement pension is strictly occupational. Compared with the ordinary disability pension, the definition of disability for the individual early retirement pension places less emphasis on purely medical criteria and more emphasis on the overall capacity to continue working and to the length of the working career.

The individual early retirement pension is normally paid as a full pension. However, if the earnings of a beneficiary of such a pension exceed a certain allowable limit (EUR 219 in 2002), the pension may be reduced to a partial pension or its payment suspended. So far only very few of these cases have occurred.

Table 2: Earnings-related disability pensions in the private sector in 2001

	Ordinary disability pension		Individual early retirement pension	All disability pensions
	No time limit	Cash rehabilitation benefit		
Full pension	154 800	10 800	22 500	188 100
Partial pension	10 200	700	-	900
All	165 000	11 500	22 500	199 000

In 2001, ordinary disability pensions made up 89% and individual early retirement pensions 11% of all earnings-related disability pensions. In the 55-64 age group the proportion of individual early retirement pensions was 17%. Most of the pensions had been granted without a time limit: only 7% of ordinary disability pensions were temporary cash rehabilitation benefits. However, in recent years cash rehabilitation benefits have constituted a growing proportion of the new ordinary disability pensions: in 1997 about 35% of new disability pensions were granted as cash rehabilitation benefits, while in 2001 this figure was 44%. As Table 2 shows, the number of partial pensions is also quite small. Under the earnings-related scheme in the private sector, 6% of ordinary disability pensions are partial.

The extensive reforms agreed between the social partners include the termination of the individual early retirement pension for those born in or after 1944. Thus, after 2006 there will be no more new awards of this pension. The individual early retirement pension will be merged into the standard disability pension by relaxing the eligibility criteria for those aged 60 and over.

2.3 *Work injuries, traffic accidents and military injuries*

Statutory disability pensions are also payable on the basis of work injuries, occupational diseases, traffic accidents and military injuries. For these injuries there are separate insurance systems.

On-the-job injuries and occupational diseases are covered by the legislation on workers' compensation insurance. Employers are required to insure their employees with a non-life insurer. The workers' compensation insurance premium rate is calculated on the basis of the employer's payroll and varies according to the employee's occupation. The premium rates of large employers are directly affected by claims experience. The average premium rate is 1.3% of total pay.

Under statutory workers' compensation insurance, a disability pension compensates for the loss of earnings if a work injury or an occupational disease still causes disability after a one-year period of daily allowance. The definition of disability is similar to the earnings-related scheme in the private sector. However, a person is entitled to a partial disability pension on the basis of work injury if at least 10% of work capacity has been lost. A full disability pension on the basis of work injury is 85% of yearly earnings, and the partial pension is proportional to the reduction in the work capacity. In general, the disability pensions based on military injuries also follow these rules.

Under the Motor Liability Insurance Act all owners of motor vehicles are required to take out a motor liability policy. The insurance companies determine the premiums independently, although they are obliged to inform the Insurance Supervision Authority about the policy terms prior to their introduction. The premiums are dependent on, for example, the type, make, model and use of the vehicle, but are also linked to a no-claims discount rate. This no-claims bonus may be as much as 70%.

A disability pension is paid under the compulsory motor liability insurance if a traffic accident causes a permanent reduction in earnings. In principle, the loss of earnings is fully compensated, but if the injury has been caused wilfully or out of gross negligence on the part of the injured person, the compensation may be reduced or even refused altogether.

In 2001 there were about 10 000 recipients of disability pensions based on work injuries, traffic accidents and military injuries.

2.4 Calculation of disability pensions

Currently, the earnings-related pension accrual is calculated separately for each contract of employment and period of self-employment, and the accrued pension rights are combined into one pension. Before 1996, pensionable earnings were calculated on the basis of earnings during the four final years of each contract of employment. Now the last ten years of each contract of employment are taken into account. The pension normally accrues at the rate of 1.5% of pensionable earnings per year of gainful employment. However, for those over 60 years of age, the earnings-related pension accrues at the rate of 2.5% per year of employment.

In 2005, this calculation will be changed. In line with the new reforms, the earnings-related pensions will be calculated on the basis of the salary and the pension accrual rate for each year. The method of calculating the pension separately for each contract of employment will be abandoned. Salaries from previous years will be adjusted by wage coefficient. The pension will accrue at the current rate of 1.5% per annum up to the age of 53. From age 53 to 62 the rate will increase to 1.9%, with a further increase to 4.5% from age 63 on.

The disability pension also accrues for the period between the onset of disability and the retirement age of 65 if the disability occurs within a year of the termination of employment. This period is extended if there have been periods of daily allowance due to rehabilitation, sickness, parenthood or unemployment. During the time between the onset of disability and the general retirement age, pension accrues at the rate of 1.5% per year until the age of 50, 1.2% between the ages of 50 and 60 and 0.8% per year between 60 and 65 years of age. These rules are also affected by the new reforms. From 2005 on the time between the onset of disability and age 63 will always be included in the accrual period. The pension for the post-contingency period will be calculated on the basis of earnings during the five years before the onset of disability. The accrual rate for the post-contingency period will equal the current 1.5% per year until the age of 50, after which it will be 1.3%.

There is no pension ceiling for earnings-related pension or for pensionable earnings. However, presently the maximum amount of the statutory earnings-related pension is limited to 60% of pensionable earnings by integrating the pensions accrued under different systems, also taking into account the benefits paid on the basis of work injury, traffic accident and military injury. These benefits take priority over the statutory earnings-related pension, so that an earnings-related disability pension becomes payable only to the extent that it exceeds these other benefits. In the future, because of the accelerated accrual rate of those over 63, it will be possible for the statutory earnings-related pension to amount to more than 60% of the salary.

The pension benefits of state and municipal employees used to be better than the benefits in the private sector. The maximum pension in the public sector was 66% of wages, and the pension accrued 2.2% per year. During the 1990s the differences between the pension benefits of the public and private sectors were gradually reduced. During the transition period, however, older employees in the public sector still managed to retain some of their former privileges.

All statutory pensions are index-linked. National pensions are linked to the consumer price index, while the index adjustments of earnings-related disability pensions – as well as other earnings-related pension benefits while the beneficiary is under the age of 66 – are in line with the average changes in wage and price levels. For beneficiaries over the age of 65, the index gives more weight to the price level than the wage level. Starting from 2005 the latter index, where the weighting of the consumer price index is 80% and the wage index 20%, will also be applied to beneficiaries under the age of 65. In addition, an age-specific coefficient will be introduced to increase the pensions of those who become disabled at a young age.

2.5 Pension application and assessment of disability status

An ordinary disability pension is preceded by payment of sickness allowance for 300 weekdays, during which the application for a pension is filed. However, applicants for an individual early retirement pension usually still work (or are unemployed) while applying for the pension. They may receive advance notice of the decision on their eligibility for the individual early retirement pension. This advance decision is valid for at least nine months, during which time the applicant must stop working in order to receive the pension. A similar advance decision also applies to the case of a partial disability pension application.

Disability status is assessed by a pension institution on application. The disability pension application always includes a medical report that explains in detail the health status of the applicant. A general practitioner or a specialist responsible for treatment of the applicant may write the report. One application may include reports by several doctors. In addition to the medical report, a disability pension application also includes information on the work and working conditions of the applicant. Often a written statement by the employer on the applicant's work performance is attached. At the pension institution, the medical examiner assesses the applicant's work capacity on the basis of the documents filed with the application. This assessment provides the basis for the decision to grant a pension or reject the application.

Even though medical factors are of primary importance in the assessment of disability, other factors may also influence the assessment. According to the definition of disability, the work capacity must be determined in relation to the actual possibility of the applicant finding work. However, it is not necessary that a job suitable for the applicant be vacant in the locality at the time; a sufficient condition is that suitable jobs are normally available in the labour market. In the same way, a partial disability pension may be granted if the applicant, despite his or her illness, has real opportunities to become partially employed, even if he or she does not have a part-time job at the time. Thus, to some extent labour market considerations are included in the assessment of disability although, as it is stated in the manual of the Central Pension Security Institute, "in general the assessment of work capacity should be independent of economic fluctuations" (Työkyvyttömyyseläke, 1997).

In addition to the availability of suitable jobs, the person's education, training, working career, age and regional ties are considered in the assessment of disability. These factors usually have more influence on the assessment of work capacity of older applicants.

The different pension schemes are coordinated in such a way that it is necessary for disability pension applicants to send in only one application, even if they are applying for a national disability pension and an earnings-related disability pension. However, the national pension organization and the earnings-related pension institutions assess the disability status separately. Conflicting decisions by the national and earnings-related schemes are minimized by negotiations on individual cases between the schemes. If the applicant has had several employment contracts or periods of self-employment in the private sector, the pension institution with which the applicant was last insured processes the application. This principle also applies to cases in which applicants have had both public and private employment contracts. To ensure that all earnings-related pension institutions interpret the disability definitions in a consistent manner, a special advisory committee for disability pensions discusses and issues recommendations on ambiguous cases.

If the pension application is rejected, the applicant may appeal against the decision. National pensions and earnings-related pensions in the public and private sectors each have their own appeal arrangements. The Insurance Court is the highest court of appeal for all pension schemes.

2.6 *Rehabilitation benefits*

During the 1990s, rehabilitation became a matter of great importance in preventing early exit from the labour market. Rehabilitation benefits and services are offered through insurance companies, pension institutions, the Social Insurance Institution, employment administration, educational systems, occupational health services, and the health care and social services of municipalities. Insurance companies pay the rehabilitation benefits, which are based on work injuries, occupational diseases or traffic accidents.

Pension institutions arrange rehabilitation to prevent disability or to improve reduced work capacity. To receive a disability pension either through the earnings-related pension scheme or the national pension scheme, the applicant's prospects for rehabilitation must have been investigated. If the applicant is eligible for a disability pension but it is likely that rehabilitation would enable him or her to return to work, the disability pension is granted as a time-limited *cash rehabilitation benefit* (see section 2.2 above). A *rehabilitation increment* of 33% may be granted to a recipient of an earnings-related disability pension for the active rehabilitation period if the rehabilitation is financed by an earnings-related pension institution.

Pension institutions also support rehabilitation of persons who are still participating in the labour market, but whose work capacity is deteriorating. An *earnings-related rehabilitation allowance*, which corresponds to a disability pension increased by 33%, may be granted to a person who does not receive a disability pension and whose rehabilitation is financed by an earnings-related pension institution. A partial rehabilitation allowance will be introduced in 2004.

In the national scheme, i.e. if the rehabilitation is arranged by the Social Insurance Institution, the benefit paid for the period of rehabilitation is called rehabilitation allowance, whether or not the person is receiving a disability pension or still in the labour force. For a person receiving a national disability pension, the rehabilitation allowance amounts to the size of the pension increased by 10%, and for a non-pensioner it corresponds to the daily allowance of sickness insurance.

Rehabilitation in the earnings-related pension scheme is usually vocational but, if needed, supporting medical rehabilitation can be arranged. The Social Insurance Institution provides both vocational and medical rehabilitation. The volume of rehabilitation services of the Social Insurance Institution is considerably larger than that of the earnings-related pension institutions. In 2000 about 54 000 persons received rehabilitation allowance from the Social Insurance Institution and 3 300 from the earnings-related pension institutions.

Currently the earnings-related pension institutions are not required to provide rehabilitation, although since early July 1999 they have been obliged to investigate the rehabilitation prospects of those employees and self-employed persons aged 58 and 59 who are in danger of losing their work capacity due to illness. Employees themselves or, for example, the occupational health service may take the initiative for this investigation. The aim is for the investigation of rehabilitation prospects to occur at an early stage, before actual sick leave is needed. The pension reform will extend the legal obligations of the earnings-related scheme to provide rehabilitation. From the beginning of 2004 there will be a statutory right to vocational rehabilitation under the scheme when the person's work capacity is at risk due to illness.

2.7 Unemployment benefits in comparison with disability pensions

An unemployed jobseeker may receive either unemployment allowance or labour market support. The *unemployment allowance* is payable to an unemployed person who has been employed for at least 43 weeks during the previous two years. For members of unemployment funds the unemployment allowance is earnings-related and for others it is a flat rate. In 2002, the basic flat-rate allowance was EUR 21.91 per day. The earnings-related allowance is the basic amount plus 45% of the daily earnings that exceed this basic amount. If the monthly earnings are more than EUR 1,971.90, the percentage is only 20. The period of earnings-related unemployment allowance entitles the recipient to an incremental earnings-related pension.

The unemployment allowance is payable for up to five days per week for a maximum period of 500 days. However, an unemployed person who is at least 57 years of age upon exhausting his or her right to the unemployment allowance receives an automatic extension of the allowance to the age of 60. At that age, an unemployed person may be eligible to unemployment pension (see section 2.8 below).

If a person is only partially unemployed, he or she may be eligible for a partial unemployment allowance. Thus, anyone who receives a partial disability pension but does not have a job may simultaneously receive a partial unemployment allowance.

If an unemployed jobseeker does not fulfil the employment criteria for the unemployment allowance or has received the maximum amount of the allowance, he or she may receive *labour market support* as long as the unemployment lasts. Labour market support is comparable with the size of the flat-rate unemployment allowance, but unlike the allowance it is usually means-tested.

The earnings-related unemployment allowance is based on the earnings during the previous 43 weeks of employment, and the replacement rate is lower for higher earnings. On the other hand, the earnings-related disability pension is dependent on the length of the working career, the earnings of the previous 10 years of each employment contract and the age at the onset of disability. Thus, whether the disability pension or the unemployment allowance is higher is greatly dependent on the individual life situation. For example, if a person is already approaching the general retirement age, has a long working career and above-average earnings, his or her disability pension is likely to be higher than the earnings-related unemployment allowance. On the other hand, a short working career (pre- and post-contingency periods together) with average earnings would indicate a higher unemployment allowance than disability pension.

2.8 Disability pensions compared with other early retirement pensions

In addition to disability pensions there are several other early-retirement options available to elderly employees and self-employed persons, the most common presently being the *unemployment pension*. Under current legislation, this pension may be awarded to a long-term unemployed person between the ages of 60 and 64 who has received unemployment allowance for the maximum period of 500 days (plus a possible extension between the ages of 57 and 60) and who has been employed at least five of the previous 15 years. According to the agreement of November 2001 the unemployment pension will be terminated for those born in or after 1950, but it will be replaced by an additional period of unemployment allowance. The extension of the allowance will be possible between the ages of 59 and 65.

Until early 2000 a further condition of the unemployment pension was that the time until the general retirement age could be counted as pensionable time, and the pension was calculated the same way as a disability pension including a post-contingency period (see section 2.4). Since early 2000 calculation of the unemployment pension has been based only on periods of gainful employment, and the time between pension contingency and the age of 65 is not included. Thus, an unemployment pension is smaller than the disability pension that the beneficiary would have received had he or she become disabled instead of being made redundant.

Another early retirement option, which is also payable under both the national and earnings-related schemes, is the *early old-age pension*. Anyone 60 years of age or older may draw his or her old-age pension before the general retirement age. However, if the old-age pension is taken early, it is reduced permanently. Owing to this reduction, the early old-age pension is always smaller than a disability pension based on the same working career. From 2005, a reduced old-age pension will be available only at the age of 62.

Under the statutory earnings-related pension scheme, the early retirement options also enable the combination of work and pension. An employee or self-employed person with a long working career who cuts down on working considerably and who has reached the age of 56 may be entitled to *part-time pension*. For those born in or after 1947 the age limit has been raised to 58. The part-time pension represents 50% of the difference between full-time and part-time earnings.

3 Development of the disability pension system from the 1960s to the 1980s

3.1 Expansion of the disability programme

During the 1960s and 1970s there was a period of rapid expansion in the number of disability pensions (Figure 1). This expansion was largely due to maturing of the statutory earnings-related pension scheme, which came into force in the private sector in 1962. In 1970 the scope of the scheme was enlarged to cover not only wage-earners but also farmers and other self-employed persons. This extension of the pension scheme was a reflection of the dramatic changes occurring in the Finnish industrial structure. Agriculture was rapidly diminishing, and services and the information sector in particular were growing. The new pension scheme for farmers, and especially the disability programme of the scheme, made it possible for industrialization to advance at a higher speed than would otherwise have been the case.

In addition to the general extension of coverage of the earnings-related pension scheme, the scope of the disability programme was also extended. In 1973 partial disability pensions were included in the earnings-related pension benefits. However, the proportion of partial disability pensions has never been large. During the 1970s slightly over 10% of all disability pensions in the private sector were partial, and since then the proportion has been even smaller. During the 1970s especially, but also later on, partial pensions have been received most commonly among farmers.

In connection with the introduction of partial pensions, the definition for disability was amended. The criteria of loss of work capacity by at least two fifths for partial and three fifths for full disability pension were included. The idea that the disability status should be assessed in relation to available work was also added to the definition. Thus, the assessment of disability was to some extent made vulnerable to labour market considerations.

Figure 1: New disability pensions under the private sector earnings-related pension scheme, 1970-2001

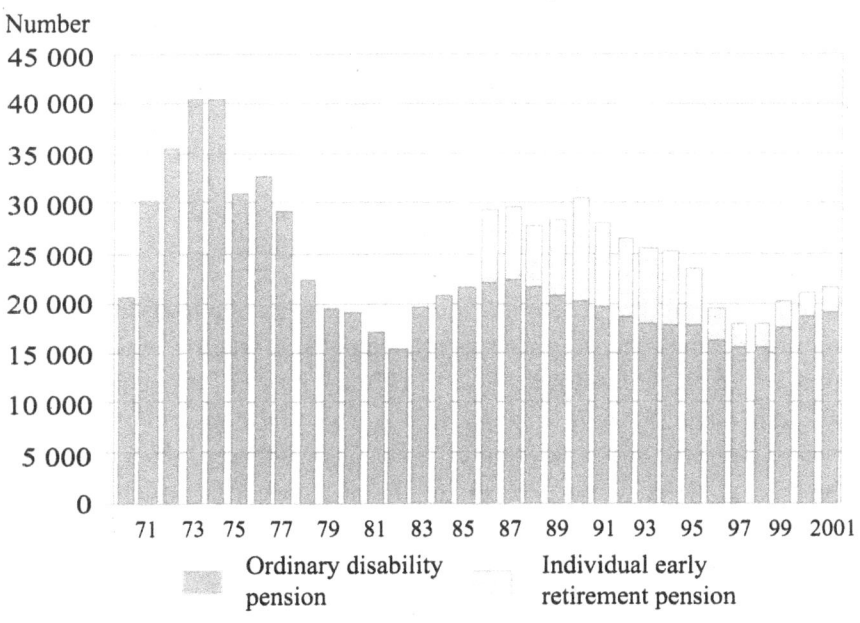

3.2 Growing unemployment – declining number of disability pensions

During the late 1970s and early 1980s, the number of new disability pensions declined (Figure 1). This development was due to labour market changes, a fall in the compensation level of the sickness allowance and probably also stricter assessment of the disability status (Notkola, 1980; Gould, 1985; Hytti, 1995). In the mid-1970s the economic situation in Finland deteriorated: unemployment reached its peak in 1978 and was further followed by structural unemployment. Contrary to the belief that the disability pension programme would expand especially in times of poor employment prospects, in Finland high unemployment contributed to a fall in the disability pension incidence.

One explanation that has been offered for this development has been the blurring of the distinction between disability and unemployment protection. During the recession, persons working in sectors of industry where fixed-term contracts were the norm and whose labour market position was unstable were likely to become unemployed and remain so even with deteriorating health. On the other hand, workers with permanent employment contracts were likely to end up applying for disability pension rather than becoming long-term unemployed in the event that they lost their job. Moreover, around 1980 the earnings-related unemployment allowance was generally higher than the sickness allowance, which normally precedes the disability pension for a period of one year. This discouraged unemployed persons with health problems from shifting over to the disability programme (Hytti, 1995).

3.3 Introduction of the individual early retirement pension

A new expansion of the disability programme occurred during the 1980s (Figure 1). This was due, for example, to the reform of sickness insurance, which raised the compensation level of the sickness allowance. More relaxed eligibility criteria in the form of the individual early retirement pension, as well as general attitudes and policies favouring early exit, also promoted the growth of the disability programme. Economic growth during the 1980s created an atmosphere that supported the expansion of the welfare state. Promoting early retirement was the prevailing policy, and several new early retirement measures were introduced.

The individual early retirement pension – a disability pension with less stringent medical criteria designed for elderly employees (see section 2.2 above) – came into force in 1986 under the national pension and the private sector earnings-related schemes, and in 1989 in the public sector. This new type of disability pension was aimed at facilitating the transition to early retirement after the end of the working career of elderly employees in a period of rapid industrial change and new production demands (Eläkeikäkomitean esitys, 1983). The individual early retirement pension immediately became very popular. With the introduction of this new pension benefit, the total number of new disability pensions granted each year grew by 35% from 1985 to 1986. Ageing employees welcomed the individual early retirement pension as a decent way to withdraw from the changes and growing demands of the modern economy. And employers found it a practical and morally justified tool for company policies focusing on personnel reduction.

One reason for the popularity of the individual early retirement pension was the relatively low age limit originally set. During the 1980s when this benefit was introduced, the age limit was 55 years. Later, it was gradually raised to 60 years.

The individual early retirement pension was by far the most popular, though not the only one of the new early retirement benefits introduced in the 1980s. In the private sector, the early old-age pension was introduced in 1986 simultaneously with the individual early retirement pension, and the part-time pension came into force one year later. In the public sector all of these new benefits took effect in 1989.

4 Disability pensions in the 1990s and the new millennium

4.1 Pension restrictions and programmes for maintaining work capacity

During the early 1990s the total number of disability pensioners was over 300 000. This was approximately 9% of the total Finnish population aged 16-64. In the older age groups the percentage was considerably higher: 36% of those aged 55-64 were receiving disability pension.

The rapid increase in the number of new disability pensioners caused great concern over the economic consequences of the expansion of the disability programme. In December 1989, only a few years after implementation of the individual early retirement pension, the Finnish Government appointed a committee to consider how the early retirement schemes could be amended to promote employment instead of early exit from the labour market. The proposals of this committee led to several pension amendments, many of which had a direct influence on disability pensions.

The qualifying ages for the individual early retirement pension and the part-time pension were changed. The age limit for the individual early retirement pension was raised from 55 to 58 in 1994, and further to 60 in 2000. These changes markedly reduced the number of new recipients of the individual early retirement pension. The age limit for the part-time pension was lowered with the idea of favouring part-time pensions at the expense of disability pensions and other full-time early retirement benefits. The age limit for the part-time pension was lowered from 60 to 58 in 1994, and again from 58 to 56 in 1998. After lowering the age limit, the popularity of the part-time pension increased rapidly. In 1999 the number of new part-time pensions already exceeded the number of new earnings-related disability pensions granted to persons aged 56-64.

To reduce the attraction of full-time early retirement, the qualifying conditions for the unemployment pension were also tightened. In 1994 the employment criterion was introduced (to qualify, the unemployed person must have been employed at least five of the previous 15 years), and the required number of unemployment allowance days preceding the pension was raised from 200 to the present 500 days. These changes caused a temporary drop in the number of new unemployment pensions in 1994.

Some additional general amendments were also made to the pension schemes. In 1994 the higher accrual rate of 2.5% per working year, instead of 1.5% was introduced for those who continue to work beyond the age of 60. In 1996 lower accrual rates were introduced for the part of the pension which is calculated on the post-contingency period, for example from the onset of disability to the general retirement age.

The pension reform of the new millennium will continue the policy orientation to restrict pension benefits and to promote employment. The range of early retirement programmes will be reduced as the unemployment and individual early retirement pensions will be abolished. The substantial bonus accrual rate for those over 63 is intended to serve as an economic incentive to continue employment.

In addition to changes in the qualifying conditions and calculation rules, an effort was also made to alter the practices that result in applying for a disability pension. At the start of the 1990s the Federation of Employment Pension Institutions conducted an information campaign called Respect for Work Ability. The purpose of this campaign was to encourage favourable attitudes towards the promotion and maintenance of work capacity.

In spring 1995 the central labour market organizations agreed to balance the financing and benefits of the earnings-related pension scheme. According to this agreement, the time-limited disability pension was changed in 1996 to the cash rehabilitation benefit, which always includes a treatment or rehabilitation plan. It was also agreed that, in general, the assessment of work incapacity would in future favour use of rehabilitation measures. For this purpose, the social partners and the earnings-related pension institutions planned and carried out an extensive training programme, i.e. 'Work Ability for Tomorrow'. Within this programme thousands of doctors throughout the country were trained in assessing work capacity, with the emphasis on adopting a new perspective: instead of concentrating on proving their patient's incapability of working, they were encouraged to support the remaining work capacity of the patients (Nikkarinen et al., 1998).

In the 1990s early rehabilitation and measures to maintain work capacity were further developed. In 1995 a working group on disability pensions concluded that participating in measures designed to maintain work capacity was appropriate for the character of the earnings-related pension scheme. "The earnings-related pension institutions have natural contacts with workplaces based on customer relations, an extensive knowledge of working life, and long and versatile practical experience of assessing work capacity" (Tola 1995). According to these ideas many of the pension institutions developed their own programmes for promoting the work capacity of the employees in their customer companies. These institution-specific programmes include customized coaching and advice for management, personnel services and occupational health care in activities for maintaining work capacity.

Among the most comprehensive institution-specific programmes are the early rehabilitation activities of the State Treasury, which is a public sector pension institution for those employed by the State. The State Treasury's activities for promoting work capacity emphasize the importance of the workplace and the work community. Some of the activities are individual-oriented, but most of the early rehabilitation occurs in groups, such as musculoskeletal, relaxation and stress, lifestyle, working community, and supervisory staff groups. Group rehabilitation means simultaneous development of the individual employee and the working community (Rissa, 1998; Väänänen-Tomppo et al., 1999).

In general, the volume of rehabilitation services increased considerably during the 1990s. Between 1990 and 2001 the number of rehabilitation beneficiaries of the Social Insurance Institution doubled, and in 2001 the number of earnings-related rehabilitation beneficiaries had increased tenfold compared with 1992. The statutory right to vocational rehabilitation under the earnings-related pension scheme, which will take effect in 2004, will further increase the volume of the earnings-related rehabilitation.

The effectiveness of rehabilitation services may be evaluated on the basis of the re-employment rate of the participants. In this respect, the rehabilitation pursued by the earnings-related pension institutions has been fairly successful: in 2001 about 1 800 persons finished their vocational rehabilitation and nearly half returned to work (Saarnio, 2002). The beneficiaries of the earnings-related rehabilitation are fairly well motivated and in their peak working years, mostly 35-44 years of age. In a less employment-oriented population the success of rehabilitation services has been far more modest. Results of an evaluation study of the service needs of the older long-term unemployed, of which many also had health problems, suggest that participation in rehabilitation services neither increased nor decreased re-employment among the participants (Järvikoski et al., 2000).

During the 1990s, promotion of work capacity and employment opportunities became an important target of Finnish public policies. In addition to the activities of the pension institutions and changes in pension policy, a number of comprehensive national or company-level programmes for promoting work capacity were launched (see e.g. Ilmarinen, 1999). Some of the most comprehensive nationwide programmes in this field have been the National Programme on Ageing Workers and the Well-Being at Work Programme. A new programme called 'Pull' aims, in particular, to increase the attractiveness of work. According to the Working Life Barometer, activities restoring, maintaining or promoting work capacity have gained a significant foothold in Finnish workplaces during recent years. In 2001 about 60% of workplaces had health-related programmes, 75% had special work safety programmes, and also 75% had programmes aimed at improving the skills and knowledge of the employees (Ylöstalo, 2002). These programmes appear to have made a difference: the percentage of employees with poor or decreased work capacity is significantly lower in workplaces where activities maintaining work capacity have been carried out (Ylöstalo, 2000).

4.2 Effect of high unemployment on disability pensions

During the 1990s Finland witnessed extraordinarily high unemployment. The peak of mass unemployment was reached in 1994, at which time the unemployment rate was 17%. For those aged 55 to 59 the unemployment rate was even higher, over 20%, and remained at that level for several years, even after the employment situation in general had begun to improve.

As in the previous recession of the 1970s, the number of new disability pensions in the 1990s began to decline along with growing unemployment. In the private sector earnings-related pension scheme, the incidence of new disability pensions (including individual early retirement pensions) in the age group 55-64 was 9% in 1990 and less than 4% in 1997, turning to a slight increase again at the very end of the decade (Figure 2). This development indicates improvement in the work capacity of employees and successful use of the new rehabilitation-oriented methods, but even more, it demonstrates the effect of permanent unemployment benefits on removing pressure from the disability programme. At times of high unemployment, unemployment benefits are widely used. They also provide financial protection for many of those whose unemployability is related to impaired work capacity, and thus reduce the need for disability pensions. This applies especially to the ageing unemployed who have access to unemployment pensions. As Figure 2 shows, the fall in the incidence of disability pensions through the early-mid 1990s was mirrored by a rise in that of unemployment pensions.

Figure 2: Incidence of new recipients of earnings-related pensions in the private sector, 55-64 years of age

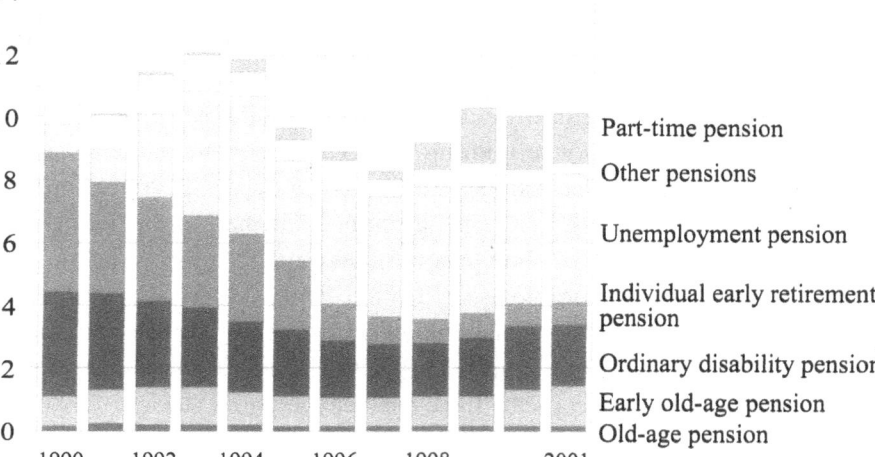

Towards the end of the decade the growth in the part-time pension programme may have also influenced the incidence of disability pensions, for example by preventing or slowing down the deterioration in work capacity and thus postponing the need for a full-time pension benefit. However, there are also signs that part-time pensioners have been in good health, and without this partial pension option they would probably have continued in full-time employment (Takala, 1999).

In the younger age groups the incidence of disability pensions mainly reflects the health and working conditions of the employed population. But in the ageing population, early retirement trends in the 1990s suggest that the extent of the disability pension programme was largely influenced by the consequences of economic and industrial change and the availability of alternative benefit programmes. Disability pensions, other early retirement benefits and unemployment allowance make up a combination of pathways for early exit from the labour market. How popular the different exit pathways are is dependent on the eligibility criteria, but also on other factors such as the replacement level, benefit costs and the attitude taken towards the various early retirement and unemployment benefits. The field of industry and the economic, cultural and structural factors of the company also direct the choice of an exit pathway (Hytti, 1995, 1998; Gould, 1997).

Some empirical findings support the idea that elderly employees prefer the disability pension to unemployment benefits. For instance, many of the ageing persons who have ended up as long-term unemployed first tried to enrol in the disability programme, but their pension application was rejected (Gould, 1995). On the other hand, there are also findings indicating that many of the long-term unemployed with declining health have remained in the ranks of the unemployed and have not applied for a disability pension (Lind, 2000).

The preference for a particular early exit pathway may be related to its general image, but also to its financial incentives. As mentioned in section 2.8, the disability pension and unemployment pension were the same amount until 2000. Currently, since a new disability pension may include a post-contingency period but a new unemployment pension does not, the compensation level of the former benefit is higher. The sickness allowance, which also precedes the disability pension, is in most cases slightly higher than the earnings-related unemployment allowance, thus creating an incentive to apply for a disability pension instead of remaining unemployed. However, depending on the age, working career and income level of the beneficiary, the unemployment allowance may be either higher or lower than a disability pension. This comparison may affect the choice between unemployment benefit and individual early retirement pension in particular. On the whole, it appears that in Finland financial incentives do not have an important effect on the probability of becoming a disability pensioner, since entering into the disability pension programme is strongly affected by the applicant's health status (Hakola, 2000).

According to some empirical findings, it appears that ageing unemployed persons who are just below the age that would entitle them to automatic extension of the unemployment allowance and afterwards to an unemployment pension are more likely than others to apply for a disability pension (Gould and Nyman, 1998). Since the prospects of re-employment are very small in that age group (Forss, 1999), it is likely that unemployed persons with some reduction of work capacity try to secure their earnings-related income until retirement age with a disability pension. On the other hand, for those recipients of the unemployment allowance who are old enough to be on the way to an unemployment pension, the probability of becoming a disability pensioner is significantly smaller than for others in the same age group (Gould and Nyman, 1998; Hakola, 2000). For these unemployed persons, extension of the unemployment allowance followed by the unemployment pension guarantees income security until retirement age, thus reducing the need to apply for a disability pension. In conclusion, it appears that there exists a certain amount of substitutability between unemployment benefits and disability pensions.

In addition to the preferences of the potential beneficiaries themselves, the preferences of employers in the form of benefit costs also influence the choice between unemployment and disability programmes. In Finland the principle by which large employers are responsible for the early retirement expenses of their own employees is applied to the financing of private sector earnings-related pensions. Until 2000, the employers' share of the costs of unemployment pensions was only half that for disability pensions, which made the unemployment pension much more favourable to large employers. Presumably this arrangement has had an important influence on the widespread use of the unemployment pension programme (Hakola, 2000; Romppanen, 2000). Since early 2000, cost-sharing for the disability and unemployment pensions has been harmonized so that a large employer's full liability for both pension types is 80%. However, since employers' responsibility for the unemployment pension does not cover the period of unemployment allowance, this option is still less expensive for the employer than the disability pension.

4.3 Illnesses causing reduction in work capacity

The findings of successive surveys conducted by the National Public Health Institute indicate that the self-perceived health of middle-aged Finns has gradually improved since the late 1970s. However, the proportion of people with reported chronic illnesses increased slightly from the 1960s to the 1990s. This increase not only reflects changes in morbidity levels but also the increased use of services and changing diagnostic and treatment practices. Disease categories also differ with respect to the development in reported long-term illnesses. One of the categories in which incidences in the adult population have increased is that of musculoskeletal diseases, whereas the incidence of circulatory diseases has decreased (Aromaa et al., 1999).

The decrease in the incidence of circulatory diseases is also reflected in the numbers of new disability pensions. In 1985 one in five of the new earnings-related pensions was based on circulatory diseases, while during the late 1990s the proportion was only one in ten. Also the age-standardised incidence of disability pensions based on circulatory diseases decreased (Figure 3). Nevertheless, circulatory diseases make up the third-largest disease category of disability pensions. The second-largest disease category of earnings-related pensions is musculoskeletal diseases, which constitute a third of all new earnings-related pensions. Since musculoskeletal diseases are most common in the older age groups, their proportion rose markedly during the late 1980s when large numbers of new pensioners were elderly recipients of the individual early retirement pension.

The largest disease category of new disability pensions is mental disorders. In fact, this is the only one of the three main disease categories in which the incidence of new earnings-related disability pensions was higher in 2001 than in 1990 (Figure 3). Compared to the 1980s the incidence has grown considerably (Aromaa et al. 1999). Among the mental disorders, depression is becoming more and more prevalent. In the private sector earnings-related pension scheme the yearly number of new disability pensions based on depression has increased from 1 000 to nearly 3 000 in the last ten years.

The decrease in the incidence of disability pensions based on circulatory diseases is mainly attributable to the general development of this disease group. The category of tumours is another example of a disease group where the incidence of disability pensions has developed consistently with the general trend of the disease. The incidence of cancer in the Finnish population has not changed much in recent decades (Aromaa et al., 1999), and neither has the proportion of new disability pensions based on this disease group. Thus, it appears that adaptation of the disability programme to new situations – changes in pension programmes and in the economy – has been most prominent in the more flexible disease categories, such as mental illnesses and musculoskeletal diseases.

Figure 3: Incidence of ordinary disability pensions by disease category under the private earnings-related scheme, 1990-2001 (age-standardised)

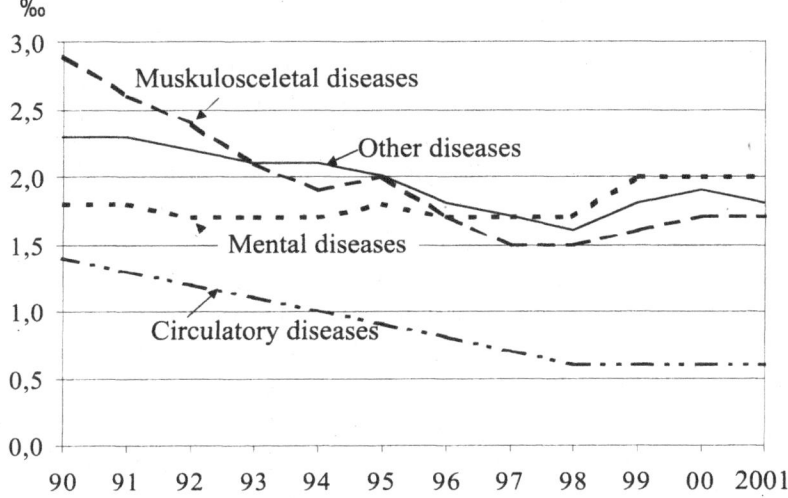

4.4 Growing rejection rate of disability pension applications

During the last three decades, disability pension rejections have often given rise to heated public debate. The representatives of pension organizations have been accused of not understanding the real situation of the applicants, and the applicants have been accused of being unwilling, instead of unable, to work. In the light of the rejection rate for disability pension applications, there is some discrepancy in the views of the applicants and their doctors, on the one hand, and administrators of the disability programme, on the other. In the private sector earnings-related pension scheme for 2001 approximately one in five applications for the ordinary disability pension was rejected, and for the individual early retirement pensions the rejection rate exceeded one in four. In the public sector and national pension programmes, the rejection rates were quite similar.

The rejection rate is higher for the younger age groups and for women than men. Moreover, of the three largest disease categories, it is highest in musculoskeletal diseases, close to the average in mental disorders and lowest in cardiovascular diseases (Table 3). Of these differences, the higher rejection rate for women especially has been debated extensively. To some extent, it has been assumed to be attributable to gender differences in illness behaviour. Women more often than men suffer from indefinite symptoms, and they are more active than men in using health services. Thus, it is possible that women apply for a disability pension at an earlier and more ambiguous stage than men and in that way may be more prone to rejections. However, it is also possible that female occupations may be valued less and their requirements and conditions may not be known as well as those of the male occupations, making the disability assessment for women more difficult (Naisten ja miesten työkyvyttömyys, 1993).

Table 3: Rejection rate for new earnings-related disability pensions in the private sector in 2001 (in %)

Sex, age and disease category	Ordinary disability pension	Individual early retirement pension
Men	16.4	24.1
Women	23.4	28.1
-44	24.0	-
45-54	20.6	-
55-59	18.2	34.6
60-64	9.2	19.7
Musculoskeletal diseases	27.4	24.5
Mental disorders	18.9	28.6
Circulatory system diseases	9.9	24.7
All	19.1	25.9

During the 1990s, particularly in the first half of the decade, the rejection rate for disability pension applications increased. In 1990 the rejection rate for ordinary disability pensions in the private sector earnings-related scheme was slightly less than 14%, but in 1997 it was 21%. Correspondingly, the rejection rate for individual early retirement pensions rose from 37% to 46% between 1990 and 1994. It has since declined, mainly due to the rise in the age limit, which eliminated the youngest applicants who were most likely to be rejected (Figure 4). The trend has also been similar in the public sector and in the national pension scheme.

The rejection rate rose for both men and women for all ages, although mostly for those applicants over 45 years of age, and for all major disease categories. Thus, the increase cannot be explained by demographic changes in the applicants. Neither was it caused by a growing inclination to apply for a disability pension: in the 1990s the proportion of new applicants in the insured population declined (Nyman and Gould, 1996; Gould and Nyman, 1998). The most probable explanation for the increase in the rejection rate appears to be the economic recession. During the 1990s, growth in the rejection rate coincided with growth in unemployment. Likewise, the previous rapid increase in the rejection rate occurred during the recession period in the 1970s (Figure 4). Moreover, a study on the determination of disability pensions in the 1990s shows that in the 50-59 age bracket the rejection rate was one and a half times higher for unemployed applicants than for others (Gould and Nyman, 1998). It is assumed that the effect of unemployment on the inclination to apply for a pension and on the assessment of disability has been an important cause for the more stringent practice in the decision-making procedure of the pension institutions.

Figure 4: Rejection rate for new earnings-related disability pensions in the private sector and unemployment rate 1970-2001

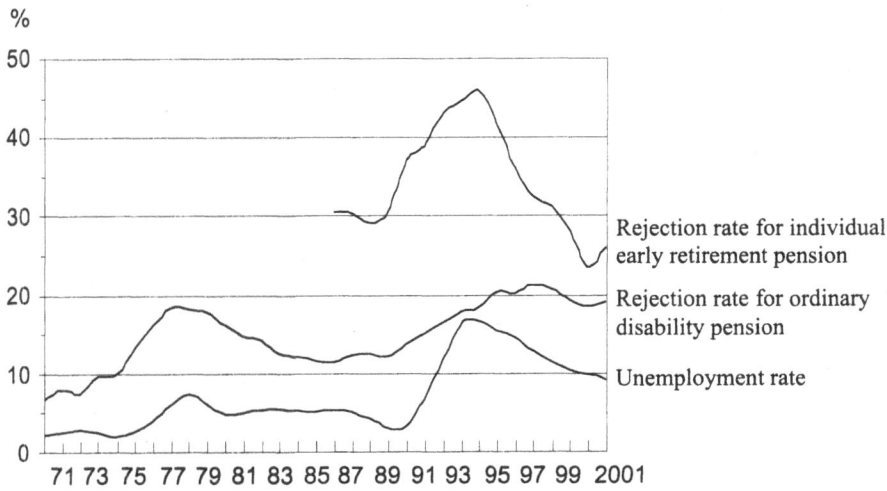

During the 1990s, about half of the private sector disability pension applicants whose application had been rejected by the pension institution appealed to the Pension Board. In general, the reversal rate of these cases was less than 10%. Of those cases that ended up in the Insurance Court, approximately one quarter were reversed. Some rejections may already be reversed before the appeal process through the self-correction procedure of the pension institutions.

The rejection of a disability pension means that the applicant is still regarded as retaining at least three fifths of his or her work capacity. Using this work capacity to find employment has turned out to be difficult, however. Studies on the post-rejection careers of disability pension applicants show that two or three years after the rejection only a small minority is still in employment (Juntunen et al., 1996; Gould and Nyman, 1998). For example, of the applicants for the individual early retirement pension whose applications were rejected in 1992 while they were 55-60 years of age, only 15% were still working two years later. A quarter of them had reapplied or appealed successfully and were receiving an individual early retirement pension or an ordinary disability pension. However, most of them were either unemployed or on unemployment pension (Gould and Nyman, 1998). Thus, rejections have slowed down the process of retirement, but their effect on the extension of working careers has been very small. In most cases, a disability pension rejection has prompted the applicant to choose an alternative pathway of early exit from work: the applicant has become unemployed instead of a disability pensioner.

5   Conclusions

During the last two decades, the general trend in disability pensions in Finland has been a downward one. The proportion of disability pensioners in the population aged 16 to 65 was nearly 9% in 1980, but by 2001 it had dropped to a little over 7%. According to a national health survey, also the self-reported work incapacity has decreased (Aromaa and Koskinen, 2002). The incidence of new disability pensions was highest during the first half of the 1970s and in the late 1980s. Both these peaks resulted from legislative changes. During the early 1970s the scope of the disability programme was enlarged by the inclusion of self-employed people and by changes in the definition of disability. During the 1980s, the individual early retirement pension was introduced with less stringent eligibility criteria than the ordinary disability pension. These extensions of the disability programme can be seen as reflections of the rapid changes in industrial structure, growing demands on working life and need for promoting competitiveness in the economy.

The general downward trend in disability pensions is, in part, attributable to the favourable trends in the health of the working age population, especially in the incidence of circulatory diseases. However, both periods of rapid decrease in the number of pensions were also periods of economic recession. Owing to the large number of unemployed, the conflict between work demands and poor health was less explicit and unemployment benefits provided a substitute for disability pensions. The declining number of pensions and the growing rejection rate of pension applications during periods of high unemployment suggest that in times of economic recession disability pensions were not used as a labour policy instrument to any great extent. Instead of expanding the concept of work capacity towards the concept of employability, medical criteria remained the chief determinants in assessing disability status.

In addition to high unemployment and improvements in health status, policy changes also influenced the downward trend in new disability pensions. On the grounds of the rejection rate, decision-making by pension institutions grew stricter both during the late 1970s and the 1990s. Moreover, during the early 1980s the compensation level of sickness allowance was low, thus discouraging would-be beneficiaries from applying for disability pension. In addition, during the 1990s pension restrictions, growing emphasis on rehabilitation, and the policy orientation towards promoting employment contributed to a decrease in number of new disability pensions.

However, the rehabilitation-oriented disability policy still faces many challenges. In recent years, Finnish employees have reported higher work stress, tighter schedules and growing demands of work. Moreover, in 2001 nearly one in five employees 55 years of age and over believed that because of health problems they could hardly continue working for a further two years (Ylöstalo, 2002). In addition, there have already been signs of changes in the disability trend: at the end of the 1990s, while the unemployment rate eventually began to decrease for the ageing labour force, the number of new disability pensions slightly increased. It therefore remains to be seen whether the decrease in onset of disability pensions in the 1990s was just a temporary phenomenon caused mainly by the economic trends, or whether it is a more lasting effect of the integrative measures of the policies pursued.

References

Aromaa, Arpo/Koskinen, Seppo/Huttunen, Jussi (eds.) (1999) *Health in Finland*. Helsinki: National Public Health Institute, Ministry of Social Affairs and Health.
Aromaa, Arpo/Koskinen, Seppo (eds.) (2002) *Terveys ja toimintakyky Suomessa*. Publications of the National Public Health Institute B3/2002. Helsinki.
Eläkeikäkomitean esitys joustavasta eläkeiästä (1983) Mimeo.
The Finnish Statutory Earnings-Related Pension Scheme (1999) Helsinki: The Central Pension Security Institute.
Forss, Mikael (1999) *The Ageing Baby-Boomers and the Labour Market in Finland*. Papers 1999:30. Helsinki: The Central Pension Security Institute.
Gould, Raija (1985) *Työkyvyttömyys – erivapaus työstä vai työttömyydestä*. Studies 1985:1. Helsinki: The Central Pension Security Institute.
Gould, Raija (1995) *Mitä eläkehylkäyksen jälkeen*. Studies 1995:4. Helsinki: The Central Pension Security Institute.
Gould, Raija (1997) 'Pathways of early exit from work in Finland in a period of high unemployment', in: Kilbom, Åsa/Westerholm, Peter/Hallsten, Lennart/Furåker, Bengt (eds.), *Work after 45?* Volume I. Arbete och Hälsa 1997:29. Solna: Arbetslivsinstitutet.
Gould, Raija/Nyman, Heidi (1998) *Työkyvyttömyyseläkeratkaisut 1990-1997*. Papers 1988:25. Helsinki: The Central Pension Security Institute.
Hakola, Tuulia (2000) *Navigating through the Finnish pension system*. Discussion papers 224. Helsinki: Government Institute for Economic Research.
Hilkamo, Pauliina (ed.) (2000) *Toimeentuloturva 2000*. Helsinki: Varma-Sampo.
Hytti, Helka (1995) 'Determinants of disability pension incidence', *Yearbook of Population Research in Finland* 32 (1994-1995): 54-69.
Hytti, Helka (1998) Varhainen eläkkeelle siirtyminen – Suomen malli. Studies in social security and health 32. Helsinki: The Social Insurance Institution.
Ilmarinen, Juhani (1999) *Ageing workers in the European Union*. Helsinki: Finnish Institute of Occupational Health, Ministry of Social Affairs and Health, Ministry of Labour.
Juntunen, Juhani/Hänninen, Kari/Lundqvist, Bo (1996) *Työkyvyttömyyseläkehakemus on hylätty – entä sen jälkeen?* Publications 28:1996. Helsinki: Employment Pension Fund.
Järvikoski, Aila/Peltoniemi, Jyri/Puumalainen, Jouko (2000) 'Eriytyvätkö pitkäaikaistyöttömien elämäntilanteet arviointi- ja kuntoutuspalvelujen tuloksena?', in: Rajavaara, Marketta (ed.), *Yksilölliset palvelut ja ikääntyneiden pitkäaikaistyöttömyys*. Studies in social security and health 54. Helsinki: The Social Insurance Institution.
Lind, Jouko (2000) 'Koettu terveys ja työkyky ikääntyneiden pitkäaikaistyöttömien työllistymisedellytyksenä', in: Rajavaara, Marketta (ed.), *Yksilölliset palvelut ja ikääntyneiden pitkäaikaistyöttömyys*. Studies in social security and health 54. Helsinki: The Social Insurance Institution.
Naisten ja miesten työkyvyttömyys (1993) *Equal Rights Publications*, Series A: Studies 2/1993. Helsinki: Ministry of Social Affairs and Health.
Nikkarinen, Tuuli/Broms, Ulla/Säntti, Janne/Brommels, Mats (1998) *Saattaen vaihdettava. Työkyvyn arviointikoulutuksen loppuraportti*. Public Health publications M 134:1998. Helsinki: University of Helsinki.
Notkola, Veijo (1980) *The development of cause-specific disability pensions in Finland 1972-1978*. Working papers 14. Helsinki: University of Helsinki.
Nyman, Heidi/Gould, Raija (1996) *Disability pension refusals over the years 1990-1995*. Papers 1996:14. Helsinki: The Central Pension Security Institute.
Rissa, Kari (1998) *Hyvinvointia valtion töihin*. Helsinki: The State Treasury.

Romppanen, Antti (2000) *Ikääntymisen vaikutuksista työmarkkinoilla.* Discussion papers 224. Helsinki: Government Institute for Economic Research.

Saarnio, Leena (2002) *Työeläkekuntoutus vuonna 2001.* Helsinki: The Central Pension Security Institute.

Takala, Mervi (1999) *Työnteon ja eläkkeellä olon yhdistäminen. Vaihtoehtona osa-aikaeläke.* Studies 1999:1. Helsinki: The Central Pension Security Institute.

Tola, Sakari (1995) Työeläkekuntoutuksen varhentamisen ja työkyvyn arvioinnin kehittämisen toimintaohjelma. Työkyvyttömyyseläketyöryhmän raportti, Liite 6. Mimeo.

Tuomisto, Tarja (ed.) (1999) *The Finnish statutory earnings-related pension scheme for the private sector.* Helsinki: The Central Pension Security Institute.

Työkyvyttömyyseläkkeet (1997) Circular A23/91 (revised). Helsinki: The Central Pension Security Institute.

Väänänen-Tomppo, Irma/Janatuinen, Esa/Törnqvist, Riitta (1999) *Kaikki hyvin työssä?* Helsinki: The State Treasury.

Ylöstalo, Pekka (2000) 'Ikääntyminen ja työelämän laadun muuttuminen 1990-luvulla', in: *Kansallisen Ikäohjelman seurantaraportti.* Publications 2000:15. Helsinki: Ministry of Social Affairs and Health.

Ylöstalo, Pekka (2002) *Työolobarometri. Lokakuu 2001.* Labour Policy Studies 241. Helsinki: Ministry of Labour.

CHAPTER 6

Disability Pensions in Germany

Holger Viebrok

1   Introduction

More than a century ago, in 1889, the German statutory pension scheme started as an old-age and invalidity pension scheme for blue-collar workers. Many of the rules have changed since then and the term 'invalidity' itself almost disappeared. But some of the characteristic features have remained valid, in particular the close connection with gainful employment. Now as ever, disability (and old-age) pensions aim at replacing the loss of earned income. Since the 1957 reform, an even closer relationship has existed between pensions and insured earnings during the whole working life.

The German Parliament (Bundestag) recently changed the rules for disability pensions in Germany. This change was part of a major pension reform as of the end of 2000 / beginning of 2001 which consists of various acts.[1] Besides reforming disability pensions, the general pension level was reduced (old-age pensions as well as survivors' and disability pensions), the rules for surviving spouses' pensions changed, and the general conditions for supplementary private pensions reformed.[2] Concerning the latter, taxation and subsidizing of occupational pensions and private old-age pensions have changed especially. The modifications with regard to private pensions have been discussed extensively, amongst other things because these elements lead to more capital funding within the total system of old-age provision. By contrast, the reform of disability pensions has taken place almost silently, although these modifications are at least as significant as those regarding old-age pensions. The reform abolished own occupation assessment for younger cohorts and led to a significant cut of the disability pension level especially in the case of older workers. As a result, workers have to bear still more risks or are forced to make provisions on their own, respectively.

This paper outlines characteristics of the German pension scheme for workers. Disability benefits are described in more detail. The paper refers to the law valid until 2000 as well as to important changes introduced by the recent pension reform.

2 Research on disability pensions in Germany

Only a relatively small number of German studies have investigated why people become disabled or why they are receiving disability pensions, respectively. Regarding the latter, it is not very surprising that the main reason for receiving disability pensions is the health status, because poor health status is a necessary (but not sufficient) condition of eligibility for disability benefits. Therefore, the question is which other characteristics influence the presence of disability. We can distinguish between studies that investigate the importance of job characteristics, studies that refer to the role of 'gatekeepers' and those that investigate economic incentives.[3] Some studies are designed as case-studies without statistically significant results.

Although there appears to be an evident link between stress and pension frequency, it is not easy to make firm conclusions from the existing studies. However, most of them were carried out in the 1980s. Naegele (1992: 80) concludes that the effect of growing stress at work is significant, but that it is overshadowed by the influence of the labour market situation.

Recent results based on the National Health Survey of the German Cardiovascular Disease Prevention (Nationaler Gesundheitssurvey der Deutschen Herz-Kreislauf-Präventionsstudie, DHP), and on the German Socio-Economic Panel (GSOEP) indicate that some factors have a significant influence on health-induced early retirement. These are (a) hard manual work, time pressure and being forced to make rapid decisions – this applies to both sexes, (b) VDU work, boring and monotonous work and strong rivalry among colleagues – this applies especially to women, and (c) inconsistent demands and unbalanced physical demands – this applies especially to men (Behrens/Elkeles/Schulz, 1998: 206). But it is not possible to determine clearly how this is linked to an increase in *total* early retirement.

Based on longitudinal data of the GSOEP, Riphahn (1995) investigated the effects of financial incentives (that is, the replacement rate) on the likelihood of receiving disability pensions. She concludes that the effect is minimal. According to her results, the strongest determinants are old age, health, working income and unemployment. Börsch-Supan investigated the impact of actuarial old-age pension deductions (also using GSOEP data), treating disability and other early retirement benefits as competing risks. He concludes that these incentives are also important in the presence of disability pensions (Börsch-Supan, 1999: 23).

Braun/Knödel noticed clear structural differences between labour-market induced cases and non labour-market induced cases. The diagnoses were found to be different, as were the length of service, income level and pension level (Braun/Knödel, 1983: 651). Concerning diagnoses, an above-average frequency of bone diseases was observed in the case of labour-market induced disability. In addition, the pension level was found to be lower on average.

Approaches that rely on one explanation alone cannot adequately explain the development of disability pension frequency. Useful results can be achieved only if relationships between individual circumstances and disease, effects of the pension scheme and company-specific characteristics such as the method of production and the staff policy (in particular career management) are taken into account (Behrens/Elkeles/Schulz, 1998; Morschhäuser, 1999; Behrens, 1999). Therefore, it is important to understand disability as being not an absolute but a relative notion, that is, to look at it as being connected with the specific job characteristics. Changes in the method of production have consequences for the ability to work, even if health status remains unchanged, because less jobs are available for disabled persons (Behrens, 1999: 74).

How long someone is able to work depends amongst other things on the company's staff policy. Companies have to take into account that qualifications possibly become outdated, workers become discouraged or lose credit. Various case studies (ibid.) have distinguished three patterns of response: (a) changing or modifying the workplace, (b) company or external career policy or (c) separating older employees from work (by change of employer, including outsourcing, unemployment, early retirement). Behrens et al. assume that setting the course very early could possibly prevent health problems, but the pension scheme influences these decisions by providing a cost-effective way of separating disabled employees. However, studies that could check these hypotheses are still missing.

However, as Burchardt (2000: 4) pointed out for the United Kingdom, many studies "have focused on disability benefits rather than disability itself"[4]. Furthermore, the German example shows clearly that disability itself is a rather vague notion (see below). As Kidd et al. note, all measures of disabilities that are related to work limitations are endogenous as well, "since the extent to which any condition or impairment is disabling depends on the type of activity under review" (Kidd et al. 2000: 965). Another important problem is that many aspects of disability are unobservable.

Thus, some additional basic research is necessary in order to develop indicators to represent the complex structure of causalities including effects of health, human capital, workplace characteristics, household characteristics, physicians, social law (including fulfilment of eligibility criteria), industrial law and financial incentives caused by wage discrimination, subsidies, other benefits and so on. The following sections focus on the institutional settings, in particular the concept of disability and the distinction between it and unemployment risks, because these have been the most important topics of the discussion in Germany and, as Börsch-Supan demonstrated, their neglect "can severely bias the estimates of incentive effects" (Börsch-Supan, 1999: 3).

3 Disability benefits within the social insurance system in Germany

3.1 Components of the social insurance system

The German national social insurance system is divided into the following branches:
- health insurance
- pension insurance
- industrial injury insurance
- unemployment insurance
- long-term care insurance

The various acts regulating these branches form the 'Sozialgesetzbuch' (SGB,[5] code of social law).

Disability risks are mainly covered by the statutory pension scheme ('Gesetzliche Rentenversicherung', GRV). The GRV is primarily an old-age pension scheme, but provides disability benefits and rehabilitation programmes as well as pensions for surviving relatives (widows, widowers and orphans). According to the Ministry of Labour, 36 041 000 men and women were economically active in 1999 (BMA, 2000). Some 90.17% of them were employees, the rest self-employed or cooperating family members. Among the employees, 7.3% were civil servants, 54.3% white-collar workers and 38.3% blue-collar workers. Civil servants are covered by an independent pension scheme ('Beamtenversorgung') without paying contributions of their own. The following sections deal with the German statutory pension scheme for blue- and white-collar workers (GRV).

3.2 Insured persons and financing

The following groups are insured by the statutory pension scheme:
- paid employees or persons during vocational training
  except for:
  - civil servants, judges, soldiers and other groups entitled to old-age provision
  - persons, who work less than 15 hours and earn less than one seventh of the reference income (EUR 325 in 2002, this amount will no longer be adjusted in the future)
  - trainees
  - old-age pensioners
- people receiving wage replacements such as sick pay, unemployment benefits, transitional payments during rehabilitation measures, early retirement benefits and so on
- severely handicapped persons and juveniles within certain institutions who are unable to work
- several kinds of self-employed persons, for example teachers and educators without employees, nurses, midwives, pilots, artists, journalists etc.
- craftsmen (members of a guild), who can opt out after 18 years of contributions

  Other insured persons are:
- parents during the first three years of child care
- non-professional care-givers (under certain circumstances)
- persons during military or alternative national service

The self-employed and some other persons can apply for compulsory insurance (but this is used very rarely). On the other hand, it is possible to become insured on a voluntary basis, provided that the person does not belong to one of the exceptions listed above.

Only a small number of people are covered by special schemes for freelancers, which insure the self-employed and their employees to a certain extent. However, self-employed persons as well as civil servants, freelancers and their employees often have pension claims from past employment periods. In 1994, 84% of the male and 82% of the female population aged 20 to 64 had paid contributions to the GRV at some point in their working life (BMA, 1998: 254).

The social security institutions are financed by pay-as-you-go (PAYG) contributions. In most cases these contributions are calculated in proportion to earned income, but they are also based to some extent on additional kinds of income in health and long-term care insurance. Industrial injury insurance is financed by risk-graduated contributions paid solely by the employer.

A contribution ceiling exists in all branches of the social security scheme except for industrial injury insurance. Except for health insurance, people earning above the ceiling remain compulsorily insured. In the pension scheme and in unemployment insurance, this 'ceiling income' amounts to about 1.8 to 1.9 times the average income of all insured.

3.3 Organizational aspects of disability insurance

The approval process usually starts with an application to the pension scheme administration and a medical certificate from the family doctor or a specialist. In many cases, workers have received sick pay up to the maximum duration (normally six months) before being referred to the pension scheme administration in order to apply for a disability pension. A medical investigation follows.

Responsibility for the medical opinion is with the social-medical service, which is part of the pension scheme's administration. In order to prepare its opinion, it will often consult with external experts. Responsibility cannot be given to a physician who has already dealt with the applicant before. The opinion assesses the occupational performance of the applicant. The Ministry of Labour and Social Affairs has drafted guidelines for medical experts.[6] The classification is based on ICD 10 (WHO).

The opinion is based on the relevant medical questions, for example, whether and how long (daily working time) someone is able to work on his job or how long the disability will probably last. An important question is whether it is possible to avoid pension payments by means of rehabilitation measures.

The statutory pension scheme is divided into several institutions with regional or substantive competence. Although they have limited self-government (supervisory board, consisting of representatives from trade unions and employer's organizations) they act according to uniform rules concerning pensions.[7] The decisions on disability are made by officials within these institutions.

3.4 Concepts of disability in Germany

Up to the year 2000, the concept of disability in the German statutory pension scheme (GRV) consisted of two important notions:
- *Occupational disability* ('Berufsunfähigkeit')
- *Incapacity to work* ('Erwerbsunfähigkeit')

From 2001 on, a new notion of disability was introduced:
- *Decreased ability to work* ('Verminderte Erwerbsfähigkeit')

In the following section, unless explicitly stated otherwise, 'disability' is used as a general term for all three notions. In addition, the German law contains at least two more notions:
- Being *severely handicapped* ('schwerbehindert'). The extent is assessed by the degree of handicap. The notion relates to functional disability. If this is more than 50%, a person is called severely handicapped. They are then protected against unlawful dismissal,[8] have tax allowances and several other privileges. They are also entitled to a special old-age pension with a lower pension age.
- *Decrease in the ability to work* ('Minderung der Erwerbsfähigkeit'). This is similar to the term used above, but is especially used in industrial injury insurance and with regard to support for war victims. The ability to work relates to the possibilities "in the complete area of employment'.[9]

The main terms are defined as follows:

Someone is *'occupationally disabled'* if his ability to work has decreased to less than *half* of that of a physically, intellectually and mentally healthy person with similar training and equivalent knowledge and abilities, result-

ing from an impairment (§43 SGB VI).[10] The ability is assessed on the basis of specific possibilities for gainful employment. This means that someone who cannot become gainfully employed in his occupation or cannot be referred to another reasonable job is not just 'occupationally disabled' ('berufsunfähig'), but also *'incapable of work'* ('erwerbsunfähig') and hence entitled to a higher pension, provided that the other relevant requirements are met. Note that occupational disability pensions are designed to compensate for a partial loss of ability. The applicant should therefore find a part-time job. But this is often impossible, in particular for men in poor health. Not surprisingly, a lot of jurisdiction relates to these definitions. The following questions are very important when judging the ability to work:
- To which jobs can people be referred and which jobs are considered reasonable?
- To what extent are labour market conditions relevant?

In the case of a blue-collar worker, the notion of 'reasonableness' is connected to a hierarchical scheme, in other words, workers can be referred only to a job that is one degree lower in the hierarchical scale. In the past, several schemes have been used, but in most cases (see also the Ministry of Labour, BMA, 1998: 286), the following hierarchical degrees of qualification are used: (a) superior/highly-qualified worker, (b) skilled worker, (c) semiskilled worker, (d) unskilled worker. Because it is possible to refer unskilled workers to all jobs that can be found on the labour market, they cannot receive occupational disability pensions at all. In the case of white-collar workers, no such explicit scheme existed, but in practice a similar procedure was often applied.

As mentioned above, according to the 'concrete view' in contrast to the 'abstract view'[11] when assessing disability, it is necessary to consider the specific job situation.[12] In other words, if an insured person is occupationally disabled (according to medical categories), the administration has to prove that a part-time job is in fact available. In practice, the pension scheme administrators ask the employment office whether this is possible or not. In the past two decades, it was not possible in most cases unless the person continues in his original job. Thus, the share of occupational disability pensions was very low during this period. But, as Figure 1 shows, the declining share of occupational disability pensions seems not to be linked to the labour market situation, because it had already decreased in the period between 1963 and 1972 (men) or 1979 (women), respectively, whereas the job situation did not deteriorate until the late 1970s.[13]

Figure 1: Share of occupational disability pensions in all new disability pensions 1960-1999 (West Germany, since 1993 the whole of Germany)

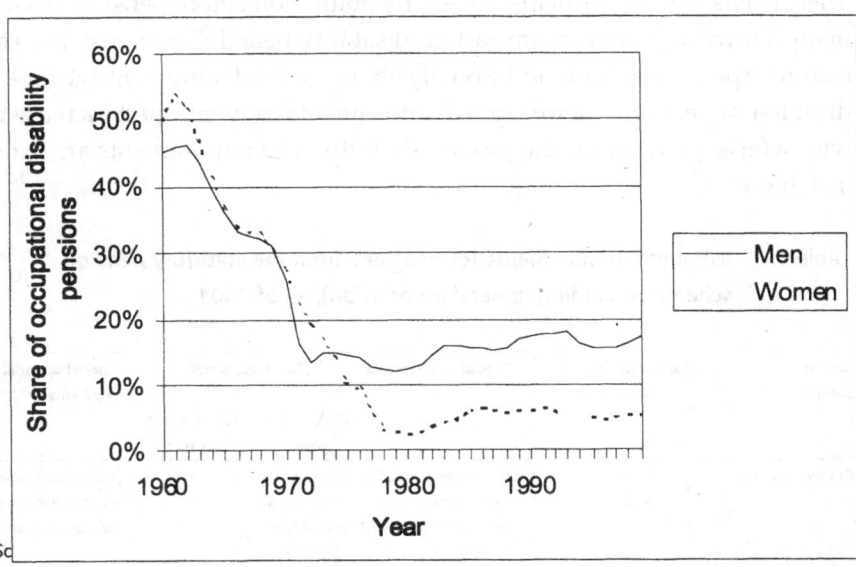

People are *incapable of work* if they are not able to work on a regular basis or not able to receive income from work above one seventh of the 'reference income' ('Bezugsgröße')[14] because of illness or handicap (§ 44 SGB VI). The job situation is also decisive when assessing incapability to work.

This concept of disability in the statutory pension scheme led to the situation that about one third of the pensions because of incapacity to work have been paid because of the labour market situation. Besides this, the occupational disability pension was often too low, given the fact that workers had to reduce the amount of time they worked (and hence the earned income) to less than a half in order to meet the requirements. Many people also feel that the existence of occupational disability pensions is not justified at all, because unskilled workers are forced to pay the same amount of contributions as skilled workers but cannot claim for an occupational pension themselves.

In December 2000, the German Parliament decided on the first of several pension reform acts, which featured significant changes in the rules for the disability pensions (see section 4.3 below).

3.5 Disability benefits from the statutory pension scheme

There exists a strong principle called 'rehabilitation before pension' in Germany. However, the most important disability benefits are pensions. The statutory pension scheme additionally offers a special retirement age for the disabled or severely handicapped, and the above-mentioned increase in widow(er)s' pensions in the case of disability. The requirements are listed in Table 1.

Table 1: Minimum requirements for pensions from the statutory pension scheme (excluding miners' association), as of 2001

Kind of pension	Earliest beginning of the pension	Special requirements	Qualifying period		Special actuarial requirements***
			Contribution years*	Total credited years**	
Disability pensions	No limit (until 65)	Occupational disability, incapacity to work (until 2000), decreased ability to work (from 2001 on)	5 before the beginning of disability or 20 before application	-	3 years of compulsory insurance during the previous 5 years
Old-age pension for severely handicapped	60	Severely handicapped, disability	-	35	-
Old-age pension after unemployment or part-time-in-old-age work	60	1 year of unemployment during the past 1 1/2 years or 2 years of part-time-in-old-age work	15	-	8 years of compulsory insurance during the previous 10 years
Old-age pension for women	60	Only for women	15	-	10 years of compulsory insurance after age 40
Old-age pension for long-term insured	63	-	-	35	-
Standard old-age pension	65	-	5	-	-

Notes
* Including periods of maternity/paternity leave (1 year before 1992, 3 years as of 1992) and certain replacement periods (military service, captivity, expulsion and others).
** Contribution periods and certain periods without contributions (periods of illness, pregnancy, legal protection for nursing mothers, unemployment, training, etc.).
*** The timeframe is extended in the case of sickness, unemployment or under several other conditions.

Source: Viebrok, 1997 (updated)

3.5.1 Requirements for disability pensions

Claimants are entitled to disability pensions if they meet certain medical and actuarial criteria. In order to check the employment status, special actuarial requirements are used in the case of disability and some old-age pensions.

These conditions require that a claimant has worked within a certain timeframe, that is, a period of several years prior to the beginning of the disability (or the beginning of an old-age pension, respectively). In the case of disability, at least three years of insurance within the last five years are necessary. The reason is that only employees should be eligible for wage replacement benefits. As mentioned above, the job situation also plays an important role, namely in the concept of disability.

Table 1 shows the actuarial requirements for old-age and disability pensions that can be drawn from the statutory pension scheme. Normally, five years of insurance prior to the beginning of the disability are required to become eligible for a disability pension. Because persons who became disabled during childhood would never have a chance to become eligible for a disability pension, they are also allowed to receive a pension after 20 years of insurance.

The 'standard pension age' for old-age pension is currently 65 or 63, respectively (see also Table 2). Table 1 also shows the earliest retirement age, which may be earlier than the standard pension age, in which case deductions of 0.3% apply for every month the pension starts earlier.

In addition to the benefits listed in Table 1, an increase for disabled survivors exists. Widows and widowers aged under 45 can claim only for a 'small' widow's pension, as it is called,[15] amounting to about two thirds of the level of the 'large' one. But they are also entitled to a large pension as long as their children are not older than 18 years or if they are disabled. As a result, in 2000 only 0.42% of widow's pensions were small pensions.

Own income (including an own disability pension) that exceeds an allowance of EUR 668.29 (early in 2002)[16] is subject to an earnings test. Forty per cent of the excess income is deducted from the widow's pension.

3.5.2 Calculation of disability pensions

As mentioned above, two different notions of disability existed in the statutory pension scheme until 2000,[17] called 'Berufsunfähigkeit' (occupational disability, in the following abbreviated OD) and 'Erwerbsunfähigkeit' (incapacity to work, IW). *IW pensions* are calculated in the same way as old-age pensions except for a partial compensation for missing insurance periods until age 60 (see below). *OD pensions* are about one third lower. Both disability pensions turn automatically into old-age pensions at age 65 (or earlier, if someone applies for that).

The calculation of pensions in Germany is based on 'earnings points', which are in principle simply the quotient of individual insured income and average income of all insured persons in a particular year. The amount of the monthly pension is proportional to the total earnings points. This sum is multiplied by the 'actual pension value', that is the value of one earnings point. The product is the monthly pension. The actual pension value determines the general pension level. Until 1999 it was adjusted annually according to the development of average net earnings. Pension deductions have to be taken into account if the pension begins earlier than the standard pension age.

The standard pension age has been gradually raised to 65 since 1997, beginning with the old-age pensions after unemployment (see Table 2). Pension deductions amount to 0.3% per month of an earlier beginning. Because old-age pensions can start at age 60 at the earliest, the maximum deduction amounts to 18%.[18] If the pension begins later than at age 65, it is accordingly increased by 0.5% per month.

Until 2000, no pension deductions existed for disability pensions, in contrast to old-age pensions. It is true that most old-age pensions were not yet subject to deductions (see Table 2), but a strong incentive to apply for disability pensions was expected. It was reduced by the Pension Reform Act 2000/2001 (see below).

The standard pension level is a measure of the general pension level, based on a model pensioner who has 45 earning points. Until 1998 such a 'standard pensioner' gained 70% of the average net earnings of all employees (but not necessarily of his own last earnings, because the pension depends on his complete earnings record).

As mentioned above, missing insurance periods before age 60 are completed by additional fictive insurance periods. This complementation amounts to 100% until age 55 and in addition one third of the remaining period until age 60. For example, someone who has been insured since age 16 and becomes disabled before age 55 has a maximum insurance period of 39 years + 20 months = 40 1/3 years. If he earned exactly as much as the average wage (receiving exactly one earnings point per year of insurance, in other words), he would accumulate exactly the same number of earnings points. This corresponds to a pension level of 70% x 40.67 / 45 = 63% of the average net earnings of all employees. The maximum possible pension is about double the standard pension because of the effect of the contribution ceiling.

Table 2: Raising the retirement age in Germany (as of December 2000)

Pension	Former pension age	Beginning of the increase (year)	End of the increase (year)	Resulting standard retirement age	Earlier beginning possible from age ... on	Maximum deductions
Old-age pension after unemployment or part-time-in-old-age work	60	1997	2002	65	60	18%
* Old-age pension after unemployment or part-time-in-old-age work	60	2001	October 2004	60 10/12	60	3%
Old-age pension for women	60	2000	2005	65	60	18%
Old-age pension for long-term insured	63	2000	2002	65	63	7.2%
** Old-age pension for long-term insured	63	2001	2006	64	63	3.6%
Old-age pension for severely handicapped	60	2001	2004	63	60	10.8%

Notes   Transitional rules for:

* Unemployed persons born before 14 February 1941 or those born before 1 January 1942 with 45 years of compulsory insurance (§ 237 SGB VI).

** Persons who receive early retirement benefits and were born before 14 February 1941 or those born before 1 January 1942 with 45 years of compulsory insurance (§ 236 SGB VI).

Source: Listed according to SGB VI.

Figure 2 shows that the average amount of new pensions for men because of incapacity to work increases with age, despite the effect of additional insurance periods. This is caused by the increasing earnings profile of men during their working career, whereas many women work full-time when younger and part-time when older, so that their average earnings (related to the complete insurance record) tend to decrease.[19] The rapid downward slope after age 60 is the result of selection mechanisms, because old-age pensions often become available at this age.

Figure 2: Pensions because of incapacity to work: average pension by age at the beginning of the pension (new pensions 1999)

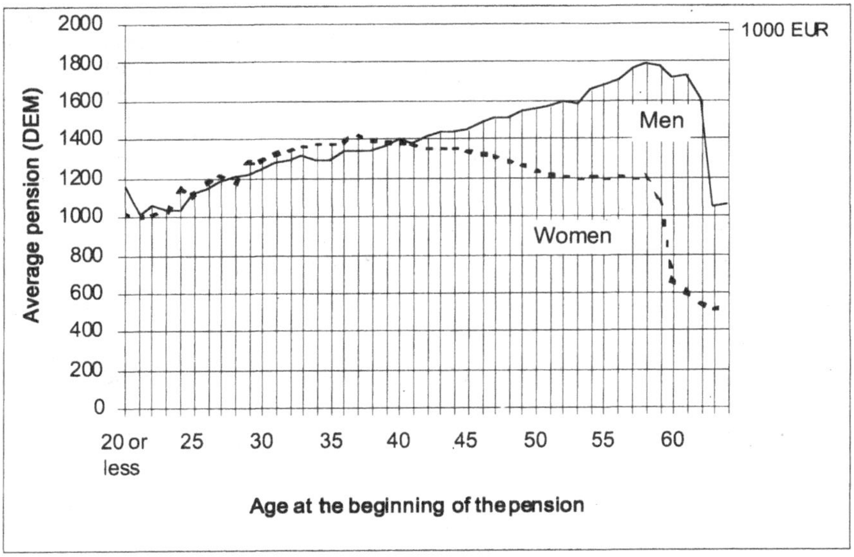

[Figure: Line chart showing average pension (DEM) on y-axis from 0 to 2000 (with 1000 EUR marker on right), and age at the beginning of the pension on x-axis from "20 or less" to 60. Two lines plotted for Men and Women.]

Source: Calculations based on Verband Deutscher Rentenversicherungsträger, 2000

Until 2000, disability pensions were granted temporarily only if there was a good chance of curing the applicant of the disability in the foreseeable future, or in the case of pensions connected with the labour market situation (§ 102 SGB VI). The time limit was set at three years, but it was possible to repeat the limitation up to a total of six years at most.

There is no extra allowance for spouses or children. Children's allowances are paid by a special federal administrative body. In most cases, pensions from the statutory pension scheme are not taxed, except for those that are very high or begin at a very young age.

3.5.3 Possibilities of combining disability pensions and working income

The occupational disability pension is designed to supplement a reduced (part-time) working income. It was also possible to combine a pension because of incapacity to work with working income. Since 1 January 1996 an earnings test has been applied in both cases. It is possible to claim for one third or two thirds of the full pension. Every option is combined with a specific earnings limit.

If the pensioner received a full pension because of incapacity to work, he was allowed to earn up to one seventh of the reference income.[20] Since 1999, this limit (marginal income limit) has remained fixed at DEM 630 (EUR 325 since 2002). If the earned income exceeded this limit, an IW pension was reduced to an OD pension (about one third lower).

Every OD pension is subject to the earnings test. The earned income limit relates initially to the earned income in the year before the beginning of the disability and is then indexed according to the adjustment of the pension (the 'actual pension value' and the last earnings point are elements of the calculation[21]). In simple terms, it is possible to express the earnings limit as a share of the most recent net earned income[22] for years between 1992 and 1998.[23] The resulting income limits for an average earner until 2000 are shown in Table 3.

Table 3: Earnings limits as a function of the share of the occupational disability pension being drawn (until the end of 2000)

Share of the pension drawn	Earnings limit as a percentage of the last net earnings	Minimum earnings limit as a percentage of the average net earnings of all insured
One third	136%	68%
Two thirds	109%	54%
Full pension	82%	41%

Source: Own calculations based on SGB VI

3.5.4 Rehabilitation benefits

Rehabilitation benefits are granted if they can reduce impairments to the ability to work, prevent workers from a premature exit from working life or re-integrate them into working life. Benefits exist in the form of medical as well as occupational rehabilitation measures, supplemented by special transitional payments, subsidies for employers wishing to integrate disabled workers, medical after-care and financing of research.

Medical rehabilitation consists of medical treatment, medicine, dressing, other remedies like physiotherapy, therapeutic exercises, occupational therapy and speech therapy as well as board and lodgings at a clinic (§15 SGB VI). The pension scheme institutions carry out medical rehabilitation measures in their own clinics.

Other components of *occupational* rehabilitation benefits include education and training or retraining, respectively, and board and lodgings in the case of in-patient measures. Supplementary benefits include subsidies for housekeeping, travelling expenses, physical education, examination fees and work clothes.

Benefit recipients have to contribute EUR 9 per day from their own resources up to a maximum of two weeks, except for the case of occupational rehabilitation.

An applicant automatically meets the *actuarial requirements* if he already receives a disability pension or the pension increase for widow's pensions or after 15 years of insurance. If these requirements are not yet met, it is sufficient to fulfil the following conditions:
a) In the case of medical rehabilitation:
   – Six months of compulsory insurance within the previous two years, or
   – five years of compulsory insurance in the presence of disability (but no pension yet).
   – Special rules exist for persons at the start of their working career.
b) In the case of occupational rehabilitation:
   – If the requirements for disability pensions are met.
   – If occupational rehabilitation measures are necessary after a medical rehabilitation.

Medical rehabilitation measures are granted for up to three weeks, but can afterwards be prolonged. Up to 1996 a repetition was possible after a period of three years, after which the period was extended to four years. There is no time limit for the length of occupational measures, although they should not exceed two years.

During the rehabilitation measures *transitional payments* are made if working income decreases. The payments differ depending on whether the applicant has children or not. Applicants with children are eligible for payments of about 60% of their most recent gross working income. Applicants without children get about 54%. Several special rules exist for various cases.

3.6 *Relationship between disability pensions and unemployment benefits*

The distinction between disability and unemployment risks is difficult, because the concept of disability in Germany also includes labour market criteria. But despite this fact, programmes other than disability pensions are used mainly to cope with labour market problems in Germany, particularly job-creation measures including subsidies (up to 100%) paid to the employer.

The calculation of unemployment benefits[24] differs considerably from the calculation of pensions. The disability pension is based on the complete working career, whereas the unemployment benefits are based on the earned income within the previous 52 weeks. Unemployed persons are eligible for unemployment benefits, in most cases for one year (see Table 4 below). These benefits are not means-tested. After the claims are exhausted, unemployment relief starts. The unemployment relief is granted without time limit, but in contrast to unemployment benefits it is means-tested.

The unemployment benefits amount to 67% of the calculation basis if the unemployed person has children up to age 18. The basis is formed by standardized net earnings. Childless persons or those with adult children receive 60%. In case of an average earner the resulting replacement ratio is similar to that of disability pensions, but it varies owing to different assumptions with regard to the working career.

Table 4 shows the duration of the unemployment benefit as a function of age and length of service. Unemployment benefits as well as relief are limited until the respective person is entitled to an old-age pension, at maximum until age 65.

Table 4: Duration of unemployment benefits according to length of service and age

Requirements (to be met simultaneously)		Duration (months)		Requirements (to be met simultaneously)		Duration (months)
length of service (months)	minimum age			length of service (months)	minimum age	
12		6		40	47	20
16		8		44	47	22
20		10		48	52	24
24		12		52	52	26
28	45	14		56	57	28
32	45	16		60	57	30
36	45	18	(continuation–>)	64	57	32

Source: § 127 SGB III

The unemployment relief amounts at the beginning to 57% or 53%, respectively. Then the individual calculation basis (and hence the unemployment relief) decreases by 3% per year.[25] There is a lower limit based on earnings amounting to about half of the average earnings. As mentioned above, unemployment relief is means-tested.

There is also social assistance in the case of poverty in Germany. Social assistance consists of recurrent as well as non-recurrent payments, in the case of special needs.

The combination of labour contract termination (based on redundancy schemes) with severance payments, unemployment benefits, and the old-age pension after unemployment very often led to an early retirement that was financed by unemployment insurance and old-age pension insurance. The earliest starting age is 57 2/3. Such solutions have been tolerated for a long time by the government. Besides, older unemployed persons are not forced to seek a new job. Thus, many workers believed they are 'entitled' to this special pathway to retirement.

Various minor reforms have aimed at cutting off this pathway, but it became less attractive when in recent years pension deductions gradually came into force and since severance pay has been partially deducted from unemployment benefits. But in view of the poor job prospects, especially for older workers in Germany, another benefit was introduced, namely the 'part-time-in-old-age work'. This should not be confused with true part-time work. Although the latter is possible as well, in most cases it is used as 'blocked' part-time, that is, the complete period of several years is divided into working full-time during the first half and not working during the second half. The complete period lasts six years at most, if a corresponding collective agreement exists (otherwise three years), that is, the period without working lasts up to a maximum of three years (or 1 1/2 years, respectively). The worker receives at least 70% of the most recent earnings from the employer, but the labour office pays compensation to the employer of 20% of most recent earnings. After that the old-age pension begins.

3.7 Distinguishing between the statutory pension scheme and statutory industrial injury insurance concerning disability

Statutory industrial injury insurance is provided by 35 industrial and 20 agricultural professional associations. Other public associations take care of scholars, students, rescuers and others.[26] The associations pay benefits only in the event of industrial accidents, accidents that happen on the way to the place of work, and occupational diseases. Industrial injury insurance covers the legal liabilities of the employer, including compensation for personal suffering. Therefore, benefits are relatively generous, provided the disabled worker is entitled to benefits at all. But as contributions are paid by employers only and are differentiated according to risks, industrial injury insurance is very restrictive when it comes to granting benefits. In particular, the question of whether a disease has been caused by the job or not is very often the object of legal conflicts. Although the definition of disability used by industrial injury insurance refers in principle to all jobs 'in the area of working life', there is a contradictory phrase, meaning that the insurance has to compensate for the devaluation of qualification. This is another possible reason for conflicts.

The insurance covers the consequences of an injury only if it results in a decrease in the ability to work of at least 10%. Pensions are granted only if the decrease amounts to at least 20%, otherwise lump-sum payments are provided. Pensions are in principle permanent. The pension amounts to two thirds of the annual gross income in the case of a 100% decrease in the ability to work, otherwise to the degree of disability. Seriously injured persons (at least 50%) who are not eligible for a disability pension from the statutory pension scheme are granted an additional 10%. Conversely, the pensions are taken into account in the pension scheme: the upper limit of the sum of both pensions together amounts to 70% (47% in case of occupational disability) of the income on which the injury pension is based. The pensions are adjusted yearly on the basis of the pensions received from the statutory pension scheme.

4 Disability pension reforms in the past three decades

4.1 Changes before 2000

The law regarding disability remained almost unaltered for three decades until late 2000. However, decisions on rules for disability pensions in Germany are made not only by the legislator but also by the federal courts. A very important conflict deals with the notion of 'concrete view' ("konkrete Betrachtungsweise") when looking at the job situation (see above).

The 'concrete view', whereby the administration has to take the concrete job situation into account when deciding on disability, has its origin in two decisions of the Federal Social Court of 11 December 1969 and 10 December 1976. In particular, skilled women after a long break from work – and hence with fewer chances on the job market – gain by the concrete view and by the protection of their occupational status. Thus, in many cases, diseases related to old age together with the worse job situation beginning in the mid-1970s, were sufficient to give an entitlement to a pension because of incapacity to work. At that time, a claim for an old-age pension required 15 years of service. Hence it follows that there was a strong incentive to apply for disability pensions.

This development did not lead to a redefinition of disability but to a significant change in the actuarial requirements for disability pensions. The legislator introduced a status check in the form of the requirement that there had to be at least three years of compulsory insurance within a five-year period immediately prior to the beginning of the disability. At the same time, eligibility criteria for the standard old-age pension (retirement age 65) became less stringent: the required length of service was reduced from 15 to 5 years with (compulsory or voluntary) contributions during the complete working life. Finally, the legislator decided on a far-reaching redefinition of disability in late 2000.

The 1972 Pension Reform Act resulted in major changes regarding old-age pensions, especially in the introduction of 'flexible' old-age pensions. These are pensions that may begin before age 65 (see Table 1). One of these new 'flexible' old-age pensions was the pension for disabled persons. It could be drawn at age 62 until 1978, at age 61 (1979) or 60 (1980 and later on).

Some changes occurred regarding rehabilitation measures. A reform act in 1974 adapted the benefits from different institutions. An act in 1977 excluded civil servants from rehabilitation benefits within the statutory pension scheme. Furthermore, occupational rehabilitation measures were transferred in part to the unemployment insurance system. However, the responsibility for rehabilitation measures is still unclear. In 1982, the conditions for rehabilitation measures changed. They were then granted only if the capacity to work was *considerably threatened*, whereas before even the *preservation* of the capacity to work was sufficient. Since 1 July 2001, various acts relating to rehabilitation and severely handicapped persons have been combined in the SGB (Social Code) IX (see also below).

The actuarial requirements for disability pensions changed significantly in 1984, as mentioned above. This led to an increase in applications in 1983, because women in particular tried to obtain a pension before the law came into force (Rehfeld, 1994: 483). On the other hand, since 1 January 1986 more women have become eligible for a pension because the periods of bringing up children are counted as periods of compulsory insurance (initially one year, since 1992 three years per child at most). Since 1995, care-giving has also counted towards the contribution periods.

The 1992 Pension Reform Act led to numerous changes in the calculation of pensions. For example:
- The 'virtual' periods of insurance, granted in lieu of contribution periods, were cut ("Zurechnungszeit").
- The maximum sum of payments in the case of concurrent pensions from the statutory pension scheme and industrial injury insurance was reduced from 80% to 70% of the most recent earnings. On the other hand, special allowances were introduced.
- The (until then) fixed earnings limits for pensions drawn before age 65 were replaced with partial old-age pensions (similar to the partial disability pensions described above, but with lower earnings limits). However, the percentage of partial old-age pensions is less than 1%.
- The periods of training taken into account were reduced from 13 to 7 (since 1997 to 3) years.
- The pensions were linked from then until 1998 to the development of average net earnings (instead of gross earnings).
- The gradual raising of the standard pension age to 65 was prepared (planned from 2001 on, but later on advanced and accelerated).
- Earnings limits and partial disability pensions were introduced in the year 1996.

4.2 Changes regarding other insurance branches

From 1 April 1984 until 31 December 1988 a pre-retirement act for workers from age 58 was in force. This act changed in particular the perception of early retirement in Germany. After 1986 workers aged 58 received unemployment benefits without being forced to seek a new job. As a successor of the pre-retirement act, a first part-time-in-old-age act came into force in 1989.

It was claimed very rarely and was withdrawn in 1993. Workers took advantage of other benefits in order to retire early, in particular unemployment benefits combined with old-age pension from age 60.

In eastern Germany (former GDR), from 3 October 1990 until 31 December 1992 (for new cases), a special pre-retirement scheme was in force. Workers aged 55 or older could apply for transitional old-age payments ('Altersübergangsgeld'), which lasted five years at most. They were entitled to receive an old-age pension after this period (just like unemployed persons in western Germany).

Because these (official and non-official) pre-retirement schemes became very expensive, on 14 February 1996 the new part-time-in-old-age act came into force. A reform act in the field of unemployment insurance as of 1 April 1997 raised the age limits at which the duration of unemployment benefits increases (Table 4 above showed the results) by three years. Besides, rules for the deduction of severance payments from the unemployment benefits became stricter. Because of transitional rules they have been introduced gradually. Furthermore, the level of unemployment relief has depended since then on the duration of the payments.

4.3 The 2000/2001 pension reform and the introduction of the new social code for disabled persons (SGB IX)

The debate on disability pensions in Germany during the past decades has been dominated by questions relating to the definition of disability, especially concerning occupational protection (occupational disability) and consideration of the labour market situation. The recent disability pension reform act, which came into force on 1 January 2001, changed the rules significantly. It replaced the former controversial notions.

The new pension for decreased ability to work now consists of two steps relating to the number of hours of work per day that the claimant is still able to perform. The limits are at six and three hours. In other words, if someone is not able to work more than three hours, he is called 'fully disabled'; and between three and six hours he is 'partially disabled'. A person who is able to work at least six hours at some job does not qualify as 'disabled'. The pension in case of partial disability is half of the full pension. In contrast to the former law, self-employed persons are also eligible for a pension. The actuarial requirements remained almost unaltered.

The occupational disability pension was abolished for cohorts born in 1961 or later. Older skilled workers who are only able to work between three and six hours in their occupation but full-time in some other job are now entitled to the partial disability pension without being forced to perform a job of lower status.[27]

Labour market criteria still hold in the case of partial disability pensions (Wollschläger 2001: 280), but expenses are partly refunded by the unemployment insurance. The incapacity-to-work pension has been replaced by a decreased-ability-to-work pension. It is very important that – except for the expiring OD pensions mentioned above – all available jobs are now considered as being 'reasonable', regardless of the job-specific skills.

Figure 3: Effect of the 2000 reform on the disability pension level

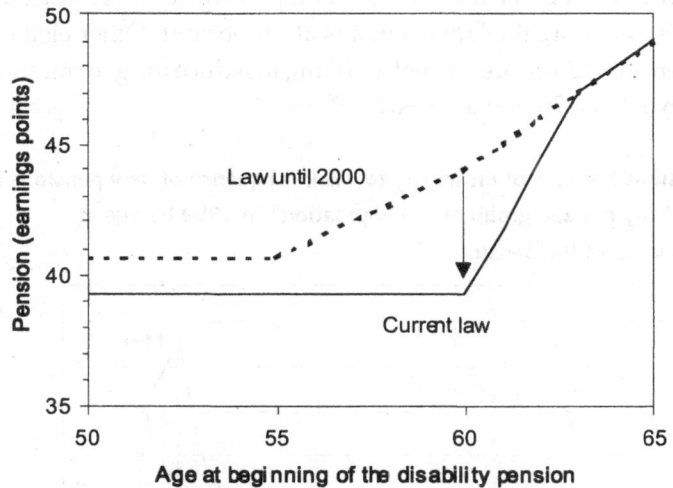

Note: The graph is based on a person entering the insurance scheme at age 16. The disability pension starts at the age on the x-axis. Until then average earnings are assumed.
Source: Own calculations based on SGB VI.

In addition, several new rules concerning the pension level have been added. Disability pensions are now reduced as a result of pension deductions in the same way as the old-age pensions. Therefore, the standard retirement age for disability pensions is assumed to be 63 and the pension decreases by 0.3% for every month it starts earlier to a maximum of 10.8% (equivalent to a pension that starts at age 60). Insofar, disability pensions are now treated like old-age pensions for severely handicapped persons. The financial incentive to switch to disability pensions is reduced, but not neutralized: the deductions applied to other old-age pensions amount to 18% at most. On the other hand, more 'virtual' insurance periods are granted until age 60 in order to offset missing contribution periods. That means that the complete period from 55 until 60 is taken into account now, in contrast to one third according to the former rules.

This results in a cut of earnings points, mostly at the age of 60 (see Figure 3). As can be seen in Figure 4, most disability pensions begin at age 52 to 60 with a peak at age 57. After this age the frequency decreases.[28] Old-age pensions after unemployment are affected by deductions of up to 18%, thereby giving an incentive to shift to disability benefits. The reform is likely to prevent workers from shifting to disability pensions, but at the cost of a decreasing pension level. The more the general pension level is reduced by other measures, the more the latter remains all important. Other elements of the recent pension reform are currently aiming to reduce the general standard pension level from 70% to about 64%.[29]

Figure 4: Pensions because of incapacity to work: frequency of new pensions in Germany per age group of the population* in 1999 by age at beginning of the pension

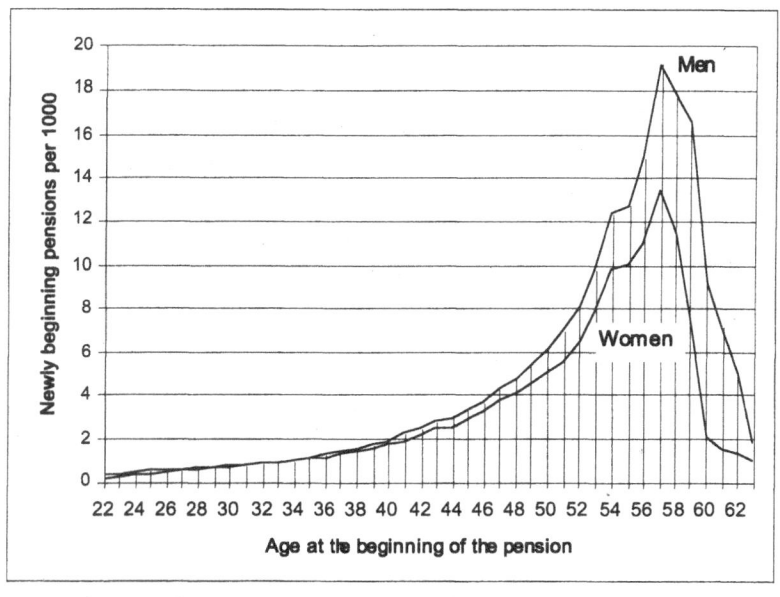

Note: * Population at 31 December ... of each age group
Source: Verband Deutscher Rentenversicherungsträger 2000

Other important elements of the pension reform are:
- Partial disability pensions and corresponding earnings limits have been reorganized in the sense that four steps (including the full pension) are now available. As described above, earnings limits depend on individual earnings. In case of an average earner, almost the entire earned income above EUR 325 is now deducted from the pension. Thus there is no longer an incentive to earn more than a marginal working income.
- A new means-tested flat-rate benefit ('bedarfsorientierte Grundsicherung', literally: needs-oriented basic protection) has been introduced to prevent people from poverty. Disability pensioners as well as elderly persons (over 65) are eligible for this new benefit.

The new SGB IX came into force on 1 July 2001. This new part of the Social Code integrates many existing regulations in the field of rehabilitation and for severely handicapped persons into one law. The reform has many improvements in detail and in the organizational structure of the social system. It also represents a new line of thought by emphasizing participation in society and working life.[30] One of the more practical changes is that it aims at more out-patient than in-patient treatment in the case of rehabilitation measures.

5 Conclusions

This paper provides a brief outline of the situation in Germany. As in other countries, expenditures for disability benefits have risen in Germany in the past three decades, but the increase is relatively moderate compared with other countries. The law has barely changed since 1969, except for an important modification of the contribution requirements in 1984, leading to more stringent access. Although labour market criteria play an important part when assessing disability, other programmes – such as longer duration of unemployment benefits for older workers, job creation, and official as well as unofficial early retirement schemes – largely financed by the unemployment insurance have been used for the most part to cope with unemployment.

Nevertheless, the underlying relationships influencing the frequency are not really clear at all, particularly as the dynamics of the relationships between health and work and the complex structure of determinants influencing disability are still almost unexplored. Additional research is necessary because understanding the determinants is very important for preparing and evaluating policy measures.

Notes

1. 'Gesetz zur Reform der Renten wegen verminderter Erwerbsfähigkeit' (BGBl. I, No. 57 23 December 2000, p.1827), 'Altersvermögensgesetz' (BT-Drucksache 14/5970 9 May 2001), 'Altersvermögens-Ergänzungsgesetz' (BGBl. I No.13 26 March 2001, p.403), 'Gesetz zur Verbesserung des Hinterbliebenenrentenrechts' (BT-Drucksache 14/6043 15 May 2001).
2. Schmähl (2000) outlines the debate on the pension reform in Germany.
3. Besides social law, jurisdiction plays a decisive role in the general conditions relating to the assessment of disability. The very important question whether a 'concrete' or 'abstract' view of the labour market situation is used when assessing disability is outlined below.
4. Dwyer et al. (2001) found that in the United States "2.9 % of the general population not receiving disability benefits [...] satisfy the SSA's definition of disability" (ibid.: 39). In addition, they demonstrate the importance of choosing the correct estimate.
5. The different acts are provided with roman numerals, for example SGB VI contains the rules for the statutory pension scheme.
6. Bundesministerium für Arbeit und Sozialordnung, Referat Öffentlichkeitsarbeit, Berlin, Germany.
7. Special rules exist for employees in the mining industry and for artists.
8. Wagner et al. (2001) analysed the impact of the protection on job dynamics in small firms and found that the law "does not seem to have the kind of strong negative influence on job dynamics [...] that is often attributed to it in public debates" (ibid: 12).
9. "Arbeitsmöglichkeiten auf dem gesamten Gebiet des Erwerbslebens", § 56 SGB VII.
10. Special rules for employees in the mining industry exist but are not discussed here.
11. In German 'konkrete' and 'abstrakte Betrachtungsweise'.
12. Voges (1994) did not observe a significant effect of a federal court's decision of 1976 with respect to this, but he could investigate cases only until 1978. The Association of Statutory Pension Insurances (VDR) and the unemployment insurance did not reach agreement about the treatment of applications after the court's decision until December 1978. However, an analysis of the frequency of new pensions also showed no substantial changes (Braun/Knödel 1983: 650). The probable reason is that the 1976 decision was only a confirmation of the older decision of 1969 (see section 4.1 below).
13. The reasons for this decrease are not fully clear. The figures are influenced by gradual behavioural responses to the important 1957 pension reform as well as by the fact that until 1984 people of age 70 became eligible for pensions because of incapacity to work.
14. The reference income corresponds to the insured person's average income.
15. This kind of pension is limited to a period of 24 months by the 'Altersvermögens-Ergänzungsgesetz', a part of the pension reform acts 2000/2001.
16. This allowance follows the development of the pensions.
17. Section 4.3 outlines the recent reform.
18. As of the year 2002, this may be the case for pensions after unemployment or part-time-in-old-age work, but transitional rules apply for long-term insured persons.
19. The distribution is probably influenced by cohort effects (younger cohorts have a higher relative earnings position), particularly in case of women.
20. That is about one fifth of average *net* earnings of all insured. This special earnings limit still holds today. The other limits changed with the recent pension reform but not the principle itself.

21 See the descriptions above. At least half an earnings point is taken into account in order to improve the situation of workers with very low earnings.
22 Differences arise depending on earnings because of progressive taxation.
23 The standard pension level decreased as of 2000, when the pension adjustment was linked to the consumer price index for one year.
24 Apart from the case of unemployed occupational disability pensioners there was no possibility to combine disability benefits from the statutory pension scheme with unemployment benefits, pre-retirement benefits or old-age pensions in Germany before 2000. Normally, the first case also led to a pension because of incapacity to work.
25 On the other hand, the general level is being adjusted according to the statutory pensions, so that the nominal decrease is in fact somewhat less.
26 Civil servants are covered by the State instead of industrial injury insurance. Their pensions are calculated in another way.
27 Note that the old limit was half the normal working time and that the former occupational disability pension amounted to two thirds of the pension because of incapacity to work. Hence it is easier to get the pension, but its level is lower.
28 The reason for this is not clear. Possible explanations are that benefits from unemployment insurance are available from age 57 2/3 onwards or because people feel that they have a good chance of 'getting through' the remaining years until age 60 without a pension.
29 The exact value relates to the definition of net earnings, which was changed at the same time. This figure refers to the former definition.
30 These changes seem to be inspired by the philosophy of 'welfare to work' in the United Kingdom (Burchardt, 1999: 9), but in fact no further conclusions are drawn relating to the requirements for disability benefits, except that disability benefits are in principle to be time-limited.

References

Behrens, Johann (1999) 'Länger erwerbstätig durch Arbeits- und Laufbahngestaltung: Personal- und Organisationsentwicklung zwischen begrenzter Tätigkeitsdauer und langfristiger Erwerbstätigkeit', pp. 71-115 in: J. Behrens/M. Morschhäuser/H. Viebrok/E. Zimmermann (Eds.), *Länger erwerbstätig – aber wie?*. Opladen: Westdeutscher Verlag.

Behrens, Johann/Elkeles, Thomas/Schulz, Detlef (1998) 'Begrenzte Tätigkeitsdauer und relative Gesundheit – Berufe und betriebliche Sozialverfassungen als Ressourcen für Tätigkeitswechsel', pp. 196-228 in: W. Heinz/W. Dressel/D. Blaschke/G. Engelbrech (Eds.), *Was prägt Berufsbiographien? Lebenslaufdynamik und Institutionenpolitik*. Beiträge zur Arbeitsmarkt- und Berufsforschung, 215. Nürnberg: IAB.

Behrens, Johann/Voges, Wolfgang (1990) 'Labilisierende Berufsverläufe und der vorzeitige Übergang in den Ruhestand', pp. 201-219 in: W. Dressel et al. (Eds.), *Lebenslauf, Arbeitsmarkt und Sozialpolitik*, Beiträge zur Arbeitsmarkt- und Berufsforschung, 133. Nürnberg: IAB.

Börsch-Supan, Axel (1999) 'Incentive Effects of Social Security under an Uncertain Disability Option', *NBER Working Paper* No. 7339. Cambridge, MA.

Braun, Roland/Knödel, Peter (1983) 'Die Arbeitsmarktlage und die Gewährung von Renten wegen Berufs- und Erwerbsunfähigkeit im Spiegel der Statistik', *Deutsche Rentenversicherung* 9-10: 621-651.

BMA (Bundesministerium für Arbeit und Sozialordnung) (1998) *Übersicht über das Sozialrecht*. Bonn: Eigenverlag.

BMA (Bundesministerium für Arbeit und Sozialordnung) (2000) *Statistisches Taschenbuch 2000 – Arbeits- und Sozialstatistik*. Berlin.

Burchardt, Tania (1999) 'The Evolution of Disability Benefits in the UK: Re-weighting the basket', *CASEpaper* 26. London School of Economics.

Burchardt, Tania (2000) 'The Dynamics of Being Disabled', *CASEpaper* 36. London School of Economics.

Dwyer, Debra/Hu, Jianting/Vaughan, Denton R./Wixon, Bernard (2001) 'Counting the Disabled: Using Survey Self-Response to Estimate Medical Eligibility for Social Security's Disability Programs', *ORES Working Paper Series* 90. Washington: US Social Security Administration.

Kidd, Michael P./Sloane, Peter J./Ferko, Ivan (2000) 'Disability and the Labour Market: An Analysis of British Males', *Journal of Health Economics* 19: 961-981.

Morschhäuser, Martina (1999) 'Altersgerechte Arbeit: Gestaltungsaufgabe für die Zukunft oder Kampf gegen Windmühlen?', pp. 19-70 in: J. Behrens/M. Morschhäuser/H. Viebrok/E. Zimmermann (Eds.), *Länger erwerbstätig – aber wie?*. Opladen: Westdeutscher Verlag.

Naegele, Gerhard (1992) *Zwischen Arbeit und Rente*. Augsburg.

Rehfeld, Uwe (1994) 'Verrentungsprozeß und versicherungsbiographische Fakten für Geburtsjahrgangskohorten – Analyse der Rentenzugangsdaten 1973 bis 1990 für Versichertenrenten', *Deutsche Rentenversicherung* 7: 471-526.

Riphahn, Regina T. (1995) 'Disability Retirement among German Men in the 1980s', *Münchener wirtschaftswissenschaftliche Beiträge*, Arbeitspapier. München: Ludwig-Maximilians-Universität.

Scheerer, Reinhard (1976) 'Berufsunfähigkeit: ein impraktikabler Rechtsbegriff', *Deutsche Rentenversicherung* 1: 9-19.

Schmähl, Winfried (2000) 'Increasing Life Expectancy, Retirement Age, and Pension Reform in the German Context', *Journal of Aging & Social Policy* 11 (2/3): 61-70. Binghamton N.Y.: The Haworth Press.

Verband Deutscher Rentenversicherungsträger (VDR) (1993) 'Grundsätze zur Berufs- und Erwerbsunfähigkeit in der gesetzlichen Rentenversicherung', *Deutsche Rentenversicherung* 8-9: 493-636.

Verband Deutscher Rentenversicherungsträger (VDR) (2000) *VDR-Statistik*, Statistics on CD-ROM. Frankfurt am Main.

Viebrok, Holger (1997) 'Opfer und Opfergrenzen, Einkommens- und Arbeitsanreizeffekte von Vorschlägen zur Reform der Invaliditätsrenten', *Zeitschrift für Sozialreform* 43 (3): 227-251.

Voges, Wolfgang (1994) *Mißbrauch des Rentensystems? Invalidität als Mittel der Frühverrentung*. München: Campus.

Wagner, J./Schnabel, Claus/Kölling, Arnd (2001) 'Threshold Values in German Labor Law and Job Dynamics in Small Firms: The Case of the Disability Law', *Arbeitsbericht* No. 233. Lüneburg: Fachbereich Wirtschafts- und Sozialwissenschaften, University of Lüneburg.

Wollschläger, Frank (2001) 'Gesetz zur Reform der Renten wegen verminderter Erwerbsfähigkeit', *Deutsche Rentenversicherung* 5: 276-294.

Zweng, Johann/Scheerer, Reinhard/Buschmann, Gerhard (Eds.) (1991) *Handbuch der Rentenversicherung*. Stuttgart etc.: Kohlhammer.

CHAPTER 7

Disability Pensions in Italy: The Law and the Numbers

Emanuele Baldacci and Gustavo De Santis

Introduction

This chapter deals with the issue of disability benefits in Italy. The main focus is on monetary benefits granted within the social security system to people of working ages (15-64 years), but to better understand this part it is necessary to look as well at the broader and rather complex picture of how protection against physical impairment impeding work in the active age span is organized in Italy. Beyond social security, reserved for people who belong to the workforce and pay insurance contributions, monetary transfers may originate within the broader welfare system covering all residents; apart from monetary transfers, several kinds of non-monetary provisions exist; and, finally, several disability benefits designed for other age classes and in particular the elderly (65+) may indirectly accrue to the working-age population instead through the family system or through the mechanism of survivors' pensions. Sections 1 and 2 deal with the normative framework (the current situation and the main reforms of the past 30 years); in section 3 we present and discuss the available data on disability; and in section 4 we draw some conclusions.

1 The national disability protection system in Italy at the end of the 1990s

1.1 Disability pension schemes in Italy: a general overview

The guidelines for the disability protection system currently in force in Italy were established in the 1960s and, with a few important modifications, have survived to this date. The system is rather complex for two main reasons: first, because in each case several variables interplay simultaneously, such as cause and degree of invalidity or contributory and in some cases general economic status of the injured person; second, because the current situation derives from successive adjustments of existing laws with the further complication that in most cases new laws were applicable only to new cases but previously conceded benefits were not repealed and will therefore last as long as any of the original beneficiaries are still alive.

Figure 1: How to access a disability benefit in Italy

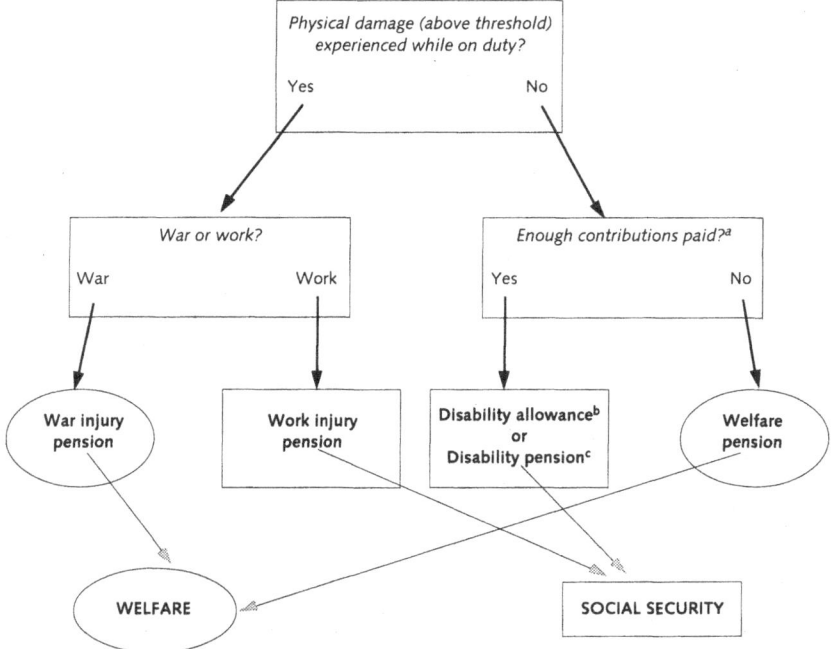

Notes: a) Five full years of contributions, three of which during the last five calendar years. b) 67-99% disability, checked three times before it becomes permanent. c) 100% disability (a permanent condition).

Currently the situation is as follows (cf. Figure 1): once physical impairment (above various possible thresholds – see below) is officially ascertained, the main dividing line is whether it occurred while on duty (work or war) or on some other occasion. If the former is the case, the injured worker has a right to a compensation (or indemnity) pension within the work or war injury programme.

If it is not a war[1] or a work injury, another fundamental question arises: is the injured person a worker who has paid enough contributions (meaning: at least five full years, three of which in the last five years)? If this is the case, the injured person is eligible for the social security system and can obtain either a partial (and potentially temporary) *disability allowance* (67-99% disability), which will later turn into an old-age pension (if the eligibility conditions for this benefit are met), or a total (and assumedly permanent) *disability pension* (100% disability).[2] If, on the other hand, the answer is no (either the disabled person was not in the labour force or he/she was in the labour force but had not paid enough contributions), the injured person takes the other route and is eligible for a *welfare pension*.

So, two parallels emerge. One is the difference between pension payments which do or do not compensate for a work injury (or a work-related illness). The other is the difference between what is labelled and statistically classified as social security or welfare (Table 1). The main difference between the two is that social security benefits depend on and are generally related to previously paid contributions whereas with welfare no contribution is requested: the system covers every resident individual and is financed through general fiscal revenues. Two further differences may be noted: welfare benefits are means-tested while social security benefits are not; and welfare benefits are not generally portable to survivors[3] while social security benefits are.

Who exactly is a disabled person? To be officially recognized as such, persons claiming to have suffered from a permanent and sizeable reduction in their physical or mental capability must apply to an officially recognized medical commission[4]. This commission examines each applicant, who is designated (officially) as disabled if his or her degree of disability exceeds one or more of the conventional thresholds operating in Italy. Note that there are several thresholds, and they also generally differ in the various cases: this complicates the picture considerably but has the advantage of allowing a gradual increase in the protection granted to persons who become more and more seriously disabled. Incidentally, this also reduces the distortions

Table 1: Pension benefits provided to disabled people (or their survivors) in Italy in year 2000: a general overview

Nature	Scheme	Disability (c) 0-17	Disability (c) 18-64	Disability (c) 65+	Work injuries (d) 0-14	Work injuries (d) 15-64	Work injuries (d) 65+	Survivors 0-14	Survivors 15-64	Survivors 65+
Social Security (a1)	Old Age			Old-age pension (c2) (C)						
	Disability	(A)	Disability allowance (c1)-> (B)	Disability pension (c3)	(D)	(E)	(F)			
	Survivor							(G)	Survivor pension (H)	(I)
	Indemnity						Direct indemnity (d)		Indirect indemnity	
Welfare (a2)	Welfare (b1)	Allowance (c4)	Pension (c5) + allowance (c6)		"Social" pension + allowance (c6)					
	War-injury indemnity		Direct indemnity						Indirect indemnity	

Notes:

- *General notes:*
  - Work allowed, except where noted.
  - Not 'means-tested', except where noted.

- *Specific notes:*

a1) Financed through, and related to, contributions (necessary anyway); a2) Financed through taxes, and means-tested.

b1) Not portable to survivors.

c) At least 67% disability for social security; at least 74% for welfare. c1) 67-99% disability. Physical damage suffered while not on duty, and checked three times before it becomes permanent. Evolves into (c2) at retirement age. Not portable to survivors. If low, raised to 'social minimum'. c2) No work allowed. c3) 100% disability. Portable to survivors. Higher than disability allowance. No work allowed. c4) For school attendance. c5) The blinds' pension is independent of age (and never evolves into a 'social' pension). c6) For accompanying person.

d) And work-related illness. At least 11% disability, caused by a work accident.

that would emerge if only one or very few dividing lines existed to separate 'normal' (excluded from all benefits) from disabled citizens (entitled to all of them).

Apart from war-injury-related payments, monetary flows may go under three basic labels, sometimes with further specifications: disability pensions/allowances, work indemnities and other welfare benefits. Let us consider them in greater detail.

1.2 Disability pensions/allowances

Disability pensions/allowances are regular (monthly) payments to workers[5] whose work capacity has been impaired by an accident incurred while not 'on duty'.

Since 1984, an important dividing line has been drawn between (total) disability *pensions* and (partial) disability *allowances*.

a) (Total) disability *pensions* are granted to workers whose physical impairment reaches 100% and who cannot (and anyway are not allowed to) work any more. This condition is considered permanent and so is the benefit, which does not evolve into an old-age pension and is portable to survivors (survivor pensions).

b) (Partial) disability *allowances*, first introduced in 1984, are given to people who, despite sizeable physical impairment (67-99%), still continue to work, although they do not necessarily have to. Partial disability (67-99% of work capacity lost) is in principle a temporary status which gives the right to a partial disability allowance and which must be reviewed every three years. If, however, the person has not recovered at the time of the third medical examination (i.e. six years after the first visit), his/her status is recognized as permanent and lasts up to legal retirement age. At that point, if minimum contribution conditions are met, which is generally the case, the disabled individual starts receiving an old-age pension; if, on the other hand, they are not met, the individual maintains his partial disability allowance.[6] People with (temporary) partial disability allowances can continue to work until they reach retirement age.

Before 1984, the definition referred to the 'earning capacity' of the individual: this encouraged a very broad interpretation of the concept, which sometimes led to misuse or even abuse. Especially in regions with high unemployment rates, social considerations mingled with medical ones and induced very generous treatments of applicants. Things changed in 1984, when a reform indicated that impairment of the *work* (not *earning*) capacity was the only thing that mattered, but benefits conceded before the 1984 reform were never repealed, and it is estimated that it will take another ten years for beneficiaries of the former scheme to become of scarce statistical and economic relevance.

Two kinds of pension can thus be provided under this scheme: partial disability allowances (67-99% disability) and total disability pensions. In both cases, the calculation formula is complicated by the circumstance that rules have changed repeatedly. The last reform (concerning all, not just disability, pensions) dates back to 1995.

Currently, i.e. in year 2000, partial disability allowances depend on the number of years of contribution and on the average wage of the worker (average of the last five years). The amount of the benefit is obtained by multiplying the average wage by the number of years of contribution by a 2% coefficient (lower for higher wages). If the calculated values are lower than the *minimum pension*[7] value (about 10 million lire per year, less than 5 000 euros) the partial disability allowance is integrated by an extra sum provided by the social security administration in order to reach this minimum (and, actually, 77% of partial disability allowances benefit from this allowance).

From the year 2002 on, the new allowances will be paid according to the new contributory system introduced by the 1995 reform. According to the new rules, the amount of the benefit will be the product of two terms: the sum of the accrued lifetime contributions and a discount factor, inversely related to the claimant's life expectancy at retirement. The accrual (discount) rate to be considered for each year in the calculation is the five-year average of the GDP growth rate.

As mentioned above, partial disability allowances are not portable to survivors, and evolve into an old-age pension when the beneficiary reaches retirement age, provided there are at least 15 years of (actual or virtual) contributions.[8] It should be noted, finally, that partially disabled individuals receiving a disability allowance are allowed to work: however, since 1996, they have been implicitly discouraged from doing so, because the more they earn, the less they receive in terms of disability benefits; in fact, reductions can be as high as 50%.

Calculations for a total disability pension, on the other hand, differ sharply from those of a partial disability allowance. The value of the disability pension is the sum of two parts: a) one part of the pension is identical to that currently in force for partial disability allowances and is determined by multiplying the 2% factor by the number of contribution years of the pensioner by the average wage; b) a second part is then added, and this is calculated by multiplying the number of years of extra seniority by the average wage by the 2% factor. This extra seniority is the difference between the legal and the actual age at retirement of the disabled pensioner.[9] As with partial disability allowances, a minimum pension of, currently, some 10 million lire per year is guaranteed anyway. On top of that, a special allowance (called *maggiorazione sociale*) is also provided to disability pensioners older than 60 or 65 with low incomes.

Total disability pensions are portable to survivors and proportions vary from 60% (only the spouse survives) to 100% (spouse with dependent children) of the former benefit. Disability pensioners and partial disability allowance beneficiaries who have low incomes and dependent children are also eligible for special family allowances (about 2.5 million lire per year, slightly more than 1 000 euros, for a pensioner with two children and a yearly income of 30 million lire, less than 15 000 euros).

Disability pensions/allowances are part of the *old age, disability and survivor (OADS)* insurance programme, which is compulsory for all employees and for the self-employed. A minimum contribution is required to be eligible for the disability pensions, and this is what makes it *social security* in national accounts data. The OADS scheme provides its services to workers on a contributory basis. Coverage is the same as that of the old-age pension system (i.e. the whole workforce) and participation in the scheme through contributions is compulsory.

Beneficiaries can be of any age – even older than 65 – because, as explained above, not all benefits provided under this scheme transform into an old-age pension at retirement age. Pensions for this group are provided by different social security funds, the largest among them being the National Institute for Social Security (or INPS: Istituto Nazionale per la Previdenza Sociale).

1.3 Work-injury compensation programme

The work-injury compensation programme includes both monetary and non-monetary provisions. The latter basically consist of health assistance;[10] the former are of two kinds: daily indemnities (for days not spent at work because of a work injury) and compensation for physical loss or impairment incurred while on duty. (In principle this should resolve in a single lump-sum payment but it takes the form of an annuity instead.) Beneficiaries can be persons of any working status (i.e. they can work while benefiting from the provision) and any age.

As for work injuries, there are a few important definitional differences from the disability cases discussed above. In the first place, only workers whose occupation is considered to be particularly exposed, i.e. the industrial, health and agricultural sectors plus a few branches in the service and the public sectors, are insured against work injuries by *ad hoc* agencies (but mainly INAIL: Istituto Nazionale per l'Assicurazione sugli Infortuni sul Lavoro – National Institute for Work Injury Insurance).[11] However, *all* workers who suffer from injuries while going to or coming back from work are insured against traffic accidents, in which case they receive not only health assistance but also an indemnity, which is generally paid by INAIL (but sometimes by other institutions, e.g. for railway workers or other publicly-owned companies).

Apart from this case (commuting accidents), disability is only considered for indemnity if caused by an accident that happened at work and because of the occupational task (or by an illness contracted in connection with work).

Monetary benefits are of two kinds:
1. Daily indemnities are paid by INAIL as a percentage of the last wage as follows: 60% for the 4th to 90th day of forced absence from work; 75% thereafter. For the first three days of absence from work 100% of the salary is generally paid by the employer but provisions depend on the contract of employment.[12]
2. Compensation for disability: benefits vary from 50% to 100% of the last wage depending on the degree of disability (for which a minimum of 11% is required).

Since 1996, the same event (e.g. a work accident) cannot give rise to more than one payment: the injured person, however, will receive the benefit that is most favourable for him/her (e.g. partial disability allowance or work injury indemnity).

Funding for the work-injury protection programme comes from a few *ad hoc* institutes, the most important of which is the National Institute for Work Injuries Insurance – INAIL: Istituto Nazionale per l'Assicurazione sugli Infortuni sul Lavoro. Protection is extended to most but not all productive activities for which social insurance is compulsory (and the presence of contributions makes it a social security expenditure according to statistical classifications). Contributions levied on employers depend on the salary mass of each enterprise and on the productive category so that those economic branches where work injuries are more frequent or serious or both pay higher premiums.

1.4 Welfare benefits

Welfare benefits are provided by INPS and some regional administrations[13] to residents with low incomes and at least 74% disability. Disability is officially ascertained by *ad hoc* commissions, who must refer specifically to the person's ability to work or cope with everyday life. Re-tests are always possible, however, especially in the frequent cases where the disabled person claims a deterioration in his/her degree of disability. Welfare disability pension coverage is universal but all cases covered by other pension schemes are automatically excluded from welfare services, e.g. war or work accidents or accidents occurring to people already insured within the OADS scheme. Benefits depend on income and on the type and degree of disability, with special provisions for those who suffer from more than one disability or from disabilities considered particularly impairing.[14]

Welfare disability pensions are provided until 65 years of age, when the pension is automatically transformed into a 'social' pension (*assegno sociale*), i.e. a minimum income (currently about 8 million lire per year, less than 4 000 euros) granted to all elderly persons.[15]

1.5 Disability allowances and other kinds of benefits

1.5.1 Disability allowances and unemployment benefits

In Italy there are different types of unemployment insurance, none of them covering all of the working population. Short-term unemployment is mainly covered by the *indennità di disoccupazione* (unemployment indemnity), granted to workers insured by INPS (most of the workforce). It generally lasts six months (or one year at most) and amounts to 30% of the previous wage.

If unemployment is caused by an industrial crisis, the unemployed worker can receive a special benefit called *integrazione salariale* (wage allowance) amounting to 80% of the last wage and payable for a maximum of two years (and only for enterprises with more than 15 employees, which are the only ones participating in the scheme).[16]

It may be interesting to compare a partial disability allowance with the unemployment benefit. The comparison is complicated by the fact that, even if we take an average wage-earner, the ratio between the two benefits (partial disability vs. unemployment) depends on the type (short- or long-term) and on the number of years of work (cf. Table 2). All in all, however, partial disability allowances are more generous, especially in that they can become permanent, whereas unemployment benefits last for two years at most.

Table 2: Ratios of disability allowance to unemployment benefits

Kind of unemployment	Years of work			
	10	20	30	40
Short-term	67%	133%	179%	266%
Long-term	25%	50%	67%	100%

Source: Own elaborations on Istat data.

Combination of partial disability and unemployment benefits is possible, but only with partial disability allowances (67-99% disability).

1.5.2 Disability pensions and early retirement

Currently, a double retirement system exists in Italy. Older workers (e.g. people having already worked at least 18 years in 1995 – the year of the latest reform) had a variety of regulations regarding their pension, including varying legal retirement ages, depending on the branch of their economic activity, their sex, etc. For these persons, however, the legal retirement age is being progressively increased: currently it is 59 for women and 64 for men, and from year 2008 onwards it will be 65 for both sexes.

Younger workers, on the other hand, will have to retire between the ages of 57 and 65 – but the younger they retire, the lower will be the amount of their pension, with a reduction based in principle on their residual life expectancy.

For younger workers, a relatively early retirement (at the age of 57) will therefore be possible in the future. Under the present system, which concerns only relatively older workers, those who prefer to retire earlier than the legal retirement age can resort to a different mechanism called *seniority pensions*. This is a special benefit provided on request to workers who, although below the standard legal retirement age, have worked[17] for a given number of years. Requirements, once extremely loose (cf. section 2), have recently been tightened: currently, dependent workers need 37 years of seniority (or 35 years of contributions and an age of 54 years); self-employed workers need 40 years of seniority (or 35 years of contribution and an age of 57 years). For public employees (civil servants) early retirement is possible for workers with lower seniority, but in this case pensions are reduced by an amount proportional to the difference between the standard and the actual number of years of contribution.

A combination of disability and early retirement benefits is not normally possible. However, a seniority retirement is easier for persons who leave the labour market because of work injuries. In this case only the 35-year-contribution condition counts with no age requirement.

1.5.3 Other legal provisions concerning disability

In 1992, an important law (No. 104) set out the general principles regarding the rights of handicapped persons. The law does not distinguish between those handicapped since birth and those who became handicapped later and does not generally address economic issues.[18] It talks about prevention, health assistance, general and professional education, removal of architectonic barriers, etc. Incidentally, this law gives local authorities most of the responsibility for organizing (and supporting financially) such 'local' services as mental homes, sanatoriums, centres for the disabled, etc. This may appear logical and desirable on the one hand, but it is also a cause for concern: once these services are run on a totally local basis, there is a possibility that the large regional differences that exist today in terms of both quantity and quality of these services will increase even further (Kazepov, 1997).[19]

Some of the provisions of Law 104/1992 directly affect the labour market. For instance, article 22 abolishes the previously required medical certificate of good health for a job in the public sector, which prevented many disabled people from applying for jobs as civil servants.[20] Article 33 prescribes a series of advantages for handicapped workers (who, among the alternatives available within that particular enterprise, can choose the working place he/she prefers) and for workers who are cohabiting with and responsible for handicapped persons, in particular children: they have a right to a reduction in working hours and are privileged in the choice of the working place.

In the same vein as the aforementioned 1992 law on handicapped persons and in application of some of its provisions, another important bill was passed in 1999 (Law No. 68 – Working rights of the disabled). Since some of its implications were very far-reaching, it was to become fully effective only 300 days after its publication, which means that it has been in force since 17 January 2000.

The law replaces an earlier law (No. 482 of 1968), which placed greater demands on employers[21] but which, in practice, was largely ignored. The most important provisions of the new law are as follows:

1. A certain percentage of working places[22] is reserved for the disabled[23].
2. Workers who have suffered a not totally impairing work injury (or a job-related illness) cannot be dismissed and must be kept at least at the same salary (and possibly also at the same or at a comparable working position) they had before the accident (or illness).
3. Companies are given financial incentive to comply through tax and contributory relief.
4. Non-complying companies are penalized twice: through fines and through disqualification from tendering in public contracts of any kind.

2 Major reforms in the system since 1970/1980

2.1 *Disability pensions*

The two most important reforms in partial disability pensions themselves took place in 1984 and in 1995, while the reform of 1992, which concerned social security in general, affected disability pensions only marginally.

Before 1984, only one kind of disability pension was envisaged within the social security scheme. Disability was defined as the loss of *earning* capacity of the insured worker and the benefit was proportional to wage, seniority and the degree of disability. The broad definition used for disability allowed or even encouraged misuse of the benefit, particularly in those parts of Italy with high unemployment rates (southern Italy, notably). In fact, the loss of earning capacity of individuals of working age could also be caused by an industrial crisis, as happened very often during the 1970s and the 1980s.

The 1984 reform tightened eligibility conditions (disability could refer only to the loss of one's *work* capacity) and considerably reduced benefits for those not totally disabled, although the old provisions were maintained for those who already enjoyed them and although, as mentioned, some 77% of partial disability allowances, in theory lower than the minimum pension, were raised to that level. Two different benefits, 'partial disability allowance' for partial (possibly temporary) and 'total disability pension' for total (assumedly permanent) disability, were introduced.

The 1992 social security reform did not concentrate specifically on disability pensions, but they were affected by some of the general rules that the new law introduced. The most relevant change concerned the indexation rule for pension amounts, which until 1992 took into account salaries (that is, price *and* real wage changes). From 1993, however, it considered only price variations, measured through the *CPI* (consumer price index). In 1992, moreover, retirement ages for old-age pensions started to increase gradually, from 60 years (males) and 55 years (females) to 65 years (males) and 60 years (females), with some effects on the calculation formula for disability pensions.

In 1995, another relevant social security reform took place, changing the calculation system of old-age, disability and survivor pensions. Before 1995, pension values were calculated according to the earnings-related formula described earlier ([reference wage] times [working years] times 2%), while the 1995 reform made contributions the sole criterion, although it was decided that the change to the new system would be gradual. The amount of the pension will eventually be determined by multiplying the accrued value of lifetime contributions by a discount factor inversely proportional to life expectancy at retirement. Another important rule introduced by the 1995 reform concerns the possibility of combining several disability pensions and benefits with working income. According to the new rules, only a partial combination of wage and partial disability allowances is possible, and, in principle, one disabling event cannot give rise to more than one disability benefit.

Important changes also took place in the period under examination for *welfare* pensions. The flat-rate benefits were first introduced in the early 1970s for individuals suffering from blindness, deaf-dumbness and other impairing disabilities. Originally, only very low benefits were granted, but in 1980 these were significantly increased and a new allowance was introduced for the totally blind that was not subject to means-testing. This allowance (called *indennità di accompagnamento* or reimbursement for an accompanying person) was relatively generous, almost twice as high as the pre-1980 benefit. In 1988 the value of these benefits was further increased and new allowances were introduced for persons who were totally blind or deaf-mute. Moreover, it became possible to combine these benefits with other incomes, including labour income. During the 1990s, only minor reforms took place, increasing the value of benefits and introducing new allowances for disabled persons attending rehabilitation courses.

Between 1996 and 1999, the annual budget law (*legge finanziaria*) introduced new formal procedures to verify the real disability status of welfare and war pensioners and to test the income conditions of the beneficiaries. Random controls were carried out and results were striking: about 25% of the welfare pensioners sampled for control had disability degrees lower than those required by the law and some 10% of war pensioners had incomes exceeding the limit foreseen for those benefits.

The new procedures adopted since 1996 proved effective in that they stopped the rapid increase in the expenditures for welfare pensions that had emerged since at least 1984 and later even curbed the number of (presumably unwarranted) recipients.

2.2 Other social security schemes

No relevant changes in unemployment legislation took place during the period. True, in the 1980s and in the early 1990s special laws enlarged the share of workers eligible for special unemployment benefits due to industrial crises, but these decisions did not constitute a true reform since they were adopted on an *ad hoc* basis to solve specific economic crises. No change was introduced during the period in the level of benefits, while the average payment period was increased for some special occupational groups more at risk of unemployment (e.g. agricultural sector, mechanical and iron industry). A general reform of unemployment benefits aiming at the introduction of a minimum income for the long-term unemployed is currently under discussion.

Relevant changes in early retirement pensions were adopted only after 1992. After the 1992 Social Security Reform Act, early retirement was temporarily suspended and eligibility rules for seniority pensions were drastically changed in 1995. Before 1995, seniority pensions were accessible to workers in the private sector with at least 35 years of contributions, the average benefit being around 60-70% of the last wage. In the public sector workers could retire even earlier, with as few as 15 years of contribution (for married women) or 20-25 years (for men), benefits in this case being about 30-40% of the last wage. In some cases, seniority pensioners could combine those incomes with labour incomes, and benefits were calculated according to the general rules without any reduction due to the young age at retirement of beneficiaries.

After 1992, a proportional pension reduction for people retiring with fewer than 35 years of seniority was introduced to stop the increase in the number of seniority retirements in the public sector by persons who were generally very young (so-called *baby pensions/pensioners*).

Since 1995, the new seniority pension rules described in the preceding sections (40 years of seniority or both 57 years of age and 35 years of seniority) have applied, while seniority pensions are supposed to disappear after the year 2010.

The new pension system will be adopted only gradually. Workers with at least 15 years of seniority in 1992 will continue to come under the old rules, while only those starting to work in 1996 or later will come completely under the new system when they retire (the rest of the workforce being in an intermediate state). However, when the new rules are fully in force, flexible retirement between 57 years and 65 years for both sexes will be introduced. People retiring early (e.g. at 57) will benefit from the pension for a longer period than people retiring later (say, at 65). For this reason the former will have to accept a proportional cut in the value of their benefit, depending on their life expectancy at retirement.

3   Disabled and disability expenditure in Italy

When analysing data on the disabled or disability expenditure in Italy, it is important to define exactly what one is talking about, since numbers can change abruptly from one case to the next. At the same time, it is useful to consider all kinds of disability benefits because, especially until not so long ago, the boundaries between the various forms were not so well defined: people often received more than just one benefit, and attempts to exclude some beneficiaries from one kind of payment resulted in an increased number of people tapping other viable sources. In particular, as we will document below, since 1984 social security disability pensions (OADS type) have become much more difficult to obtain: however, while their number and amount started to decrease, especially for the population of working age (15-64), welfare disability pensions started to increase, finally resulting in an almost flat global trend of disability pensions and payments (to people of all ages), which displayed a clear downward tendency only recently.

As for social security (or OASD) disability pensions,[24] the number of beneficiaries in the working (15-64) age span has declined dramatically in recent years: from almost 3.5 million in 1980 to about 650 000 in 1998 (Figure 2). Since these are stock data, where momentum plays an important role, the abrupt decline is better appreciated in terms of new entrants: from over 230 000 by the mid-1970s to less than 5 000 by the end of the 1990s (Figure 3).

In both cases, there are practically as many women as men, which is surprising since women are underrepresented in the labour force: formerly (in 1975) they represented less than 30% of the total labour force and in spite of a sizeable relative and absolute increase they still account for less than 40% (Table 3).

Figure 2: Beneficiaries (aged 15-64) of Social Security disability pensions in Italy, 1975-1998

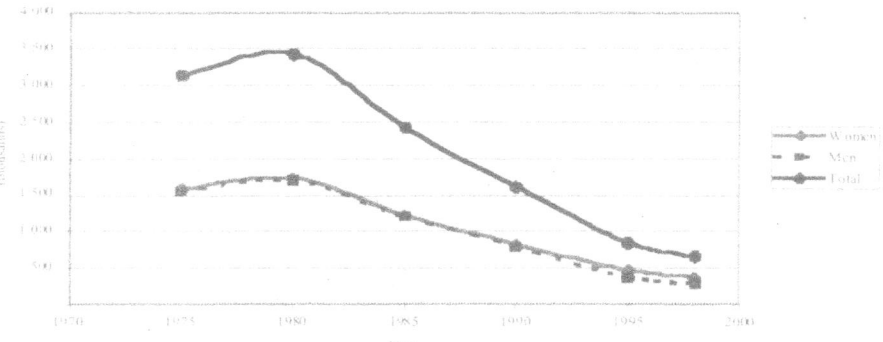

Figure 3: New beneficiaries (aged 15-64) of Social Security disability pensions in Italy, 1975-1998

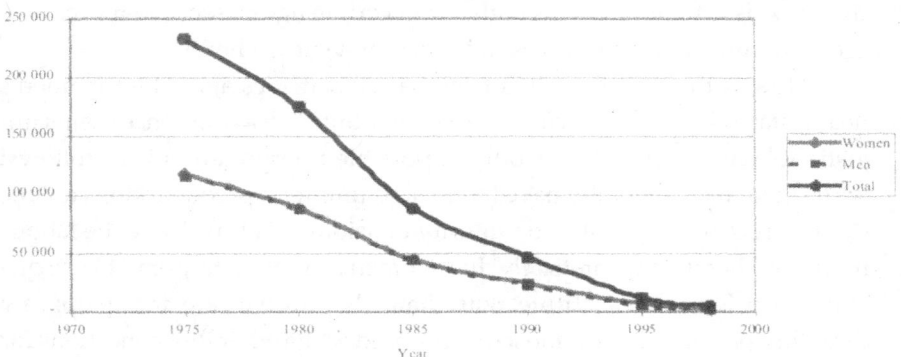

Table 3: Labour force and disability pensioners in Italy, by gender (age: 15-64)

	1975	1980	1985	1990	1995	1998
Labour force (stock) (thousands)						
Women	5 442	7 289	8 066	8 747	8 399	8 677
Men	13 803	14 442	14 753	14 740	14 018	14 158
Total	19 245	21 731	22 819	23 487	22 417	22 835
Disability pensioners (stock) (thousands)						
Women	1 578	1 725	1 220	820	470	368
Men	1 558	1 702	1 204	787	370	288
Total	3 136	3 428	2 425	1 607	840	655
New disability beneficiaries (yearly flux)						
Women	117 128	88 213	44 295	23 768	6 823	2 661
Men	115 579	87 047	43 710	22 832	5 371	2 080
Total	232 707	175 260	88 005	46 600	12 194	4 741
Rate of disability pensioners (stock)						
Women	29.0%	23.7%	15.1%	9.4%	5.6%	4.2%
Men	11.3%	11.8%	8.2%	5.3%	2.6%	2.0%
Total	16.3%	15.8%	10.6%	6.8%	3.7%	2.9%
Incidence of new disability pensioners (yearly flux)						
Women	2.15%	1.21%	0.55%	0.27%	0.08%	0.03%
Men	0.84%	0.60%	0.30%	0.15%	0.04%	0.01%
Total	1.21%	0.81%	0.39%	0.20%	0.05%	0.02%

Source: Istat.

So, the 'risk' of becoming disabled is much higher for women than for men, in terms both of stock (total disabled/workforce) and flow data (newly disabled/workforce; in both cases over the 15-64 age span) (Table 3). The relative 'risk' is roughly twice as high but in certain age classes (50-64 years) it grows to three to four times as high (data not shown here).

How is this possible? It is true that all statistics agree that women's health status is generally worse than men's, but such a difference seems unjustifiable in objective terms only. A possible interpretation is as follows: while men, who generally have longer and uninterrupted working careers, can resort more frequently to seniority pensions and thus leave the labour market earlier than theoretically due, women cannot so they tend to use disability pensions as a substitute. Both channels, however, are drying up: new disability pensions have almost disappeared while eligibility conditions for seniority pensions, as remarked in the previous sections, are becoming more and more stringent and the very possibility of accessing this side exit from the labour market should theoretically disappear in some ten years (or earlier if politically feasible).

It may be worth remarking at this stage that at least during the 1990s, the rate of rejection for disability pension applications has been relatively steady (and high: 70% of applications are rejected, as opposed to a rejection rate for pensions of other kind of about 35%). Thus, declining trends are brought about basically by a declining number of applicants, probably discouraged by the stricter requirements of the law.

Thus far we have considered only social security (or OASD) disability pensions. There are two other kinds of benefit to be considered, however. In 1998 (latest year for which data are currently available) almost 1.3 million work injury indemnities were paid, amounting to some 7 700 billion lire (0.4% of GDP). About 1.2 million payments went directly to the disabled, while the rest accrued to survivors (spouse or dependent children of a deceased worker). The 1.2 million injured workers may roughly be broken down by age groups as follows: 20% are aged 14-49 years, 10% 50-54 years, 12% 55-59 years, 15% 60-64 years, and 43% 65 years or more.

In 1995, figures were somewhat higher: about 1.8 million indemnities overall, roughly 1 million of which accruing to persons aged 15-64. On the other hand, welfare pensions, merely 400 000 in 1980, amounted to roughly 1.5 million in 1995. Of these, it can be estimated that about 1 million accrue to persons in the 15-64 age span. To summarize, there were some 7 million disability payments (of three kinds: social security, welfare and indemnities) in Italy in 1995, of which some 2.7 million benefited people in the 15-64 age span.

These figures are remarkably high: in the same year, a representative household survey carried out by the Bank of Italy (for different purposes) revealed that the disabled were about 3.3 million overall, and about 1.4 million were in the 15-64 age span. In Italy, there are therefore roughly twice as many disability payments as there are disabled: this explains why, since 1995, efforts have been made to make sure that in a not-so-remote future only the truly disabled receive assistance and in the form of just one kind of payment.

The data of the 1995 survey of the Bank of Italy also help us understand how disabilities affect people of different ages and sexes (Figure 4). Not surprisingly, disability risks grow with age and may become as high as 20% for those aged 65 or more. It should be noted, however, that disabilities are generally reported more frequently for men except in the oldest age group, where women seem to be more affected. This contrasts with what other statistics say (excess of women receiving disability pensions) and calls into question the true health status of men and women – and the quality of the Bank of Italy data with respect to disabilities.

Indications that disability pensions are (or at least were) used as a form of compensation for allegedly disadvantaged conditions of other kind also come from an analysis of their geographical distribution: the proportion of (social security) disabled in the South is more than twice as high as in the North, with the Centre lying somewhere in between (Table 4).[25]

Figure 4: Percentage disabled by sex and age group, Italy 1995

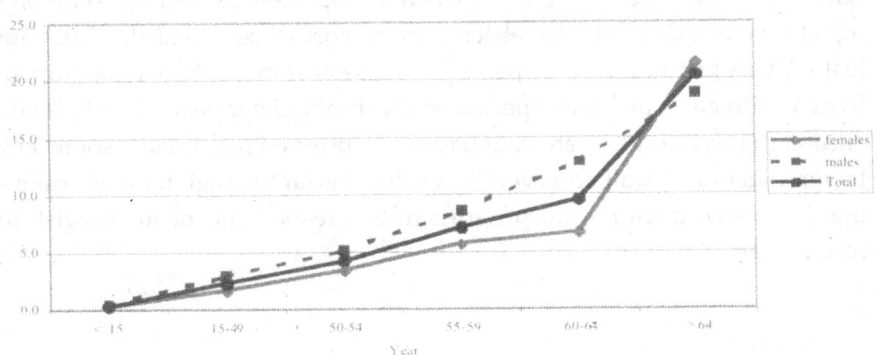

Source: Bank of Italy Household Survey, 1995.

Table 4: Incidence of disability and unemployment in Italy, by geographical area (age: 15-64)

	1975	1980	1985	1990	1995	1998
	Rate of disability pensioners (stock) (%)					
North	12.3%	11.2%	7.4%	4.5%	2.4%	1.8%
Center	18.0%	17.6%	11.5%	7.5%	4.1%	3.2%
South	20.4%	20.2%	14.1%	9.5%	5.7%	4.4%
Italy	16.0%	15.3%	10.4%	6.7%	3.7%	2.8%
	Rate of unemployment (stock) (%)					
North	1.0%	0.8%	2.0%	1.2%	2.9%	2.8%
Center	1.1%	0.7%	1.6%	1.6%	3.8%	3.7%
South	1.8%	1.4%	2.5%	3.3%	7.5%	7.4%
Italy	1.3%	1.0%	2.1%	2.0%	4.4%	4.3%

Source   Istat.

The existing differences in the productive structure (more agriculture and construction in the South) cannot possibly explain the discrepancy. A more likely explanation is the geographical distribution of unemployment, which principally affects the South and much less the Centre and the North (Table 4).

So, one possible (though admittedly negative) interpretation is that disability pensions were conceded to ease tensions on the labour market. But this is a subject for the next section.

One final note on work accidents is in order. Between 1995 and 1999 (latest year available), the trend of accidents reported to INAIL (and involving at least one day of forced absence from work) was practically flat, with just under one million cases per year. These cost more than 1 000 human lives and create some 30 000 permanently disabled per year (INAIL, 2000). Although this is lower than what had been observed previously (some 30% lower than in 1988), all observers agree that it is far too high for a self-defining developed country and progress in this respect has been sluggish in recent years.

4   Interpretation of trends, expectations for the future

Article 38 of the Italian Constitution (1946) states that

> All citizens unable to work and lacking the resources necessary for their existence shall be entitled to maintenance and social welfare.
> Workers shall be entitled to adequate insurance for their needs in case of accident, illness, disability, old age and involuntary unemployment.
> Disabled and handicapped persons shall be entitled to education and vocational training.

So the Italian Constitution foresees but implicitly distinguishes between welfare protecting citizens and social security protecting workers (who have paid contributions). However, the boundaries are far from clear, both theoretically (what is adequate? what is disability? and so on) and even more so empirically. Moreover, the current Italian statistical classification system tends in some cases to blur the distinction between disability and old-age benefits: disability pensions, for instance, remain such even after beneficiaries have reached retirement age.

At a cursory glance, statistics seem to indicate that Italy spends a lot (and, hence, also 'cares' a lot) for its disabled and injured persons: some 7 million pensions, amounting to roughly 57 billion lire (3% of GDP). However, if properly re-organized, for instance along the ESSPROS lines adopted by the new Italian system of statistical pension classification (SCPP; Baldacci and Milan, 1997), data show that more than half of the pensions formally accruing to the disabled actually go the elderly: they may be disabled (see below, however) but they would be insured anyway, either by social security (with an old-age pension) or by the welfare system (with a social pension). So what is actually taking place in most cases is a simple re-labelling of monetary flows accruing to the aged.

Another problem with the Italian 'disability package' is its misuse – or sometimes even abuse. The first studies showing (and denouncing), among other things, the biased use of the disability protection system date back to 1976 (Castellino, 1976); several other studies have followed since (e.g. Beltrametti, 1996; Baldacci and Milan, 1998). What these studies indicate is that before 1984 disability in several cases was very clearly a shortcut to early – sometimes very early – retirement, or in other words an improper substitute for life-long unemployment plus old-age benefits. In part, it was the law itself that justified such an approach, making reference to *earning*, not just *work* impairment. The studies mentioned and others on the same lines (and Table 4 above) did not use individual data but showed that 'disability' payments were highly concentrated in areas with high unemployment rates and notably in the South. It is true that these are also areas with (formerly) high emigration rates so that return migration of disabled workers may partly explain the distortion. Also, these are areas where 'risky' economic activities (especially agriculture and construction) prevail, which justifies part of the excess – although these cases should primarily affect work-injury indemnities rather than disability pensions. But these explanations can account for only a very small fraction of the excess: the rest was very clearly due to a distorted use of the system by which, sometimes with open fraud, a sort of compensation was accorded to economically deprived areas.

Since 1984, things have changed: the new law made explicit reference to *work* not just *earning* impairment as a basis for a disability pension. Moreover, apart from the totally disabled (100%), the principle was introduced that injured persons were to undergo three different medical checks before their disability status could be considered permanent: this allowed for possible cases of recovery but its main, though unconfessed, purpose was to make sure that claimants were really needy and that one inaccurate (or bribed) medical check would not transform a potential worker (with a temporary injury) into a permanent burden for society. Needless to say, saving money was another objective, because partial disability is compensated less than total disability.

The innovation, however, did not affect what had happened before: so two main effects emerged. The first was that the bulk of disability beneficiaries, with only very few new entrants, started to decline, although only slowly. There were still 5.4 million of them in 1980 and 3.5 million in 1997. Most of the beneficiaries, however, are now elderly: indeed, when limited to those of working age (15-64), numbers are very different: from 3.4 million in 1980 to just 0.7 million in 1998. On top of that, the flow of new entrants (aged 15-64) is still decreasing: from over 200 000 in 1980 to less than 100 000 in 1985 (immediately after the reform) to as few as 5 000 in 1998.

The second consequence is that the problem of misuse of the disability protection system, while not disappearing, has at least in part changed: instead of passing through the social security system (protection accorded to workers having paid at least five years of contributions, three of which in the last five years) abuse has in part moved towards the other available channel: welfare. There were only 0.4 million welfare pensions in 1980 but nearly 1.5 million in 1995, more than half of these accruing to people of working age. The outlays for these pensions tripled in real terms from 1975 to 1995, passing from 1 billion lire (0.1% of GDP) to 6.3 billion lire (0.3% of GDP), both because of the increased number of beneficiaries and because of the more and generous treatment accorded to each case, especially during the 1980s. It should be pointed out that conditions for a welfare disability pension are generally more stringent than those for social security disability: a disability of as much as 74% is required to be eligible for them as opposed to 67% under social security.

Since 1996, however, controls have tightened on these pensions as well: the very first sample check in 1996 indicated that some 25% of the welfare 'disabled' either were really not such or had incomes exceeding the admitted ceiling, and roughly the same percentage (25 to 30%) emerges whenever new samples are extracted and checked from this subgroup of the population. As a consequence, even welfare pensions have considerably slowed down in Italy in the last two to three years: for those aged 15-64, for instance, estimated outlays have scaled down from 6.3 to 5.5 billion lire (1995 to 1998).

According to all available evidence, these data reflect both objectively improved health status and enhanced capacity of control on the part of the responsible agency (INPS –National Social Security Institute for the social security part; Ministry of Internal Affairs for most of the rest). The health status of the population of working age, and workers in particular, has improved for a number of reasons. In the first place, economic activity has progressively moved away from the sectors most at risk (agriculture and construction and industrial activity in general) towards the service sector, where accidents are considerably rarer and not as damaging. Second, greater attention has been given to the issue of safety, both in the workplace and elsewhere: the steadily decreasing number of accidental deaths is a very clear indicator in this sense and one on which changing statistical definitions have relatively little influence. More generally, a number of studies have been carried out to test whether increased life expectancy goes along with improved life quality. Results are mixed with regard to the final years of life: it is not totally clear whether, at that point, we are merely 'adding years to our life, or also adding life to our years', as a commentator once put it. But in the active (15-64) age span there can be little doubt: life quality has improved.

However, what has proved most effective in curbing the number and outlays of disability pensions in Italy has not been improved life quality but improved control on old (welfare) beneficiaries and new (welfare and social security) claimants. This seems to be due, in good part, to the changed political climate, which has been brought about, amongst other things, by a very high and rapidly growing fiscal pressure, rightly interpreted as (at least in part) the consequence of past abuses, including those in the disability field. Technically speaking, improvements also depend on the fact that although the number of agencies issuing disability pensions is still high, rules and regulations have been progressively reduced to a uniform and common standard.

What the Italian experience seems to show therefore is that easy access to a given facility (disability benefits in this case, but several other examples would work equally well, like the national health service or seniority pensions) will soon lead to over-exploitation and abuse. Another lesson to be learned is that when there are two more or less parallel channels leading in the same direction (a disability benefit), it is of little use regulating only one of them (social security in this case), because people will soon try to tap the other source (welfare). The third conclusion is that once a mechanism is set in motion it is very hard to bring it to an immediate halt: all those who are already benefiting from it, although in some cases through extensive interpretations or abuse, will most likely continue to enjoy their privileges for the rest of their lives, which may mean 20 or 30 years. But even for new entrants, earlier rules, no matter how distorted, create an expectation that is generally very difficult to eradicate: the continuously decreasing number of new beneficiaries of social security pensions suggests that, apart from improved safety conditions in general, doctors have adapted only slowly to the new rules formally in force since 1984.

The history of the last 20 years of disability pensions in Italy, along with the fact that public deficits are now under stricter scrutiny than they were in the past (because of the enormous public debt in Italy – slightly higher than the GDP – and because of the fiscal rules of the European Union) suggest that in the future the problem of the abuse of disability pension should diminish and might even virtually disappear, thus leaving some room for a more adequate treatment of those who are really needy. Currently, in fact, also because of the large number of beneficiaries, disability benefits are discouragingly low: OADS pensions, for instance, average less than 1 million lire per month (less than 500 euros) gross, that is some 30% of an average salary. Recourse to several pensions and, especially, reliance on the family network has thus far protected the (really) disabled, but both channels are drying up. Since 1995, in principle, only one pension has been (or is going to be) available for each disabled person, while the family, though traditionally and culturally still strong in Italy, has been eroded in the last 15-20 years by several factors, including low fertility, increased female work participation, decreasing marriage and increasing divorce rates.

One reason for concern should not be totally overlooked, though: early (including seniority) retirements have recently become an important way out of the labour market in Italy and it can be argued that this is one of the reasons why workers have had less frequent recourse to disability facilities – which, it may be worth noticing, are tapped especially after the age of 50. The 1992 and, even more so, the 1995 and 1997 pension reforms in Italy,[26] however, tend to conflict with this tendency: early retirements of all kinds should virtually disappear and only ordinary retirement in the age span 57 to 65 should take place. This will create a potential for people who, especially in the case of labour market difficulties, could lobby to have another side and easy exit towards an early pension, however labelled – be it seniority, disability or whatever.

Thus, the struggle between the general public interest in an orderly access to whatever benefit is foreseen by the law in favour of the needy and several private interests, each one trying to obtain special treatment for his/her own allegedly special case, is not over yet.

Notes

1. In the rest of our contribution we will disregard all forms of payments related to the war-injury programme. It should be noted, however, that contrary to what might be imagined after 55 years of peace, war injury compensation is far from irrelevant in our country: in 1998, for instance, there were still some 475 000 war pensions, costing some 2 400 billion lire (1.2 billion euros), that is more than 0.1% of GDP. These figures include those injured in wars after World War II, e.g. Italian soldiers acting as 'blue helmets' for the UN peacekeeping force, or medical and religious personnel injured in war zones all over the world. About 10% of beneficiaries, who are often survivors (wives and children in particular), are estimated to be between 15 and 64. This provision, like all welfare provisions in Italy, is means-tested to exclude individuals with yearly incomes above a given threshold, which currently amounts to some 8 million lire (or 4 000 euros) per year (but some kinds of income are excluded from the computation: for instance, social pension (see below), interest on government bonds and imputed rent (if a person owns the dwelling he/she lives in). War-injury related payments are always included in statistics on pensions and, broadly speaking, disability pensions in Italy.

2. Respectively named 'assegno di *invalidità*' (for partial disability) and 'pensione di *inabilità*' (for total disability). However, 'invalidity' and 'disability' do not seem to have consistently distinct meanings in Italian (or in Italian disability laws, for that matter) and we will only use the term 'disability' here.

3. Indemnities for war injuries constitute an exception in this respect: they are labelled as welfare but are portable to survivors.

4. Although operating locally, these commissions are centrally appointed (by INPS or INAIL or other responsible agencies) and, at least in principle, follow the objective evaluation criteria described in specific, legally-valid disability tables. In all cases, the official recognition of a disability status is a centrally controlled decision taken by the responsible agency itself.

5. Having worked (and paid contributions) for at least five years, at least three of them in the last five years.

6. But this change is only of statistical relevance, the amount of the pension being practically unaffected.

7. This minimum pension for retired workers (10 million lire per year, less than 5 000 euros) is different from and higher than the welfare minimum (8 million lire per year, less than 4 000 euros), which, as discussed below, is granted to all elderly persons (over 65) without income of their own.

8. These years are calculated as the sum of years of contribution (seniority) and the number of years spent as a beneficiary of the allowance.

9. The assumption here is that the disabled person would have kept on working until the legal retirement age had the disabling accident not occurred.

10. In 1978, however, the National Health Service came into being, which extended (basically) free health coverage to all Italian residents. So the role of INAIL in this respect has been somewhat reduced to (a) contributing to the NHS and (b) compensating the worker for those expenses not covered by the NHS.

11. Other categories of workers are partly insured against work accidents: they get a 'privileged pension' – which means that an extra amount of varying (albeit generally limited) importance is added to their ordinary (disability or old-age) pension.

12   If a worker gets sick (not because of a work accident or a work-related illness) and cannot go to work, he/she gets paid (by INPS) but this provision is classified within the health assistance programme, not within the disability protection programme in Italy.
13   Until 1998, provisions of this kind were also granted by the Ministry of the Interior.
14   For instance, all blind persons of any age who do not benefit from any disability pensions beyond the base, flat-rate pension (if they are relatively poor), also receive a special monthly allotment called *indennità di accompagnamento* (or allowance for an accompanying person), which is worth mentioning because it is the only example of a welfare provision that is not means-tested.
15   Old people having some sort of income of their own receive only what is necessary to raise them to this 'minimum' threshold.
16   Longer periods can be covered by other *ad hoc* unemployment benefits.
17   Or, at least, have paid special extra contributions for eligible periods (e.g. years spent at university).
18   Indeed, expenditure of public money is foreseen only 'in cases where strictly necessary and for periods as short as possible' (article 5, paragraph 1h).
19   Another issue that will likely emerge is that of admission criteria: since these services are financed locally, a difference will probably be made between the residents (and possibly those who have been resident and have paid local taxes for a minimum number of years) and the rest of the population.
20   They did apply, actually, but only for those jobs explicitly reserved for the disabled: see further in the text.
21   Companies with at least 35 dependent workers were supposed to have at least 15% of them selected from the 'protected' categories – which included orphans, widows and disabled. Both the old and the new law apply to all kinds of employers, public or private, in any branch of economic activity.
22   One place if the dependent workers are 15 to 35; two places if they are 36 to 50; 7% if they are over 51. Note, however, that 50-60% of these workers can be chosen by the employer (the rest being provided by local public-work agencies), whereas formerly this practice (of selecting preferred individuals among the disabled) was explicitly prohibited.
23   Article 1 details who is to be considered disabled: this rather long list includes those who have at least 45% disability (down to 33% if due to a work injury); those who have suffered from war injuries; the blind and deaf mutes.
24   In this section, for the sake of simplicity we will not distinguish between full disability pensions and partial disability allowances.
25   An analysis by single administrative region reveals even more marked anomalies: cf. Beltrametti (1996) or Baldacci and Milan (1998).
26   In 1997, a few relatively minor adjustments were introduced to equalize treatment and accelerate the transition from the old regime to the new rules foreseen by the 1995 reform.

References

Aquila, C./Pracanica, A./Pracanica, G. (1994) *Invalidità, sordomutismo e cecità civile*. Milano: Pirola.

Baldacci, E./Lugaresi, S. (1995) *The New Pension System in Italy: Gainers and Losers under Different Macroeconomic Assumptions*. Documenti n. 4. Roma: Istat.

Baldacci, E./Milan, G. (1997) *La classificazione delle pensioni per funzione e centro di spesa: metodologia e definizioni*. Documenti n. 19. Roma: Istat.

Baldacci, E./Milan, G. (1998) 'Gli effetti di redistribuzione territoriale della spesa pensionistica di invalidità', in: Rossi, N. (ed.), *Il lavoro e la sovranità sociale*, 1996-97. Bologna: Il Mulino.

Beltrametti, L. (1996) 'Le pensioni di invalidità in Italia: effetti redistributivi tra le regioni italiane (1951-1993)', *Politica economica* 12 (3): 391-403.

Bonati, G./De Ritis, F./Gremigni, P./Montemarano, A./Rizzardi, R./Rodà, G. (1995) *La riforma delle pensioni*. Milano: Pirola.

Castellino, O. (1976) *Il labirinto delle pensioni*. Bologna: Il Mulino.

Ceccato, F. (1998) *La classificazione funzionale dei trattamenti pensionistici*, Documenti, Istat n. 19. Roma: Istat.

Eurostat (1981) *European System of Integrated Social Protection Statistics (ESSPROS). Methodology*, vol. 1.

Eurostat (1992) *Digest on Statistics on Social Protection in Europe. Partial disability/Disability*.

Ferrera, M. (1993) *Modelli di solidarietà*. Bologna: Il Mulino.

Franco, D. (1994) *L'espansione della spesa pubblica in Italia*. Bologna: Il Mulino.

INAIL (2000) *Rapporto Annuale 1999*. Roma.

IRS (1995) *La spesa pubblica per l'assistenza in Italia*. Milano: Franco Angeli.

Istat (1981) *I conti della protezione sociale 1975-79. Aspetti metodologici e prime elaborazioni*, Supplemento al Bollettino Mensile di Statistica, n. 8.

Istat (1996) *Rapporto Annuale. La situazione del Paese 1995*. Roma: IPZS.

Istat (1997) *Le pensioni di invalidità in Italia. Anni 1980-94*, Argomenti n. 8. Roma: Istat.

Istat (1998) *Rapporto Annuale. La situazione del Paese nel 1997*. Roma: Istat.

Istat (several years) *Trattamenti pensionistici*, Informazioni. Roma: Istat.

Istat, INPS (1998) *Il sistema pensionistico italiano: beneficiari e prestazioni*, Informazioni n. 91. Roma: Istat.

Kazepov, Yuri (1997) *Le politiche locali contro l'esclusione sociale*, Commissione di Indagine sulla povertà. Roma: IPZS.

Matteuzzi, M. (1996) *Strumenti di assistenza pubblica e politica sociale*, Note di lavoro n. 9605. Bologna: Prometeia.

Monacelli, D. (1998) 'Per una riforma dello stato sociale: le politiche di assistenza', *Politica economica* 14 (1): 97-153.

Negri, N./Saraceno, C. (1996) *Le politiche contro la povertà in Italia*. Bologna: Il Mulino.

OECD (1988) *Ageing of Population. The Social Policy Implications*. Paris: OECD.

Pizzuti, F.R./Rey, G.M. (1990), *Il sistema pensionistico. Un riesame*. Bologna: Il Mulino.

Russo, G. (1996) *Il calcolo delle pensioni*. Milano: Pirola.

Scalia, R. (1992) *Le pensioni di guerra*. Roma: CieRre edizioni.

Scorda, M. (1997) *L'invalidità civile nella vigente legislazione*. Roma: AMNIC.

CHAPTER 8

The Dutch Disability Experience

Leo Aarts and Philip R. de Jong

1 Introduction

Comprehensive European welfare states are facing hard times. The loss of productivity and the growing tax burden that are by-products of large social welfare systems are gradually eroding their popular support. While social equity is still a major goal of public policy in these countries, the real social costs of achieving it are now so high that even traditional supporters of the welfare state have begun to call for reform.

A country like the Netherlands, which was once looked upon as a model of the modern democratic welfare state, has come to acknowledge that more of the same is no longer possible. Like other European countries it experienced unprecedented postwar levels of transfer dependency and slow growth in the 1980s and early 1990s. It also had to come to terms with the competitive pressures of a single European market and the budget deficit restrictions that European Union members had to meet to satisfy the requirements for entry into the European Monetary Union in 1999.

To these social, economic and fiscal pressures must be added the less immediate but very real presence of ageing populations. The ageing baby boomers add a major long-term dimension to the growing public debate on the need to make existing social welfare systems more sustainable. In the Netherlands, changes in disability policy have been at the centre of this debate.

In the second half of the 1990s, a sustained policy of moderate wage growth combined with benefit cuts and stricter eligibility standards – which was started in 1982 – finally proved successful. Employment grew faster than anywhere else in continental Europe, and the official unemployment rate was nowhere as low as in the Netherlands. At the turn of the century, the Dutch economy was in good shape, the labour market was tight and the prospects were reasonable. But one issue remained unresolved: the numbers entering the Dutch disability scheme were growing again, and among the OECD countries the Dutch had one of the largest disability beneficiary populations.[1] According to OECD data 9% of the Dutch working age (20-64) population were disability beneficiaries in 1999. Only Poland had a higher prevalence.[2]

In this chapter we look into the Dutch disability problem. We first describe the Dutch social welfare system. Next, we discuss specific aspects of the Dutch sickness benefits and disability insurance schemes, how they were amended and why the numbers are growing again despite those amendments.

2   Social welfare programmes in the Netherlands

The Dutch social welfare system includes both insurance (contributory) and welfare (non-contributory) programmes. The insurance programmes flow from the vision of *Bismarck* – the designer of legislatively established insurance funds to cover *risques professionnels*. The welfare programmes flow from the vision of *Beveridge* – the designer of a national safety net to protect against poverty by covering more general *risques sociaux*.

These two types of programmes are administered and financed differently. Social insurance programmes mandate participation of legally defined groups, and are usually financed by compulsory contributions under a pay-as-you-go system. The insurance programmes are administered by institutions supervised by boards in which trade unions and employers' organizations are represented. Means-tested welfare programmes, on the other hand, are financed by general revenue, and administered by local governments. Insurance programmes can be further divided into national programmes, covering all residents, and programmes that only cover employees. Civil servants used to have their own arrangements but were integrated into the earnings-related insurance programmes that cover private sector workers in 1997.

The principle of solidarity and its legal counterpart – the constitutionally established responsibility of the State to protect its residents from poverty – is a hallmark of the Dutch social welfare system. This is achieved by two provisions of the system: wage replacement and minimum income guarantees. Wage replacement is based on mutual solidarity among employees and their employers to protect the employees' acquired standard of living. The wage-replacement programmes cover loss of earnings due to unemployment, sickness, or disability.

Flat benefit insurance programmes and means-tested welfare programmes safeguard the subsistence levels of all residents. Old-age insurance provides a flat benefit income to men and women aged 65 and over. Separate disability insurance programmes for the self-employed and for those whose handicap started before age 18 provide a flat benefit income for those of working age who suffer a health impairment. Survivor insurance provides flat benefits to the surviving spouse and dependent children. These have been means-tested since 1996. Unemployment insurance provides a wage-related benefit of limited duration to those who lose their jobs. Public assistance provides protection to those with insufficient income and to those whose unemployment coverage runs out. A new scheme, introduced in 1998, which integrated various existing programmes, aims at support and vocational rehabilitation of handicapped residents by supplying subsidies and in-kind transfers.

In addition to income maintenance, medical expenses, including medical rehabilitation, are also covered by insurance-based programmes. The health costs of private sector employees earning below EUR 29 200 per year in 1999 are covered by the health cost insurance programme. Exceptional medical expenses, such as long-term institutionalization, are also covered by public insurance. Finally, a quarterly childcare allowance is financed by general revenue.

2.1 The social minimum

The social minimum is defined as the amount of money necessary to provide for basic needs. Basic needs are assumed to depend on household composition. The social minimum is linked to the after-tax statutory minimum wage. It establishes the level of the safety net in the social welfare system. In 2001, the social minimum for a household consisting of a couple with or without a child is 100% of the after-tax minimum wage, or about EUR 920 per month. For single-parent families the social minimum is between 70 and 90% of this amount; and for single persons it is between 50 and 70%, depending on need. While the purchasing power of the statutory minimum wage is usually adjusted in accordance with the average wage index, social welfare benefits follow the minimum wage.[3]

2.2 Sick pay

When a Dutch worker is unable to perform his or her job because of illness or injury, irrespective of its cause, he or she is entitled to sick pay. Sick pay replaces 70% of gross wage earnings, but most collective bargaining agreements between employers and employees stipulate that sickness benefits are supplemented to the level of net earnings. Sick pay ends after 12 months.

Since 1996, employers have been fully responsible for financing sick pay. They may reinsure their sick pay liability with a private insurer but are not obliged to do so. Employers are mandated to contract with a private provider of occupational health services to manage absenteeism. After the onset of a lasting disability the employer may be unable to offer a commensurate job, for instance if the company is small and the range of jobs is restricted. Because the occupational health service has a contract with the current employer, it usually cannot mediate towards placement in a new firm. It then transfers the employer to the public social insurance agency whose task it is to help find a suitable new job.

Before 1996, all sickness benefits were administered by the same public agencies that run disability and unemployment insurance (for details, see below).

2.3 Disability benefits

Under the Dutch ruling any illness or injury entitles an insured person to a disability benefit after a mandatory waiting period of 12 months. While other OECD countries distinguish people with disabilities by whether the impairment occurred on the job or elsewhere, only the *consequence* of impairment is relevant for the Dutch disability insurance programme.

Compensation for loss of earning capacity due to long-term or permanent disablement is provided by three separate disability insurance programmes targeting different social groups. The first, and by far the biggest, programme covers employees and awards wage-related benefits. The other two address the self-employed and those handicapped from youth. These provide flat rate, social minimum, benefits from age 18 onwards. Otherwise, the design and administration of these two programmes are similar to the wage-related programme.

The degree of disablement is assessed by considering the worker's residual earning capacity. Since 1994, capacity has been defined by the earnings flowing from any job commensurate with the claimant's residual capabilities as a percentage of pre-disability usual earnings. The degree of disablement, then, is the complement of the residual earning capacity and defines the benefit level. Before 1994, only jobs that were compatible with a claimant's training and work history could be taken into consideration. The medical definition of disability has also been tightened: under the new ruling, the causal relationship between impairment and disablement has to be objectively assessable.

Wage-related benefits are based on age and earnings. Previously, coverage did not depend on age as an approximation of work history or any other count of insurance coverage years. This meant that every member of the population at risk was fully covered. When an applicant was found fully (80-100%, see below) disabled, the statutory replacement rate was equal to that of sickness benefits, i.e. 70% of before-tax earnings. As part of the reforms of 1994, the amount and entitlement period of the earnings-related disability benefit is now dependent on age to simulate a contribution years requirement (for details, see below).

Partial benefits can be combined with labour earnings up to the level of the pre-disability wage. If recipients of a partial benefit are unable to find gainful employment they are entitled to a partial unemployment benefit. Combination of disability and unemployment benefits never replaces more than 70% of earnings lost.

The Dutch disability programme for employees is unique in that it distinguishes seven disability categories from less than 15%, 15-25% disabled, and so on to 80-100% disabled. The minimum degree of disability giving entitlement to benefits is a 15% loss of earning capacity. Benefit amounts depend on the degree of disability: a 20% disablement gives entitlement to a benefit of 14% of covered earnings; 30% disablement to 21%, and so on. Disability benefits are capped by a maximum amount of covered earnings which equals about EUR 36 300 per annum (in 1999). This is also the maximum amount of income taxable for disability (and unemployment) insurance.

The other two disability schemes – for self-employed and handicapped youth – have six disability categories: they skip the first category so that entitlement starts at a degree of disability of 25%.

Until 2002, the Dutch disability plan differed from other national programmes, not only because it has no separate work injury scheme and has a more elaborate system of partial benefits, but also because it was run by social insurance agencies under contract with the National Institute of Social Insurance. Each firm was directed to one of these agencies by law. Each agency, therefore, holds a legally protected sectoral monopoly. In 1999, after a drastic revision of previous plans, the current Cabinet proposed to replace these agencies by one public service in 2002. This is the (national) Social Insurance Institute (UWV) which administers the Disability and Unemployment Insurance benefit programmes.

2.4 Unemployment benefits

Coverage for unemployment insurance benefits requires gainful employment for at least 26 weeks before unemployment. Unemployment insurance benefit amounts depend on two work history requirements: a 'weeks' requirement and a 'years' requirement. The first requirement stipulates that one should have been employed for at least 26 weeks during the 39 weeks preceding unemployment. The 'years' requirement states that the employee must have been employed for at least four years during the five years preceding the year of becoming unemployed. If only the 'weeks' requirement is met, entitlement is restricted to a flat benefit at the social minimum level for six months at most. If both requirements are met the unemployment benefit is 70% of before-tax pre-unemployment earnings. Duration of these earnings-related benefits depends on a combination of age and work record in the past five years, with a minimum of six months for those below age 23 and a maximum of five years for those over age 59.

Apart from a work history requirement, an unemployed worker is only eligible for a benefit if the unemployment is not at the applicant's fault. Continued entitlement requires (proof of) active job search and the willingness to accept all suitable job offers. Whether a particular job offer is considered suitable depends on a worker's education, work history, age, previous income, residence and length of unemployment.

The law is ambiguous regarding these criteria. Hence, what is suitable is often determined by the courts. As a rule, the longer the spell of unemployment the broader the set of jobs that are considered suitable. General economic and social conditions may also be considered. Lay-offs are subject to the approval of public employment administrators. In general, employers will not be permitted to lay off a worker unless the job – not the worker – can be proven to be redundant or unless personal work relations have been seriously damaged.

Unemployment insurance is administered by the same Social Insurance Institute that runs the disability insurance scheme. A separate body of Public Employment Service agencies is responsible for supporting job search activities and investments in employability through schooling and subsidized employment.

For those who are not entitled to unemployment insurance benefits, or who exhaust their entitlement, social assistance is available. This is a welfare – or social safety net – programme at the subsistence level as defined by the social minimum. Every job-seeking resident over 21 is entitled to these benefits, independent of work history. They are fully means-tested. To obtain and keep eligibility, an unemployed worker must register at a local branch of the Public Employment Service and be willing to accept any job. Social assistance is administered by municipalities under the supervision of the Ministry of Social Affairs. It is paid for out of the government budget.

2.5 Early retirement

Dutch early retirement programmes have no statutory basis; they emerged as an element of collective bargaining agreements between trade unions and employers in 1975. Their original purpose was to increase employment opportunities for unemployed youths by encouraging the early retirement of older workers. But during the 1980s, early retirement was increasingly used by older workers as an alternative to unemployment or disability programmes for exiting the labour force. What started as a solution to the youth unemployment problem became a very popular exit path for older workers, subsidized by their younger colleagues through pay-as-you-go.

All civil servants are covered by early retirement programmes, as are about 70% of private employees, especially those in large firms. Eligibility criteria differ from industry to industry. The average minimum age of eligibility in most industries is 60. Eligibility also depends on job tenure. Under most programmes, a worker must have at least ten years of tenure with the firm. In general the after-tax benefit-wage ratios are about 90%. Hence, replacement rates are higher than those under social insurance. Like disability benefits, early retirement benefits end at age 65 when the retired worker enters the old-age pension system.

The tremendous growth in early retirement plans in the past, the expected fiscal pressure of an ageing workforce and benefits being paid out of pay-as-you-go funds called for changes in these actuarially unbalanced programmes. An increasing number of these – collectively bargained – plans are now being transformed into capital-funded flexible pension schemes with a much closer link between contributions and pension rights.

3 Selected aspects of the Dutch sick pay and disability insurance programmes

3.1 Disability assessments

There is strict separation between medical doctors who treat the sick and disabled and the gatekeepers who check the legitimacy of their claims to the sickness and disability programmes. This separation is meant to protect both the independence of the gatekeepers and the confidentiality of the relation between patients and their treating physicians.

As a consequence, the health status and prognosis of a worker who reports sick is checked by a medical examiner who works for an occupational health service (OHS) contracted by the employer of the sick worker.

Disability insurance claims are adjudicated by teams consisting of a specialized medical examiner and a vocational expert. They jointly determine the degree and permanency of disability and the worker's rehabilitative potential. These experts are employed by the Social Insurance Institute.

3.2 Labour market considerations in disability assessment

Disability benefit adjudicators, using the definition of disability in the appropriate disability programme, often find it difficult to make assessments within the discrete disability categories laid down in law. Theoretically, estimates of remaining earning capacities have to be made on the basis of a claimant's medical and vocational characteristics and their impact on all suitable jobs, whether such jobs are actually available or not. Theoretical assessments, however, diverge from actual earning capacities if suitable jobs are not made available to persons with partial disabilities. Sometimes employers discriminate against partially disabled people or, during economic downturns, may be reluctant to employ them.

A second problem of disability assessment, then, is to determine whether a person with a partial disability is unemployed because of impairment or because of an inextricable combination of impairment, discrimination and economic conditions. Before the 1987 social welfare reform, the law recognized the potential discrepancy between theoretical and actual earning capacities. It stipulated that adjudicators, in their assessments of the degree of disability, should take account of the difficulties that persons with partial disabilities might experience in finding commensurate employment. This legal provision is usually referred to as the "labour market consideration" in the two disability programmes.

In practice, however, accurate assessment of impairment and unemployment turned out to be difficult. In 1973, the insurance agencies solved this administrative problem by assuming that poor employment opportunities resulted from discriminatory behaviour, unless the contrary could be proven. The ensuing administrative practice was to treat partially disabled applicants as if they were fully disabled. This interpretation of the law made an accurate assessment of theoretical earning capacity unnecessary, as a minimum earnings loss of 15% was sufficient to entitle a person to full benefits.

The result was an administrative culture that stressed income maintenance at the expense of rehabilitation and economic independence. The social partners running the insurance agencies considered these procedures to be in conformity with their group interests. Employers found this a relatively easy and cheap way to release low-productivity or redundant workers. Trade unions found it a means of providing adequate income for people with severe disabilities and a generous unemployment and early retirement option for workers with health complaints that were difficult to verify.

As a consequence of these liberal procedures, the full award rate increased steadily until 1990. In 1986, the year before the 1987 social welfare reforms were enacted, the share of new disability beneficiaries declared fully disabled and receiving a full award of 70% of gross earnings had increased to 88%. Only 12 % were awarded partial benefits. After a series of changes that were effected in the first half of the 1990s, the share of partial awards went up to 43% in 2001.

3.3 Rehabilitation

When the disability insurance programme was initiated in 1967, claims were adjudicated by a separate Joint Medical Service using the fine grid of seven disability categories to meet explicit rehabilitative aims. The Explanatory Memorandum that accompanied the new Disability Insurance Act stated that disabled workers would be provided benefits according to their loss of earnings capacity and that the Joint Medical Service would help find them employment commensurate with their residual capabilities. In this way, it was hoped that people with a disability could return to the workforce despite of their impairments.

Macro-economic labour market forces frustrated this noble aim. An increasing supply of youths and married women and a very inflexible wage structure put heavy pressure on the Dutch economy's ability to create jobs. In response, the disability programme became an easy and generous early retirement programme for redundant labour. In contrast to other countries with similarly comprehensive disability systems, such as Germany and Sweden, income security started to take precedence over job security in the Netherlands. One of the goals of the 1987 social welfare reforms was to redress this bias in Dutch disability policy by eliminating the legal basis for using labour market considerations in the evaluation process.

If used as intended, the Dutch partial benefit system, together with a broad variety of rehabilitative instruments, might have encouraged the re-employment of workers with disabilities. For instance, a set of in-kind provisions is meant to support job accommodation and training costs to promote re-employment of workers with disabilities. But for lack of mandates that force disabled employees and their employers to use these re-employment instruments, spending on vocational rehabilitation is low. In 1996,

EUR 6.35 million was spent on provisions to support the employability of workers with disabilities, a mere 0.5% of the total disability budget of EUR 9.5 billion. The comparable German percentage of the total budget is 4.2%. In Belgium the comparable figure is 1.4%.

In 1986 the Handicapped Workers' Employment Act was enacted. This act contained a number of measures promoting the re-entry of workers with disabilities into the labour force. Employers were mandated to accommodate job demands and work conditions for employees with disabilities. The employer was entitled to financial support for making such accommodations. In addition, it required employers to pay workers with disabilities the same wage rates received by other employees in similar employment. However, if an employee with disabilities proved incapable of equivalent performance, employers could be given permission by the Social Insurance Agency to reduce wages proportionally. These agencies could grant firms a wage dispensation to compensate for productivity losses they might incur when employing workers with partial disabilities. The act also established a disabled employment quota of between 3 and 7%. This quota system was not enforced.

In July 1998 the Handicapped Workers' Employment Act was replaced by the Reintegration of Work Handicapped Persons Act (REA), adding wage subsidies to the existing set of rehabilitation instruments. Work-handicapped persons are all those who:
- have a disability that reduces their productive capacity, and
- are entitled to a disability benefit or have lost their entitlement fewer than five years previously;
- are entitled to an in-kind provision or subsidy to maintain or restore their productivity, or have lost their entitlement to such provision fewer than five years previously;
- belong to the group targeted by the Sheltered Work Provision Act;
- do not belong to any of the above-mentioned groups but have been assessed (through medical examination at a social insurance agency) as being work-handicapped.

The status of work-handicapped is allowed for five years, after which it has to be re-established. REA excludes all those work-handicapped persons who have an employment contract, unless they have reached the 12-months sickness limit, with or without a disability insurance award, and those who have not reached this limit but are unable to resume with their current employer.

1. REA covers expenses incurred by companies to maintain or restore the productivity of workers who have the status of work-handicapped. Such subsidies may cover schooling, training and (job) coaching; accommodation of the workplace or the work conditions.
2. Companies can get a replacement subsidy of NLG 8 000 if a worker who is unable to do his old job is placed in a new, commensurate job.
3. Companies that hire a work-handicapped worker can get a total subsidy of NLG 24 000, spread over three years: NLG 12 000 in the first year of employment; NLG 8 000 in the second year, and NLG 4 000 in the third year.
4. If a company can prove that the cost of maintenance or restoration of the productivity of a work-handicapped worker surpasses the standard subsidies mentioned before, it can apply for a tailor-made package; this package may also include a wage subsidy covering one third of the gross wage.
5. In principle, a work-handicapped worker is entitled to an equivalent wage; however, if his productivity is lower than that of an able-bodied worker in an equivalent job, the company may ask for wage dispensation – paying a lower wage; the wage reduction may be compensated by a partial disability benefit.
6. Sickness benefits for work-handicapped persons are collectively covered; in other words, companies that hire a work-handicapped person do not bear the financial risk of continued payment of (part of the) wage when he/she is sick.
7. Companies whose share of work-handicapped persons is larger than 5% of the payroll are exempt from paying the base disability insurance premium for those workers. If this share is 4 or 3%, they are awarded an exemption of two thirds or one third, respectively, of the base premium.

Social insurance agencies can now contract individual reinsertion plans with private rehabilitation service organizations. These plans are financed out of the REA budget and cover both the reintegration instruments and the effort of the rehabilitation service. In 1999 – the first full year in which REA was in operation – about 48 000 reinsertion programmes were contracted; 72% of those concerned sickness and disability beneficiaries; the others were unemployed disabled (with or without an unemployment transfer income). In other words, plans were made for about 3% of the disability beneficiary population.

As of April 2002, the responsibilities of the sick employee, his/her employer, and the occupational health service are legally specified, and mandate a structured approach to early intervention. After a maximum of six weeks of absence the occupational (health service) doctor has to make a first assessment of the medical cause and the functional limitations and give a prognosis regarding work resumption. On the basis of these data, employer and employee draft a vocational rehabilitation programme in which they specify an aim (resumption of current/other job under current/accommodated conditions) and the steps needed to reach that aim. They appoint a case-manager, and fix dates at which the programme should be evaluated, and modified if necessary. The rehabilitation programme should be ready by the 8th week of sickness. It is binding for both parties, and one may summon the other when proven negligent. After 35 weeks of sickness the Social Insurance Administration sends a Disability Insurance application form to the sick employee. Disability Insurance claims are only considered admissible if they are accompanied by a rehabilitation report, containing the original rehabilitation plan, and an assessment as to why the plan has not (yet) resulted in work resumption.

Employment regulations in the Netherlands are meant to encourage the continued employment of people with disabilities. A disabled employee may be dismissed only if employment in his or her current job or in alternative work within the company would put an unreasonable financial strain on the employer. An absolute dismissal ban is in force for the first two years following the onset of a disability. At the end of this period the employer is usually granted permission to dismiss a worker. A comparison among 10 European welfare states, the United States and Japan shows that the Dutch system of job protection during sickness is much stronger than in any of the 12 countries (Bakkum and Desczka, 2002).

Industrial pension plan policies, however, offer strong incentives to workers who have become disabled on the job to leave the workforce, since the accrual of pension rights related to the last job continues even after the person enters the disability rolls. In addition, most pension plans do not require disability beneficiaries to pay pension premiums. Such contract rules discourage re-entry into the labour market by creating a gap in pension accrual rights. Until 1999, strict labour contract rules also discouraged employers from hiring people with disabilities, because they permitted only a very short probationary period and offered strong dismissal protection for workers with fixed contracts.

Finally, to encourage re-employment, the Government provides sheltered workshops for those who are difficult to employ in the regular job market. In 1998, about 90 000 persons (1.3% of the Dutch labour force) were employed by these workshops. Although disability beneficiaries are not obliged to accept such employment, almost 50 000 (5.5% of all beneficiaries) do; 44% of them have been disabled from birth, e.g. as a result of Down's syndrome. Sheltered workshop wages are, in general, higher than full disability benefits.

4 Recent amendments

4.1 Benefit cuts

Since August 1993, disability has been more strictly defined (see above), and the disability status of all beneficiaries who were under 45 at that time has been reviewed according to the new standards. These reviews affected about 30% of the 1995 beneficiary volume and were completed in 1998. In 1994 and 1995, 91 500 beneficiaries under the age of 40 were reviewed; 29% of those reviewed had their benefits terminated, and 16% were reclassified in a lower disability category and saw their benefits reduced accordingly. According to a sample taken at the end of 1995, one year after the reviews, 23% of those who had suffered a loss of benefit income had increased their work effort. More specifically, among those 54% who were not in paid employment at the time of the review, 30% held a job one year later. Most of the others were still dependent on some form of transfer income. These results show that the reviews have been successful in reducing the beneficiary volume but less so in increasing the work effort of those who had a full award before they were re-examined using the stricter rules.

Under the new benefit calculation system, which became effective under the same law as the stricter eligibility standards, the disability benefit period is divided into two chronologically linked parts. The first is a short-term wage-related benefit, which uses, as before, the pre-disability wage as the basis for calculating benefits. The duration of this wage-related benefit depends on age at the onset of disablement. It varies from zero for those under 33 to six years for those whose disability started at age 58 or beyond.

The second part is a follow-up benefit with a lower income base and hence a lower replacement rate with respect to the pre-disability wage. During the follow-up period, the income base for benefit calculation is the minimum wage *plus* a supplement depending on age at onset according to the formula: 2% times [age at onset − 15] times [wage − minimum wage].

The new benefit rules meant a sharp break with a quarter century of disability entitlement to wage-related benefits of unlimited duration. Age now serves as a proxy for work history, or "insurance years", introducing a quasi-pension element into the disability system. The reduction in government-provided disability insurance has generated a lively market in which private insurers compete with corporate and industry pension funds to fill the gap between the old system, with a statutory replacement rate of 70%, and the new calculation scheme with age-dependent replacement rates. Private coverage of these supplements is capital-funded and financed by premiums that are differentiated according to risk at the level of individual workers or firms. Specific firms and even complete branches of industry sign collective bargaining agreements that readjust the gap between the old and new replacement rate so that a majority of employees are covered by such gap insurance. The new supplements replaced additions to the previously prevailing statutory replacement rate of 70%, which led to effective benefits that covered up to 100% of lost earnings for many employees. All in all for most workers the resulting replacement rates are lower now than they used to be before the 1993 amendments.

Employers showed a surprisingly strong willingness to purchase gap coverage. Apparently, their stated interest in reducing labour costs was outweighed by their desire to maintain a generous exit option for their redundant workers. The eagerness of private insurers to offer supplementary coverage is less surprising. After all, the new benefit calculation formula implies that younger and better-paid workers face a lower replacement rate. In other words, groups with a low disability risk are hardest hit by these cuts. Under such favourable self-selection conditions, coverage of these cuts up to the original 70% replacement, or even higher, is an attractive proposition for private insurers.

4.2 Privatization of sickness and disability benefits

Sick pay

In 1994 employers were mandated to cover the first six weeks of sick pay themselves and to contract with a private provider of occupational health services. These services monitor sick spells, advise firms on the nature and extent of the health risks to which their manpower is exposed and on how to reduce these risks.

In March 1996, the Sickness Benefit Act was abolished altogether, and employers' responsibility for coverage of sick pay was extended to a maximum of 12 months, after which disability insurance takes over. Under the Civil Code, companies are obliged to replace 70% of earnings lost to sickness. They may choose whether they want to bear their sick pay risk themselves or have (part of) it covered by a private insurer. Most small businesses buy such insurance.

This is a remarkable change. A fully regulated monopoly market to which private insurers had no access has been transformed into a deregulated one on which private insurers freely bid for contracts with companies seeking to insure their sick pay liabilities. As a result, sickness absence rates (excluding pregnancy and maternity leave) dropped from 6.5% in 1990 to 4.6% in 1997. It then increased 6.0% in 1999. The increase between 1997 and 1999 could well be related to an increasingly tight labour market. Therefore, to get a proper indication of whether privatization of sick pay has structurally reduced absenteeism the 1999 figure should be compared with the top of the previous business cycle – 1990. This gives a reduction of about 8% in absence rates (from 6.5% to 6.0%).

A more contentious effect of this drastic form of privatization is that employers scrutinize the health of job applicants more strictly than before, making the labour market less accessible for people with disabilities. Under the 1998 Reintegration of Work Handicapped Persons Act, however, the sick pay of handicapped workers is covered by a collective residual sickness benefit scheme. This new regulation is designed to fight discriminatory behaviour of employers.

Disability insurance

Beginning in 1998, the experience rating of firms has been phased into the disability insurance scheme. Pre-1998 benefits are still funded by the existing uniform pay-as-you-go contribution rates but the first five years of disability benefit recipiency of new beneficiaries will be paid out of premiums that are levied according to the "polluter pays" principle. If an employee is awarded a disability benefit, the company faces a higher contribution rate, and vice versa if a company employs a disability beneficiary. Moreover, companies are allowed to opt out of the public insurance system, but only with respect to the coverage of the first five years of benefit recipiency.

4.3 Changing the administration

Disability insurance

In the debate on disability policy, the focus gradually shifted from the programme itself towards the programme administrators. In 1993, a multi-party parliamentary committee investigated the operations of the insurance agencies with special attention to the administration of the disability insurance scheme. A vast number of current and former administrators, civil servants and political decision-makers were publicly interrogated by the committee. The picture that emerged from the nightly televised summaries was devastating for the image of the insurance agencies. What had been most suspected, and what had already been shown by research, was now publicly confirmed. The committee's report created broad political support for drastic changes regarding, in particular, the dominant and autonomous position of the trade unions and employers' representatives in the management of social insurance.

In 1995, as a result of the committee's recommendations, an independent supervisory body was set up. It publishes annual reports on the efficiency and legality of the administration of the social insurance programmes. In 1997, the public insurance agencies that were run by the social partners were privatized and regrouped into five organizations. Apart from their traditional tasks of administering public (unemployment and disability) insurance programmes, they set up a range of private activities offering medical and vocational rehabilitation and occupational health and employment services.

The original plan was to create a competitive market in which these five agencies, as well as new entrants to this market, would compete for contracts with companies or groups of companies to administer wage-replacing unemployment and disability insurance. The trend was towards offering full-service packages that would cover the legally mandated social insurance liabilities as well as pensions and health insurance. The public debate on this model of private delivery of social insurance revealed several problems.

First, while disability risks are privately insurable, unemployment is not. Therefore, a competitive insurance market for mandatory coverage of the disability risk could be viable and efficient if private insurers were allowed to control all the links in the insurance chain, from prevention to rehabilitation. Insurers could offer companies tailor-made packages by varying elements such as the extent of co-insurance, the quality of claims management and the intensity of damage control through prevention, swift rehabilitation and monitoring activities. One crucial element in this chain is the assessment of the degree of disablement. A political majority was unwilling to subject disability assessment to the business interest of private insurers. As a consequence, a hybrid model was proposed in which the whole chain was privatized except disability assessment, which was to be done by a separate public (medical) agency.

Second, privatization would not obtain an efficient market for unemployment insurance. Employers are likely to be interested only in the cheapest unemployment insurance administration contract because they do not profit from investment in quick re-employment of workers whom they have made redundant. Putting disability and unemployment risks in one basket, therefore, would result in a (socially) sub-optimal outcome.

Third, private agencies that cover the mandatory (public) insurance are likely to offer additional related insurance services, such as health insurance and pensions. To the extent that the portability of such employee benefit packages is limited, employees are locked into the company. Likewise, companies may find it difficult to change providers of employee benefits.

And finally, private agencies that get data on covered workers because they run public schemes may abuse it for other commercial activities. Similarly, they may use money from mandatory public insurance for their private business. Auditing such hybrid organizations is complex, controversial and expensive.

For these and other reasons, a political majority pulled the plug on this privatization plan in the summer of 1999. In 2002 a public monopoly, i.e. the Social Insurance Institute, was established to run the disability and unemployment insurance programmes. Only rehabilitation is contracted out to private firms. This could offer an opportunity for the existing occupational health service companies that now manage sickness benefit claims to broaden their scope.

Unemployment benefits

Since 1996 the Dutch labour market has become increasingly tight. The unemployment benefit rate, the number of benefit recipients per 1,000 employed, dropped from 0.152 in 1995 to an estimated 0.085 in 2000. This is the result, among other things, of a sustained policy of wage moderation. During the 1990s employment grew by 25%. Long-term unemployment is increasingly concentrated among those with low education and ethnic minorities.

In agreement with EU directives, the long-term unemployed, who are mostly on social assistance, are now offered a reintegration plan. Depending on the qualifications of the individual client, the plan aims at reinsertion in the labour market or social reintegration. Municipal social service agencies that administer the social assistance scheme may contract commercial employment agencies or private rehabilitation companies to effect welfare-to-work plans.

The interest of municipalities in reducing their assistance benefit expenditures was heightened by increasing their co-payment rate up to 25%. Previously this rate had been only 10%. The other 90% were covered by the State budget. Moreover, annual lump-sum grants to municipalities to cover their general budget are dependent on a set of factors that include socio-economic strength. And strength is measured by the number of persons on social assistance. Municipalities, therefore, have no financial interest in reducing their social assistance dependency rates. The possibility of further increasing the financial responsibility of municipalities in funding social assistance benefits is under study.

5   Trends

Evidence that the new rules were biting is that benefit terminations due to recovery, i.e. being found fit for generally accepted work, doubled from 4% in 1990 to 8% in 1995. The stricter regime also affected the incidence of new disability awards. Among men, new awards as a percentage of the labour force decreased from 1.7% in 1990 to 0.9% in 1995. Among women the disability benefit incidence rate dropped from 2.4% in 1990 to 1.4% in 1995. The decrease in awards may well be the combined result of increased stringency of the gatekeeper and lower application rates because disability benefits lost part of their financial appeal on account of the lower benefits and stricter eligibility requirements.

A smaller number of awards and a steep increase in benefit terminations resulted in a 7% decrease in the disability beneficiary population over the three years between 1994 and 1996. So far these are the only years in which the number of beneficiaries has declined since the introduction of the comprehensive disability insurance scheme in 1967.

Since 1995 the beneficiary volume has been growing again, especially among younger women. Male incidence rates grew from 0.9% in 1995 to 1.2% in 1999, and those for women from 1.4% to 2.0%. Young women (younger than 35) show the steepest rise in incidence rates: from 1.1% in 1995 to 1.5 in 1999.

But the share of partial benefits increased continuously over the 1990s, from 15% in 1990, to 19% in 1995 to 30% in 2001. Moreover, almost half (46%) of the partial beneficiaries were working in 1998, as well as 13% of recipients of a full benefit (Lisv, Trendrapportage arbeidsongeschiktheid, 2000: 63). In 1999, however, the recovery rate was back at its previous level of 4%. All in all, the number of beneficiaries in full benefit equivalents (corrected for partial benefit recipiency) as a percentage of the labour force dropped from a peak of 11.4% in 1990 to a level of 10% in 1995, where it has remained until now.

6 Discussion

Dutch disability insurance differs from other disability transfer programmes in several ways. First, it does not distinguish according to whether disablement is caused by a professional or another risk. Before 1967 the Netherlands, like other countries, had separate benefit schemes for industrial injuries and occupational diseases, on the one hand, and a general disability programme for other ("social") risks. The unique comprehensive disability insurance programme (WAO) introduced in July 1967 took the more generous one of the two schemes – the (Work) Injury Act – as its model.

As a consequence, the WAO had high (gross) benefits (80% of the gross wage), causing an even higher after-tax replacement rate in the case of full

(80-100%) disablement. It also took its fine grid of disability classes, starting at 15% disablement, from the compensation schedule of industrial injuries. Next, the WAO copied the Work Injury Act by measuring disability as the extent of earning capacity loss. Most other disability benefit programmes use work capacity as their central concept. Earnings capacity is a more complex notion because it requires translating functional limitations into residual capacity into jobs commensurate with the residual capacity and the earnings that go with suitable work.

Each of these conceptual links adds to the complexity of the measurement of disability, increases the burden on the gatekeepers and broadens the scope for claimants to become eligible for the programme. To these elements can be added the ruling that explicitly stipulated consideration of the potentially weak position of partially disabled on the labour market. It opens the gates of the programme even further (see section 3.2). A last element derived from the Work Injury Act, which (still) makes the Dutch programme more accessible than those elsewhere, is the absence of a required contribution period before a worker is fully covered. Such absence is normal under a work injury scheme because a construction worker who falls from a scaffold on the first day on the job has to be covered. Like the United States Social Security Disability Insurance, general disability benefit programmes in other EU countries require a certain contribution payment period, which may be as long as five years before full coverage is obtained (Bakkum and Desczka, 2002).

Apart from the fact that the Dutch fit all disability contingencies into a work injury type scheme, there are three more aspects that make the WAO uniquely accessible. First, the Dutch system is the only one that adheres to a strict separation between treating physicians and those who check the legitimacy of absence from work (occupational health service, and social insurance, doctors). A worker who is sick for more than three or four weeks will visit one or more treating doctors and an occupational health service doctor. The purpose of these visits is to establish the nature and extent of incapacity. While the treating doctors accept symptoms and declarations of ill health by the patient as a basis to work towards full recovery, occupational health service doctors carry the burden of proving the absence of incapacity. But for this proof they depend on the information they get from the curative sector. Normally, the contracts under which they operate are so limited that they do not have a (time) budget to collect such information or do a thorough examination themselves.

Although the sickness and disability schemes have been thoroughly revised, disability entry rates are growing again. By making sick pay the financial responsibility of the individual employer and by introducing experience rating, companies have to deal with the full cost of disability. But the possibilities for them to act on these financial incentives are limited. First, under Dutch privacy ruling employers are not allowed to get information on the health status of their sick-listed employees from the doctors working for occupational health service agencies. Likewise, sick-listed workers are not obliged to inform their employer about the expected duration of their absence, their health limitations, and necessary accommodations to speed up work resumption.

Second, companies depend on the quality of the contract they have with their occupational health service agency and on the quality of its claims management under a given contract. Despite the fact that companies now carry the full financial risk of sick pay, they do not seem interested in contracting an extensive occupational health service (OHS) package, which would allow OHS doctors to monitor absenteeism more thoroughly. One reason for this may be the fact that most companies are too small to have bad experiences with long-term sickness – and why would they invest in reducing risks that they consider negligible? Among larger companies, investments in adequate prevention and claims management vary widely. A conclusion might be that mandating companies to contract an OHS agency is superfluous. The financial risk that companies now run could well be a sufficient incentive to contract an adequate OHS package voluntarily. Making it mandatory may give the wrong signal and could lead to strategies that run counter to what is socially desirable.

Third, workers who report sick with a health complaint that is not clear-cut and does not allow for an unambiguous work resumption prognosis are left on their own. They rarely get treatment by specialists and OHS doctors lack the budget to design and implement reintegration plans. After about two months, most companies have replaced a worker with an unclear prognosis. They weigh their sick pay and disability premium liabilities against investment in reintegration with an uncertain return and often decide to let the employee continue on the path to disability benefit. OHS agencies have no discretion to mediate towards new employers if an employee is unable to resume with his/her current employer. In those cases employees are directed to the social insurance agency whose capacity to help them find a new employer has been shown to be limited.

Fourth, social insurance doctors seem to find it difficult to deny disability benefits to employees with vague health complaints. This is in conflict with the 1993 law stipulating that the medical cause of disability should be objectively assessable. But under political pressure this rule has been attenuated. The trends suggest that the "health route" towards continued benefit dependency (first covered by sick pay, followed by disability benefits) is still the easiest way out for all parties involved. For certain groups of employees who lack career prospects and whose households are not solely dependent on their earnings, the possibility of benefit recipiency may still be attractive, although the benefit is considerably lower than it used to be. This may partly explain the rise in the disability incidence among married women.

The Donner report

In May 2001, a National Advisory Commission on Disability proposed to drastically revise the current scheme. It carries the name of its chairman, i.e. the Donner Commission. The proposal takes as a starting point the mutual responsibility of employer and employee to promote work resumption and prevent benefit dependency. The employer is obliged to take care of the necessary accommodation of the current job, or to offer another job, inside or outside the firm. The employee has to provide the medical information necessary to adapt employment conditions, and has to accept any job offer earning 70%, or more, of his previous wage. The sufficiency of the return to work efforts of employer and employee will be judged by the Social Insurance Institute (UWV). Insufficiency will be sanctioned. If the employer is held liable he will have to continue payment of sickness benefit until he has taken the steps judged necessary by the UWV. If the employee proves unwilling to collaborate with reasonable plans and job offers, the employer may dismiss him/her.

This system of mutual obligations to effect work resumption is underscored by a new risk definition of the Disability Insurance. People are only awarded a disability benefit if they can be considered permanently severely disabled. Partial disability is not covered anymore by the public Disability Insurance programme. It is expected that this measure alone will reduce the inflow rate by two thirds.

Notes

1. On the Dutch disability policy in a broader macro-economic setting see Bovenberg (2000) and de Jong (1999).
2. See Prinz (forthcoming), Chart 3.13.
3. (Full) indexation of the legal minimum wage and social transfers may be omitted if the number of social welfare beneficiaries is large relative to the workforce.

References

Bakkum, H./Desczka, S. (2002) *De nederlandse WAO in internationaal perspectief* (The Dutch WAO in International Perspective). The Hague: Ministry of Social Affairs and Employment, Werkdocument no. 241.

Bovenberg, A.L. (2000) 'Reforming Social Insurance in the Netherlands', *International Tax and Public Finance* 7 (3): 345-368.

de Jong, Ph.R. (1999) 'Reforming Social Policy: Learning from the Dutch Experience', *Swiss Journal of Economics and Statistics* 135 (3): 253-271.

Lisv / Landelijk Instituut Sociale Verzekeringen (2001) *Trendrapportage 2000*. Amsterdam: Lisv.

Prinz, Christopher (ed.) (forthcoming) *Transforming Disability into Ability*. Paris: OECD.

CHAPTER 9

Disability Pensions and Social Security in Norway

Svenn-Åge Dahl and Hans-Tore Hansen

1   Introduction

Norway is normally classified as a part of the Nordic welfare regimes (Esping-Andersen, 1990, 1999; Kuhnle, 1990), which feature a universal pension system covering all residents and an earnings-related supplementary pension system for employers and the self-employed. Others have added the high participation in the labour force by older people and women (including those with small children) as characteristic of the Nordic welfare regimes (e.g. Kolberg, 1992). After a long period of steady incremental growth, during which social security programmes were gradually extended, the Norwegian welfare system has recently witnessed a period of reform, with the first sign of major curtailment of entitlements in some areas. However, there has also been continued expansion and even further developments in that direction are being discussed. The evolution in Norway has to be seen in the light of the economic situation. Compared with the other Nordic countries and also many other Western countries, Norway has been in a favoured situation, basically because of its high oil and gas revenues. There seems to be agreement among Norwegian politicians that the welfare system should be kept more or less as it is,[1] and surveys of the population indicate that there is consensus about continued public responsibility for welfare provision (Hatland et al., 1994).

The Norwegian authorities are, however, concerned about the high and still growing number of new disability pensioners.[2] This not only increases expenditure; it also reduces the working population and thus the capacity to finance public welfare. The demographic changes, with an increasing share of elderly persons in the population, combined with higher average pension benefits, together with the growing tendency to early retirement make the authorities worried about the expected expansion in pension expenditure in ten years time. It is a political intention to reduce the increasing number of disability pensioners and persons on sick leave. Much emphasis has been put on incentives to work and the intended change from passive benefits to active participation.[3] Along with this change of emphasis in goals, there has been more focus on better prevention, more rehabilitation, incentives and more flexible benefit schemes.

In this chapter we will give a detailed presentation of the Norwegian welfare state, with emphasis on the social security system and the disability pension system in particular. Both the changes in the system in earlier years and possible changes in years to come will be discussed. Our presentation is based on official regulations, governmental documents and research related to disability pension.

2 Description of the disability pension system and related social security schemes

2.1 *The National Insurance Scheme*

The Norwegian welfare state has developed over a long period of time (Bjørnson and Haavet, 1994; Seip, 1994). To be precise, the National Insurance Scheme was established with the National Insurance Act of 17 June 1966 and the Act on Special Supplements to Benefits from the National Insurance Scheme of 19 June 1969. According to these laws, all residents in Norway (employers, self-employed, pensioners, housewives, children, students, etc.) are independent members of the national insurance system. People working in Norway without being residents are also members of the system, and so are Norwegian seamen on Norwegian ships and some other groups. Membership of the National Insurance Scheme is compulsory. It is not possible to contract out.

The National Insurance Scheme is organized as a pay-as-you-go system, and it is financed by contributions from the State, employers, employees, and self-employed and other members. Parliament decides contribution rates and State grants.[4] Total expenses of the National Insurance Scheme in 1999 were NKr 159 235 million. This represents approximately 13% of the gross domestic product. The State grants to the National Insurance Scheme in 1999 amounted to NKr 44 262 million. The national insurance system manages about 30% of the Government revenue.

All insured persons are granted free accommodation and treatment, including medicines, in hospitals. The patient has to pay a share of the cost of treatment by a general practitioner or a specialist outside hospital, for treatment by a psychologist, for prescriptions of important drugs and for transportation expenses in connection with examination or treatment. The municipality and/or the national insurance cover the main part of the expenses. Necessary medical examinations during pregnancy and after confinement are free.

2.2 The disability pension system

Coverage and access to the system

The disability benefit programme in Norway is universal, and insurance is provided by the National Insurance Scheme. To be eligible for a disability pension, claimants have to be between 18 and 67. Those under 18 are supposed to be supported by their family and those over 67 receive an old-age pension. Recipients must reside in Norway and must normally have contributed to the social security system for at least three years.

The income/working capacity has to be permanently reduced by at least 50%.[5] All jobs that the claimant is able to manage are supposed to be taken into consideration. The disability assessment is based on an estimation of education, abilities, age, working experience and working possibilities (including those available in another place). The evaluation is thus made on an individual basis and not on the basis of employment status. According to the rules, disability pensions should not be awarded if there is a chance of getting the disabled person into some kind of employment. In practice, however, the rules have not been strictly applied, especially to older applicants and those who are closely attached to the place where they live, or when employment opportunities are small or non-existent. It is known that the disability pension has acted at times as a remedy against geographical and structural unemployment. Labour market conditions may influence the evaluation of the individual's actual possibilities for returning to work. For those working at home ("housewives"), the disability pension compensates for loss of capacity to do work at home.

An essential condition is that the disability must be attributable to "illness, injury or defect", i.e. the disability must have a medical cause. Both physical and mental ailments may entitle a person to a disability pension. There has been some doubt regarding problems such as alcoholism and drug addiction, but today most doctors regard these problems as illnesses. A disability pension is often provided in particular in those cases where the applicant has other ailments as well.

Disability pension is a permanent status with no re-test. Normally a disability pension is granted up to the age of old-age pension (67 years). In 1997, 21 258 disability pensions were terminated. Of those, 15 768 ended with old-age pension, 3 095 ended with death, 2 039 ended for unknown reasons, and 356 ended for "other reasons". Among the two latter groups, some may have returned to work. The disability status may be re-tested if there is a major change in the working capacity. During temporary vocational training, the pensioner may retain the pension. During a probationary work period the pensioner retains the right to return to disability pension within a limit of three years.

Organizational aspects of the disability pension system

The assessment of disability status is made by the local social security office, based on statements from the treating doctor, if necessary with assistance from consulting doctors working for the national insurance authorities. The procedure is that the claims first go to the local social security office. Afterwards, applications are sent to the regional social security office, where most of the cases are settled. Some cases are sent further to the National Insurance Administration (NIA), and in the last instance the case may go to the Social Security Tribunal.

The disability benefit programme

The disability pension consists of a basic pension and a supplementary pension and/or special supplement. The basic pension and the special supplement are calculated on the basis of the insurance period and is independent of previous income and contributions paid.

The basic pension – a key to the system

Disability pensions are granted, like other long-term benefits (e.g. old-age pension), by the National Insurance Scheme and are calculated in relation to a basic amount. Parliament adjusts this amount each year in accordance with changes in the general income level. The main adjustment takes place on 1 May each year. On 1 May 1999 the basic amount was NKr 46 950. In the case of partial disability, the pension is reduced proportionally.

All persons who are insured for pension purposes and who have a total insurance period of three years between the age of 18 and the year they become 66 are entitled to a basic pension. The current insurance requirement does not apply to persons who have been insured for at least 20 years (on the basis of periods of residence, etc.) or are entitled to a supplementary pension. The basic pension is independent of previous income or contributions paid. A full basic pension requires a minimum insurance period of 40 years, with a proportional reduction if the insurance period is shorter. Persons not insured for pension purposes and who have less than 20 years of insurance are entitled to supplementary pension benefits. The basic pension is calculated on the basis of the same number of years as the supplementary pension.

For an unmarried pensioner or a pensioner whose spouse is not a national insurance pensioner, the full basic pension equals the basic amount for that year. A pensioner supporting a spouse (or a cohabitant to whom s/he previously was married or with whom s/he has children) who is not a pensioner may be entitled to a supplement of up to 50% of her/his basic pension. The supplement is means-tested and reduced by 50% of income in excess of the minimum pension for couples plus 25% of the basic amount.

If both spouses are pensioners, the full basic pension is 75% of the basic amount for each. The same applies to cohabitants who were previously married to each other or have children together.

Supplementary pension

A supplement of up to 50% of the pensioner's basic pension is granted under certain circumstances for a supported spouse. A supplement of up to 30% of the basic amount is granted under certain circumstances for each supported child under the age of 18. These supplements are means-tested. A guaranteed supplement is provided for benefits granted before the introduction of means-testing. Persons born disabled or becoming disabled before reaching the age of 24 are granted a guaranteed minimum supplementary pension on the basis of a final pension point of 3.3, corresponding to an earned income of 4.3 times the basic amount.

The aim of the supplementary pension scheme is to prevent a marked decline in the standard of living upon retirement. A person is entitled to a supplementary pension if the annual income exceeded the average basic amount of any year for three years after 1966. Full credit (pension points) is given for income up to six times the basic amount. Furthermore, one-third of the income between 6 and 12 times the basic amount is credited as pensionable income for these years. Income exceeding 12 times the basic amount is disregarded. Before 1992 income up to 8 times the basic amount was credited at the full rate and income between 8 and 12 times the basic amount at one-third. The amount of the supplementary pension depends on the number of pension-earning years and the yearly pension points. As a general rule, a full supplementary pension requires 40 pension-earning years. In case of less than 40 pension-earning years, the pension is reduced proportionally.

A full annual supplementary pension acquired for years prior to 1992 is 45% of the amount obtained when the current basic amount is multiplied by the average pension point figure for the person's 20 best income years (final pension point). If the person concerned has earned pension points for fewer than 20 years, the average of all pension point figures credited is used. From 1992 the supplementary pension percentage has been 42%. Insured persons born disabled or becoming disabled before reaching the age of 26 are credited future pension points to a minimum of 3.3 (corresponding to an earned income of 4.3 the basic amount) if the beneficiary was born after 1940.

Persons belonging to older age groups have had no possibility of earning a full supplementary pension since the system was established in 1967. In consequence, special transitional provisions have been introduced for these groups. Persons who are taking unpaid care of children under seven years of age and of disabled, sick and elderly persons at home are credited a pension point figure up to 3.00 in the supplementary pension scheme.

Pensioners supporting children under 18 years of age may receive a supplement of up to 25% of the basic amount for each child. The supplement is means-tested.

Special supplement

Those who have no or only a small supplementary pension are entitled to a special supplement from the National Insurance Scheme. A full special supplement is payable if the insurance period is at least 40 years. The special supplement is reduced proportionally if the period is shorter. A supplementary pension is deducted from the special supplement.

For an unmarried pensioner or a pensioner whose spouse is not a national insurance pensioner, the special supplement is 61.55% of the basic amount (ordinary rate). If the supported spouse is 60 years or older, the special supplement is 123.1% of the basic amount. If both spouses receive a minimum pension, the special supplement is the same as for singles, i.e. 61.55% of the basic amount each.

For a pensioner married to a pensioner who has a supplementary pension higher than the special supplement, the special supplement is 55.85% of the basic amount (minimum rate). However, the total supplementary pension and special supplement may not be lower than twice the special supplement according to the ordinary rate, i.e. 123.1% of the basic amount. The same provisions apply to cohabitants who were previously married to each other or have children together.

OTHER SUPPLEMENTS
The disability pension benefit may be supplemented by collective bargaining agreements. Municipal and State pension schemes – with a levy of 2% of income – are coordinated with the statutory benefit and may never account for more than approximately two-thirds of the former income. Private pension schemes usually contribute approximately 20% of former income, which comes on top of the statutory benefit without any coordination.

TAXATION OF DISABILITY BENEFITS
Special tax provisions apply to disability pensioners with income below a certain minimum limit. Persons within these groups are not liable to pay tax or national insurance contributions on income. Pensioners with income exceeding the minimum limits are liable to tax calculated according to special tax limitation provisions. Consequently tax and national insurance contributions on net income for this group may not exceed 55% of the income in excess of the minimum limits. Disability pensioners with income exceeding the limits for which the special tax limitation provisions apply are entitled to a special deduction in income, reducing the tax on the net income by NKr 4 939 (1997). In addition to the special tax provisions, pensioners are liable to pay a lower national insurance contribution than employees.

COMBINATION OF DISABILITY BENEFITS AND INCOME FROM WORK

The size of the disability pension depends on how much the ability to earn an income (or do housework) has been reduced. If the ability to earn an income has been totally lost, the person is granted a 100% disability pension. In the case of partial disability, the pension is reduced proportionally. If a person has not been granted a 100% disability pension, the disability pension may be combined with work or other types of benefits (i.e. unemployment benefit, sickness benefit and rehabilitation benefit). Disability pensioners can have some income from work before their disability is re-evaluated. A small income from work at a maximum level of one basic pension may be combined with a full disability pension. If the income is greater than the basic pension, the disability grade may be re-evaluated. Disability pensioners may engage in vocational training for up to three years without losing their entitlement to a disability pension. Their disability pension is reduced according to how much they work. There has been some experimentation allowing a disability pension of less than 50%. The argument has been that those with work capacity lower than 50% may have an incentive to be classified with a loss of work capacity above 50% to get a disability pension. Those with a work capacity under 50% might also work less than they could in fear of losing their disability pension. So far, however, not many people have used this possibility.

SOCIAL ASSISTANCE

Local authorities (municipalities) are responsible for providing a means-tested safety-net for adults (over 18) who cannot provide for themselves (or their children), thus including disability pensioners.[6] Support is normally given in the form of cash grants. Such grants may be given in addition to benefits from the National Insurance Scheme and are very common, since half of those receiving social assistance also receive some kind of benefit from this scheme.

2.3 Characteristics of the sickness benefit programme

An insured person who is incapable of working owing to sickness, who has an annual income of at least half the basic amount and whose occupational activity has lasted for at least 14 days is entitled to sickness benefit.[7] A self-reported illness is allowed four times a year for short periods of three days.

Apart from this, the treating doctor must assess all absence caused by sickness.[8] The doctor's statement is regarded as a recommendation to the NIA, which formally makes the decision about sickness benefit payment. Doctors employed by the NIA may not issue medical reports.

For employees, statutory sickness benefits are 100% of pensionable income and are paid from the first day of sickness for a period of 260 days (52 weeks).[9] The employer pays the sickness benefits for the first 16 days and the National Insurance Scheme pays the remainder. For persons with chronic diseases and frequent sickness absence, the National Insurance Scheme takes responsibility for sickness benefits during the whole sickness period, including the first 16 days ordinarily paid by the employer. Income exceeding six times the basic amount is not taken into account. Collective bargaining agreements are often made for employees with an income above this level, however. With partial work incapacity (minimum 20%, before 1994 the minimum limit for partial sickness benefits was 50%), partial sickness benefits may be given. Persons receiving sickness benefits may enrol in rehabilitation or training programmes to prevent long-term disability. Special regulations are given to ensure early intervention; for instance, active sick leave was introduced in 1994 with modified tasks at the regular place of work or vocational rehabilitation.

There is no specified mandatory sickness period before a disability benefit can be claimed, but it must be documented that the claimant has undergone appropriate medical treatment and vocational rehabilitation. Furthermore the work capacity must have been reduced by a minimum of 50% for medical reasons.

2.4 *Benefits in the case of occupational injury*

The National Insurance Act regulates work injury benefits, which are administrated by the NIA and local insurance offices. The NIA is responsible and decides on all claims for benefit. The treating doctors as well as medical-vocational experts advise the benefit administration. The work injury programme in the National Insurance Scheme is financed by ordinary contributions from employees and members and is not risk-rated. Insurance is provided by the NIA with supplementary compensation from private insurance companies.

An insured person who is the victim of an occupational injury is entitled to the same benefits as the ordinary rules, but on the basis of special and more favourable rules. With regard to pensions, for instance, the benefits are not reduced because of missing insurance periods (insufficient earnings or failure to complete the qualifying period), but are always granted at full rates. Disability pensions may be granted provided that the earnings ability has been reduced by 30%, otherwise 50%. Compensation for non-financial loss (reduced quality of life) may be granted provided that the medical nature and degree of the injury is more than 15%. The receipt of a work injury benefit does not preclude participation in vocational rehabilitation. The injury benefits are usually granted permanently and there are no regular re-tests. If there is a substantial change in the circumstances taken into account in determining the disability pension, the case may be re-examined and the pension recalculated or terminated. As a rule there is no qualifying period, but disability pensions are normally preceded by a year with sickness benefit. Compensation for non-financial loss should not normally be applied for until a year has elapsed. Partial benefits are available, depending on the degree of disability. Lump-sum awards are available for disability pensions of less than 50% and compensation for non-financial loss.

The Occupational Injury Compensation Act No. 63 of June 1989 was a major reform, as it made employers liable to compensate financial loss in excess of the compensation offered by the National Insurance Scheme in the case of occupational injury or disease. The supplementary compensation from insurance companies is funded by contributions from the employers and is risk-rated. All employees are covered by this Act, regardless of the type or size of the company they work for. Pensioners and unemployed workers can claim compensation from the insurance company of their last employer. Payment is also guaranteed if the employer is bankrupt.

The Working Environment Act contains several provisions that implicitly or explicitly protect disabled persons/employees. For instance, an employee who is absent from work owing to accident or illness may not be given notice for that reason for a fixed time (6 months/12 months) after becoming unfit for work. There are no laws protecting disabled people such as anti-discrimination in employment in the Working Environment Act, and the Act does not regulate the employee's right to subsidies, wages, national insurance, etc. According to the internal control regulations/system the manager is responsible for taking the initiative and providing motivation and follow-up of health and safety activities. This system is meant to encourage prevention, early identification and risk evaluation of health and safety problems at the workplace.

2.5 Characteristics of the unemployment benefit programme

Providing re-employment services to benefit recipients has the highest priority in the Norwegian labour market policy. Such services are offered by the public employment service, which also administers the unemployment benefit system.[10] The unemployment benefit scheme is financed through the National Insurance Scheme. It covers all wage-earners up to 67 years of age. Previously self-employed persons over the age of 64 are also entitled to unemployment benefit until the age of 67.

Daily cash benefits during unemployment compensate loss of income because of unemployment. Working hours must have been reduced by at least 40% and the claimant has to be capable of work and registered at an employment office. Previously earned income is a condition for entitlement to daily cash benefits. The claimant has to have an income from work of at least 1.25 times the basic amount for the preceding calendar year or an income from work at least equal to the basic amount as an average during the three preceding calendar years.[11] The right to unemployment benefit is not based on a certain length of contribution payment.

Benefits may be temporarily suspended if the claimant refuses to take a suitable job or participate in labour market measures or fails to attend the employment office when summoned. The job search intensity is usually checked through reporting forms to be completed by the beneficiary and sent in to the employment service every two weeks. If the unemployment period extends over a long period, the local employment office interviews the beneficiary.

The calculation of daily cash benefits is based on income from work, income from labour market measures and income from daily cash benefits during unemployment, sickness, maternity and adoption. The calculation basis is the highest income of the preceding calendar year or the average over the three preceding calendar years. The maximal benefit basis is six times the basic amount. The benefit rate per day is 0.24% of the calculation basis and is paid five days a week. This will normally give an annual compensation of 62.4% of the calculation basis. Persons over the age of 64 are guaranteed a calculation basis of at least three times the basic amount, and benefits are paid without time limitation until the age of 67. Supplements for dependent children under the age of 18 are provided. Graduated unemployment benefit can be combined with part-time work when ordinary weekly working hours have been reduced by at least 40%. Such benefit may also be combined with partial disability benefit.

The benefit period varies depending on earlier income from work. Income from work amounting to at least twice the basic amount gives a benefit period of 156 weeks (three years). Income from work amounting to less than twice the basic amount gives a benefit period of 78 weeks (1.5 years). When the initial benefit period has expired, a subsequent benefit period may be granted immediately provided that the requirements concerning previous income are met.[12]

2.6 Rehabilitation benefits

An insured person under 67 years is entitled to rehabilitation benefits if he/she is a resident in Norway and has been insured for three years immediately prior to claiming the benefit. An insurance period of one year is sufficient if the claimant has been physically and mentally capable of performing normal work during that year. Rehabilitation benefits are granted if the working capacity has been permanently reduced or if opportunities in the choice of occupation or place of work are substantially limited. Benefits are also granted for improvement in the general functional capacity if this is substantially reduced because of illness, injury or defect.

A rehabilitation allowance is granted to an insured person entitled to daily cash benefits in case of sickness after the period of entitlement to daily cash benefits has expired. It is also granted to an insured person who is not entitled to daily cash benefits in case of sickness, but who has been unable to work for one year. It is generally only granted for a period of 52 consecutive weeks. A vocational rehabilitation allowance is granted to an insured person who is undergoing vocational rehabilitation. It is also granted during periods before rehabilitation measures start and after rehabilitation before suitable work is found. A temporary disability benefit may be granted before a final decision is made on a disability pension.

The level of the rehabilitation allowance, vocational rehabilitation allowance and temporary disability benefit corresponds to the disability pension. However, during continued medical treatment after the payment period for sickness benefit has expired, a partial rehabilitation allowance may be granted if the work capacity is reduced by 20% or more. No special supplement is granted, but supplements for supported spouse and children are provided.

Rehabilitation benefits are granted to cover the insured person's expenses in connection with rehabilitation measures. Benefits are granted for education in schools, courses or business enterprises, if this has a decisive influence on the insured person's working possibilities. A person who has substantially and permanently reduced general functional capacity may be granted the necessary and appropriate benefits (e.g. interpretation services, guide dogs, etc.) in order to improve the ability to manage daily life. Expenses for technical aids and the purchase of vehicles are covered. Transportation expenses and expenses incurred through technical aids are covered through the basic benefit.

2.7 Vocational rehabilitation strategies

The current principle is that vocational rehabilitation should be tried before disability pensions are made available. All labour market programmes for vocationally disabled persons and general labour market programmes may be used, depending on the individual's needs and motivation. Programmes include information, guidance, ordinary labour market measures and job-placement assistance. In addition, the vocationally disabled persons may utilize schemes that have been specially developed for disabled job seekers. Measures outside the public employment service, e.g. ordinary schools, may also be used.

There are two main paths to vocational rehabilitation: 1) through a long sickness period and benefits from the National Insurance Scheme, and 2) unemployed persons who are defined as vocationally disabled because of a social or medical handicap. For the first group, the social security office assesses whether medical conditions for occupational rehabilitation apply. The public employment office then decides whether occupational rehabilitation is necessary and appropriate to find or maintain a job and, if so, which labour market measures may be suitable. Thus, the employment office has the final say as to whether labour market measures are needed and relevant.

Local labour market authorities are responsible for vocational rehabilitation, which may include (1) educational measures in schools/courses, (2) training or job training in visiting positions, (3) wage subsidies and contributions to operating costs received by ordinary employers, (4) supported employment and (5) sheltered employment.[13] Wage subsidies are open to disabled persons and persons who have finished a medical rehabilitation process, as well as other exposed groups of unemployed. Some subsidies are reserved for the weakest groups. Supported employment programmes are for persons with extensive disabilities.[14] Private organizations may be involved as employers or as organizers of training measures. Also, private schools may be involved in the arrangement of educational measures. No sections of the open labour market are reserved for the employment of disabled people and there are no employment quota systems imposing certain obligations on employers.[15]

During rehabilitation, the persons involved have the right to take part in measures as long as is necessary and appropriate to find a suitable job. Generally, there are variations in length – from three months to three years – within the different measures. Rehabilitative measures are temporary, however. The traditional course was to introduce vocational rehabilitation measures between long-term sickness benefits and disability benefits. The aim is increasingly to intervene early, e.g. through activity during sickness, to introduce rehabilitation measures at an early stage and to increase reintegration for persons on disability benefits through rehabilitation measures. It is possible to enrol in a rehabilitation programme while receiving sickness or disability benefits and rehabilitation can be combined with subsidized, supported or sheltered work.

2.8 Early retirement provisions

The standard pension age in Norway is 67. The old-age pension consists of a basic pension, a supplementary pension and/or a special supplement and possible supplements for children and spouse (means-tested). A minimum old-age pension consists of a basic pension and a special supplement. It may be partly deferred until the age of 70. If the insured person maintains an earned income exceeding the basic amount, the pension is reduced by 40% of the exceeding income. For persons over 70 there is no reduction in pension because of wage income.

There are no provisions for early retirement under the National Insurance Scheme and, in contrast to many other countries, partial retirement and bridge jobs play a minor role in the transition from work to retirement in Norway. There are, however, possibilities for large groups to exit from the labour force before the retirement age of 67. Calculations indicate that the mean age for retirement in Norway is about 61 years (NOU, 1994: 2). A disability pension is one possibility. This possibility differs from other routes in that it depends on medical criteria.

Next to disability pensions, the most important possibility for early retirement is the "Early Retirement Pension Agreement" (AFP). This agreement-based pension is not part of the National Insurance Scheme. It is a privately negotiated early retirement scheme based on an agreement between trade unions and employers' organizations and came into effect on 1 January 1989. Over the years the scheme has expanded to other groups, including the public sector. AFP is not available for self-employed persons. The retirement age under AFP has been gradually reduced from 66 years in 1989, 65 years in 1990, 64 years in 1993 and 63 years in 1997 to 62 years in 1998. The use of the scheme has increased as the retirement age has dropped, and it has also been extended to new groups in the labour market as the replacement rate and the knowledge of the scheme have improved. Today about 60% of the labour force has the possibility for early retirement through AFP. According to the current rules it is possible to retire fully on AFP or partially with the option of going back to work at a later stage. The financial burdens of the AFP scheme are shared by the State (40%) and employers (60%) for private sector workers aged between 64 and 66. For private sector workers in the 62-63 age group there is no direct government contribution. For government employees in the 62-66 age group the Government bears the full cost, while the municipalities bear the full cost for municipal workers in the same age group.

The AFP scheme is open to applicants with at least ten years of social security contribution and an annual income of at least the basic amount at the time of claiming benefit. The pension is also conditional on an average income of at least twice the basic amount during the ten best income years since 1966. Only persons who are actually employed at the time of claiming benefit are eligible.

The AFP pension is calculated in the same way as the disability pension. The pension is the same as the full pension entitlement, but income taxation is less favourable than a full old-age pension. The AFP replacement rate varies between 50 and 60%. Receivers of AFP continue to earn rights to old-age pension.

Under both public and private occupational pension schemes, certain occupational groups are subject to special age limits, entailing the retirement of a number of persons with a full pension before the age of 67. Examples of special age limits in the public sector are firemen, police and military, who have to retire at 60, and cleaning staff, prison officers, air traffic controllers, nurses, railway workers and government drivers, who have to retire at 65.[16] About one-third of the employees in the public sector are subject to these special age limits. In the private sector the proportion is considerably lower. Examples from the private sector are pilots and divers, who have to retire at 55. The rules where groups are subject to special age limits are part of occupational pension schemes. All employees in the public sector are covered by different occupational pension schemes. About 35% of the employees in the private sector are covered by an occupational pension scheme.

Occupational pension schemes are usually funded, except for the scheme for government employees where it is a pay-as-you-go system. Contributions are paid by members of the pension scheme and by employers. The pension schemes for civil servants are financed by contributions from the employees (2% of earned income), employers and financial support from the State.

A fourth possibility for leaving the workforce before the age of 67 may be through a longer period of sickness absence (up to one year) following periods of rehabilitation. As mentioned earlier, persons above the age of 64, including the self-employed, may receive unemployment benefits without time limitation until the age of 67.[17] Private insurance and financial situations may provide other possibilities for early retirement.

Table 1: Number of new early retirees aged 60-66 years by early retirement regime, 1993-1997

	1993	1994	1995	1996	1997
Disability pension	7 291	7 142	6 913	6 769	7 417
AFP private	1 773	2 012	2 007	2 300	3 659
AFP State	1 040	1 513	1 235	1 280	1 634
AFP municipal	1 090	1 504	1 276	1 414	1 968
Special age limits – State	808	734	586	700	624
Special age limits – municipal	818*	513	350	515	641
Readjustment State	911	932	775	444	378
Seamen's pension	1 109	1 104	1 106	1 059	979
Total	14 840	15 454	14 248	14 481	17 300

Note: * Number of pensioners for the second half-year is multiplied by 2 because of missing information for the first half-year.
Source: NOU, 1998: 19 *Fleksibel pensjonering*.

Table l gives a survey of the number of pensioners under the age of 67 in the different early retirement schemes. As the table shows, among new pensioners in the 60-66 group in 1997, 7 400 received disability pension and 7 300 were early retired through AFP (private sector, governmental and municipalities). As mentioned, the AFP scheme covered persons between 65 and 66 years of age until 1993, after which the scheme also covered those who were 64 years old.

3   Major reforms during recent decades

After a long period of steady, incremental growth, involving a gradual extension of social security programmes (i.e. reduction of old-age pension age from 70 to 67 years in 1973, guaranteed supplementary benefit for those born with a disablement and those who become disabled before the age of 20), the Norwegian welfare system has recently witnessed a period of reform with the first sign of major curtailment of entitlements in some areas, but with continued expansion in other areas. In official terms, the attempt has been made to change the system from a passive support line ("trygdelinjen") to a new active work orientation line ("arbeidslinjen"). The term was first used in the Green Paper on Rehabilitation (*Stortingsmelding* nr. 39, 1991-92). The change involves a move away from the passive doling out of money to the active linking of benefits to efforts on the part of the claimant to become self-sufficient. Along with this change of emphasis in goals, there has been a greater emphasis on incentives and a focus on the possible disincentives embodied in generous welfare arrangements.

Up to the beginning of the 1990s, the criteria for obtaining a disability pension were liberalized, partly as a result of amendments to existing laws. After a longer period of liberalization regarding what counted as "illness, injury and defect", a period of dramatic growth in the number of disability pensioners was followed by a period of retrenchment at the beginning of the 1990s. From January 1990 disability pensions as a result of old age among claimants aged between 64 and 67 were no longer allowed. At the same time requirements for re-education, work rehabilitation and geographic movement became stricter. In 1991 Parliament decided to tighten the condition that the disablement must be attributable to "sickness, injury or defect", i.e. that disability must have a clear medical cause.

The age limit for being classified as young and disabled was raised to 24 years in 1992, and to 26 years in 1997. In 1998 the lower age limit for disability pension was raised from 16 to 18 years. In addition there were also changes in the sickness benefit system and rehabilitation. As we shall discuss later, there is a difference in opinion as to the degree the reforms contributed to the sharp decrease in the number of new claimants that was observed in the beginning of the 1990s, especially among women. Whatever the reason, lately there has again been a large growth in the number of new claimants.

However, there have also been extensions of the entitlements. Benefits for the congenitally disabled have been increased in the form of a guaranteed minimum addition to the basic pensions. Also, points towards eligibility for supplementary benefit have been made available to those with responsibility for caring for dependants. More lenient rules have been provided for the degree of disability required for entitlement for housewives in part-time work.

In 1997 the minimum age for guaranteed supplementary benefit was adjusted to 26 years, and the supplementary benefit was increased to 3.3 times the basic amount. There have also been some experiments with a disability grade lower than 50%, and it has been made easier for disability pensioners to take part in work training programmes without having to make a new application if the programme fails. In 1997 the free income level was raised from 50 to 100% of the basic amount and the period of suspension of benefit during testing of work ability was extended from one to three years.

There has also been a restriction in the medical criteria for sickness benefit. The NIA specified in June 1993 that problems such as grief, financial difficulties, normal ageing and marital problems do not in themselves create entitlement to sickness benefit. This reform is seen as significant because it involves a reversal of a trend towards liberalization in terms of symptoms acceptable as legitimate reasons for sick leave. Other restrictions in sick leave were also imposed. While doctors have always enjoyed great autonomy in determining eligibility, the reform also involved a shift of responsibility for such determinations to the local national insurance administration. After an initial period of 12 weeks sick leave, the administration is required to verify continued eligibility. The administration may also check the doctor's decision to award a benefit. Furthermore, after the 12-week period, the administration must draw up a plan for the possibilities for rehabilitation of the person on sick leave. The most important extensions of eligibility are where the employee has parental responsibilities. Between 1991 and 1993 three different reforms granted longer periods of sick leave to parents whose children are sick.[18]

Unlike Sweden, Norway has not introduced cut-off periods in sickness benefit. Instead the social partners agreed in 1990 on a programme aimed at reducing sick leave by 10% in the following year. This agreement was a result of increasing pressure to reform the existing system, which paid a full 100% earning from the first day of sickness.

In January 1994, the National Insurance Act was amended to give the labour market authorities overall responsibility for active vocationally orientated measures aimed at vocationally disabled persons.[19] The aim was to increase the priority given to active measures rather than passive income maintenance in order to promote integration of the vocationally disabled into the ordinary labour market. This change has been accompanied by reforms in the cash benefit system. The allowance for extra needs has been abolished, and claimants are now asked to approach the local social assistance agency for such help. The time on medical rehabilitation was also limited to one year. Before, there was no time limit on this benefit. The reform did not involve any major changes in detailed regulations covering subsidized and/or supported employment.

The 1994 rehabilitation reform stressed the job-training and formal training role of labour market enterprises. This applies particularly to phase 2, where the primary objective is to improve prospects for transition to ordinary work. To prevent phase 2 becoming a permanent measure, a maximum duration of two years for this phase was introduced. Also, any one enterprise should have a minimum of 50% of its workers in phase 2. This also sets limits to the number of persons in phase 3 (permanent sheltered employment). There are plans to simplify the funding administration of work co-operatives.

Since 1980 various changes have taken place in the unemployment benefit programme, mainly of a minor character. Under the initial unemployment legislation, unemployment benefit was paid for 80 weeks, followed by a cut-off period of 26 weeks. During this period, recipients had to rely on social assistance or their own resources. This period was reduced to 13 weeks in mid-1991. In May 1992, the 80-week rule ceased to be applied automatically and at the same time the cut-off period was abolished in cases where the employment office was unable to offer either work or training schemes for the unemployed person. In 1997, some substantial changes were implemented. Among other things, these concerned the required minimum income from work qualifying for unemployment benefit, which was raised from 0.75 to 1.25 times the basic amount the preceding calendar year or 100% of the basic amount as an average during the three preceding calendar years. Furthermore, income from participation in labour market measures no longer qualified for unemployment benefit. The rules concerning the length of the benefit period were also changed. While the maximum benefit period previously had been the same for all benefit recipients (normally up to 186 weeks), it now varies depending on earlier income from work. Income amounting to at least twice the basic amount gives a benefit period of 156 weeks. Income less than twice the basic amount gives a benefit period of 78 weeks. The reason for these changes was a political desire that the unemployment benefit programme should motivate active job-seeking by the benefit recipients and encourage them to shift from passively receiving benefits to ordinary work. Currently no reforms of a more substantial nature in the unemployment benefit programme are under consideration.

The whole area of labour market measures is currently being reviewed. The aim is to simplify the number and types of measures, to remove unnecessary differences between programmes available to the unemployed and the vocationally disabled persons and to reconsider the length and level of support within the various measures. It is also an aim to increase the number of participants in vocational rehabilitation/training in order to counteract the increasing number of disability pensions.

In April 1999 the Government established a Royal Commission including representatives of the largest employer and employee organizations, civil servants and scientists to propose reforms in the sickness benefit and disability pension schemes. The reason for this work was the strong growth in the disability pension and sickness cash benefit schemes during the previous years. The Commission was asked to propose measures to reduce sickness absence and the number of persons receiving disability pension and to evaluate reforms and actions that had been applied previously to reduce the duration of absence and early retirement related to disability. The Commission submitted its report 15 September 2000 (NOU, 2000: 27). An entire package of reforms was suggested: (1) earlier intervention and better methods for following-up people with sickness benefit; (2) reduced benefit level in the event of sickness and increased employer contribution to sickness benefit (20% of the benefit after the first 16 days); (3) extension of today's shielding of employers from employees suffering from chronic illness; (4)

increased requirement for vocational rehabilitation before disability pension can be granted; (5) dividing the disability pension into a temporary disability benefit (for a limited period of four years) and a permanent disability pension, which should be granted only to those with a 100% disability. A bill is planned for submission to the Storting (Parliament) in 2001, probably without many of the mentioned suggestions.

4 Review of national studies

4.1 Introduction

All OECD countries have experienced a drop in the average age of retirement. Extensive early retirement and the use of disability pension are the most important explanations. Since 1950 the average age of transition to inactivity among men has dropped 3.2 years to 63.8 years in 1995, and 8.8 years to 62.0 years for women in Norway (Blöndal and Scarpetta, 1998). The National Insurance Act was passed in 1967, and since then the number of disability beneficiaries has more than doubled, from 98 645 in 1967 to 279,573 at the end of the year 2000 (183% increase). Some 9.9% of the population aged 18-67 years now receive disability pension (11.5% of the women, 8.3% of the men). Measured in fixed prices (1996), the average pension has increased a lot – from NKr 40 000 (1967) to NKr 90 000 (1996), and the expenditure for disability pension has increased by almost 440% in terms of fixed prices (1996). In recent years the number of disability beneficiaries has been growing at a rate of 1 000 (net) each month. The number of employees aged 55 years and more has dropped. This decline is due to reduced labour force participation among men. The labour force participation for Norwegian women, on the other hand, has increased slightly and is relatively high compared to other countries, especially among older persons.[20]

This development will change the age structure of the labour force and will therefore affect labour costs and competitiveness. In addition, early retirement causes concern for the financing of welfare states in the immediate future. Thus, the use of disability pension and other early retirement schemes is an important topic on the political agenda in Norway as in several other countries. Until 1989 disability pension was the only early retirement scheme in Norway. As mentioned previously, a privately negotiated early-retirement scheme (Early Retirement Pension Agreement – AFP) came into effect from 1 January 1989. The pension age in the scheme has been gradually reduced over the years and has been set at 62 as of 1 March 1998. The use of the scheme has increased as the retirement age has been reduced and at the end of 2000 there were 31 578 persons receiving an AFP pension.

Norwegian research on the causes of the growth in disability pensions (and early retirement) has traditionally focused on push factors, but pull factors got more attention in the 1990s (e.g. Kohli and Rein, 1991). The economic-oriented pull view assumes that early exits are the result of social policies that have created attractive exit possibilities, for example, by lowering age boundaries and opening new institutional pathways. Sociological theory, on the other hand, focuses on the push factors generated by the organization of work. This framework assumes that the process of early retirement is driven by the evolution of the labour markets, especially by the high rates of unemployment, and by deeper structural features such as rationalization and outsourcing, accompanied by the growth of subcontracting and the increased use of temporary workers. In this view early retirement takes place regardless of what institutional pathways are available and, accordingly, no social policy can stop early retirement from occurring. In the following sections we shall give a short overview of Norwegian studies on disability pension in recent years.

4.2 *Labour market studies*

The conditions on the labour market have been the central explanation for the growth in the number of disability beneficiaries. The focus has been on unemployment, and the underlying perspective in most of the research on disability pension in Norway is the idea that it is hidden unemployment insurance (Abrahamsen, 1988). Persons who are fully capable of working have been granted disability pensions because there is no possibility for a new job in the area. The requirement to move to other parts of the country (where there are jobs) has not been pushed, i.e. the conditions on the labour market are used as a "medical diagnosis".

The model that has received most attention in the analysis of the relation between the labour market and disability pension in Norway is the "social exclusion model" (Halvorsen, 1977, 1980). The main thesis in this model is that the process of change in the economy (industrial structure) leads to "social exclusion" of marginal workers because of increased demands and workloads. Workers are excluded for social reasons, and the possibility of obtaining a new job is small. It is a situation in which the possibilities for choice are constrained because of the individual resources concerning health, age, education, and professional experience.

Kolberg (1991) has tested the model empirically and concludes that the model's logic is too simple and at best can explain certain aspects of the disability pension. For example, he asks how this model can explain the growth in the use of disability pensions in the public sector by pointing to the logic of capitalism. It is a fact that there has been a greater increase in disability beneficiaries in the public sector, especially among women (Stokke, 1993). Rationalization and downsizing are not just a private sector phenomenon.

Several indications point to the importance of macroeconomic conditions for the disability frequency. Kolberg (1974, 1976) and Kolberg et al. (1977) showed at an early stage that there were clear regional differences in the recruitment to disability pension (see also Bogen, 1981 and Halsteinslid, 1988). But there are also large differences within municipalities (NOU, 1990: 17). The industrial structure and differences in unemployment level explain the regional differences. Municipalities with a high percentage of disability beneficiaries are situated in northern Norway (fisheries), and in municipalities where service industries dominate in less central parts of the country. Municipalities with a low percentage are situated along the western coast and in central parts of eastern Norway. Low average income and education, high use of social assistance allowances and a high percentage of unemployed and disabled are significant indicators of the increasing number of disability beneficiaries (Christoffersen, 1995). It is possible that there are institutional differences in the way the social security offices treat disability applications.

Berg (1987) shows that it takes between 1.5 and 3.5 years before a change in the unemployment has an effect on disability pensions. For every third unemployed person a disabled person is generated. This finding is supported by Rødseth (1990), who found that the number of disabled increased by approximately 90 per 1 000 unemployed last year, and Bowitz (1992a, 1992b, 1997) who concludes that the entry rates for disability pension depend (positively) on the unemployment (especially long-term) level. Unemployment was an important variable in explaining why people entered the disability system during the period 1973 to 1991. In a recent study with data from 1980-

1997 Bragstad et al. (2000) found that the level of unemployment four to six years earlier influences the inflow to the disability pension system. The commonest diagnosis among the unemployed is musculoskeletal health problems (Berg, 1987). Manual workers have the highest incidence (Berg, 1994).

Immigrants account for only a small part of the disabled – 3% in 1992 (Lajord and Flittig, 1995). Relatively fewer immigrants are disabled than ethnic Norwegians (5% and 9% respectively), but there are considerable variations. Among immigrants from Pakistan, Turkey and Morocco, and from Asia and Africa in general more persons receive disability pension than among ethnic Norwegians (Grünfeld and Noreik, 1991, 1992). This is interpreted as an expression of the higher unemployment level among these groups and the lower general age for old-age pension in these countries.

Dahl et al. (2000) analyse early retirement pathways (disability pension, unemployment benefits and out of the labour market) for male and female workers. Family characteristics, expected income in different end states, and push factors such as industry attachment and local unemployment are found to be important for the early retirement process. The explanatory variables have different effects on the different exit routes for males as well as females. The hypothesis that disability and unemployment are interchangeable pathways into early retirement is therefore rejected.

The evidence regarding the effects of the replacement rate is less conclusive (see also Thøgersen et al., 1998). Hanssen (1994), Hansen (1996) and Tysse (1996) support these results, all of them using data from the KIRUT database[21], as they show that unemployment increases the risk of becoming a disability pension recipient. The disability pension is used as an instrument in labour market policy to reduce the number of (elderly) unemployed.

There have also been several studies on the importance of downsizing and closing of factories. The most famous of these is Westin's study (1981, 1990) of the closure of a sardine factory. He summarizes his findings this way (Westin, 1990: 75): "The results of this study demonstrate that a factory closure and its ensuing unemployment can have long-lasting effects on the laid-off workers with regard to future employment, usage of social security benefits, health-related behaviour and social readjustment. The laid-off workers contributed far less to paid work than did the controls over all ten follow-up years, they used more sick leave in the first follow-up year, their risk of receiving a disability pension was more than three times higher than for the controls during the first four follow-up years, and the women retreated to their housewife roles more often than did the controls."

These results are supported by several other studies (Bjørndal et al., 1990; Noreik et al., 1990; Dahl 1991, 1996; Rønsen et al., 1991). There tends to be an increase in claims for disability pensions from workers in companies that downsize or close the plant. To increase the replacement rate (often up to 80%) many companies have paid a small company pension in addition to the disability pension (Dahl, 1991; Halvorsen and Johannessen, 1991; Halleraker, 1994). This gave incentives to apply for a disability pension. The replacement rate can also be increased because, besides being insured under the National Insurance Act, around 50% of the Norwegian labour force is insured in collective pension schemes covering disability and old-age pensions. Being insured in such a scheme increases the replacement rate for the employee. If an employee leaves on a disability pension, the employer does not have to pay the insurance premium. Because of the profile of the insurance premium over time – the insurance premium is highest in the last years before the employee reaches standard retirement age (67 years) – the savings for the firm will increase with the age of the employee. For some companies this is an important argument when it comes to choosing a downsizing strategy (Dahl and Nesheim, 1998). Downsizing employees through disability has several advantages because avoiding lay-offs means fewer conflicts with the trade unions, it protects the firm's reputation, and the firm gets rid of the oldest part of the workforce. From the late 1980s downsizing increased in Norway and disability pensions were an attractive option for both employers and employees (Dahl, 1991, 1996; Thøgersen et al., 1998).

It is also important to note that sickness insurance has a replacement rate of 100%, which means that if a worker is downsized he has incentives to go to the doctor instead of the employment office (12 months of sickness insurance is a prerequisite for disability pension). It is also considered less stigmatizing to be disabled than unemployed. Doctors often help the unemployed coming to their offices – lesser diseases are described as serious so as to be accepted by the social security office. It is a case of securing income for the patient (Westin, 1990; Dahl, 1991).

There has also been some discussion about the importance of the working environment. The hypothesis is that physical and psychological strains lead to sickness absence and disability. A bad working environment can influence sickness absence directly by leading to sickness and indirectly by making it more difficult to work when the health or the ability to function is already reduced for other reasons. Tellnes et al. (1990) found that both patients and doctors assessed the physical workload to have contributed to the health problems leading to sickness certification in 48.4% of the sickness absences. Correspondingly, psychological factors were considered contributory causes of sickness in 32.1% of the cases. Several studies show that the probability of becoming a disability pensioner varies with occupation (Kolberg, 1991; Bjerkedal et al., 1995). The variation in occupational transition rates to disability pension indicates that characteristics of the working environment are of importance. This supposition is supported by Kolberg (1991) who found that a bad physical working environment has an effect on entry into disability pension status. On the other hand, he was unable to confirm the influence of the psychological working environment on the probability of becoming a disability pensioner. There are no signs that the physical working environment has become worse since 1980 and most indicators for the psychological working environment also show signs of stability (NOU, 2000: 27). The exception is that more and more employees feel that the pressure of work has increased over the period. About 50% of the employees interviewed reported increased working speed and pressure to increase the quality of the products (Grimsmo and Hilsen, 2000).

4.3 Health and sickness

Changes in health status and sickness are obvious explanations for the observed increase but there are no medical studies investigating this hypothesis. The development in people's health is found to be stable with signs of improvement. Even though seven out of ten report that they have a chronic disease, 80% of the men and 76% of the women say that their health is good, a small increase for both sexes since 1985. An explanation of this paradox is that people's perception of health includes more than sickness and that several serious diseases are not permanent. Twelve per cent of the population say that permanent disease or disablement influences their everyday life to a high degree.

The life expectancy for Norwegian women and men has risen by two and three years over the last 20 years, and was 81.3 years for women and 75.5 years for men in 1997. The health in the population varies with socio-economic position, education, occupational class, sex and income. The standard of health follows a hierarchical social pattern, where those who are best off also have the best health. Dahl and Birkelund (1999) found that the differences between the social classes in health remained unchanged between 1980 and 1995 and that employed persons had better health than non-employed.

The most used indicator of changes in health status and sickness over time is mortality. But mortality is declining, which means that the health status of the population is better. Mortality is especially declining for disability beneficiaries and exits from disability pension are therefore reduced (Abrahamsen, 1988). The result is an increase in the number of persons receiving a disability pension. But there has also been an increase in diseases that are not deadly, for example musculoskeletal diseases and mental disorders (depression, etc.), and a reduction in accidents and cardiovascular diseases among both men and women.

Amundsen (1988) concludes on the basis of studies of health surveys (1975 and 1985) that changes in sickness cannot explain the increase in the number of disability beneficiaries. In these surveys people were asked about their health, and there are, as we know, methodological problems with such an approach, as it is not objective (Bound, 1991). The Health Survey (1995) registered more persons than before who reported being sick more than once, especially in the 16-44 age group. Some 66% of the population aged 16 years or more reported having a chronic disease. It is possible that there is a "reserve" of persons with health problems in the population that may lead to an increase in the number of disabled. With increased job requirements, a person's health problem becomes relatively worse and can "force" the employee out of work (Westin et al., 1989).

4.4 Gender and family

Changes in the family structure (more divorces and one-person households) are other explanations for the observed growth. Amundsen (1988), Kolberg (1991) and Hansen (1996) show that marital status has a great impact on who becomes disabled. The risk is significantly less for married than unmarried persons. Family life protects against social problems. Selection is an alternative explanation – those who are not married or get divorced have more problems than persons who are married. The mentioned studies did not test for selectivity.

Some studies discuss the causes of the strong growth in female disability beneficiaries from the mid-1970s (Abrahamsen, 1988; Kjeldstad, 1990; Solheim, 1989).[22] Abrahamsen (1988) found that the disability incidence (high incidence) among females was highest in manufacturing and service work. She therefore posits a relationship between a dangerous and arduous working environment and disability. The increase is also a result of more women being eligible for disability pension because of higher labour force participation (Kjeldstad, 1990, 1991). Kjeldstad's results also show that stable labour force attachment over many years, especially in low-paid jobs, increases the probability of becoming a disability pension recipient. Solheim (1989) asked 27 disabled women what led to their disability. They had physically arduous, low-paid, low-status work with few chances of advancement. Their labour market career was unstable because of childbirth and caring work at home. The probability of receiving a disability pension varies a lot between different occupational groups among women and is highest among women with heavy work.

4.5 Administrative practice and the sickness/disability concept

The medical concept of sickness is relative and the definition depends on a number of factors, such as cultural traditions, people's ability to tolerate pain and existing methods of treatment (Kjønstad, 1987). The concept of disability has been liberalized, as groups that were originally excluded from disability pension have been included. Alcoholism, drug addiction and psychopathy are now regarded by the medical profession as sickness and give right to disability pension. These changes have led to a small increase in the number of disability pensioners (Ellingsen and Kjønstad, 1988). Housewives were not originally included because they had no income of their own, but the practice was liberalized in the 1970s. It has been shown that this liberalization had some effect on the number of disabled, but it cannot explain the strong growth in female disability pensioners (Ellingsen, 1988; NOU, 1990: 17). More important is probably the acceptance of "diffuse illnesses", fibromyalgia being the most frequent diagnosis among new female disability pensioners in 1997.

The number of disability beneficiaries reached a temporary peak in 1991 (238,519). As a result of the strong increase over the preceding years, the medical conditions in the eligibility criteria were tightened in 1991. Capacity for work was defined in relation to the labour market as a whole rather than to suitable work, as had been the case before. Sickness had to be the main reason for reduced work capacity, the concept of sickness had to be scientifically based and commonly accepted in medicine, and if objective signs of disease could not be demonstrated, at least two doctors had to agree on the presence of sickness. The restrictions were aimed especially at applicants with "diffuse illnesses". This hit women harder than men because these diffuse illnesses are "female diseases" (musculoskeletal, minor psychological and mental diseases). The law also had new and stricter requirements concerning geographical and occupational mobility and the rehabilitation efforts were increased. The effect was immediate and for the next couple of years the number of persons receiving disability pension decreased. It also affected women harder than men. For several years a majority of the new disability beneficiaries were women, but in the period 1991 to 1994 the number was equal to men and lower than in the preceding years. Applications for disability pensions decreased and rejection rates increased immediately both for men and women. But the effect was short-term, as the number of new disability beneficiaries started to increase rapidly again from 1995 and onwards, with more new female than male disability pensioners, and the total numbers of new entries reached new heights in 1998 and 1999. One of the reasons for the increase was a verdict in the Social Security Tribunal[23] in 1994, which overruled the medical criteria definitions introduced in 1991. The verdict came after a woman brought her case before the Tribunal after having been denied a disability pension with the diagnosis fibromyalgia. Claussen (1998a) argues that the restriction of disability benefits most affected applicants with the fewest resources and seems to have contributed to the ongoing process of marginalization of the weaker section of the population. In view of the increase in the number of disability beneficiaries and growth in expenses, the changes can hardly be said to have been a great success – because we are here talking about a growing economy with a low unemployment rate.

The National Insurance Act is based on rights. This means that the applicant has to meet certain requirements to receive benefits. Nevertheless, there is room for judgement, especially for disability pensions, and doctors and social security administration officials' assessments and practice can be of importance for the development in the number of disability pensioners. The doctor's role varies between being an advocate for the patient or a consultant for the NIA (Hvinden, 1994), but it would appear that doctors feel more loyalty towards their patients than to the NIA (Dæhlie, 1993). However, in an analysis of doctors as gatekeepers, Claussen (1998b) found that they were willing to be gatekeepers even when the medical criteria were tightened.

On the other hand, doctors do not agree on who meets the medical criteria. Terum and Nergård (1999) constructed two histories of sickness and got 360 doctors to consider them for disability pension. The doctors disagreed on whether or not the medical criteria were met, on the reduction of the work capacity and whether rehabilitation had been tried to a sufficient degree. These variations were to a large degree dependent on the doctors' personal values and moral concepts. It has also been shown that there are differences between general practitioners and doctors employed by the NIA (Getz, 1994; Getz and Westin, 1995).

4.6 Incentives, norms and work ethics

Views that attitudes and behaviour are changing, that the work ethic is not as good as it was and that people have less inhibitions in applying for pensions are widespread. The more people who live on a disability pension, the more common and the less stigmatizing it becomes. The research on this is scant and there is no systematic research on attitudes to applying for social security. Changes in behaviour need not come from changes in attitudes, because the available alternatives have also changed. Higher replacement rate and liberal eligibility criteria may increase people's choice – weighting the inconvenience of working with health problems against the reduced income living on a disability pension. As we shall see, econometric studies do not support this explanation as a cause for the increase in the number of disability beneficiaries.

In recent years the KIRUT database, as mentioned above, has been used to analyse the transition to disability pension. Hanssen (1994) and Dahl et al. (2000) both find that the probability of disability increases with age and education. Higher alternative income to disability pension leads to lower probability of transition to disability for women with subjective diagnoses as compared with women with objective diagnoses. Bratberg (1996a) found differences between men and women – the differences in elasticity with respect to expected income and expected benefits were much larger for males. Furthermore, females are more responsive to changes in benefits and the replacement rate than are males (Dahl et al., 2000). The results indicate that labour force status one year after entering long-term sickness is more sensitive to changes in expected wages than expected benefits. There is no clear evidence that having a "subjective" diagnosis increases the probability of becoming a beneficiary. In another paper Bratberg (1996b) modelled return to work and disability entrance as alternative destinations from sickness. In the observation period the rules for disability benefit eligibility had been tightened (1991), as previously mentioned, making it possible for him to assess the effect of a "natural experiment". One result was that the effect of previous earnings on transition back to work was statistically significant and positive. Furthermore, individuals entered disability and rehabilitation with higher rates when they were in a second spell of sickness. The results regarding the natural experiment indicate that the duration of all long-term sickness spells increased after the reform, suggesting unintended costs in connection with the reform. The tightening of the law in 1991 reduced the inflow because more applications were rejected, but the number of applicants did not go down (Andersen, 1995).

Hansen's (1996) results show that married women have a higher risk than men of becoming disabled (see also Enjolras and West Pedersen, 1997). Persons with a history of sickness, unemployment and rehabilitation have a significantly higher probability of becoming disabled. He also found that the replacement rate was important for the transition to disability pension.

But the transition to disability pension has been studied using data other than KIRUT. Christoffersen and Nervik (1991) compared transition to disability pension among persons receiving social assistance with other clients. Persons who leave social assistance to disability pension have less labour force experience and lower education than those who leave for work or education. It may be more legitimate to receive disability pension than long-term social assistance – it is less stigmatizing to receive a disability pension.

Becken (1996) investigated characteristics of young (20-40 year) disabled. Two out of three were women and 56% lived in eastern Norway. The difference in age and education between men and women was small, but women were more often married than men. The most important diagnoses were mental disorders, musculoskeletal, connective tissue diseases and diseases of the nervous system and sensory organ. Most of them preferred to work, and one-quarter had paid work.[24] A couple of other studies also show that disability pensioners are willing to work (Ruud et al., 1973; Kildal, 1976).

These studies are supported by Øverbye (1998), whose results show that new young disabled have a clearer connection to the labour market than earlier, and that men are more inclined to have income in addition to the disability pension than women. About 20% of all persons receiving disability pensions had paid work (1996), but the percentage decreased over time. Young (less than 36 years) disabled had increased their labour market participation, while it was decreasing for disabled over 47 years. The disabled adjusted their work effort to changes in the amount they could earn without losing some of the disability pension.

4.7 *Demography*

The most important explanation for the growth in disability pension in Norway *at the moment* is an ageing population and an ageing workforce, but no research considering these explanations has been carried out to date. The large numbers of persons born after 1944 are now close to the age where the risk of disability rises steeply, as the part of the population aged 50 to 66 increases. It is predicted that the number of disability beneficiaries will grow to 344,000 by 2010 and 366,000 by 2030 (NOU, 1998:10).

The use of disability pension increases with age, and the increase is very marked after the age of 50 (NOU, 2000: 27). When trying to explain the use of social security benefits in the light of demographic changes, two types of changes are discussed: changes in the age structure of the population, and changes in the occupational frequency of the different age groups. In the period 1993 to 1998 the number of employees increased by 45% for the 50-54 age group and 34% for the 55-59 age group. The growth in the population in the same age groups was 37% and 18% respectively. The age groups with the largest growth are the groups where the inflow to disability pension is highest. This indicates that changes in the age structure of the working population can explain some of the increase in the number of persons receiving disability pension. Calculations show that 50% of the growth in the period 1993-1998 can be explained by demographic changes. An age structure as in 1993 would have given an estimated 12 700 fewer disability pensioners.

4.8 Disability pension vs. AFP

In Norway the privately negotiated early retirement scheme (AFP) has stimulated research, as the use of the scheme has increased the last years. The tightening of the eligibility criteria for disability pensions coincided with a reduced pension age and an improved replacement rate in the AFP scheme. Substitution between the schemes seems to have taken place. The AFP scheme relieves some of the pressure on the disability pension (15%) and unemployment insurance (8%) systems (Thøgersen et al., 1998). Compared with persons receiving an AFP pension, the disability beneficiaries have low education, low income, weak health and work in the private sector (Visher and Midtsundstad, 1993; Rødseth and Bjørsvik, 1994). The process leading to early retirement and disability pension is different because of the importance of health for the transition to disability pension, which is not important for the transition to AFP (Dahl and Midtsundstad, 1994).

4.9 Conclusion

Norwegian research on disability pensions covers several areas and professions (medicine, sociology, economics and political science), but the focus has mostly been on the development in the labour market. In the last ten years, the number of studies has increased substantially as more money has been put into research on social insurance. Research has also been stimulated by better data, and a new database, called FD-Trygd, with event history data for the whole population for the years 1992-2000, is now in operation. The database contains detailed information on socio-economic background, labour market participation and social insurance payments. This makes it possible to study transitions of individuals between jobs, education, social insurance benefit schemes and social assistance.

Compared with other countries, the standard pension age in Norway is high (67 years), and until recently most employees had no early-retirement option other than a disability pension. As in several other countries, the disability pension has therefore functioned as an informal early retirement pension. In many countries, Norway included, difficulties in getting a new job have been used as eligibility criteria for disability pension. If disability were considered only in accordance with strict medical criteria, there would be no possibility of using such a scheme for early retirement.

Over the years several measures have been tried to reduce the inflow, such as tightening the eligibility criteria and more active rehabilitation (work line), but with limited success, as the growth, except for a couple of years, has not slowed down substantially. Several explanations have been put forward by researchers, politicians and bureaucrats, but there are no simple answers. As we have seen, the reasons for the observed growth are complex and the process leading to disability pension is a multi-dimensional phenomenon governed by medical as well as a variety of non-medical factors.

Notes

1. It should be added that there has been much political controversy in Norway in recent years concerning a "cash-for-care programme".
2. Three recent reports dealing with these issues are NOU 1998:10 *Fondering av folketrygden*, NOU 1998:19 *Fleksibel pensjonering*, and NOU 2000: 27 *Sykefravær og uførepensjonering*.
3. The terms for changing the system from a passive support line ("trygdelinjen") to a new active work orientation line ("arbeidslinjen") was first used in the Green Paper on Rehabilitation (*Stortingsmelding* nr. 39, 1991-92).
4. The employer's contribution is assessed as a percentage of gross wages, differentiated according to geographical regions, and with an additional contribution for wages exceeding "the basic amount". The contribution is 7.8% of pensionable income for employees, and 10.7% of pensionable income (with an upper income limit) for self-employed persons. The contribution rates are uniform.
5. Between 1997 and 2003, trials are being carried out to test a minimum limit of 20% partial disability.
6. Social assistance is in principle an individual right. However, according to the law, spouses are financially responsible for one another and parents are also responsible for looking after their children until they are 18 years old. Married persons and their dependant children are thus considered as one economic unit with regard to social assistance.
7. An insured employee may also be absent from work in order to care for a sick child.
8. In 2000 on a trial basis, chiropractors/physiotherapists were given the right to issue medical reports.
9. Self-employed persons receive sickness benefits equivalent to 65% of pensionable income from the 15th day of sickness for a period of 250 days (50 weeks). By voluntarily paying a higher contribution, they may obtain 65% of pensionable income from the first day of sickness or 100% from the 15th day of sickness or the first day of sickness. There are special rules in the case of employees who take care of sick children or close relatives at home. Between 1991 and 1993, three different reforms granted longer periods of sick leave to parents whose children are sick. An insured woman who has been working for six out of the ten months preceding delivery is entitled to daily maternity cash benefits at 100% for 42 weeks or 80% for 52 weeks.

10 From 1 July 2000 private employment agencies were allowed to offer re-employment services.
11 Special rules apply to persons having completed compulsory military or civilian service during the previous 12 months. They may receive unemployment benefits regardless of the conditions above concerning previous income.
12 Under the initial unemployment legislation, unemployment benefits were paid for 80 weeks, followed by a cut-off period of 26 weeks. During this period, recipients had to rely on social assistance or their own resources. This period was reduced to 13 weeks in mid-1991. In May 1992 the 80-week rule ceased to be applied automatically and at the same time the cut-off period was abolished in cases where the employment office was unable to offer either work or training schemes for the unemployed person.
13 Sheltered employment may be provided through labour market enterprises or work co-operatives. Work co-operatives offer permanent employment in sheltered sectors for persons with special needs or extensive disabilities who cannot benefit from other labour market programmes and who are receiving (or will receive) disability benefits. This includes the mentally retarded. Labour market enterprises aim at the vocationally disabled and consist of three phases: (1) testing of work capacity and prospects for on-the-job or educational training, (2) job training or formal training to improve employability and prospects for transition to ordinary work, (3) permanent employment in sheltered enterprises for disabled persons with limited prospects for ordinary work. In the first phase participants receive a training allowance or benefits from the National Insurance Scheme and in addition they may receive a small wage or bonus from the employer. In phases 2 and 3 standard wages are offered. Sickness benefits are often the only source of income in labour market enterprises during phase 1, while disability benefits are the only source of income in work co-operatives. It is possible to combine work in sheltered or reserved employment with sickness or disability benefits.
14 Supported employment started out as a three-year project initiated by the Ministry of Labour and Government Administration with the objective of developing new approaches to integrating people with vocational disabilities into ordinary jobs. The project was completed by the end of 1995 and became established early 1996 as a regular labour market measure.
15 Whereas the main rule in public sector recruiting is that the best qualified is employed, the Civil Servants Act gives the State employer the chance to choose a sufficiently qualified handicapped person before a more qualified non-handicapped person.
16 In the public sector occupational pension scheme it is also possible to retire three years before the special age limit if the sum of time in service and age amounts to 85 years or more.
17 The scheme where people retire early because of unemployment is not part of the public pension scheme but part of the unemployment scheme. However, both schemes are part of the National Insurance Scheme.
18 There has been a gradual extension of maternity leave from 18 weeks in 1977 to a maximum of 52 weeks in 1993. In order to gain full entitlement to benefit, it is now a requirement that the father draws benefit for at least four weeks. From 1994 parents can take part of their leave in form of a "time account".
19 The National Insurance Scheme has a medical definition of disability (disability, injury or defect), while the public employment service applies the term "vocationally disabled" to job seekers who have a physical, mental or social handicap that reduces their job opportunities. Thus, a disabled person without problems in the labour market would

not be included among the vocationally disabled. Also, measures are not linked to specific types of disability, but are considered on a case-by-case basis.

20   The participation rate for men aged 55-66 dropped from 81% to 66% in the period 1972-97. At the same time the labour force participation rates for women (aged 55-66) increased from 40% to 54%.

21   The KIRUT database contains data on a 10% random sample of the Norwegian population aged 16-67 years from the NIA, Directorate of Labour and Statistics Norway. It covers the years 1989 to 1996. KIRUT is a Norwegian acronym that roughly translates as "clients into and through the social insurance system".

22   At the end of 2000 57% (160 413) of the disability pension recipients were women.

23   The Social Security Tribunal settles disputes between two parties – the claimant and the social security system. The Tribunal is an independent institution, and the judges are lawyers, doctors, rehabilitation experts and laymen. If a person is dissatisfied with the decision of the Tribunal, s/he may bring an action before the ordinary courts.

24   It is possible to have an income of 0.5 G (approximately NKr 24 500 in 2000) and at the same time receive maximum disability pension.

References

Abrahamsen, Bente (1988) *1980-årenes uførepensjonister*. Rapport 88:10. Oslo: ISF.

Andersen, Erik (1995) *Årsaker til redusert tilgang til uførepensjon. Perioden 1989-1993*. Trygdeforskningsprosjektene rapport nr. 5 1995. Trondheim: Institutt for samfunnsmedisinske fag, Universitetet i Trondheim.

Amundsen, Ellen (1988) *Individuelle faktorer ved rekruttering til uførepensjoneringen - En empirisk studie 1977-1983*. Rapporter 88/16. Oslo: SSB.

Becken, Lars-Erik (1996) *Unge uførepensjonerte. En beskrivelse av kjennetegn ved uføre som er mellom 20 og 40 år*. Notat 1996: 3. Oslo: INAS.

Berg, Jon E. (1987) *Mellom arbeid og trygd*. Oslo: Sosialøkonomisk institutt, Universitetet i Oslo.

Berg, Jon E. (1994) 'Disability pensions granted form 1988 to 1990 in two municipalities in Norway: the importance of occupational status', *Scandinavian Journal of Social Welfare* 3: 14-18.

Bjerkedal, Tor/Michaelsen, Grete/Wergeland, Ebba (1995) *Yrkesspesifikk uførepensjonering i Norge 1993*. Rapport nr. 1/95. Oslo: Rikstrygdeverket.

Bjørndal, A./Johnsen, B./Clemetsen, P.I. (1990) 'Konsekvenser av innskrenkninger ved en Hjørnesteinsbedrift', *Tidsskrift for den Norske Lægeforening* 110: 239-242.

Bjørnson, Øyvind/Haavet, Inger Elisabeth (1994) *Langsomt ble landet et velferdssamfunn: trygdens historie 1894-1994*. Oslo: Ad Notam Gyldendal.

Blöndal, Sveinbjörn/Scarpetta, Stefano (1998) *The retirement decision on OECD countries*. Working paper AWD 1.4. Paris: OECD.

Bogen, Ingrid (1981) 'Ikke-medisinske årsaker til uførhet', *Tidsskrift for samfunnsforskning* 22: 309-330.

Bound, John (1991) 'Self-reported versus objective measures of health in retirement models', *Journal of Human Resources* XXVI: 106-138.

Bowitz, Einar (1992a) *Offentlige stønader til husholdninger. En økonometrisk undersøkelse og modellanalyse*. Sosiale og økonomiske studier nr. 80. Oslo: SSB.

Bowitz, Einar (1992b) 'Arbeidsledighet og uførepensjon', *Økonomiske analyser* 8: 7-13. Oslo: SSB.
Bowitz, Einar (1997) 'Disability, benefits, replacement ratios and the labour market. A time series approach', *Applied Economics* 29: 913-923.
Bragstad, Torunn/Sagsveen, Anne/Thorup, Edvard (2000) *Geografiske variasjoner i tilgang av nye uførepensjonister 1980-1997 etter fylke*. Rapport 06/2000. Oslo: Rikstrygdeverket.
Bratberg, Espen (1996a) 'Short run exits from long term sickness', in: Bratberg, Espen, *Incentives in Social Insurance*. Dissertations in Economics, No. 11. Bergen: Department of Economics, University of Bergen.
Bratberg, Espen (1996b) 'Sickness duration and disability eligibility', in: Bratberg, Espen, *Incentives in Social Insurance*. Dissertations in Economics, No. 11. Bergen: Department of Economics, University of Bergen.
Christoffersen, Lise (1995) *Uførepensjonen på 80-tallet. Nasjonal vekst med lokale varianter*. Rapport 1995: 2. Oslo: INAS.
Christoffersen, Lise/Nervik, Jon Arve (1991) 'Sosialkontoret – uførepensjonens venteværelse?', in: Hatland, Aksel (ed.), *Trygd som fortjent?* Oslo: Ad Notam.
Claussen, Bjørgulf (1998a) 'Restricting the influx of disability beneficiaries by means of law: experiences of Norway', *Scandinavian Journal of Social Medicine* 26: 1-7.
Claussen, Bjørgulf (1998b) 'Physicians as gatekeepers: will they contribute to restrict disability benefits?', *Scandinavian Journal of Primary Health Care* 16: 199-203.
Dahl, Espen/Birkelund, Gunn E. (1999) 'Sysselsetting, klasse og helse 1980-1995. En analyse av fem norske surveyer', *Tidsskrift for samfunnsforskning* 40: 3-32.
Dahl, Espen/Midtsundstad, Tove (1994) 'Hvorfor går eldre arbeidstakere av før ordinær pensjonsalder: vil de eller må de?', in: NOU (1994: 2), *Fra arbeid til pensjon*. Oslo: Statens forvaltningstjeneste.
Dahl, Svenn-Åge (1991) *Dekruttering og trygd*. SNF-report 13/91. Bergen: SNF.
Dahl, Svenn-Åge (1996) *Dekruttering - fra kriseløsning til strategi?* SNF-report 20/96. Bergen: Foundation for Research in Economics and Business Administration (SNF).
Dahl, Svenn-Åge/Nesheim, Torstein (1998) 'Downsizing strategies and institutional environments', *Scandinavian Journal of Management* 14: 239-257.
Dahl, Svenn-Åge/Nilsen, Øivind Anti/Vaage, Kjell (2000) 'Work or retirement? Exit routes for Norwegian elderly', *Applied Economics* 32: 1865-1076.
Dæhlie, Bjørg (1993) 'Diagnostisk rasjonalitet. Primærlegers mening og fibromyalgidiagnosen', *Tidsskrift for Den norske lægeforening* 114: 2827-2830.
Ellingsen, Dag (1988) 'Uførebefolkningen i utvikling', in: Kjønstad, Asbjørn (ed.), *I uførepensjonens og sosialhjelpens gråsone*. Oslo: Universitetsforlaget.
Ellingsen, Dag/Kjønstad, Asbjørn (1988) 'Uførepensjonistenes diagnoser', in: Kjønstad, Asbjørn (ed.), *I uførepensjonens og sosialhjelpens gråsone*. Oslo: Universitetsforlaget.
Enjolras, Bernard/West Pedersen, Axel (1997) *Forventet pensjoneringsalder og pensjoneringsmønstre blant seniorene i staten*. FAFO-notat 1997:20: Oslo: FAFO.
Esping-Andersen, Gøsta (1990) *The Three Worlds of Welfare Capitalism*. Cambridge: Polity Press.
Esping-Andersen, Gøsta (1999) *Social Foundations of Postindustrial Economies*. Oxford: Oxford University Press.
Getz, Linn (1994) *Trygdemedisinsk diagnostikk – er den pålitelig?* Trygdeforskningsprosjektene rapport nr. 3 1994. Trondheim: Institutt for samfunnsmedisinske fag, NTNU.
Getz, Linn/Westin, Steinar (1995) 'Rådgivende legers og primærlegers vurdering av komplekse uførepensjonssaker', *Tidsskrift for Den norske lægeforening* 115: 1748-1753.
Grimsmo, Asbjørn/Hilsen, Anne Inga (2000) *Arbeidsmiljø og omstilling*. AFIs skriftserie nr. 7. Oslo: Arbeidsforskningsinstituttet (AFI).

Grünfeld, Berthold/Noreik, Kjell (1991) 'Uførepensjonering blant innvandrere i Oslo', *Tidsskrift for Den norske lægeforening* 111: 1147-1150

Grünfeld, Berthold/Noreik, Kjell (1992) 'Bruk av helsetjenester og trygdeytelser blant immigranter i Oslo', *Tidsskrift for Den norske lægeforening* 112: 365-367.

Halleraker, Morten (1994) *Bruk av gavepensjoner ved førtidspensjonering*. Arbeidsnotat nr. 1/1994. Bergen: SNF.

Halsteinslid, Hilde (1988) *Trygd og økonomi. En modell for studiet av endringer i uføreandeler*. SSEF arbeidsnotat 4/88. Bergen: Institutt for økonomi, Universitetet i Bergen.

Halvorsen, Knut (1977) *Arbeid eller trygd?* Oslo: Pax.

Halvorsen, Knut (1980) 'Utstøting som forklaring på sanering av arbeidskraft', in: Halvorsen, Knut (ed.), *Arbeid og sysselsetting foran 80-åra*. Oslo: Pax.

Halvorsen, Knut (1983) 'Kritikken av utstøtingsmodellen', *Sosial trygd* 8/9.

Halvorsen, Knut (1994a) 'Those who cannot have what they want must want what they can get. The experience with company-based early retirement pension schemes in Norway', *Scandinavian Journal of Social Welfare* 3: 50-60.

Halvorsen, Knut/Johannessen, Asbjørn (1991) *Når bedriften ikke har bruk for deg lenger. Førtidspensjonering som individuell velferd, personalpoligikk og sosialpolitikk*. NKSH-rapport nr. 91:2. Oslo: NotaBene.

Hansen, Hans-Tore (1996) *Trygd – en midlertidig bro, eller en vei ut ar arbeidsmarkedet?* Avhandling for dr. philos. Bergen: SNF.

Hanssen, Astrid L. (1994) *Overgangen fra arbeid til uførepensjon – sannsynligheten for å bli uførepensjonert ved klare vs. diffuse diagnoser*. Bergen: SEFOS.

Hatland, Aksel/Kuhnle, Stein/Romøren, Tor Inge (1994) *Den norske velferdsstaten*. Oslo: Ad Notam Gyldendal.

Hvinden, Bjørn (1994) *Divided against Itself: A Study of Integration in Welfare*. Oslo: Scandinavian University Press.

Kildal, Nanna (1976) *Velferd og menneskeverd. En undersøkelse av uførepensjonister i en utkantkommune (Lyngen)*. Oslo: Universitetet i Oslo.

Kjeldstad, Randi (1990) *Yrkesdeltaking, yrkesinntekt og uførepensjonering*. INAS-rapport 90:3. Oslo: INAS.

Kjeldstad, Randi (1991) 'Overgang til uførepensjon. Konsekvenser av kvinners yrkestilpasning over livsløpet', in: Hatland, Aksel (ed.), *Trygd som fortjent?* Oslo: Ad Notam.

Kjønstad, Asbjørn (1987) *Norwegian Social Law*. Oslo: Norwegian University Press.

Kohli, Martin/Rein, Martin (1991) 'The changing balance of work and retirement', in: Kohli, Martin/Rein, Martin/Guillemard, Anne-Marie/van Gunstern, Herman (eds.), *Time for retirement. Comparative studies of early exit from the labor force*. Cambridge: Cambridge University Press.

Kolberg, Jon Eivind (1974) *Trygde-Norge*. Oslo: Gyldendal.

Kolberg, Jon Eivind (1976) *Hvorfor kom så mange på trygd – og langt flere enn forventet. Om årsaker til uførhet*. Tromsø: Universitetet i Tromsø.

Kolberg, Jon Eivind (1991) 'En empirisk utprøving av utstøtingsmodellen', in: Hatland, Aksel (ed.), *Trygd som fortjent?* Oslo: Ad Notam.

Kolberg, Jon Eivind/Kildal, Nanna/Viken, Arvid (1977) *Levekårsundersøkelsen. Uførepensjon og samfunnsstruktur*. NOU 1977: 2. Oslo: Universitetsforlaget.

Kolberg, Jon Eivind (ed.) (1992) *The study of welfare state regimes*. Armonk, New York: M.E. Sharpe.

Kuhnle, Stein (1990) 'Den skandinaviske velferdsmodellen – skandinavisk? Velferd? Modell?', in: Hovdum, A. R./Kuhnle, S./Stokke, L. J. (eds.), *Visjoner om velferdssamfunnet*. Bergen: Alma Mater.

Lajord, Jorunn/Flittig, Else (1995) *Innvandrere og uførepensjon.* Notat 95/20. Oslo: SSB.
Noreik, Kjell/Grünfeld, Berthold/Sundby, Per (1990) 'Notat om uførepensjonsordningen', in: NOU (1990: 17), *Uførepensjon.* Oslo: Statens Forvaltningstjeneste.
NOU (1994: 2) *Fra arbeid til pensjon.* Oslo: Statens forvaltningstjeneste.
NOU (1998: 10) *Fondering av folketrygden.* Oslo: Statens forvaltningstjeneste.
NOU (1998: 19) *Fleksibel pensjonering.* Oslo: Statens forvaltningstjeneste.
NOU (2000: 27) *Sykefravær og uførepensjonering.* Oslo: Statens forvaltningstjeneste.
Øverbye, Einar (1998) *Pensjonister i arbeid. En undersøkelse av uføre- og alderspensjonisters aktivitet på arbeidsmarkedet.* Skriftserie 5/98. Oslo: NOVA.
Rødseth, Tor (1990) *Trygd og effektivitet.* SEFOS notat 46. Bergen: SEFOS, UiB.
Rødseth, Tor/Bjørsvik, Geir (1994) 'Uførepensjonering og AFP-pensjonering', in: NOU (1994: 2). Oslo: Statens forvaltningstjeneste.
Rønsen, Marit/Westin, Steinar/Goldstein, Harald/Strøm, Steinar (1991) *Long-Term Effects of a Plant Closure: A Multistate Duration Analysis of Event History Data in a Ten Year Follow-Up Study.* SNF-rapport 30/91. Bergen: SNF.
Ruud/Lie (1973) 'En gang uføretrygdet - alltid uføretrygdet?', *Sosial trygd* 1973/5.
Seip, Anne-Lise (1994) *Veiene til velferdsstaten: norsk sosialpolitikk 1920-75.* Oslo: Gyldendal.
Solheim, Liv (1989) *Uføretrygda kvinner – vegen fram og livet etterpå.* Bodø: Norlandsforskning.
Stokke, Liv Jorunn (1993) *Uførepensjonistar i offentleg sektor.* FAFO-rapport 153. Oslo: FAFO.
Stortingsmelding nr. 39 (1991-92) *Attføring og arbeid for yrkeshemmede. Sykepenger og uførepensjon (Attføringsmeldingen).* Oslo: Statens forvaltningstjeneste.
Tellnes, Gunnar/Bruusgaard, Dag/Sandvik, Leiv (1990) 'Occupational factors in sickness certification', *Scandinavian Journal of Primary Health Care* 8: 37-44.
Terum, Lars Inge/Nergård, Trude B. (1999) 'Medisinsk skjønn og rettstryggleik', *Tidsskrift for Den norske lægeforening* 119: 2192-2196.
Thøgersen, Øystein/Bratberg, Espen/Holmås, Tor Helge (1998) *Normer, incentiver og tidligpensjonering.* SNF-report 33/98. Bergen: SNF.
Tysse, Tone Ingrid (1996) *Ledighet blant eldre arbeidstakere – en forløpsanalyse.* Bergen: Institutt for økonomi, Universitetet i Bergen.
Visher, Mary/Midtsundstad, Tove (1993) *Utgang fra arbeidslivet. En studie av eldre arbeidstakere førtidspensjonering og AFP.* FAFO-rapport 154. Oslo: FAFO.
Westin, Steinar (1981) 'Legene og arbeidsmarkedspolitikken', in: Brunstad, Rolf/Colbjørnsen, Tom/Rødseth, Tor (ed.), *Sysselsettingen i søkelyset.* Bergen: Universitetsforlaget.
Westin, Steinar (1990) *Unemployment and health: Medical and social consequences of a factory closure in a ten-year controlled follow-up study.* Trondheim: TAPIR.
Westin, Steinar/Norum, Dag (1978) *Når sardinfabrikken nedlegges.* Sosialdepartementets sammendragsserie nr. 6.
Westin, Steinar/Schlesselman, James J./Korper, Mieko (1989) 'Long-term effects of a factory closure: Unemployment and disability during ten years' follow-up', *Journal of Clinical Epidemiology* 42: 345-441.

CHAPTER 10

Invalidity Pensions:
Trends and Policies in Poland

Stanislawa Golinowska
Katarzyna Pietka

1 Definition of the term *invalidity*

According to the Polish law, the definition of invalidity contains two core elements: a medical factor relating to physical disability, and an economic one relating to the inability to work. Until the passage of the disability assessment reform in 1996, the medical element was the dominant factor of the assessment. A new definition making the ability to work the dominant assessment criterion was introduced in 1997.

The law of 28 June 1996, which enforced the disability assessment reform, defines an individual incapable to work as a person who has partially or completely lost his/her ability to work as a result of disability[1] and will not regain this capacity after retraining. An individual who is partially incapable of work is a person who has significantly lost his/her ability to perform work commensurate with his/her qualifications. An individual who is completely unable to work is a person who has lost his/her capacity to perform any type of work. Major detriment to physical ability requiring permanent or long-term care and the assistance of another individual to satisfy basic needs is regarded as complete inability to work and to pursue an independent existence.

Polish regulations on disability assessment do not commit the assessing institution to estimate the percentage of the detriment of health, which would be tantamount to benchmarking disability. An invalidity benchmark of 50% was assumed until 1996. It is quite possible that the overwhelming majority of doctors still continue to perform assessments on the basis of the 50% criterion. The process of standardizing the criteria and assessment procedures has just begun. For that reason, even if the benchmark were raised above 50%, it is unlikely that there would be any immediate effects in terms of limiting the number of disabled persons. An investigation of the assessments by the Institute for the Medicine of Labour has shown that only 30 to 50% of the cases were assessed according to the standard rules. This prompted the authorities to provide doctors with relevant training and start working on standardizing assessment procedures.

Table 1: Structure of assigned invalidity pensions by the degree of incapacity for work

Year	Total	Permanent incapacity for work and independent existence	Permanent incapacity for work	Partial incapacity for work
		in per cent		
1995	100.0	11.4	41.5	47.1
1996	100.0	12.0	41.3	46.7
1997	100.0	12.7	41.5	45.8
1998	100.0	12.9	40.9	46.2

Source: State Social Insurance Institute/ZUS data (1999, 1998, 1997, 1996).

Incapacity for work is assessed on the basis of all the following criteria:
- the nature and course of the disease and its impact on the physical condition,
- the mental and physical ability of the organism and the degree of adjustment to anatomic losses, disability, consequences of the disease,
- demonstrated qualifications, age, occupation, performed work and working conditions, and the capacity to continue working, and
- the possibility of regaining the capacity to work through treatment and rehabilitation or retraining.

The goal of the new definition of incapacity for work was to relieve the social insurance system from the need to grant invalidity pensions on confirmation of the deterioration of health (medical criterion). Under the regulations in force, if a doctor performing assessments for the Social Insurance Institution certifies blindness of one eye of a white-collar worker (an economist for instance), the worker is recognized as being able to work. Under the former act of 14 December 1982, the decision would classify him/her as a disabled person of the third category eligible for an invalidity pension.

Despite the amendment of the definition of incapacity for work, the categories of incapacity currently in force much resemble the earlier definitions of disability groups (see Table 1, column 1).

Occupational incapacity for work is applied in case of farmers. The act on social security of farmers does not contain the term 'invalidity', but refers to farming disability. Consequently, farmers are not expected to perform other occupations, even if invalidity is partial and does not prevent an individual from taking up another type of work.

The pension/benefit system for farmers – more favourable than for other occupational groups – is a transitional instrument of great importance. The policy of stimulating restructuring in agriculture through the pension system started in the 1960s and was intensified in the 1970s. The prerequisite for receiving a pension from the social system was to cede the farm to the Treasury or a qualified (in terms of farming skills) successor. In 1990, during the introduction of a free market and democracy, this rule was relaxed. Under the law of 20 December 1990, a farmer applying for the pension was required to stop working on the farm with no restriction on what he should do with the farm. Such liberty stemmed from the general rules of the Civil Code, and allowed for selling or renting the farm as well. Also, regulations concerning the agreement between the farmer and the successor were established in order to clearly define the relationship between them. Older generations of farmers in Poland have very low professional skills and have no chance of qualifying for a new job in the non-farming sector, which has been subject to very strong modernizing pressures. Providing those farmers with pensions eases the restructuring process as a whole. With the upcoming integration of Poland into the European Union, this process will have to be speeded up as well.

2 Coverage and eligibility

The right to an invalidity pension – both accident benefits and pensions resulting from general insurance – is granted to persons insured within the social security system, i.e. the employed, the self-employed and farmers (farmers in a separate system).

2.1 Eligibility within the employment system (employed and self-employed, State Social Insurance Institute/ZUS)

Eligibility for an invalidity pension is determined on the basis of the following three criteria:
- work incapacity,
- record of minimum required contribution and non-contribution periods,
- occurrence of disability during periods of employment or considered as employment, or within an 18-months period after completion of these periods.

Under the present law on ZUS pensions and benefits (act dated 17 December 1998), a minimum period covered by contributions or not covered by contributions but considered as an insurance period (e.g. during school time) is required. This requirement is similar to that found in earlier provisions:
- 1 year prior to completion of 20 years of age,
- 2 years at the age of 20-22 years,
- 3 years at the age of 22-25 years,
- 4 years at the age of 25-30 years,
- 5 years at the age of over 30 years, with the work disability occurring within the 10 years preceding the application.

The non-contribution period should not exceed one third of the period covered by contributions.

2.2 Eligibility for farmer's pension (Farmers Social Insurance Fund/ KRUS)

Under the 1990 law, the core eligibility criterion for invalidity pension is long-term (at least six months) incapacity for work on the farm. Under the earlier law, pension rights were granted as a consequence of total incapacity for work. Because of the fact that amended regulations have eased the criteria, the document specifies two types of incapacity – permanent and long-term incapacity. A permanent pension is granted to individuals who have been officially recognized as permanent invalids. It is also allocated automatically to those who are classified as "completely incapable of work and independent existence" (according to the latest definition) and are five years from the legal retirement age.

An additional condition for eligibility for an invalidity pension is termination of farming activities. An individual who fails to cease his/her farming activities may be punished with partial or total suspension of his/her invalidity pension.

The law does not specify the length of the insurance period required to claim farmer's pension from general insurance, but notes that the period should be within the ten years prior to the occurrence of the disability.

Both spouses working at the farm and other household members are entitled to separate pensions.

3 Organizational aspects of the invalidity system

As a consequence of the changes introduced in the 1990s, there are now three categories of institutions assessing medical disability:
1. institutions performing assessments for the employed and the self-employed pension system – ZUS,
2. institutions for the farmers' pension system– KRUS, and
3. institutions for non-pension-related disabilities, which, despite their name, perform assessments for pension-related purposes for individuals disabled at birth or persons who became disabled in their childhood or teens.

Table 2: Comparison: disability assessment institutions and the object of assessment

Former disability assessment system	Current disability assessment system employed by ZUS	Current disability assessment system employed by KRUS	Disability assessment for non-pension purposes, including social assistance
Disability and Employment Commission (KIZ)	A doctor performing assessments for ZUS	A doctor performing disability assessments – the first instance; KRUS Medical Commission – the second instance	District Disability Assessment Team
Disability of the first category	Complete work and independent existence incapacity	Complete and permanent incapacity to work on the farm	Major disability
Disability of the second category	Complete work incapacity		Moderate disability
Disability of the third category	Partial work incapacity	Partial and long-term incapacity to work on the farm	Minor disability

Source: Own comparisons

3.1 Current ZUS disability assessment system

ZUS-certified doctors carry out disability assessments and grant the right to disability benefits.

A ZUS-certified doctor is a medical specialist (holding the second degree) who has completed a training course recommended by the chief doctor of the Institution. A certified doctor issues his/her assessments individually, meaning that he/she is personally responsible for the contents of the assessments he/she produces. Previously, commissions of several doctors performed assessments.

In each case, before an assessment is given, the certified doctor may ask for additional medical or professional records, seek the opinion of a consultant doctor or psychologist, or perform additional tests or clinical observations.

The consultant doctor and the psychologist may issue their opinion only after direct examination of the applicant and an analysis of available medical and professional records.

Medical assessment is the sole basis on which the pension-awarding body decides whether to grant an invalidity pension or not.

With the mediation of a ZUS Division, the insured individual is entitled to appeal against the decision of the pension-awarding body to the Labour and Social Insurance Court.

The new law aims at increasing doctors' liability for the certificates they produce by reorganizing the invalidity assessment system.

The medical disability assessment procedure calls for the ZUS-certified doctor to operate in a regional ZUS division (earlier medical commissions for disability and employment were within the structure of a ZUS division, but worked independently and were often located at public healthcare establishments). This way, the social insurance institution can coordinate and supervise issues related to disability assessment.

There are 51 regional ZUS divisions in Poland. The network used to be based on the earlier regional structure of Poland (49 voyevodships). Under the administrative reform of 1999, the number of voyevodships was reduced to 16, which made the ZUS divisions' network too compact. Regional ZUS divisions are internal administrative units of the institution, i.e. the ZUS, and are not connected with the regional authority administration. The regional units are supervised by the ZUS head office in Warsaw.

3.2 Disability assessments within KRUS

After the disbanding of the Commission for Disability and Employment, which was in charge of medical assessments, KRUS organized its own (farmer-oriented) assessment institution in 1997. It performs assessments at two instances – the first instance is a doctor, and the second (higher) instance is the medical commission of KRUS. The president of the service supervises the implementation of assessments.

3.3 Disability assessment for non-pension purposes

Disability assessment for non-pension purposes (including invalidity pension benefits funded by social assistance) are performed by teams for assessment of disability categories, operating in line with provisions of the Vocational and Social Rehabilitation and Employment of the Disabled Act of 27 August 1997. Teams operate at district level[2] in local family assistance centres (PCPR), and a single team may service several districts (in line with agreements made between district authorities).

The team performs assessments at the request of the applicant, his/her legal representative or – with their consent – a social security institution.

Under the law, assessments cover:
- determination of the category of disability (major, moderate, minor),
- identification of the recommended type of benefit to which the disabled person is entitled:
  - training, including specialist courses,
  - identification of suitable employment to match the mental and the physical capacity of a given individual,
  - possibility of rehabilitation and indication of suitable forms to match individual capacity and needs (not including rehabilitation camps),
  - the need to apply for financial support from the social security service,
  - the need for orthopaedic devices and auxiliary equipment,
  - participation in therapeutic classes,
  - application for assistance during performance of everyday activities, that is, application for social and nursing services provided by a network of social assistance institutions, non-government organizations and others.

In 1999 the teams' responsibilities were expanded to enable them to perform assessments related to:
- identification of the need for permanent and direct childcare and nursing to an extent that the carer cannot take up employment or work on a farm run by an individual applying for the permanent benefit,
- meeting the criteria for admission to a nursing home specified by the Social Security Act.

Individuals are entitled to appeal against the assessment performed by the team for assessment of disability categories to a Board of Appeal at the local court.

4 Types of benefits/services offered through invalidity insurance

ZUS offers two types of benefits from the invalidity insurance:
1. benefits from the 'general' insurance, and
2. benefits in respect of work accidents.

(1) Invalidity pensions from general insurance are granted after the end of sick leave, during which an applicant was entitled to sickness benefit. Sickness benefit is granted for no longer than 180 days after medical confirmation of a temporary working disability. During the first 35 days the employer has to pay the benefit – in that respect, the benefit can be regarded as an extension of the salary. The required employment period is one month, meaning that an employee acquires the right to sick leave after one month of work. The amount of sickness benefit is equivalent to 80% of the person's wages. If after expiration of sick leave, an employee continues to be disabled, he/she is entitled to a rehabilitation cash benefit for the period of rehabilitation, if medical examinations confirm that the individual will be capable of working again within 12 months. The rehabilitation treatment may start before the end of the 180-day period, but the rehabilitation benefit (wage substitution) is paid after expiry of the right to sickness benefit.

The value of the rehabilitation benefit is equivalent to 75% of the recipient's wages. If a disorder resulted from a deliberate act or a fight, the employee is not entitled to sickness or rehabilitation benefit.

If a doctor identifies a reduced working capacity as a consequence of an illness, making the employee fit for less intense work, the employee is entitled to the compensation allowance. The allowance compensates for the difference between the wages before the partial incapacity to work and that received for the duration of the incapacity. The lower wages reflect the reduced productivity of the sick employee or correspond to those paid for a part-time job. This situation can apply to the position held before the incapacity or to a new position. The maximum period of the compensation allowance is short – three months. However, for an employee undergoing rehabilitation in parallel, the period can be extended to 24 months.

For an individual temporarily unable to work who has exhausted all the benefits he/she is entitled to (sickness benefit and possibly rehabilitation allowance) but is still unable to work, the invalidity assessment procedure determines whether the person is fully disabled or is unable to work in his/her current occupation.

New legal provisions (Invalidity Assessment Act of 1996) allow for assessment of the work disability in the previously held position and ability to work in another profession. In this case, applicants are entitled to the training benefit from the pension-granting body for 12 months. The benefit period may be extended (for no longer than 30 months) at the instigation of a job centre.

Once all of the above-mentioned possibilities have been exhausted, an employee who is disabled becomes entitled to an invalidity pension. The application for a disability pension must be submitted no later than 18 months after termination of employment (or an equivalent period of time). The pension-granting body may grant a permanent pension if permanent working disability is medically established, or a temporary pension if assessment indicates a temporary incapacity to work.

(2) A work accident invalidity pension is granted for loss of health as a result of an accident at work, on the way to and from work, or as a result of an occupational disease. Loss of health (since 1997, loss of ability to work) is determined by a certified doctor (previously medical commissions). A special law passed in 1983 specifies occupational diseases that entitle applicants to a work accident invalidity pension. Beneficiaries of such pensions are entitled to nursing allowance, rehabilitation services, professional training benefits (as in the case of pensions granted through general insurance), and the right to retire five years before reaching the legal retirement age. If an individual receives an invalidity pension granted for an accident at work, he/she may choose on reaching the retirement age to maintain the pension and claim a 50% old-age pension, or to receive 50% of the invalidity pension and all of the old-age pension. This means that his/her income at retirement could be higher than during the working period.

5 Invalidity pension formula

(1) The invalidity pension granted from general insurance to an individual totally unable to work is 24% of the basic amount plus 1.3% of the pension

calculation base for each year of contribution, plus 0.7% of the calculation base for each year of non-contribution and each year of a hypothetical period. These periods are calculated by complete months. The invalidity pension formula is as follows:

Pension = 24% of basic amount + [1.3% × Ns + 0.7% × Nns + 0.7% × Nnsb] of calculation base

Basic amount is 100% of gross average wage minus social insurance contributions.

Pension calculation base is an average base for calculating social insurance contributions based on 10 calendar years chosen by the applicant from the 20 calendar years preceding the year in which the application for pension was submitted. The total multiplier of the calculation base may not exceed 250%.

Contribution periods (Ns) are periods covered by contributions.

Non-contribution periods (Nns) are periods during which an equivalent to remuneration was received, leave without pay, university studies (up to standard university age), and the inability to work before 1989 because of political repression.

Hypothetical non-contribution periods (Nnsb) are periods that the pensioner is missing to meet tenure-related (25 years of work) and age criteria (60 years), which are required to acquire the right to an old-age pension. The difference between the legal retirement age for males and females is not taken into consideration.

Pensions granted to individuals who are partially unable to work are 75% of the pension for total work incapacity.

In no case should the amount of the pension exceed 100% of the calculation base, nor should it be lower than the minimum statutory pension.

Invalidity pensions are subject to adjustment on the basis of the CPI.

(2) Work injury benefit is equivalent to a maximum of 100% of the individual calculation base for a fully disabled person, and 75% for a partially disabled person.

The calculation base for the benefit may not be lower than 1.5 times the minimum wage.

Work injury benefits may not be lower than 80% of the wage in the case of total incapacity (individual calculation base), and 60% for partial incapacity. The 1975 provisions also specify the relation between the minimum work injury benefit and disability benefit from the general insurance. The minimum work injury benefit must exceed the minimum invalidity pension from the general insurance by at least 20%.

Work injury benefits are not terminated when the person acquires an old-age pension – both pensions are paid simultaneously.

(3) Farmers' pensions

The social insurance system for farmers uses the same formula for calculating old-age and disability pensions.

Old-age or disability pension = p * employee minimum old-age pension + 1% * insurance period * employee minimum old-age pension, where:

p = an indicator ranging from 85% to 95%, depending on the number of contribution years – the greater the number of contribution years the higher p.

The farmer's old age (disability) pension cannot be lower than the minimum employee old-age (disability) pension.

Farmers' social security contributions do not depend on income or the size of the farm but solely on the number of persons working on the farm (a farmer and his family members). The calculation base for contributions is the income of the owner of a medium-sized farm. The farming contribution

Table 3. Farming and working disability pension

Year	Average monthly farming disability pension, PLN	Average monthly working disability pension, PLN	Relation of farming to the working pension
1985	0.65	0.92	70.6
1990	47.4	52.6	90.1
1991	81.0	98.6	82.0
1992	111.9	151.3	74.0
1993	149.8	201.4	74.4
1994	218.2	277.4	78.6
1995	282.6	357.1	79.1
1996	354.1	434.9	81.4
1997	417.4	523.0	79.1
1998	476.5	598.6	79.6

Source: ZUS and KRUS.

is thus very low. Despite this fact, only 75% of farmers pay social security contributions. Contributions cover only 6% of KRUS expenditure – the rest is financed from the budget.

As a result, the levels of farming disability pensions differ from one another only to a very small extent. They are lower than disability pensions for workers (see Table 3), but the difference is smaller than between total incomes of farmers and total incomes of the working society: The ratio is 0.8 for disability pensions and 0.7 for total disposable incomes. Disability pensions are becoming a very important source of income in most farms, especially with so many of them experiencing substantial drops in productivity.

6 Invalidity pension and working

Partially disabled individuals may take up employment on the following conditions (valid since March 1999):
- If the revenue generated by work is 70% or less of the average monthly salary, the pensioner is entitled to the full amount of the pension.
- If the pay is between 70 and 130% of the average monthly salary, the benefit is decreased by any amount earned in excess of 70% of the average monthly salary, but by no more than 24%, 20.4% and 18% – for each category of disability respectively – of the basis for pension calculation (valid since December 1998 and indexed annually for CPI growth).
- If earnings exceed 130% of the average monthly wage, the pension payment is suspended.

The combination of disability benefit and income from work effectively legalized the situation in which disabled persons were working unofficially.

For those who are able to earn higher wages, the law assumes that their salaries will be enough for them to live off. It is possible that such a rule demotivates people from working in jobs generating higher incomes that would result in their losing some or their entire pension. At present, the discrepancy between disability benefits and wages is great enough for working to be advantageous for those disabled persons who are able to find a well-paid job. In any case, the linking of disability pensions with high working incomes would be too generous in a country where the people are poor and the social security system is weak.

Persons with total work incapacity may take up employment only at a sheltered workshop where working conditions meet the needs of the disabled.

The Polish labour market has a relatively large group of disabled workers, which is a direct consequence of strong incentives for employers to hire disabled individuals. There are two types of measures aimed at increasing employment of this group: an obligatory quota for disabled employees and the provision of subsidies and other benefits from the public treasury for sheltered workshops. The 1991 Employment and Rehabilitation of the Disabled Act commits employers with more than 50 employees to include 6% disabled persons on their payroll. Employers who fail to employ any disabled person or employ fewer than 6% must pay a fine to the quasi-budgetary State Fund for Rehabilitation of the Disabled (PFRON). Disabled persons with severe and moderate disabilities (according to the non-pension system criteria) have many rights: shorter working day (7 hours), longer holiday leave (additional 10 days), lower social insurance contribution (by 50%). Unfortunately, the system does not always function as the legislators had intended.

Under the Professional and Social Rehabilitation and Employment of the Disabled Act of 27 August 1997 disabled persons are entitled to business loans on highly favourable terms. The efficiency of this measure has not been yet investigated.

7   Unemployment benefit versus invalidity pension

Pension and benefit system provisions rather than unemployment benefits were the core social protection measures used to address the rapid growth in unemployment. To reduce the number of newly unemployed coming from deteriorating and restructured State companies, older persons were given the option of early retirement. A relatively liberal medical assessment system was also maintained (as late as 1997). Within this system individuals could claim invalidity pensions instead of the unemployment benefit, especially during the initial period of transformation. In the years 1989 to1992 (four years) the average number of pensioners went up by almost two million (20%), whereas the population at retirement age grew by 863,000, that is slightly over 1%. A particularly dramatic increase in the number of old age and invalidity pensions was observed in 1991, when the number of first-time benefits soared by almost 50%.

The disability system played an important role in amortizing growing unemployment, however, the criterion of the labour market situation was never officially included into the disability assessment. People exposed to the risk of losing their job were highly motivated to seek a disability pension. In view of the poor health of Polish society, especially among workers and farmers, fulfilment of the medical criteria was not difficult. Additionally, the assessment system was rather 'soft'.

Table 4: Development of unemployment and disabled levels

Year	Registered unemployment		Disability beneficiaries (in the employee and farming systems)	
	Number of people in 1 000	Growth: previous year = 100	Number of people in 1 000	Growth: previous year = 100
1990	1 126.1		2 628	
1991	2 155.6	191.4	2 835	107.9
1992	2 509.3	116.4	3 043	107.3
1993	2 889.6	115.1	3 166	111.6
1994	2 838.0	98.2	3 289	103.9
1995	2 628.8	92.6	3 391	103.0
1996	2 359.5	89.7	3 457	101.9
1997	1 826.4	77.4	3 501	101.3
1998	1 831.4	100.3	3 531	100.8
1999	2 349.8	128.3	3 500	99.1

Source: GUS – Statistical Yearbooks of the Republic of Poland.

Over the past decade, the social security policy for the unemployed has been tightened and unemployment benefits have become more restrictive. Unemployment benefits always used to be low, with very limited differentiation and they were generally short-term. They did not provide sufficient alternative social security to disability pensions, particularly because Polish unemployment is mostly structural and the proportion of long-term unemployed in the total number is growing.

- *Generous benefits only at the beginning*

The first law providing unemployment benefits, the Employment Act of December 1989, fixed the amount of the benefit at 70% of wages during the first three months, 50% for the next six months and 40% for the next nine months. It was relatively easy to obtain an entitlement to the benefit. An unemployed person who declared his/her intent to take up a job was automatically entitled to the benefit. The benefit period was basically unlimited and could be claimed until an individual received a job offer. At this time non-employed persons such as wives maintained by their husbands were also claiming the benefit. This situation (heaven for the unemployed, but not necessarily out of job) lasted slightly over six months.

The requirements were made more stringent in August 1990. Outside the farming sector, only those who had been previously employed for at least 180 days were entitled to benefits. May 1991 saw the introduction of the classification of *gminas* in terms of their unemployment rate, which meant that the entitlement to benefits depended on the unemployment rate in the region where the applicant lived. In *gminas* where the risk of unemployment was high, individuals could claim the benefit for 18 months, if they had between 25 and 30 years of qualifying employment, while in other regions the benefit was paid for 12 months.

- *Decrease in the unemployment rate*

In 1991 the unemployment rate doubled from 6% to 12%. A law, the Employment and Unemployment Act, was passed in October 1991. The right to the benefit remained unchanged, but the law provided for a considerable decrease in the amount paid to 33% of the average wage for the entire benefit period, which was kept as 12 months, or a maximum of 18 months (for employees with 25 to 30 years of qualifying employment) in *gminas* with particularly severe unemployment.

The wage-dependent benefit concept was replaced by a flat-rate formula. The change was mainly prompted by budget limitations resulting from a slump in production and a crisis in public expenditure in the initial years of transformation. Effective for short periods, this type of benefit was justified by the financial crisis (Barr, 1999).

Political opposition criticized the Solidarity government for the massive unemployment, generous benefits and passive labour market policy, and the failure to actively prevent unemployment. This criticism encouraged the Minister of Labour to issue a decree on public and intervention works on 17 December 1991 and to allocate funds to subsidized jobs for selected employee groups, e.g. the disabled.

In 1992 the unemployment rate reached 13.6% and for the first time there was some discussion as to whether the unemployed in Poland were really not working. Many people pointed to the extensive grey economy and the handsome income to be earned there. The Central Statistical Office of Poland (GUS) launched a systematic survey of the economic activity of the population (BAEL), which produced a detailed picture of employment and unemployment. Several laws were passed that year (including the two amendments to the Employment and Unemployment Act in February and October). This led to an increase in the unemployment benefit – up to 36% of the average wage – and expanded the scope of active labour market programmes and the exemptions for employees in *gminas* with severe unemployment.

In 1993 the unemployment rate rose to 16.4%, the highest level in the entire transformation period. Surveys carried out by GUS (BAEL) indicated that in terms of the total activity of the population, the rate was in fact 1 to 2 points lower. Dramatic growth in unemployment came to an end the same year.

The characteristics of unemployment observed in the initial period of transformation resulted from the imperfect unemployment benefits system. This justified the replacement of the wage-related benefit by a flat-rate benefit. Contrary to the common belief that the unemployed are often employed but illegally, the majority of beneficiaries simply failed to search for jobs and the benefit constituted a significant portion of their family's income. This conclusion was formulated on the basis of analyses of initial data generated by labour force surveys. Between 1990 and 1993, the benefit was claimed by over 80% of all registered unemployed. The overwhelming majority of this group treated the benefit system as means to improve their (and their family's) financial status without taking up employment.

Table 5 shows an assessment of the situation in the labour market in 1990 to 1995 using the Sztanderska method (Sztanderska, 1996) for evaluating the reasons for the changes.

In the first period of transition, the fundamental impact on the unemployment level was related to the fall in employment. Until 1992, the decrease in the number of employed was even higher than the inflow of the new labour force. A part of the drop in employment was related to the fact that people accepted early retirement and their workplaces being cut rather than offered to newcomers. During the three years from 1990 to 1992 the labour market balance was negative, i.e. the total number of persons leaving the labour market due to retiring (including early retiring) exceeded the number of newcomers (by 2.5 times in 1991). This implies that in that period the adverse impact of the high increases in the number of new labour market participants on unemployment was entirely absorbed by retiring. In the years of highest growth in unemployment, the high level was not influenced by demographic shifts in labour resources. Nor does the reduction in jobs available fully explain the annual rise and fall in the number of employed persons as shown in Table 5. It is possible that in the transition period people who had not worked before became professionally active. This includes people who would not have entered the labour market without the motivation of granting benefits to women who had not worked before or to school-leavers, for example.[3] This hypothesis was put forward by Sztanderska (1996), Góra (1995) and Kwiatkowski (1995).

Table 5: Balance of changes in population on the labour market – increases/decreases compared to previous year (in thousands)

Item	1990	1991	1992	1993	1994	1995
1 Employment in 000s	-1 244	-703	-432	-250	+163	+28
2 Unemployed	+1 126	+1 030	+354	+380	-52	-209
3 Professionally active (1 + 2)	-118	327	-78	+131	+111	-187
4 Inflow of new labour resources due to reaching professional activity age	563	573	598	621	640	631
5 Outflow due to retirement and disability	925	1 361	678	555	529	472
6 Pure effect of demographic changes and impact of social insurance system on professional activity (4 minus 5)	-362	-789	-80	+66	+111	+159
7 Unemployment increase due to other reasons (3 minus 6)	245	1 115	2	65	0	0

Source: Based on Sztanderska (1996) and author's own amendments.

The balance between persons who are active on the market and those who are leaving it is biased by double counting of persons combining a pension and working income at the same time. The disability and old-age pensioners group consists of people who have left the labour market, although some of these people actually stay on the market while receiving pensions. It is estimated that about 30% of all old-age and disability pensioners are still legally employed (Wiktorow, 1996). Polish regulations decreased pensioners' benefits and wages from work only if they exceeded 120% of the average wage. Only after this threshold had been exceeded did the beneficiary have to make a choice whether to work and have the benefit suspended or to continue to receive the benefit and work part-time for less money.

Many old age and disability pensioners work in the shadow economy. GUS surveys from that period on unregistered work (Kalaska et al., 1996) shed some light on the size of this phenomenon. About 6 to 10% of the population aged over 60 works illegally. Among 'younger' pensioners the figure is probably closer to the upper limit of 10%.

In 1992-1993, the annual growth in unemployment was three times lower than in 1990-1991 and the changes in the labour market were less drastic than they had been hitherto. In parallel with the declining rate of redundancies, one essential factor contributing to the slower growth in unemployment was the increasingly positive balance of demographic shifts. The new entrants to the labour market were more numerous each year than those retiring from it.

- *Diversification of rights to benefits and their amounts*

Unemployment started to decrease in 1994. Whereas in 1994 the rate of registered unemployment stood at 16%, it was lower by one percentage point in 1995, declined by three percentage points in 1996 and reached 10.3% in the fourth quarter of 1997. The declining tendency in unemployment allowed the new government to pursue a less intensive labour policy. The unemployment debate was fuelled by new topics. Although many continued to feel concerned by this new phenomenon, some argued that excessive social security measures aimed at the unemployed created a social trap which encouraged beneficiaries to remain unemployed. The government document *Strategy for Poland* stated that the demotivating effects of excessive social protection for the unemployed should be limited. Appropriate steps were taken in 1994 and incorporated in the amendment of August 1994 to the Employment and Unemployment Act. The definition of the unemployed was modified to classify them as people who were actually out of work.

New measures for older employees aimed at cutting down the number of people retiring early or applying for an invalidity pension. It was stressed that early retirement and invalidity pensions were more expensive than unemployment benefits. This argument was strongly advocated by experts from the World Bank. The criticism and the intention of providing social security for older employees were the driving forces behind the enforcement of anticipatory old-age benefits paying 52% of average wages.

To reduce the negative impact of unemployment by young people starting a family, the benefit period was extended if the unemployed maintained his/her children and the spouse was also unemployed.

In 1995 this labour market policy was continued, with the main focus on restricting the entitlement to benefits and provision of preferential security measures to selected groups threatened by unemployment. Measures to counteract the demotivating effects of social security for the unemployed were reflected by the amendment to the Employment and Unemployment Act of December 1995. The amount of the benefit was quota-based, totalling PLN 260, which at the time was equivalent to 36% of average wages. Yet, in time, with price adjustment of the benefit and wages growing faster than prices, the ratio between the benefit and the average wage decreased in real terms in 1994, for the first time in several years

Regulations on the obligation to accept jobs offered to the unemployed became stricter. After two refusals (three in the earlier law), the unemployed lost his/her right to the benefit, even if the offered jobs failed to match his/her qualifications. Job centre employees were responsible for monitoring the current status of the unemployed.

The decrease in unemployment in Poland varied considerably from one region to another. This meant that the unemployment policy had to become more selective. An analysis of unemployment was carried out by *gmina* and region. As a result, benefits and other labour market measures were adapted to the needs of the different regions. Regional authorities did their best to ensure that their regions were included in the *gminas* and regions with high structural unemployment since this status enabled them to apply for additional funds for development of infrastructure (public and intervention works), investments and/or tax exemptions for businesses.

- *Further restrictions in rights to benefits*

In 1996 the policy pursued during the previous two years was continued. It focused on diversifying the right to benefits and expanding programmes for activating the unemployed. At the same time, the Government started to implement a policy provided for under the law of 1995, which modified the definition of unemployment and provided grounds for restricting the right to benefits. After 1995, the benefit was granted exclusively to individuals with no other source of income. Previously, individuals earning a modest income up to 50% of the lowest wages had also been able to claim benefits. The formula for calculating benefits was also amended. The flat-rate benefit was replaced by a tenure-dependent one. Individuals with no more than five years of tenure were entitled to 80% of the benefit, whereas persons with tenure of over 20 years were entitled to claim 120%.

Generally speaking, active non-individual measures aimed at the long-term unemployed are not very efficient. This group of unemployed gradually loses its foothold in the labour market and becomes more and more dependent on the social security system. In 1997, benefits were claimed by 40% of the total unemployed. At the end of 1998, the figure went down to 30% and dropped further to 20.6% in mid-1999, not counting anticipatory old-age pensions and allowances. As a social protection measure aimed at employees of restructured industries, the latter type of benefits witnessed a dramatic growth in the years 1998 and 1999. The amount of the unemployment benefit slumped to approximately 30% of the average wage.

The decline in unemployment in the mid-1990s meant that the Government paid less attention to labour market policy than in the initial period of transformation. It turned more to reforms in other areas, and eventually social programmes for employees made redundant by restructured branches of the economy and industries became core labour market issues.

- *Recurring growth in unemployment*

Since 1999, unemployment has been on the increase again in Poland. By mid-2000, the unemployment rate had again reached 13.6%. At the same time, assistance for the unemployed was extremely limited. During the initial period of territorial administration reform and other social reforms[4] public expenditure on development of new institutions increased at the expense of funding for social benefits and services. At present, the average unemployment benefit is less than 30% of the average wage and is claimed by barely one fifth of the total unemployed. In these circumstances, pensions rather than unemployment benefits are a more interesting addition to income of persons threatened by unemployment.

8 Invalidity pension versus early retirement

During the real socialist era with its advocacy of total employment, early retirement was a political privilege. It was reserved for groups that contributed to the 'establishment of socialism', such as miners, railway employees, police, army, journalists, artists and teachers. It was accorded to those working in 'special conditions' (a term used to refer to working conditions that are hazardous to health) or those with a 'non-standard working profile' (term not clearly defined). Women with over 30 years of tenure were also entitled to retire five years early. As a consequence of these preferences, the actual retirement age (55 years for women and 59 years for men) was five and six years earlier, respectively, than the official retirement age (60 years for women and 65 years for men).

Invalidity pensions were an attractive benefit mainly for farmers (the number of applications for pension within the system for farmers has always been higher than in the employee system) and persons employed in non-privileged industries. Pensions were more often granted to men than to women. First-time pensioners were approximately 45 years old.

The transformation period also brought about certain attempts at changing the system. These included the removal or limiting of privileges relating to early retirement. The attempt was successful only initially (under the Revalorization Act of 1991), and thus only smaller, poorly organized and less claim-oriented groups, such as the academics, were affected by the restriction. The second attempt took place in 1999 under the radical pension reform. Following protests, mainly from miners, the Government introduced 'transitional pensions' for claimants who were entitled to the privilege but would have lost it following the reform of 1 January 1999. In line with the acquired rights principle, an alternative solution had to be found for this group. The authorities proposed the introduction of transitional pensions, i.e. benefits for persons entitled to early retirement until they became eligible for a statutory retirement pension.

The Government also introduced a solution that allowed employees to retire early if their company was forced to make personnel cuts. This solution was devised in response to the growing unemployment in the early 1990s. The problem was resolved by means of a benefit that enabled older employees under the statutory retirement age but with the required tenure to retire early. The regulation was limited to redundancies in restructured or declining companies, and eventually encouraged a large number of employees to decide on this option. It is possible that many people who retired under these regulations could have continued working. In reality, the State provided them with material security but failed to prevent their return to the labour market, with the result that many of the redundant early retirees decided to work again later.

The decree which permitted early retirement in connection with redundancy, remained in force for seven years (1990 to 1996). During that period, almost 50% of all retiring employees at the beginning and approximately 40% at the end of the period were early retirees.

This regulation was partly modelled on solutions applied in Western European countries, which also employed the pension and benefit system to suppress unemployment (during the oil crisis).

New solutions were introduced in 1995 in the form of 'anticipatory old-age benefits'. These benefits were not provided under the old-age regulations, but under the Employment and Prevention of Unemployment Act, and were financed not by the Social Insurance Fund but by the Labour Fund.[5] They were designed for elderly persons living in high unemployment areas. The level was set initially at 80% of the potential old-age pensions and from 1998 at 90%. Amendments to the Employment Act in 1998 introduced pre-retirement benefits for elderly employees at 30 to 50% higher than regular unemployment benefits.

It was thus still possible to retire early, although the option was now referred to as 'the benefit'.

In 1999, when unemployment started growing again, the demand for pre-retirement benefits and allowances increased so dramatically that the Minister of Labour was forced to apply for a loan from the Labour Fund. The number of new invalidity pensions did not increase to the same extent, however. Besides the tightening of the qualification criteria, the reform of medical assessments also created new problems. As a result of a large number of appeals by persons who had been refused the benefit, the ombudsman proposed the development of a new transitional benefit for the unemployed with poor health who were no longer entitled to the invalidity benefit under the new definition of invalidity.

The focus on invalidity pensions will increase as the eligibility for pre-retirement benefits through the labour market or social security system is further restricted. Officially, the criterion related to the situation on the labour market was not included in the system for invalidity pensions. Deterioration in conditions on the labour market is usually accompanied by an increase in the number of applications for invalidity pension and in the number of benefits granted.

9 Reforms of the invalidity pension system and related systems since 1970

Major changes in the Polish social security system were introduced by Edward Gierek, who launched the 'socialist upgrading' of the country in the 1970s. The core elements of these changes in social security were an extension of the system to the private sector and to individual farmers and craftsmen, and equal rights for blue- and white-collar workers. From a structural point of view, the most important developments included the introduction of uniform benefits through their integration and the closing of gaps in the social security network. This solution was intended to prevent situations in which an insured individual who was unable to work would be deprived of income at a certain stage of his/her disability (e.g. introduction of sickness benefit to cover the period between termination of sick leave and eligibility for an invalidity pension).

Two sets of changes took place in the 1980s. The first phase was inaugurated at the beginning of the decade. As part of the reform of the centralized social security system, an attempt was made to increase the transparency of public expenditure and the economy. The second stage was initiated during the period of martial law, when populist solutions and privileges for influential working class groups were introduced to legitimate authorities that lacked the support of society.

The 1990s, a decade marked by transformation of the political and the economic system, can be split into two stages. The first stage, which took place at the beginning of the decade, saw solutions that responded to the expectations of the new social movements (including Solidarity) regarding general principles of social justice and support for dramatic changes in the economic system, such as automatic indexation of benefits. Stage two – implemented in the late 1990s – focused on the introduction of reforms that would create more scope for greater individual precaution (propensity to save) and would permit savings in public expenditure and hence a decrease in taxes. Within the social insurance system for the disabled the definition of invalidity was redefined from biological to economic disability (detriment to health was replaced by capacity to take up an income-generating job), and one-man medical assessments (instead of commissions) were also introduced. In 1999, a revolutionary pension reform came into force, which included a compulsory capital segment and defined contribution formula. The invalidity pension formula remained unchanged, with the result that persons with a potentially modest pension in the future (low wages, gaps in employment) will benefit more from an invalidity pension. This encourages people to apply for invalidity pensions, of which there are already a large number in Poland.

Nota bene, disability pension is a life pension if the person is not eligible for an old-age pension. The right to an old-age pension is contingent on the meeting of two criteria: (1) age criterion – 60 for women, 65 for men, (2) contribution history – at least 20 years for women and 25 years for men. People with fewer opportunities on the labour market, who are thus less likely to obtain a reasonable old-age pension will be strongly motivated to seek a disability pension, even if it is based on a very minor inability to work. There is a need to harmonize the two systems (adjusting the disability system to the reformed old-age one) in order to eliminate such incompatibilities.

Comparison – fundamental provisions on social security in the event of illness and invalidity in the years 1970-2000

Year of passage	Subject of the provision	Legal format – source
1972	Introduction of unified sickness benefits replacing various sickness allowances, equal rights for blue- and white-collar employees	Law increasing benefits in the event of an illness of the employee, 7 July 1972
1974	Maintenance of acquired rights to the benefit upon cession of the farm (transfer to the State Land Bank or cession to the successor)	Law transferring farms to the State in return for pension and financial benefits, 29 May 1974
1974	Benefit Act; benefit integration and introduction of sick pension after termination of 6-month benefit period	Law on financial benefits through health insurance in the event of illness and maternity, 17 December 1974
1975	Industrial Accident Act; farmers are covered by occupational accident system, identification of insurance and compensation benefits	Law on financial benefits in respect of accidents at work and occupational diseases, 12 June 1975
1975	Definition of accidents at work and rights of victims	Decree of the Minister of Labour, Wages and Social Issues on principles and procedure for identification of detriment of health and allocation of benefits for accidents at work, on the way to and from work, and occupational diseases, 17 October 1975

Year of passage	Subject of the provision	Legal format – source
1975	Amended Benefit Act: the amount of the benefit is dependent on work tenure	
1976	Social security covers individuals pursuing economic activity, including free professions	Law on social security for persons conducting economic activity and their families, 18 December 1976
1977	Farmers are covered by social security, however disability pension equals old-age pension and there is no scaling of pensions on the basis of the level of disability	Law on old-age benefits and other benefits for farmers and their families, 27 October 1977
1982	Farmers became subject to the same criteria as employees: contributions, retirement age, legal definition of invalidity for farmers	Law on social security for farmers and their families, 14 December 1982
1982	Unification of principles, introduction of diversification – permanent and long-term disability	Law on old-age benefits for employees and their families, 14 December 1982
1983	Index of employee groups entitled to retirement privileges on the basis of non-standard work profile or work in special conditions	Decree of the Council of Ministers on the retirement age and an increase in invalidity pensions and benefits for employees working in special conditions or non-standard work profile, 7 February 1983
1983	Index of occupational diseases entitling applicants to invalidity pension	Decree of the Council of Ministers on occupational diseases, dated 18 November 1983
1990	Establishment of a separate social insurance institution for farmers – KRUS, rights to benefits upon termination of farming activities	Law on social insurance of farmers and their families, 20 December 1990
1991	Definition of invalidity and identification of obligations of employers hiring the disabled	Law on employment and rehabilitation of the disabled, dated 9 May 1991
1991	Revalorization Act; introduction of new old-age and disability pension formulas, automatic indexation of benefits, cancelling pension supplements for some of the branches	Law on revalorization of old-age benefits and pensions, principles for identification of old-age benefits and pensions and amendment of selected acts, 17 October 1991
1996	Setting the procedure and essential documents for identifying temporary working disability	Decree of the Minister of Health and Social Security on identification of temporary working disability, 17 May 1996

Year of passage	Subject of the provision	Legal format – source
1996	Disability assessment reform – modification of the term 'invalidity' and organization of medical invalidity assessment; in force from September 1997	Law on amendment of selected acts on old-age benefits for employees and their families, 28 June 1996
1996	Introduction of social pensions for disabled not covered by any of the systems	Law on amendment of the act on social security, 14 June 1996
1997	Social privileges for the disabled, including credits for their economic activity	Law on professional and social rehabilitation and employment of the disabled, 27 August 1997
1998	System Act: division of risk and insurance funds within social insurance system, identification of the nature of particular types of insurance	Law on the social insurance system, 13 October 1998
1998	Old-Age Benefit Act: identification of rights and the amount of benefits as a result of a radical pension reform, introduction of the defined contribution system	Act on old-age benefits and pensions from the Social Insurance Institution, 17 December 1998
1999	New Benefit Act, also providing sickness benefits	Act on financial benefits with respect to illness and maternity, 25 June 1999

Source: Own comparison.

Notes

1. Two kinds of physical disability are recognized: permanent and long-term; with permanent disability the health and physical condition are not likely to improve; long-term disability is a condition lasting more than 12 months from the last day of sickness benefit.
2. District (*powiat*) is an administrative level between regional (*voyevodship*) and local (*gmina*, community); there are 373 districts in Poland.
3. The principle by which school-leavers were eligible for benefits was changed by virtue of the regulation adopted on 22 December 1995 (amendment to the Employment and Unemployment Act and amendments to other laws) that came into force on 1 March 1996, making school-leavers more active (scholarship instead of benefit).
4. 1999 saw the enforcement of four social reforms: pension, healthcare, education and decentralization reforms.
5. The Labour Fund collects contributions from employers at the level of 2.5% of the wage bill in their companies. In the event of a deficit, it used to be easier to subsidize the Labour Fund from the state budget rather than raise the contribution rate. Since 1999 – a year of administrative reform and of public finances – generating such funding from the budget has become much more difficult. The next solution for the Minister of Labour is to apply for a loan.

References

Barr, Nicholas (1999) 'Reforming welfare states in post-communist countries', in: *Ten Years After: Transition and growth in Post-Communist countries*, paper to the conference organised by the Centre for Social and Economic Research (CASE) on 15-16 October 1999 in Warsaw, now published in: Orlowski, Lucjan, T. (ed.) (2001), *Transition and growth in Post-Communist countries. The ten-year experience*. Cheltenham, UK + North Hampton, MA, USA: Edward Elgar.

Golinowska, S. (ed.) (2001, forthcoming) *Zabezpieczenie spoleczne inwalidów w Polsce i w innych krajach* (Social security of disabled people in Poland and other countries). Warszawa: MPiPS /CASE.

Góra, M./Socha, M./Sztanderska, U. (1995) *Zachowanie bezrobotnych na rynku pracy. System rejestracji bezrobotnych i zasizek dla bezrobotnych* (Behaviour of the unemployed on the labour market. Registration system and the unemployment benefit). Warszawa: Zeszyty Centrum im. Adama Smitha Nr. 5.

Kalaska, M./Kostrubiec, S./Witkowski, J. (1996) 'Praca nierejestrowana w Polsce w 1995 r' (Unregistered labour in Poland 1995), in: *GUS, Studia i Analizy Statystyczne*. Warszawa.

Kwiatkowski, E. (ed.) (1998) *Przepzywy sizy roboczej a efekty aktywnej polityki panstwa na rynku pracy w Polsce* (Flows of labour force versus effects of the active labour policy in Poland). Wydawnictwo Uniwersytetu Zódzkiego.

Sztanderska, U. (ed.) (1996) *Rynek pracy w Polsce 1993-1994* (Labour market in Poland 1993-1994). Warszawa: IPiSS.

Wiktorow, A. (1996) *System emerytalno – rentowy. Przeslanki i mozliwosci reformowania* (Pension system. Premises and chances of reforming). Gdańsk: Instytut Badań nad Gospodarka Rynkowa.

ZUS (1999, 1998, 1997, 1996) *Wazniejsze informacje z zakresu ubezpiecze~ spolecznych* (Main information of social insurance). Warszawa.

CHAPTER 11

Invalidity Pensions: The Case of Slovenia

Cveto Ursic and Tine Stanovnik

1 Introduction

Probably the most distinguishing characteristic of the social security system of Slovenia is its stability, which has several facets. Thus, while most European countries in transition introduced separate and autonomous social security institutions only in the early 1990s, following the collapse of communism and the introduction of multi-party political systems, in Slovenia these institutions enjoyed an autonomous or semi-autonomous status even decades prior to economic transition. Stability of institutions is but one aspect: what is even more important is the stability of social rights granted by these institutions – and these have remained remarkably stable. This of course does not mean that the rights were (and are) immutable; it does mean that changes introduced over the past decades (from the early 1970s) have been gradual, and that the menu of rights has undergone very little change. For example, replacement rates granted by the pension system, probably the most important component of the social security system, have remained relatively stable. As for rights within the health insurance system, they are being gradually reduced. While the 1999 Pension and Disability Insurance Act (PDIA) introduces more stringent conditions for pension and disability rights, the changes will be spread out over more than a decade. Also, during this long period, names and labels have changed, but not the substance. Thus, for example, the 1999 PDIA introduced the term *disability benefit*, which in effect applies to the same population as the pre-1999 *benefit during the waiting time for part-time work and benefit during the waiting time for other suitable work*. All this does not imply that there have been no endeavours to embark on more radical reforms; it simply means that such endeavours have failed to gain acceptance.

Paradoxically, the autonomy (or rather independence from the central government budget) of the social security institutions, in this case the Institute for Pension and Disability Insurance (IPDI), has recently been reduced, since government subsidies now form a non-negligible share of the Institute's total revenues. Also, for a very brief period (in 1992) the Institute for Health Insurance (IHI) was deprived of its autonomy and integrated into the central government budget. The experiment of a 'unified' budget failed, and the IHI was quickly re-established as an autonomous institution.

The IPDI is responsible for the administration and disbursements of pensions – old age, disability and survivors – and other related compensations, whereas the IHI is responsible for health service and various sickness-related indemnities. Other forms of services and benefits are mostly financed through the central government budget. Thus, unemployment benefits (and related disbursements) are the responsibility of the Employment Service of Slovenia, which is a non-autonomous institution, in spite of the fact that parts of its revenues come from employee and employer contributions (for unemployment insurance).

In the Slovenian system, disability insurance is embedded in the pension and disability insurance scheme, which means that a single contributory rate (one for employees, one for employers) covers both contingencies. This insurance is mandatory for all employed and self-employed persons.[1] Disability insurance covers all types of disability risks, regardless of whether they are work-related or not; in principle, the benefits depend on the amount of paid contributions and years of insurance. Disability insurance also has a preventive function, in that it attempts to reduce the consequences of work disability; in this sense, disability pensions are to be viewed as an extreme measure, applicable only in the case of very severe loss of work capacity.

2 The Slovenian Social Insurance System

2.1 The pension and disability insurance system in the 1990s

Slovenia gained independence in 1991, and soon after the new parliament passed a number of fundamental acts necessary to establish the new legal foundations of the state. In 1992 a new law on pension and disability insurance was passed. The law retained the basic principles of social insurance, i.e. that the insurer's rights are based on past contributions, but it also included strong elements of solidarity (principle of vertical equity). The system provided for fairly generous old-age and disability pensions, as can be seen from Table 1, which shows the net replacement rate, i.e. ratio of net pension benefits to net average wage.

Table 1: Ratio of net old-age pension and disability pension to net average wage (in %), Slovenia, 1991-1999

Year	Net old-age pension (in % of net average wage)	Net disability pension (in % of net average wage)
1991	73.0	60.3
1992	77.8	64.4
1993	73.9	60.8
1994	75.4	62.4
1995	76.2	63.0
1996	74.6	61.2
1997	74.3	60.8
1998	74.5	60.6
1999	75.8	61.5

Source: Institute for Pension and Disability Insurance, 1999 Annual Report.

The replacement rate was quite stable during the 1990s, but the number of pension recipients increased considerably in the same time period, as can be seen in Table 2. Predictably, the net result was a large increase in total pension outlays, as can be observed in Table 3.

Table 2: Pension beneficiaries (by type of pension) and contributors (active insurers), Slovenia, 1990-1999

Year	Old-age pensioners	Disability pensioners	Survivor pensioners	Other pensioners	All pensioners	All contributors
1990	197 259	82 289	76 726	27 820	384 094	884 615
1991	227 524	87 194	78 482	25 727	418 927	816 902
1992	252 393	92 378	80 531	23 526	448 828	764 902
1993	259 525	94 739	81 764	21 517	457 545	782 570
1994	260 751	95 698	82 120	19 516	458 085	772 549
1995	262 587	96 883	83 121	17 671	460 262	768 961
1996	265 341	97 649	84 527	15 805	463 322	765 731
1997	269 958	98 146	85 970	14 142	468 216	783 196
1998	274 477	98 251	87 133	12 533	472 394	784 193
1999	279 114	98 105	88 171	11 059	476 449	801 280

Note: 'Other' refers to pensioners who receive pensions according to the agricultural pension scheme, which was discontinued in the early 1980s. The scheme is thus slowly approaching extinction.

Source: Institute for Pension and Disability Insurance, 1999 Annual Report.

Table 3: The outlays of the Institute for Pension and Disability Insurance as percentage of GDP, Slovenia, 1991-1999

1991	10.9%
1992	13.8%
1993	14.0%
1994	14.5%
1995	14.8%
1996	14.5%
1997	14.4%
1998	14.4%

Source: Institute for Pension and Disability Insurance of Slovenia, Annual Reports and Statistical Yearbooks of the Statistical Office of Slovenia.

Table 2 also shows that the trends regarding old-age pensioners and disability pensioners are quite closely related. This close relation, particularly visible during the first years of transition, is not specific to Slovenia and can be observed in other Central and Eastern European countries in transition. Generous early retirement schemes in the early period of transition increased the number of old-age pensioners, and this "coincided" with "the apparent leniency in granting disability pensions" (IMF, 1995: 14). It seems as if all doors of the pension system were wide open, in order to prevent massive unemployment among the elderly population.

The early-retirement schemes were generous both in terms of entrance conditions and pensions granted. For early retirement, the insured person was required to have at least 35 years (men) or 30 years of contributions (women); there was also an age limit, which was low, but gradually increased to 58 (for men) and 53 (for women) by 1997. In addition, the insured person had to fulfil one of the following conditions: (a) bankruptcy of the firm, with no possibility for re-employment; (b) be disabled;[2] (c) be unemployed, and have been registered at the employment office (for at least 12 months in the previous 24 months). There was a small reduction (of 1%) in pensions for each missing year to age 63 (for men) and 58 (for women). The reduction was abolished once the required age was reached.

For those who could not reach the safe haven through early-retirement schemes, other options were possible. Thus, for the elderly unemployed who were sufficiently close to qualifying for an old-age pension, the Employment Service of Slovenia would, after the regular expiration of unemployment benefits, continue to disburse unemployment benefits for a maximum of three years.

The new Pension and Disability Act (PDIA) has no provisions for early retirement; also, the 1998 amendments to the law on employment and unemployment insurance discontinued the provision of extended disbursements of unemployment benefits for persons approaching pensionable age.

2.2 Developments in Slovenia's social security system

Though we shall concentrate on the more recent developments, it is worth mentioning that Slovenia's pension and disability insurance system has displayed remarkable continuity, a 'gradualism' rarely encountered even in strongholds of the Bismarckian type of welfare states. Thus, article 2 of the 1972 Federal (Yugoslav) pension and disability insurance act, enumerates the basic rights of disabled insured persons, which include not only disability pensions but also the right to vocational rehabilitation and employment, with allowances for diminished work capacities. A similar set of rights is also stated in the federal law of 1982. Its article 17 explicitly states the right to reassignment (to other suitable jobs), the right to vocational training and the right to allowances and benefits such as rehabilitation benefits, allowance for part-time work and allowance for reassignment. These rights and the procedures for acquiring them were detailed in the 1983 Republic Act. It is thus fair to say that the foundations of the system were laid in the early 1970s. Even the aforementioned 1992 PDIA, passed by the Parliament of Slovenia, did not introduce any major changes in the existing system; it was envisaged, however, that this law would be provisional pending a more radical reform of the social security system.

The centrepiece of pension reform was the reform of old-age pensions. The reform of disability pensions was less remarkable and was relegated to discussions among professional groups during the whole debate on pension reform. The pension-reform discussion in fact entered the public domain with the publication of a *white paper on the reform of the pension and disability insurance* (Ministrstvo za delo, družino in socialne zadeve, 1997) in November 1997. This paper proposed a fairly radical pension reform, with the first pillar based on PAYG financing, and the second pillar designed as a (privately managed) mandatory savings scheme. Following protracted discussions, the reform proposals were considerably diluted and the pension act finally passed legislation in December 1999. Most of the changes concerned the first pillar, i.e. the PAYG system. Entrance conditions (such as increase in pensionable age) were cut out and accrual rates were substantially reduced. Other parameter values were also changed to provide a better actuarial balance between paid contributions and subsequent benefits (pensions). The second pillar was introduced, though not as a mandatory saving scheme but as a pillar for 'classic' occupational schemes to be initiated by employers at company level. Only for certain hazardous occupations are employer contributions for the second pillar mandatory and stipulated by law.

The 1999 PDIA also introduced changes in disability insurance; as already stated, these changes are not radical. They will be presented in detail later on, though the most important ones can be stated briefly:
- It acknowledges the 'absolute' definition of disability.
- Vocational rehabilitation has become a basic right (and obligation) stemming from disability insurance.

- Certain new rights from disability insurance are introduced. In sum, the wide range of rights has been retained, though the eligibility criteria have been severed, and the rights made somewhat less generous (Kuhelj, 2000).

The changes have in fact been postponed, and virtually the whole disability part of the 1999 PDIA will come in force on 1 January 2003; only the determination of the pension base and calculation formula for disability pensions were effective immediately, i.e. starting from 1 January 2000. The postponement is caused by the need to change a considerable number of laws that dealt with disability, such as laws on employment and labour relations, social assistance and social care, taxes and customs, health care and rehabilitation.

3 Disabled persons in society; an overview of legal provisions and definitions

In Slovenia social security for the disabled is anchored in the constitution, which states that persons with disabilities have a legal right to protection and vocational training. Children with physical and mental developmental disorders, as well as other persons with severe disabilities, have the right to education and training for an active life in society, which is financed by public resources.

The following groups of persons with disabilities are distinguished:
- *War disabled* persons are persons disabled while members of the armed forces in war or during peacetime activities, as well as civilians disabled in peacetime or war.
- *Persons with disabilities according to the law on employment and vocational training of persons with disabilities* are individuals requiring special professional assistance in training and employment. Their physical or mental disability entitles them to special social care.
- *Children with special needs* are children with disorders in mental development, blind children and those with sight and hearing difficulties, speech disorders, mobility handicaps, chronic diseases, deficiencies in specific areas of learning ability and behavioural or personality disorders, who need special education programmes carried out with additional professional assistance, or adapted educational programmes, or special educational programmes.

- *Persons with disabilities according to the law on social protection of persons with physical and mental disabilities* are moderately, severely and profoundly mentally disabled and profoundly physically disabled persons, who are unable to live and work independently and whose disability developed in childhood or adolescence before the age of 18 or during the period of regular schooling but not after the age of 26, and who need special social protection owing to their disability.
- *Disabled insured persons* are persons whose rights and obligations are stipulated in the Pension and Disability Insurance Act (PDIA). This group of disabled persons will be analysed in greater detail.

According to Slovenian legislation, the disability of an individual is confirmed by a decision issued by a legally appointed authority, which in turn is based on an opinion of a specialist in the relevant field. This decision serves as a basis for claiming rights and also for assuming obligations.

The rights (and obligations) of persons with disabilities are dealt with in approximately 70 legal acts in the fields of health care and rehabilitation, accessibility of the physical environment and information or communication systems, education, provision of financial support and social security, vocational training and employment, customs duties and taxation, etc. These laws contain special provisions for persons with disabilities (Uršič, 1999a). For example, in the taxation field, the Personal Income Tax Act provides a special tax allowance for severely disabled persons, while the Corporate Income Tax Act provides tax allowances for companies employing disabled persons.

In the past two years, a number of new regulations have been passed, certain modifications made to the existing laws and new regulations drafted. All this will have an important effect on the working and living conditions of persons with disabilities. They include laws on employment relations, training and employment of persons with disabilities, interpreters for the deaf, organizations of persons with disabilities and equal opportunities for persons with disabilities (Uršič, 1999b).

We now turn to the largest group of persons with disabilities, namely disabled insured persons.

4 Disability insurance

4.1 Definition of disability

The 1992 PDIA defined disability in relative terms, i.e. as a permanent loss of or reduction in work capacity, related only to the workplace and the position occupied by the person prior to the disability. This definition was broadened in the 1999 PDIA, whereby disability is not necessarily regarded as a permanent state. Also, disability is not narrowly defined with regard to the workplace but rather as a general reduction in work capacity for *any* kind of work. The difference between health insurance and disability insurance still remains and short-term disability is in the domain of health insurance.

The new broader definition of disability includes three categories of disability:

Category 1 includes insured persons: (a) who have lost the capacity to engage in organized gainful employment; and (b) who suffer from occupational disability and do not have any remaining capacity for work. This means that the person cannot work full-time at another job (without further impairing his disability), cannot be trained by means of vocational rehabilitation programmes for full-time work at another job and cannot perform work for at least half of the full working time. This category may be described as *full disability*.

Category 2 includes insured persons whose capacity for work in their occupation is impaired by 50% or more. This category may be described as *occupational disability*.

Category 3: includes three sub-categories, which may be labelled work, occupational and job-specific disability, respectively. These are:
(a) insured persons who have lost the capacity to work full-time, but are capable of working at a certain job at least on a part-time basis;
(b) insured persons whose capacity to work in their occupation is impaired by less than 50%;
(c) insured persons who can continue work in their occupation on a full-time basis, but cannot work at the job they have been assigned to.

Category 3 may be described as *reduced capacity*.

'Occupation' means not only the job position to which an insured person has been assigned, but also all jobs that correspond to his physical and mental capacities and for which he has the relevant qualifications (level of education, supplementary training, work experience).

4.2 Causes of disability, rights and their acquirement

The law defines the following causes for the occurrence of disability: employment injury, occupational disease, illness and off-the-job injury. In 1996, the shares (as percentage of all occurrences) were 3%, 1.1%, 90.5% and 5.3%, respectively.

Rights, stemming from the 1999 PDIA, are:
(a) disability pension,
(b) vocational rehabilitation,
(c) right to reassignment,
(d) right to part-time work,
(e) disability benefit and disability allowance.

These rights will be described in greater detail in section 5; suffice to note that these groupings, based on the 1999 PDIA, are quite similar to the groupings of the 1992 PDIA. The only noteworthy change is the introduction of the term 'disability benefits', beneficiaries being mostly unemployed disabled persons who do not receive unemployment benefits. The 1992 PDIA also included benefits for this group, which was euphemistically labelled 'recipients of benefits during the waiting time for part-time work and recipients of benefits during the waiting time for other suitable work'. This cumbersome term was intended to convey the idea that this group of disabled insured persons would soon find employment again, which in fact was not the case.

Typically, the right to active labour participation (part-time work, 'reassigned' work) or preparation for active labour participation (vocational rehabilitation) is accompanied by the right to cash benefits. Thus, persons reassigned to a new job are also entitled to disability allowance (allowance for reassignment); persons on part-time work are entitled to a (partial) disability pension; and persons on vocational rehabilitation are entitled to a rehabilitation benefit.[3]

As a general rule, a disabled person acquires rights based on disability if the disability occurred prior to the age of 63 (men) or 61 (women). Also, the person must be included in mandatory pension and disability insurance, though there are exceptions to this rule.

The procedure for granting any right from disability insurance starts with the formal application by the insured person, his doctor or a medical commission. The doctor or medical commission can refer the insured person to the disability commission if they deem that a recovery of work capacity is unlikely; the referral to a commission is mandatory after a one-year absence from work (without interruptions) on account of illness or injury. Until the procedure for granting rights from disability insurance is completed, the insured person retains his status within the health insurance and receives income compensation for temporary absence from work – all according to the health insurance regulations. The disability commission consists of two physicians and another expert (on industrial psychology, industrial safety, etc.); the employer may also participate. If the disability commission decides on vocational rehabilitation, it must also obtain the opinion of an institution for vocational rehabilitation. The rulings of the disability commission may be contested, in the final instance at the labour and social court.

5 Rights, based on disability insurance

5.1 *Disability pension*

5.1.1 Eligibility for disability pension

An insured person is granted a disability pension if he has a category 1 disability. Also, an insured person may be granted a disability pension even with a category 2 disability if he cannot engage in another appropriate job without vocational rehabilitation. This entitlement does not apply if the person is over the age of 50. Alternatively, an insured person with a category 2 or 3 disability may also be granted a disability pension if he cannot obtain adequate employment or re-employment because he is at least 63 years old (men) or 61 years old (women).

The right to a disability pension also depends on the causes of the disability. If disability is caused by occupational disease or employment injury, the insured person can obtain a pension regardless of the insurance period. However, if the cause of the disability is illness or off-the-job injury, a 'sufficient' insurance period is required. As a general rule, the insurance period must cover at least one third of the period from age 20 to the date of the occurrence of disability; this is referred to as 'years of service'. The lower age limit depends on the attained educational level. For persons with a three-year university education the lower limit starts at 23, whereas for persons with a four-year university education it starts at 26. For insured persons with higher education, military service, period of registered unemployment, training for ancillary police units and time spent at service as a conscientious objector are not counted as years of service. The right to a disability pension can be granted exceptionally even if the insured person has a shorter insurance period. This is possible particularly for persons under age 30 who have a very short insurance period.

5.1.2 Pension base for assessment of disability pension

The pension base for disability pensions is calculated in the same way as old-age pensions; it is equal to the best consecutive 18 year average of wages, salaries or other income that served as the base for payment of social security contributions.[4] The pension base is a net concept, meaning that the gross amounts are reduced to net amounts, though not using the person's actual income tax rate, but rather the average income tax rate and the social security contribution rates. For men, the pension is equal to 35% of the pension base for the minimum insurance period (15 years), plus 1.5% for each additional year of insurance. The calculation is the same for women, except that their starting level is higher, and equal to 38% of the pension base (for 15 years of insurance).[5]

Disability pension granted on the basis of employment injury or occupational disease is assessed as if the insured person had a full insurance period, i.e. 40 years for men and 35 years for women. In case of off-the-job injury or illness, the computed disability pension is somewhat higher than the old-age pension, for two reasons. First, there are no pension deductions for pensioning prior to full pensionable age (63 for men, 61 for women), and, second, the minimum disability pension is more generous – it cannot be less than 45% of the pension base for men and 48% of the pension base for women.[6]

5.2 *Vocational rehabilitation*

Vocational rehabilitation is defined as an integral process, through which the insured person is provided with professional, physical and psychosocial training (Vlada Republike Slovenije, 1998). It is intended to lead to reintegration in the work environment – either in another occupation, another job or (if the workplace is suitably adapted) even in the same occupation or same job. It is important to stress that once the right to vocational rehabilitation has been granted, the insured person must abide by the conditions specified in the rehabilitation contract, duly signed by the Institute for Pension and Invalidity Insurance, the employer and the insured person (Cvetko, 2000).

The right to vocational rehabilitation is granted to an insured person who fulfils all of the three qualifying conditions: (a) afflicted with category 2 disability; (b) younger than 50 years when disability occurred; (c) may be trained for other work on a full-time basis.

Vocational rehabilitation is tailored to the insured person and can take the form of additional education, practice in an appropriate job with an employer, etc.

These provisions are designed to encourage vocational rehabilitation, since the proportion of insured persons undertaking vocational rehabilitation has been very low in recent years (less than 2% of all disabled insured persons).

In the period between the acquisition of the right to vocational rehabilitation and its completion, the insured person is entitled to a rehabilitation benefit equal to 100% of the disability pension to which he would otherwise be entitled. Where rehabilitation takes place with his employer, the benefit is reduced to 40%. Also, after completion of the rehabilitation programme the insured person is entitled to a rehabilitation benefit equal to 100% of the disability pension he would have received; it is disbursed until the insured person starts work at a new job. As for the employer, he must provide a job commensurate with the work capacity of the person, taking into account the vocational rehabilitation that the insured person has had. It is also worth mentioning that the right to vocational rehabilitation is not a once-and-for-all right and is not conditional on the status of the disabled person: he can be an active insured person or unemployed.

5.3 Right to reassignment

The right to reassignment to another suitable workplace is granted to insured persons who meet any of the following criteria. (1) completion of a vocational rehabilitation programme; (2) category 2 disability occurring after age 50; (3) category 3 disability, specifically: (a) insured persons whose capacity to work in their occupation is impaired by less than 50% or (b) insured persons who can continue to work in their occupation on a full-time basis, but cannot work at the job they have been assigned.

When taking up a new job, persons meeting criterion (2) or (3) are also entitled to a benefit, which is computed as a percentage of the disability pension they would have received if they had been eligible for it. The percentage varies, however: it is 25% for category 3 disabilities listed above, and 20% for category 2 disabilities. We refer to this benefit as 'allowance for reassignment'.

5.4 Right to part-time work

An insured person with a category 3 disability (reduced capacity) is entitled to part-time work if he is not capable of working full-time. This right must be guaranteed by the employer, who does not have the right to dismiss this insured person. Besides the right to part-time work, the insured person is also entitled to a partial disability pension, which is in fact an allowance for part-time work.[7] It is assessed *pro rata* on the basis of the percentage reduction from full-time work. Thus, a 50% working time entitles the insured person to a partial wage and partial disability pension; the latter would be equal to 50% of the hypothetical (computed) disability pension.[8] The partial disability pension may be increased or decreased, depending on the change in the status of the insured person. If the insured person, working part-time, is reassigned to a new job, the benefit may be increased by 30%. If the insured person has terminated his employment at his own fault, it is reduced by 30%, and if the job is terminated without the employee's fault, it is increased by 40%. We refer to this benefit as 'allowance for part-time work'.

In the 1992 Pension Act an insured person (employee) working part-time received full wage compensation. This wage was paid partly by the employer and partly by the Institute for Pension and Disability Insurance. For other categories of insured persons (self-employed, unemployed, workers in agriculture, etc.) the compensation for the 'missing' part was based on the computed hypothetical disability pension.

5.5 Right to disability benefit and disability allowance

In section 4.3 we observed that the right to disability allowance is granted to certain groups of disabled insured persons when taking up a new job.[9] Also, a type of disability allowance – i.e. allowance for part-time work – is granted to disabled insured persons who are working part-time.[10] In addition, disability benefits are granted to unemployed disabled persons.[11] The base for both the disability allowance and disability benefit is the hypothetical disability pension, but the actual percentage varies considerably, from 20% to 80%, depending on the type of disability (category 2 or 3), status (employed, unemployed following disability, unemployed prior to disability etc.) and age of the insured person. For example, for a re-employed disabled insured person with category 2 disability (occupational disability) the percentage is 20%, whereas for category 3 disability it is 25%.[12] There is no time limit for this disability allowance, meaning that the employee receives it for the duration of employment. As for disability benefits, the percentage varies between 20 and 80%. The highest percentage is granted to insured persons with category 2 disability who became unemployed following disability (at no fault of their own). The lowest percentage is granted to persons younger than 53 years who became unemployed at their own fault. These are of course only the extremes, with values in between depending on the criteria outlined above.

Typically, an unemployed disabled insured person does not receive this disability benefit outright when becoming unemployed. Every insured person is first entitled to an unemployment benefit, provided he has accumulated a sufficiently long period of contributions. The duration of unemployment benefit is from 3 to a maximum of 24 months, depending on the length of the contribution period. The base is the average 12-months wage, and the percentage 70% of this base (for the first 3 months) and 60% after that.[13] Once this right has been exhausted, the disabled insured person is entitled to the rights as specified in the 1999 PDIA – meaning either a disability benefit, or possibly even a disability pension; there are no time limits for disability benefits. As for other insured persons, upon expiration of unemployment benefits there remains the possibility of means-tested social assistance.[14]

According to the 1992 PDIA, the disability benefit for unemployed persons was equal to 80% of the insured person's pension base, whereas under the 1999 PDIA the percentage varies, and it is 80% only in the most favourable case. We note that this benefit (like disability benefits for other types of insured persons) is not means-tested.

5.6 Employer obligations towards insured disabled persons

The 1999 PDIA set certain obligations for the employer, aimed at assuring certain rights of the disabled employees. Thus, the employer must, as a rule, retain the disabled employee and provide him another job commensurate with his remaining work capacity, education and training. When assigning the employee to another suitable job, the employer must take into consideration the opinion of the disability commission on the suitability of the new job or new workplace. The employer is also obliged to provide the disabled employee with the possibility of vocational rehabilitation and part-time work. These obligations are not absolute, and the employer can, for subjective or objective reasons, dismiss the disabled persons. Objective reasons might be the inability of the employer (a) to provide a job commensurate with the remaining work capacity and professional qualifications of the disabled person or (b) to provide vocational rehabilitation. Subjective reasons lie within the domain of the employee, i.e. the disabled insured person, and might include rejection of vocational rehabilitation without justifiable reason, or not completing it as scheduled. Another subjective reason would be if the disabled insured person did not start work according to the contract provisions at his reassigned position or part-time work. It should be stressed that for employers employing more than five persons, reasons for termination of a job contract are established by a special commission appointed by the Minister of Labour. It includes representatives of the IPDI, Labour Inspection Office, National Employment Office and representatives of the employers and labour unions. To sum up, legal protection of the employment status of disabled insured persons is relative and not absolute; nevertheless, disabled insured persons can be dismissed only under very narrow and clearly spelt out conditions.

6 An overview of trends in the number of beneficiaries and outlays of the Institute for Pension and Disability Insurance

6.1 Trends in various forms of provision for disabled insured persons

We have described the main bundles of rights for disabled insured persons. The financial side, i.e. cash disbursements, can be classified conveniently into the following groups:
1. Disbursements for disabled insured persons who have completely withdrawn from the labour force; these are recipients of disability pensions.
2. Disbursements for disabled insured persons who have temporarily withdrawn from the active labour force, and are (a) undergoing a vocational rehabilitation programme or (b) temporarily unemployed; these are recipients of disability benefits.
3. Disbursements for disabled insured persons who actively participate in the labour force but receive partial compensation from the IPDI, i.e. (a) persons on part-time work and (b) persons reassigned to new jobs; these are recipients of disability allowances.

The second and third group each consist of two subgroups, so we can actually speak of five different types of recipients; the trends for these recipients are presented in Table 4.

Obviously, there are different underlying trends for each of the five groups of recipients. Thus, the particularly large increase in the number of recipients of disability pensions between 1989 and 1992 was due to the economic recession, which resulted in a large increase in unemployment among the younger age groups and a large increase in the number of old-age retirement and disability pensioners. The former group entered the pension system through very favourable early retirement schemes, and the latter group through the already observed leniency of the disability commissions. The dynamics in the growth of the number of recipients of disability pensions was thus influenced by demographic trends, changes in economic conditions and presumably also by the leniency or stringency of disability commissions.

Table 4: The number of recipients of disability pensions, disability benefits and other disability-related compensations, Slovenia, 1970-1999

Year	Disability pensions	Rehabilitation benefits	Allowance for reassignment	Allowance for part-time work	Disability benefits
1970	41 868	284	3 710	1 614	746
1971	44 979	291	4 031	1 707	731
1972	47 283	252	4 195	1 890	738
1973	49 117	249	4 919	2 291	573
1974	50 493	247	6 258	2 798	512
1975	50 542	238	7 201	3 378	473
1976	51 237	302	8 702	3 960	482
1977	52 429	315	9 530	4 441	469
1978	53 939	322	10 936	5 445	433
1979	54 238	318	11 687	5 871	404
1980	56 145	300	12 552	6 451	362
1981	57 974	249	13 675	7 223	368
1982	60 826	211	13 982	7 833	339
1983	63 613	194	14 581	8 286	326
1984	66 066	126	14 141	9 337	312
1985	68 907	127	14 053	10 304	283
1986	71 324	159	14 428	11 227	438
1987	74 242	191	14 207	12 191	639
1988	77 472	221	14 193	12 834	740
1989	80 686	277	14 057	12 954	808
1990	84 000	269	12 560	11 418	830
1991	89 734	251	11 947	10 121	1 165
1992	92 943	210	11 390	10 099	1 401
1993	93 867	170	10 260	8 937	1 789
1994	94 848	162	10 643	9 447	2 582
1995	96 058	204	11 576	10 195	4 118
1996	96 850	219	12 257	10 980	5 551
1997	97 369	203	13 012	11 451	7 070
1998	97 498	191	13 626	12 060	8 955
1999	97 382	219	14 222	12 616	10 737

Note: Column 3 corresponds to cash disbursements described in section 5.2, column 4 to cash disbursements described in section 5.3, column 5 to cash disbursements described in section 5.4 and column 6 to cash disbursements described in section 5.5. As noted, prior to 1999 the recipients of disability benefits were labelled 'recipients of benefits during the waiting period for part-time work and recipients of benefits during the waiting period for other suitable work'.

Source: Statistical Department, Institute for Pension and Disability Insurance of Slovenia.

There are two reasons for the stagnant number of recipients of rehabilitation benefits. On the one hand, disabled insured persons were not really motivated for rehabilitation, since their financial position was assured even without it, as they received allowances for reassignment or for part-time work, which compensated their loss of earned income. On the other hand, employers, particularly in the last 10 years, have not been very keen on the prospect of their employees obtaining the right to rehabilitation. Restructuring and consequent downsizing of the workforce have been on employers' agendas since the late 1980s. Owing to the fact that the work protection of disabled persons was absolute, employers put great pressure on disability commissions and on the IPDI to pension off disabled insured persons. This course of action obviously solved the employers' problems, but at a high cost to society.

The large annual increases in the number of recipients of the allowance for reassignment and allowance for part-time work from 1973 up to the mid-1980s, and a subsequent stagnation since can be explained by the changes in the legal provisions regulating these two types of disability allowances. Thus, the 1972 Pension Act provided for more favourable allowances for reassignment and part-time work. This Act also granted the right to certain groups of disabled insured persons who had been ineligible hitherto. Following this steady increase, amendments to the Pension Act in the mid-1980s introduced a concept of 'change in work capacity'. These amendments resulted in stagnation in the number of recipients of these two types of allowances. Change in work capacity now applied if the disabled insured person could not perform his assigned job, but was capable of working full-time in the same company in another position commensurate with his professional training and education. Furthermore, it did not grant him the status of a disabled insured person and, consequently, his rights were not set by law but by internal company regulations.

If we confine ourselves to the most recent period, i.e. the 1990s, the increase in the number of recipients of disability benefits is quite impressive. The causes are well known: owing to massive lay-offs and closures, many disabled persons have joined the ranks of the unemployed, and their 'temporary' unemployed status appears to be of a more long-term nature. The re-employment possibilities for this category of insured persons are slim, so they actually receive disability benefits until they are entitled to a disability pension.

6.2 The structure of outlays by the Institute for Pension and Disability Insurance

The growth in the number of recipients of various disability-related disbursements provides one view of the changes that have occurred in recent years. Yet another view is provided through an analysis of IPDI outlays. For this purpose, we group expenditures of the Institute for Pension and Disability Insurance into four broad categories.

1. *Pensions and pension-related outlays*, which include old-age, disability and survivors' pensions, pensions for workers in agriculture and pensions for the military. The IPDI also honours commitments to persons who have acquired pension rights in other republics of the former Yugoslav Federation but have residence in Slovenia, and persons who have acquired pension rights in Slovenia but live in other republics of the former Yugoslav Federation. Also included in this category are means-tested supplements, special allowances for persons with physical impairment, supplements for persons requiring assistance at home, supplements for recreation, etc.[15]
2. *Income compensations for disabled insured persons and other outlays related to employment of disabled insured persons*, which include rehabilitation benefits, allowances for part-time work and reassignment, and disability benefits for 'temporary' unemployed disabled persons. Also included are payments to institutions for training of disabled insured persons and co-financing of new jobs for disabled insured persons.
3. *Health insurance for beneficiaries* includes contributions for health insurance for pensioners and other recipients of IPDI disbursements.
4. *Administrative and other costs* include postage, services of the disability commissions, financing costs and the IPDI's administrative costs.

The structure of outlays, based on these four groups, is presented in Table 5, together with the main subdivisions for the first two groups.

As can be seen, there have been certain structural changes in the 1990s. With effect from 1 March 1992, the IPDI was obliged by law to contribute towards the health insurance of pensioners and other recipients of IPDI disbursements; this caused the large increase in this share in total outlays. Also, the share of administrative costs has been decreasing since pensioners have started receiving their cheques not through the Post Office but through banks. In addition, the IPDI negotiated a reduction in the cost of postal services with the Post Office. Though the share of work-disability related outlays is still small, its steady increase is caused mostly by the increase in the number of recipients of disability benefits.

Table 5: The structure of outlays of the Institute for Pension and Disability Insurance of Slovenia, 1980-1999

Year	Total outlays (=100)	Pensions and pension-related outlays	Of which pensions:			Work-disability related outlays	Reha-bilita-tion benefit	Of which:			Health insur-ance for bene-ficiaries	Ad-min-istra-tive costs
			Old age	Disa-bility	Survi-vors			Allow-ance for re-assign-ment	Allow-ance for part-time work	Disa-bility bene-fits		
1980	100	84.4	44.7	18.1	16.1	3.0	-	1.3	1.5	-	10.8	1.8
1985	100	90.5	48.1	18.8	15.6	3.4	-	1.5	1.8	-	3.9	2.2
1990	100	92.7	52.5	17.3	13.7	2.4	-	0.8	1.4	-	1.3	3.6
1991	100	93.4	53.8	17.1	12.5	2.9	-	0.8	1.1	-	0.6	3.0
1992	100	86.9	50.5	14.7	10.6	1.9	-	0.5	0.8	-	8.9	2.4
1993	100	87.9	51.6	15.1	10.7	1.9	-	-	-	-	7.6	1.7
1994	100	88.4	51.4	15.3	10.8	2.0	-	-	-	-	7.4	1.9
1995	100	88.3	50.9	14.8	10.5	2.4	-	-	-	-	7.2	2.1
1996	100	88.0	51.0	14.5	10.5	2.8	-	-	-	-	7.6	1.7
1997	100	89.2	51.5	14.5	10.5	3.0	-	-	-	-	7.7	1.3
1998	100	88.0	51.2	14.1	10.4	3.2	0.0	1.0	1.0	1.2	7.6	1.2
1999	100	87.7	51.4	13.9	10.3	3.5	0.0	1.0	1.0	1.4	7.6	1.2

Note: – = data not available. The breakdown of the subheading *Pensions and pension-related outlays* represents only the three main subgroups; similarly the subheading *Work-disability related outlays* represents two (and later on four) of the main outlays.

Source: Institute for Pension and Disability Insurance, Annual Reports.

7 Concluding remarks

In spite of the great social, economic and institutional changes that Slovenia has experienced in the past decades, its social security system has displayed remarkable stability. The changes that have been introduced have been piecemeal and in line with the basic tenets of the system; also, they have not touched all aspects of the system to an equal degree. It seems that of all the contingencies covered by the social security system, the disability part has undergone the fewest changes. In effect, most of the rights provided by disability insurance were introduced in the early 1970s and during the past decades their name has sometimes changed but not their content. Even the 1999 PDIA has retained all the basic rights pertaining to disability insurance, though it has relabelled and repackaged some of them in the process. Furthermore, the larger part of the disability section of the 1999 PDIA will be on hold till 2003. The reason for this freeze is the need to adapt various provisions in the labour relations law, law on rehabilitation and employment of disabled persons, law on human rights of disabled persons, etc.

Obviously, the reintegration of disabled persons in society is a very complex endeavour, involving a number of policy actors and institutions, not only of the state, but also of civil society. In this respect, the role of disability and pensioner organizations is important and, together with the labour unions, has perhaps even been instrumental in preventing larger and more far-reaching changes in the pension and disability insurance system. Pensioners have also entered the political arena, and the Democratic Party of Pensioners, a member of the coalition government since 1996, acts as a watchdog and guardian of the interests of elderly and disabled persons. Thus, the strong legal and constitutional safeguards, as well as determined and highly-motivated actors within civil society and in the political arena, appear to provide a sufficient guarantee against any unwarranted intrusion into the rights of disabled persons. In spite of these jealously guarded rights, it seems that the issue of income maintenance has been over-emphasized and that the right to work has become a relative right, not an absolute one. This can best be seen from the consistently low levels of recipients of rehabilitation benefits, and quite large increases in the number of recipients of disability benefits – and these are mostly long-term unemployed disabled persons. In spite of the intentions of the 1999 PDIA, it remains to be seen whether this trend can be reversed, and the right to work reaffirmed.

Notes

1. The state is responsible for the payment of social contributions for the unemployed, to the IPDI and IHI.
2. This applied to disabled insured persons in active employment.
3. In fact rehabilitation benefit is termed 'cash benefit' for the period between the acquisition of the right to vocational rehabilitation and the completion of vocational rehabilitation, and 'temporary benefit' for the period between the completion of vocational rehabilitation and commencement of work at a new job. These two benefits are actually disability benefits in all but name, since the basis for computation is the same as for disability benefits – it is the disability pension that would have been hypothetically received.
4. The 1992 PDIA stipulated best consecutive 10 year average.
5. These are values according to the 1999 Pension Act. The 1992 Pension Act was more generous: accrual rates were 2% (for men) and 2.25% (for women). The starting level for women was somewhat higher, i.e. 40% of the pension base. Needless to say, the changes will be introduced only gradually.
6. The minimum old-age pension is 35% of the pension base for men and 38% for women.
7. The 1999 PDIA uses the term 'partial disability pension', whereas the 1992 PDIA used the term 'allowance for part-time work'.
8. Should the hypothetical (i.e. computed) pension be lower than the minimum pension for a full insurance period, the hypothetical disability pension is set at the value of the minimum pension for a full contribution period. This floor is also used in computing rights under section 5.2 (for rehabilitation benefits) and section 5.5 (for disability benefits).
9. For this group of disabled insured persons, the allowance was named 'reassignment allowance'.
10. As already noted, in the 1999 PDIA this allowance is labelled 'partial disability pension'.
11. The 1999 PDIA is a bit confusing and does not clearly distinguish between disability benefits and disability allowances. Thus, a single article – article 94 – describes the amounts of disability 'allowances' for the unemployed and allowances for re-employed disabled persons.
12. This somewhat illogical percentage – since one would expect the percentage for category 3 to be lower than for category 2 – was probably a leftover of the debris of inconsistent proposed amendments.
13. It is worth mentioning that the floor of this base is lower than the floor of the pension base, and the ceiling much lower than the ceiling of the pension base.
14. Prior to 1999, if the insured person was 'close' to pensionable age, he could receive the unemployment benefit for a further three years. Also an amendment in 1998 put an end to abuses of unemployment insurance, in that the right to unemployment benefit became cumulative, i.e. for each new unemployment spell the duration of receipt of unemployment benefits was reduced, since it took into consideration the unemployment benefit already 'used-up' and the duration of re-employment (following unemployment).
15. Though the special allowance for persons with physical impairment and supplement for persons requiring assistance at home are disability-related expenditures, they have not been described here.

References

Belopavlovič, Nataša/Cvetko, Aleksej/Kalčič, Miran/Kuhelj, Jože/Plavšak, Nina/Rangus, Bojan (2000) *Zakon o pokojninskem in invalidskem zavarovanju s kometarjem*. Ljubljana: Gospodarski vestnik, Inštitut za delovna razmerja.

Cvetko, Aleksej (2000) *Pravice iz pokojninskega in invalidskega zavarovanja po novem zakonu*. Ljubljana: Bonex.

IMF (1995) *Republic of Slovenia: New challenges confronting the social insurance system*. Washington, D.C.

Kuhelj, Jože (2000) *Zakon o pokojninskem in invalidskem zavarovanju*. Ljubljana: Uradni list Republike Slovenije.

Ministrstvo za delo, družino in socialne zadeve (1997) *Bela knjiga o reformi pokojninskega in invalidskega zavarovanja*. Ljubljana: Ministrstvo za delo, družino in socialne zadeve.

Skupščina R Slovenije (1991) Obvladovanje in razvoj invalidskega varstva v sodobni družbi (Koncepcija razvojne strategije invalidskega varstva v Sloveniji), in: Uršič, Cveto/Kroflič, Marjan (eds.) (1998), *Človekove pravice in invalidi, Zbirka mednarodnih dokumentov*. Ljubljana: Zveza delovnih invalidov Slovenije, Inštitut Republike Slovenije za rehabilitacijo.

Svetlik, Ivan (ed.) (1992) *Social policy in Slovenia – Between tradition and innovation*. Aldershot: Avebury.

Uršič, Cveto (1996) 'Social (and disability) policy in the new democracies of Europe (Slovenia by way of example)', *Disability&Society* 11 (1): 91-105.

Uršič, Cveto (1999a) 'Pravica invalidov do zdravja in zaposlitve v Sloveniji', pp. 11-14 in: *4. hrvatski simpozij o invalidima: zbornik radova*. Zagreb: Savez organizacija invalida Hrvatske, FIMITIC.

Uršič, Cveto (1999b) 'Profesionalna rehabilitacija i zapošljavanje invalida u Evropi i Sloveniji', pp. 7-24 in: Uršič, Cveto (ed.), *Profesionalna rehabilitacija i zapo ljavanje invalida – Danas i sutra*. Ljubljana: Inštitut Republike Slovenije za rehabilitacijo.

Vlada Republike Slovenije (1998) *Program usposabljanja in zaposlovanja invalidov v Republiki Sloveniji za obdobje 1998–2002*. Ljubljana.

Zakon o delovnih razmerjih, Uradni list R Slovenije, št. 14/90, 5/91, 10/91, 29/92, 13/93, 2/94, 19/94, 38/94, 29/95.

Zakon o družbenem varstvu duševno in telesno prizadetih oseb, Uradni list SR Slovenije, št. 41/1983.

Zakon o temeljnih pravicah iz pokojninsekga in invalidskega zavarovanja, Uradni list SFRJ, št.35/1972, 18/1976.

Zakon o temeljnih pravicah iz pokojninskega in invalidskega zavarovanja, Uradni list SFRJ, št. 23/1982.

Zakon o pokojninskem in invalidskem zavarovanju, Uradni list SRS št. 27/1983.

Zakon o pokojninskem in invalidskem zavarovanju, Uradni list R Slovenije, št. 12/1992, 7/1996.

Zakon o pokojninskem in invalidskem zavarovanju, Uradni list R Slovenije, št. 106/1999.

Zakon o temeljnih pravicah iz delovnega razmerja, Uradni list SFR Jugoslavije, 60/89, 42/90; Uradni list R Slovenije, št. 4/91, 10/91, 17/&91, 13/93, 66/93.

Zakon o usmerjanju otrok s posebnimi potrebami, Uradni list R Slovenije, št. 54/2000.

Zakon o usposabljanju in zaposlovanju invalidnih oseb, Uradni list SR Slovenije, št. 18/76.

Zakon o vojnih invalidih, Uradni list R Slovenije, št. 63/95, 62/96, 2/97.

Zakon o zaposlovanju in zavarovanju za primer brezposelnosti, Uradni list R Slovenije, št. 5/91, 10/91, 17/91, 12/92, 12/93, 13/93, 71/93, 2/94, 38/94.

CHAPTER 12

Social Security and Disability in Sweden

Agneta Kruse

In 1913 a general pension system was introduced in Sweden. It was aimed at providing support to those not able to support themselves by working, be it because of old age or other reasons. The system covered all people living in Sweden, men and women, and was not exclusive to those belonging to the workforce or to certain occupations. Disability and old-age pensions were integrated into a single system and remained so until the last decade. In 1994 a new old-age pension system was launched by the Swedish Parliament to be implemented in 1999. The disability pension has not undergone such a reform, although the rules have been changed a number of times and different reform options are being discussed.

One reason for the discussion of reforms is the growing number of disability pensioners, as shown in Table 1. In 1970, 188 000 persons, or 4.8% of the labour force, had a disability pension, a figure which had risen by 1998 to 423 000, or almost 10%. This occurred despite the fact that the statutory old-age pension age was lowered from 67 to 65 years of age in the 1970s and that, using increased life expectancy as an indicator of health status, the Swedish people were much healthier in 1998 than in 1970. Public expenditure on disability pensions during the last 20 years has almost quadrupled, although it has remained almost constant as a percentage of GDP.

There are (at least) two approaches to the discussion on the need for reform. According to the first one, the increased disability rate is due to physical or psychological factors relating to the working environment. The design of the system does not give incentives or oblige employers to invest in environmental precautions. The second view maintains that asymmetric information, especially moral hazard, in combination with the design of the system induces an overuse of the system. Both (or neither) of these views may be correct. In this chapter the Swedish disability pension system will be described and analysed. The information given in Table 1 will be broken down into demographic, medical and regional factors. The focus will be on eligibility and the type of protection the system gives and on its effects on incentives and efficiency.

Table 1: Public expenditure on disability pensions, number of disability pensioners and newly granted disability pensioners (in thousands)

	Expenditure		Number of pensioners		% of labour force		Newly granted	
	Million SEK	% of GDP	Men	Women	Men	Women	Men	Women
1970			99.1	88.8	4.2	5.7	26.7	17.1
1975			154.3	134.6	6.5	7.7	26.0	19.0
1980	10 500	2.0	149.7	144.0	6.5	7.4	24.1	21.2
1985	17 900	2.1	160.0	162.6	7.0	7.9	26.2	24.8
1990	28 700	2.1	167.2	194.0	5.8	8.8	23.6	26.9
1995	40 000	2.4	189.3	230.5	8.4	11.1	18.6	20.6
1998	40 000	2.2	186.7	235.0	8.4	11.6	15.9	18.6

Source: RFV. Socialförsäkring, different years; Statistikinformation Is-I, different years.

In Sweden the path to retirement from the labour market is often via a disability pension, which in turn is often preceded by a spell of sickness or unemployment (see, for example, Palme and Svensson, 1999). As these systems tend to work as communicating vessels, they will be discussed briefly in this chapter. In section 1 the benefit calculations and the decision-making process with regard to the disability pension system are described. Section 2 gives a statistical description of the stock of disability pensioners and of those who have been newly granted disability pensions. In section 3 the outcome is discussed from the point of view of distribution and efficiency. Some of the reform proposals are also reviewed.

1 Design of the disability pension scheme

In Sweden, insurance against the risk of not being able to support oneself by work is to a very large extent financed and provided by the public sector. There are occupational schemes as well as some private alternatives, but these are of minor importance. A major principle in all Swedish social insurance is the emphasis on work; it has been labelled 'workfare' instead of welfare. The systems are thus explicitly organized to facilitate the combination of part-time participation in the labour market with part-time absence on sickness leave or disability retirement. The systems are uniform, obligatory and defined benefit systems organized on a pay-as-you-go basis.[1] The workfare feature means that the benefits are based on the principle of loss of income, but of course there is a basic pension as well for those who do not have a record of market income.

Disability pensions in Sweden consist of two parts, a basic pension and a supplementary scheme (ATP).[2] The entire population aged between 16 and 64 is covered by the basic pension; to be more precise, all Swedish citizens and foreign citizens domiciled in Sweden are covered according to the National Insurance Act. In order to be covered by the ATP the person insured has to have a certain work record.

Disability pension in Sweden is granted to persons with reduced work capacity.[3] There are temporary and permanent disability pensions and a pension can be granted in full, or as three-quarter, two-thirds, half and quarter pensions. Between 1972 and 1991 persons in the labour force in the 60 to 64 age bracket could also be granted disability pensions for labour market reasons, especially if there had been long spells of unemployment. Today disability pensions are granted only on medical grounds, although until 1997 the medical judgement was more lenient for persons between 60 and 64 (so-called 'elderly rules'). To be eligible for an ATP pension, applicants must have had pension-carrying income for at least two of the previous four years.

1.1 Organizational aspects of the disability system

The decision to grant a disability pension is made by a local social insurance board. There are 21 regional social insurance offices with politically elected boards; these are the first instance. Their decision can be appealed against in higher instances. Although they are local and politically elected boards, the law, the rules and the recommendations are identical throughout the entire country, and the local offices are supervised by the National Social Insurance Board.

The application can be made by the insured as well as by the person in charge in the local social insurance board. In principle, there is no time limit on sickness benefits. However, the clerk in the local office has an obligation to investigate persons on long-term sick leave. Usually, the insured has had a long spell of sickness before receiving a disability pension. After a person has received sickness benefits for a year, the clerk in the local social insurance office should investigate the possibility of reintegrating him or her into the labour market. If this is not deemed possible, the official should try to transfer the person to a disability pension. The obligation to actively investigate persons on long-term sick leave was particularly emphasized during the 1990s. Since the sickness insurance benefits are often higher than those from the disability pension system, this effort is often met with resistance.

The disability status is assessed by a general practitioner or a specialist. The local social insurance board, which makes the decisions, can demand a second opinion and also consult a doctor employed by the board. This doctor never meets the insured person, however, but makes his/her assessment on the basis of the casebook. The assessment shall be made on purely medical criteria and should indicate whether and to what degree the person is able to work in an 'ordinary' job in the labour market. Of course there are often evaluation difficulties. In 1997, for example, 19% of the newly granted disability pensions were granted for mental illness, 43% for musculoskeletal and conjunctive diseases, where 'objective' assessment is problematic.

1.2 Types of benefits/services offered by the disability insurance

As mentioned, the main benefits offered by the disability scheme are the basic pension and the supplementary pension (ATP). For those with no or a low ATP there is a pension supplement (PTS). Other possible benefits are housing supplements, child supplements and car allowances as well as rehabilitation/reintegration measures.

1.2.1 Calculation of disability benefits

Within the Swedish social insurance system an accounting unit called *base amount* is used. Many of the benefits as well as pensionable income and so forth are calculated in terms of the base amount. It follows the CPI, i.e. the systems are inflation indexed.[4]

BASIC PENSION

The basic pension is a flat-rate, universal system; eligibility is based on citizenship or long-term residency. As explained above, the benefits are inflation-indexed by being tied to the base amount (B), which is adjusted as a function of the consumer price index (CPI). For a single pensioner the benefit is 0.9 (reduced) B. The reduced B is 98% of B. For married pensioners the benefit is 0.725 (reduced) B.[5]

Disability pensioners with low or no ATP receive a pension supplement (PTS). The maximum PTS is currently 111.5% of the base amount (since 1993 the reduced B). This supplement was introduced in 1976, for both old age and disability pensions. Originally, the supplement was the same for both categories, but after six months the supplement for disability pension was increased to twice that of old-age pensions. Since its introduction, the PTS has been increased 13 times. It is reduced krona by krona by the pension benefit received from ATP, i.e. the marginal effect is 100%.

The minimum pension for a single disability pensioner in 1997 was thus (0.9 x 0.98 x 36 300) + 1.115 x 0.98 x 36 300 = SEK 71 682 a year or SEK 5 974 a month + housing supplement.[6]

SUPPLEMENTARY PENSION (ATP)

The ATP is based on the loss of income principle, i.e. the benefit depends on previous income and work history. Pension-carrying income is earnings from work but also remuneration from social insurance, such as sickness, unemployment and parental leave benefits. To be eligible for an ATP disability pension the claimant has to have had pension-carrying income (earnings of at least 1B) during at least two of the four previous years. The benefit is calculated on the assumption that the person would have continued to obtain the same income. There is a floor and a ceiling on the benefit side (not on the contribution side) of 1B and 7.5B respectively.

Benefits from the ATP are 60% of the average income over the previous four years (or average of all, depending on which gives the highest benefit). The maximum pension benefit from ATP was SEK 141 600 in 1997. Together with the basic pension the maximum was SEK 173 600. The fee is paid on all income as a payroll tax (social security charges). The total pension fee, basic as well as ATP, and old age as well as disability, was 19.45% of the wage sum in 1985. In 1998 it totalled 20.18%; this includes a new own fee of 6.95%.

The disability benefit from the ATP is thus calculated *as if* (on the assumption that) the insured person had continued working until ordinary pension age. Thus, the benefit levels do not differ for persons becoming disabled at different ages, apart from growth effects (the benefits are indexed for inflation in relation to the base amount, not for growth) and career effects.

1.2.2 Some related benefits

The *housing supplement* is subject to a means test and is based on the housing costs. In 1997 approximately 60 000 women and 47 000 men out of approximately 422 000 disability pensioners, i.e. around one in four, received this housing supplement to their disability pension (RFV, 1999: 124). Some information on the scope is given in the table below.

Table 2: Housing supplements to disability pensions

	Average annual amount in SEK	Total Expenditure in millions SEK
1990	11 176	6 164
1995	17 401	10 440
1997	18 212	9 544

Source: RFV. Social Insurance Facts.

The *child supplement* is for dependent children under the age of 16. Since 1 January 1990 this benefit has been payable only to persons who were entitled to the benefit in December 1989. *Car allowance* was introduced on 1 October 1988. Handicapped persons (i.e. not only those with a disability pension) "who cannot move around without considerable difficulties" can get an allowance to purchase a car and to adapt it if necessary. There is also a transportation service for old and/or disabled persons, subsidized by the local municipality. Furthermore, disability pensioners under the age of 40 pay half of their hospital charges (the full fee is currently SEK 80 a day).

Rehabilitation/reintegration measures are also to be found, including a rehabilitation cash benefit when participating in occupational rehabilitation, purchase of work-related rehabilitation services; these programmes are intended for people who have not been granted a disability pension. Usually they concern persons on long-term sickness leave who are offered participation (or 'forced' to participate) in different kinds of rehabilitation programmes. Very often the local insurance board 'demands' that the insured person takes part in a rehabilitation programme before a disability pension is granted. There is no restriction on training in an occupation comparable with the one that the person used to have. If the programme fails, i.e. the insured person is not rehabilitated, he/she gets the disability pension. Since 1993 special cash benefits have been provided during the rehabilitation period. Until 1997 the rehabilitation benefit was higher than the one from the sickness insurance.

1.3 The connection between the disability pension system and other social insurance systems

A major principle in Swedish social insurance is the emphasis on work; this means that the systems linked to the disability system are also based on the loss of income principle.

SICKNESS INSURANCE

As mentioned earlier, the route to disability pension very often passes through long-term sickness. In 1995 for example, out of 45 000 persons who had been sick for more than 12 months, half were granted a disability pension.

At the lower end of the income scale, the remuneration from the disability system may be higher than that from the sickness insurance. This is due, among other things, to the extra, means-tested benefits tied to disability pensions. Of course, this also holds *a fortiori* for those who never entered the labour market or did so to a minor extent. For other income groups it would appear more profitable to stay on sickness leave rather than to transfer to disability pension. The sickness insurance has, however, undergone a number of changes. While benefits expanded during the 1980s, the opposite was the case during the 1990s. During the last decade there have been innumerable changes and reductions in the replacement rates for sickness insurance as well as the introduction of a waiting period of one day and of a sick-pay period. This has probably lessened the resistance to being transferred to a disability pension.

Unemployment insurance

Unemployment insurance is based on the loss of income principle; those who do not have a work record making them eligible for unemployment benefits are entitled to a special benefit equal to the lowest daily unemployment allowance. The maximum replacement rate was lowered during the 1990s from 90% to 75%. The lowest daily allowance is SEK 230, the highest SEK 564. There is a waiting period of five days. The maximum duration of unemployment benefit is normally 300 days, and 450 days for people in the 55-64 age group. When the unemployment period is ending, the employment office is obliged to offer the unemployed person public relief work, vocational training, etc. Participation in labour market programmes gives an entitlement to a new unemployment period.

It is possible to combine a disability pension with unemployment benefits as long as the sum does not exceed 100%. A number of factors decide whether the disability benefit or the unemployment benefit is the most favourable for the individual. The disability pension is based on historical earnings, which might have been earned many years earlier. These benefits are not indexed to growth, which of course means that a disability pensioner, especially one who becomes disabled early in life, falls behind everybody else including the unemployed. However, in the low-income brackets this has been partly allowed for by the numerous changes in PTS that have taken place since its introduction. In the short term, the waiting period reduces the benefits from unemployment insurance. According to SZW (1997), disability benefits in 1996 were higher than unemployment benefits in all income brackets.

The delineation of disability pensions and other forms of early retirement

The 'ordinary' pensionable age for both men and women is 65. There are various possibilities for early retirement; the average retirement age is thus lower than the ordinary one, although there is no reliable information on how much lower. In the early 1990s, the National Social Insurance Board reported figures on average retirement age. The calculations included retirement due to old age and disability pension, which gave an average retirement age of 59.2 in 1993 and 59.0 in 1994. The proportion of persons in the 60-64 age group obtaining benefits from the public sector due to old age is low, however: approximately 19% of women aged 64 and 10% of men of that age.

This puts emphasis on disability pension as an important route out of working life. In 1999 there were 39 600 new recipients of disability pensions. Of these 40% were in the 50-59 age group and 23% in the 60-64 age group. As seen in Table 4 below, approximately one-third of people aged 60 to 64 have a disability pension.

Old-age pension can be used for early retirement from 60 years of age (so-called 'advanced withdrawal'). The benefit will be lowered on an actuarial basis for the rest of the beneficiary's life. The withdrawal can be partial and combined with work, unemployment or disability pension. The sum must not, however, exceed 100%. Since 1976 there has also been the possibility of partial pension for those in the 60-64 age group, although the lower age has now been raised to 61. In order to be eligible, claimants have to have a certain work record and reduce their labour supply by a certain number of hours a week. The loss of income is partly replaced by the partial pension system. There have been a number of changes in the replacement rate: from 65% to 50%, then back again. From an individual's perspective, advanced withdrawal is an expensive way out of working life (see Kruse and Söderström, 1989). Accordingly, not many people make use of this possibility. In 1987 less than 4% of men and less than 3% of women aged between 60 and 64 used this form of early retirement. In 1996 these figures had increased to 6.5% and just over 3%, respectively (NOSOSKO, 1999). Partial pension has of course been more popular, see Table 3.

Table 3:   Partial pensions. Number in 1000s

		% of those eligible
1985	47	17
1990	38	15
1995	38	17
1997	14	7

Source: RFV. Social Insurance Facts.

2 Who gets a disability pension?

An increasing number of persons are becoming disability pensioners (see Table 1). This is also evident from Table 4, which shows the number of disability pensioners by sex and age as a percentage of the population. There has been an increase in all age groups. There is no clear-cut answer to the question why this is so: whether it is due to deteriorating health, increased demands on workers from the workplaces or something else. A salient feature is the increased risk of disability with age. In the youngest age brackets there is a fairly stable number of disability pensioners. This means, of course, that the increase falls almost exclusively on the elderly. Poor health, sickness and disability are to a very large extent a function of age. The percentage with a disability pension increases 10 to 12 times between the youngest and the oldest age groups. There is also a dramatic two- to three-fold increase in the disability rate from the middle-aged in the labour market (50 to 55 years) to the oldest age group. In the years before old-age retirement, approximately one-third of the population have a disability pension.

Table 4:   Disability pensioners by sex and age: percentage of population

	16-49	50-54	55-59	60-64
1975				
F	2.4	6.8	9.8	16.6
M	1.9	6.2	10.1	21.9
1990				
F	2.7	11.8	19.1	32.5
M	2.1	8.5	16.0	32.5
1995				
F	3.5	13.4	22.0	34.4
M	2.7	9.3	17.8	33.4
1998				
F	3.5	13.4	21.8	34.0
M	2.7	15.3	16.2	31.7

Source: Allmän försäkring. SOS, RFV, different years. Socialförsäkring, RFV, different years.

The disability risk as a function of age is also evident in Table 5 where newly-granted pensions are shown.

Table 5: Newly-granted disability pensions by sex and age per 1000 insured excluding disability pensioners

	16-29	30-49	50-59	60-64
1985				
F	1.3	4.5	21.1	55.2
M	1.4	3.4	21.0	78.3
1995				
F	1.3	6.0	19.1	35.0
M	1.1	4.0	16.7	41.5
1997				
F	1.4	5.6	16.6	44.9
M	1.3	3.6	13.2	60.4
1998				
F	1.6	5.6	15.6	26.4
M	1.5	3.6	12.5	28.8
1999				
F	1.7	6.4	18.1	32.4
M	1.6	4.0	13.3	30.9

Source: Allmän försäkring. SOS, RFV, different years. Socialförsäkring, RFV, different years.

Compared with most other countries, Sweden has a high labour-force participation rate in the older age groups. In 1996 Swedish men in the 55-64 age group had the fourth-highest labour-force participation rate among European OECD countries (after Iceland, Norway and Switzerland), and Swedish women the second-highest (after Iceland and on a par with Switzerland) (NOSOSKO, 1999: 11). In that year about 66% of men and 60% of women belonged to the labour force, compared, for example, with Germany, where the corresponding figures were 50% and 30%, or Italy with 42% and 15%. So, although there has been a steady decrease in labour-force participation among the elderly in Sweden and an increasing number of disability pensioners, the high participation rates are still puzzling and in need of explanation.[7] One major explanation is the general emphasis on work in all Swedish social security schemes. Instead of cash benefits, people are supposed to take part in vocational training and different kinds of labour market programmes. During this time they still belong to the labour market.

Also noticeable is the difference between men and women. In the beginning of the period there were fewer women than men with disability pensions. The increase, however, has been greater among women than among men, and during the 1990s more women than men were granted disability pensions, quite in line with a higher sick rate among women. However, women were granted a partial disability pension more frequently than men (see Table 6 and also Table 9). There is no simple explanation for this difference. Women obtained a disability pension more often than men on the diagnosis 'musculo-skeletal' disease, while men were more often diagnosed with 'cardiovascular diseases (see Table 6).

Table 6: Gender differences in newly-granted disability pensions, 1996

	Men	Women
Number, newly-granted	18 308	20 941
– of which full pension	67%	55%
musculo-skeletal disease	36%	49%
cardiovascular disease	16%	6%
psychiatric diseases, including drug abuse	22%	19%

Source: RFV (1998b).

It might be thought that the difference in frequency of part-time pensions is a form of discrimination against women, with their capacity for work being treated less leniently. However, investigations do not give strong support to this view (RFV, 1998b). One reason for the differences might be that the 'male' diseases are easy to diagnose, while the 'female' ones show more diffuse symptoms.

Not only are there differences between men and women in the frequency of disability pensions granted. There are also systematic regional differences, which are shown in Table 7. The southern part of Sweden (from Stockholm to Gotland in the list) has a much lower than average proportion of newly-granted disability pensions, while the opposite is true for the northern part (from Kopparberg/Dalarna to the end of the list). A couple of exceptions are Gothenburg, which used to be above the average, and Gotland, which has lately climbed above the average. Also worth mentioning is that in both Kopparberg/Dalarna and Västerbotten the proportion of newly-granted disability pensions has recently dropped and is approaching the average. There is still a marked difference between the northern and the southern parts of Sweden, however, and the difference remains even after adjusting for demographic differences and industrial structure (see Kruse, 1995).

Table 7: Newly-granted disability pensions in a sample of regions, per 1000 insured excluding those with a disability pension

	1986	1994	1997
Average	10.1	9.6	7.6
Stockholm	7.5	8.6	6.4
Gothenburg	11.2	12.8	5.5
Malmö county	9.9	7.7	7.5
Halland	9.0	7.9	6.1
Kronoberg	9.7	6.7	5.9
Gotland	7.4	8.7	9.0
Kopparberg/Dalarna	12.1	10.4	7.8
Jämtland	11.5	13.5	9.4
Västerbotten	11.4	15.5	8.1
Norrbotten	12.1	12.2	14.1

Source: SOS. RFV.

There is no information on disability pensions by socio-economic groups in the statistics from the National Board of Social insurance. Since we know that a disability pension is almost always preceded by a spell of sickness, however, we can use information on sickness incidence by socio-economic group as an indication of the incidence for disability pensions. This is shown in Figure 1.

Figure 1: Sick leave incidence by age and socio-economic group in 1998-1999

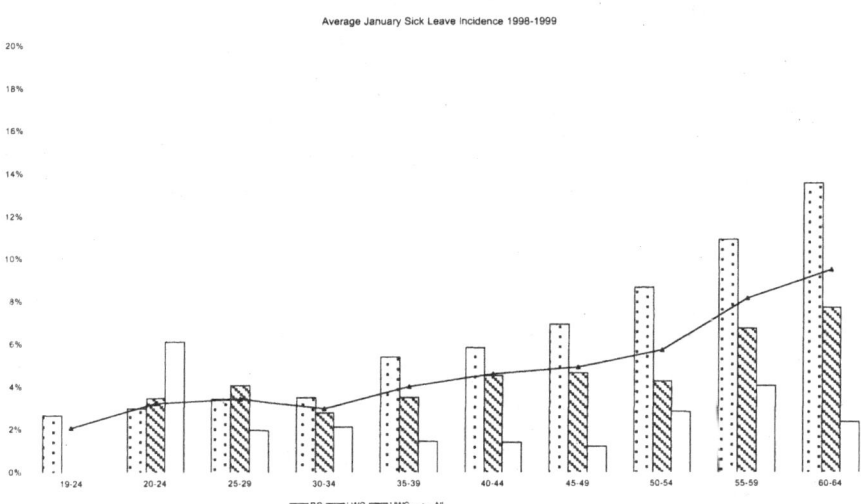

Note: BC is blue-collar workers, LWC lower white-collar workers and UWC upper white-collar workers.
Source: Edgerton et al. (2000). Based on data from Labour Force Surveys, Statistics Sweden.

We can see that apart from the youngest age groups, the risk of being on sick leave, and thus later on a disability pensioner, is much higher for blue-collar workers than for white-collar workers, and the risk is higher for lower white-collar than for upper.

There is no information in the official statistics on the frequency of disability pensions among immigrants compared with Swedish citizens either. In RFV (1996) the immigrants in the Swedish social security system are studied. Table 8 shows disability pensions by citizenship.

Foreign citizens are more likely to become disability pensioners than Swedes. The dispersion in the group is large, however. People from Latin America, Asia and Africa (except male North Africans) have a much lower disability frequency than the average.

The answer to the question "Who gets a disability pension?" is thus
- the older, the higher the risk,
- women more frequently than men,
- people living in the northern parts of Sweden,
- blue-collar workers more often than white-collar workers,

- foreigners, especially people from the Nordic countries and Southern Europe, but not those coming from distant parts of the world.

Table 8: Number of disability pensioners by citizenship. Percentage of the population aged 16-64. Age-standardized, 1994

Citizenship	Men	Women
Sweden	6.62	8.30
Other Nordic countries	11.34	12.33
of which Finland	14.09	13.69
Western Europe, USA	4.07	4.51
Eastern Europe	5.20	5.88
Southern Europe	9.28	10.61
of which Yugoslavia	15.98	20.42
Latin America	3.01	4.05
West Asia	2.45	2.68
North Africa	7.87	1.62
Rest of Africa	1.69	1.03
All with foreign citizenship	8.42	9.41
All	6.80	8.48

Source: RFV (1996).

3 Reforms and trends in the number of disability pensioners

Since the early 1970s there have been numerous changes in the rules of the disability system. During the 1970s and 1980s the changes were mostly in the direction of expansion: disability pensions became eligible for labour market reasons in the oldest age group and the pensionable age was lowered from 67 to 65 in 1976. At the same time a partial pension system was introduced. From the beginning of the 1990s the changes were in a restrictive direction. The most important changes are listed in the appendix. Table 9 shows the development of newly-granted disability pensions, where changes in rules are noticeable.

Table 9: Newly-granted disability pensions by sex. Total number in hundreds and per cent receiving a full pension

	Men total	of which full pension, %	Women total	of which full pension, %
1971	268	90	172	81
1975	258	90	197	81
1980	241	78	212	71
1985	262	82	248	77
1990	236	75	269	68
1992	283	74	301	64
1993*	304	73	321	61
1994	234	68	251	54
1995	186	65	206	53
1996	183	67	209	55
1997	200	73	212	60
1998	159	71	186	60
1999	176	71	219	61

Note: *) The levels 3/4 and 1/4 introduced.
Source: RFV (1998a), RFV (2000).

A couple of features in the table are worth commenting on. The decline in newly-granted disability pensions for men between 1975 and 1980 is most probably due to the lowered age in the old-age pension system. The female pattern does not follow the male one in these years. One reason may be that in the older age brackets female labour force participation was still relatively low but gradually increasing. As disability pensions are granted because of loss of work capacity, the incentive to apply for a disability pension is, of course, lower if you do not belong to the labour market and are not expected to support yourself in the first place. Also, the gradual decline in work capacity as a function of age seems to be harder to assess if housework is the only work performed.

The sharp increase in newly-granted disability pensions in the year 1993 and the sharp decrease in the years thereafter is due to increased efforts by employees in the local social insurance offices. As mentioned before, they were given the task of looking through the files on people on long-term sickness and trying either to put them in rehabilitation programmes or, if deemed impossible to reintegrate them into the labour market, to transfer them to disability pensions. In the decline of newly-granted disability pensions between 1997 and 1998 the increased emphasis on medical reasons and the abolishment of the 'elderly rules' show up.

The Swedish social insurance system as 'workfare' has been further accentuated lately. The emphasis on medical reasons when assessing sickness or disability is one indication. Another one is the introduction of new part-time levels. The purpose is to encourage/force people to keep in contact with the labour market. In the table above the number of newly-granted disability pensions is shown as well as the percentage granted in full. The systems are thus explicitly organized to facilitate the combination of part-time participation in the labour market with part-time retirement. If, however, a person has been granted a full disability pension, he or she is not allowed to work.

4 Reforms envisaged – discussion and conclusions

Sickness insurance, disability pensions and, to a certain extent, old-age pensions are insurances to protect against the risk of loss of work capacity and income.[8] It should be noted initially that work incapacity severely limits a person's economic circumstances. As people are risk-avert utility is increased if there is an insurance against the risk of disability. In Sweden, as in most other countries, both sickness and disability insurance are public and obligatory. There are good reasons for such a design. The information problems in the insurance market – hidden information about individual risks impossible for the insurer to assess – make a market solution either inefficient or unstable. Making the system obligatory eliminates this 'adverse' selection part of the information problem (Rothschild and Stiglitz, 1976; Barr, 1992). If the insurance is public and obligatory, it is also possible to use it as a means of redistribution, supporting 'weak people' often said to be a main objective with social insurance. A uniform insurance such as the Swedish disability system is redistributive, from low-risk to high-risk persons or activities. Such a system economizes on information, which may be difficult or costly to get. However, a uniform system may be costly in another way. Since there is no differentiation according to risk, prices are distorted and do not give correct information about true costs; high-risk activities will expand beyond the optimal level. It also tends to reduce the incentives to engage in prevention and risk-reducing activities. The number of 'weak people' referred to above will consequently increase. A uniform system might be viewed as solidarity with high-risk claimants, if it is not possible to influence the risk through behaviour or preventive activity. If it can be influenced, however, such a design causes inefficiency and economic loss. Thus, there is a trade-off between the pros and cons of a uniform system.

The insured event, work incapacity, is a state that is not always easy to observe for the insurance company. Also, it is seldom a 'none or all' state but rather a matter of degree. This asymmetric information, with some information hidden from the insurer, gives rise to the second problem of asymmetric information, the problem of moral hazard, which is one of the inherent problems in the insurance market. With moral hazard, the probability that the insured event (disability, injury) will occur is influenced by individual behaviour. There are two kinds of moral hazard: *ex ante* and *ex post*. Using sickness insurance as an example, *ex ante* moral hazard means that with an insurance the individual's incentives to engage in health care and prevention or to choose a low-risk job are lowered. *Ex post* moral hazard means that the incentive to use the insurance and to report sick with a less severe illness, is increased. In this case the remedy is not a public insurance; moral hazard is the same for both public and private systems. Instead, efficiency can be increased by mechanisms such as co-financing, for example qualifying days, replacement rates of less than 100% or control.

Within the sickness insurance scheme, reforms have been aimed at coping with the problem of moral hazard. Thus, the replacement rate has been reduced to less than its former 100%, and a qualifying day and sick-pay period (employers' period) have been introduced. The effects on sickness leave have been quite substantial (see Table 10).

These reforms also mean a partial individualization or privatization according to risk. An explicit aim was to affect incentives, and it is evident that at least in the time span of just under a decade the reforms in sickness insurance have had quite a pronounced effect.

The impact of the reforms is greatest on short-term sickness absence and may even cause an increase in long-term sickness spells. To cope with long-term sickness spells, the forerunner to a disability pension, the 'reforms' have increased emphasis on rehabilitation. Since 1992 there has been a law making rehabilitation the employer's responsibility. The responsibility for supervision and coordination rests with the local insurance board. So far, there have been no reliable evaluations of the cost-effectiveness of the rehabilitation programmes, for example, despite the fact that the resources invested in these programmes amount to just under SEK 10 billion, i.e. almost one-quarter of the expenditure on disability pensions.

Table 10: Sick leave incidence rate by sex and age, 1987-1999 (%)

Period	Sex	20-24	40-44	50-54	60-64	All
	Men	6.1	7.1	10.2	13.5	7.9
1987-91	Women	8.6	10.0	12.3	14.0	9.7
	All	7.3	8.6	11.3	13.7	8.8
	Men	4.2	5.2	7.5	12.1	5.8
1992-93	Women	4.8	8.2	10.2	16.9	8.0
	All	4.5	6.8	8.9	14.6	6.9
	Men	2.3	3.7	5.2	7.7	4.2
1994-97	Women	3.9	6.2	8.2	7.9	6.2
	All	3.1	5.0	6.8	7.8	5.2
	Men	2.7	2.9	3.8	9.9	3.6
1998-99	Women	3.9	6.2	7.5	9.2	5.9
	All	3.2	4.6	5.7	9.5	4.8

Source: Edgerton et al. (2000).

The figures showing large regional differences have led to a suspicion of severe moral hazard, even of abuse, with the employer and the employee or the employee's union together using social insurance to circumvent the laws in the labour market. Up to now, however, the reforms within the disability pension system have not increased the co-financing and not differentiated the premiums along the lines of high/low-risk firms, branches or regions according, for example, to experienced rates. Instead, the changes have been in the direction of tighter scrutiny. The aim has been to make a stricter examination before granting a disability pension, and granting it only on medical grounds. The last remnant of non-medical reasons was the 'elderly rules', which were abolished in 1997 (see appendix). The effect on the number of newly-granted disability pensions has been quite substantial, as is evident from Table 5.

New reforms within the disability pension are envisaged. Firstly, there is a need to reorganize the system, since disability pension used to be a part of the old-age pension system. As mentioned earlier, the Swedish parliament agreed in 1994 on a reformed old-age pension system, which was launched in 1999. However, the disability pension system was not reformed at the same time. The reformed old-age system is a defined contribution system instead of the former defined benefit design. The connection between contributions and benefits has been considerably tightened; exceptions are extra benefits paid for raising children and military service and a guarantee pension at the lower end of the income scale. One property in the reformed system is that there is no longer an ordinary retirement age. Instead, there is a flexible pensionable age from 60 upward. In accordance with the close connection between contributions and benefits, the pension benefit is determined in an actuarial way. Thus the workfare profile is further emphasized in the new system. The actuarial design means that the individual balances more (less) work and more (fewer) consumption possibilities in accordance with his/her preferences. A guarantee pension is not granted for early retirement pension but is calculated on the basis of the pension payable at age 65. The partial pension system will be abolished. We have seen that the majority of newly-granted disability pensioners are in the 60-64 age group. It will now be possible to retire in this age group using an old-age pension with a permanently reduced benefit level.[9] It will in many cases be a delicate task to distinguish between disability and 'natural old-age tiredness'. The unions of blue-collar workers have expressed their concern and disapproval about this part of the reformed pension system, as their members, having the highest incidence of disability, might come out badly.

The second reason behind the reform discussion stems from public budget concerns and the concern with an ageing population. The ageing problem is, of course, further increased if a large proportion of those of 'working age' retire in advance owing to disability. As mentioned earlier, despite increased longevity and despite the fact that people claim improved health in investigations and polls, the number of disability pensioners has more than doubled since the 1970s. So, keeping the workforce healthy and at work is seen as a means of preventing ageing.

In January 2000 a 'dormant disability pension' was introduced. From the individual's point of view, it is a risky step to try to re-enter into the labour market once a disability pension has been granted, which would mean putting a safe support at stake. Thus there are strong incentives not to try to re-enter. With the dormant disability pension the pensioner can try to work without risking his pension, i.e. without having to renew an application for a disability pension. So far the popularity of this reform has been limited. Instead of the 3500 pensioners who were expected to apply for a dormant pension, by August 2000 not even 500 had done so.

The disability pension system will no longer be a part of the old-age pension system. Instead, it will be integrated into sickness insurance. The Ministry of Health and Social Insurance has recently presented two reports on disability pensions, proposing some major changes (Ds 2000:39, Ds 2000:40). Again, the proposed changes stress workfare. It is proposed that the concept of disability pension should be abolished altogether. Instead, there will be 'activity insurance' for young people, 19 to 29 years of age[10] and sickness insurance for people in the 30 to 64 age group. This suggestion may be something more than a euphemism, as the intention is never to grant a permanent disability pension. Instead, the work incapacity is to be re-examined at certain intervals; it is proposed that the activity insurance for the young will be granted for a maximum of three years at a time. One line of argument is that medical and technical improvements make it impossible to know what kind of disability today will constitute a work incapacity tomorrow. The proposals are still under consideration but show the general direction being pursued in Sweden at the moment.

Notes

1   The reformed old-age pension system abandons this tradition. 13.5% of the system will be funded and both the funded and the pay-as-you-go parts are organized on a defined contribution basis (see Kruse, 1997).
2   As mentioned, there are also occupational schemes with fees and benefits negotiated between the parties in the labour market. There are four main contract areas: private blue collar, private white collar, state employees and local government employees. These are of minor importance in comparison with the social insurance schemes. Benefits are generally: 10% of income loss up to 7.5B, 60% between 7.5 and 20B (not for blue-collar workers) and 32.5% between 20 and 30B (B is base amount, see section 1.2.1). Occupational pensions are not included in the figures in the tables and will not be dealt with in this report. For further information on the occupational schemes, see Wadensjö (1997) and Edebalk et al. (1998).
3   The value of home production is treated on a par with earnings in the labour market.
4   The base amount, B, was SEK 6 000 in 1970, SEK 9 000 in 1975, SEK 13 900 in 1980, SEK 21 800 in 1985, SEK 29 700 in 1990, SEK 35 700 in 1995 and SEK 36 300 in 1997 (1 euro ≈ SEK 8.50).

5   The reduced base amount was introduced in 1993 as a means of narrowing the budget deficit during the economic crises in the 1990s.
6   For comparison it might be interesting to know that social assistance for a single person is around SEK 3 500 a month + housing supplement and that a student loan + grant is around SEK 60 000 a year.
7   This is stressed by Wadensjö, see for example Wadensjö (1996) and Wadensjö & Palmer (1996).
8   When the general pension system was introduced in Sweden in 1913, it was an invalidity insurance. For convenience, invalidity due to old age was supposed always to occur at the age of 67. In the 1970s the retirement age was reduced to 65 years of age. With the 1994 reformed old-age pension system there is no statutory age; the retirement age is flexible between 61 and 70 with benefits reduced or increased in an actuarial way.
9   This possibility also existed in the old system in the form of 'advanced withdrawal'. As there were other, subsidized retirement options, it was seldom used, see section 1.3.
10 It is proposed to raise the lower age of eligibility from today's 16 to 19. This is said to be a modernization, an adaptation to changing living conditions where almost all 18-year-olds are still at school being supported by their parents. Since the financial responsibility of parents has been extended, this factor should also be reflected in the treatment of disabled young people.

References

Barr, N. (1992) 'Economic theory and the welfare state: A survey and interpretation', *Journal of Economic Literature* XXX.
Ds (2000:39) Sjukskrivning i stället för förtidspension – Ersättning och ålderspensionsrätt vid långvarig eller varaktigt medicinskt grundad nedsättning av arbetsförmågan.
Ds (2000:40) Akrivitetsersättning. Nytt försäkringsstöd för unga med långvarig medicinskt grundad nedsättning av arbetsförmågan.
Edebalk, P-G./Ståhlberg, A-C./Wadensjö, E. (1998) *Socialförsäkringarna.* SNS.
Edgerton, D./Kruse, A./Wells, C. (2000) Designing an optimal sickness insurance. Some evidence from the Swedish experience. Paper presented at the ESPE meeting 2000 in Bonn. Forthcoming as a Working Paper, Dept. of Economics, Lund.
Kruse, A./Söderström, L. (1989) 'Early Retirement in Sweden', in Schmähl, W. (ed.), *Redefining the process of retirement.* Springer Verlag.
Kruse, A. (1995) 'Varför socialförsäkringar och vilken utformning?', in: *Ohälsoförsäkring och samhällsekonomi,* SOU 1995:59.
Kruse, A. (1997) 'Pension systems and reforms in Sweden', in: Augusztinovics, M. (ed.), *Pension systems and reforms in Britain, Hungary, Italy, Poland and Sweden.* PHARE-ACE project (EU) No. P95-2139-R.
NOSOSKO (1999) Förtida utträde från arbetslivet 1987–1996. En jämförelse mellan de nordiska ländera. Nordisk Socialstatistisk Komité, 10:1999.
Palme, M./Svensson, I. (1999) 'Social security, occupational pensions, and retirement in Sweden', in: Gruber, J./Wise, D. A. (eds.), *Social security and retirement around the world.* NBER.
RFV (National Social Insurance Board) (1996) *Invandrarna i socialförsäkringen.* RFV redovisar 1996:11.

RFV (1997) *Risk – frisk-faktorer – sjukskrivning och rehabilitering i Sverige* (Risk and health factors – sickness absenteeism and vocational rehabilitation in Sweden). A summary in English. RFV Redovisar 1997:6.
RFV (various years) *Social Insurance Facts*.
RFV (1998a) *RFV informerar*. Statistikinformation Is-I 1998:008.
RFV (1998b) *En socialförsäkring för kvinnor och män - en kartläggning ur ett genderperspektiv* (Social insurance for women and men – a survey from a gender perspective). RFV redovisar 1998:1.
RFV (1999) *Socialförsäkringsboken*.
RFV (2000) *RFV informerar*. Statistikinformation Is-I 2000:002.
Rothschild, M./Stiglitz, J. (1976) 'Equilibrium in competitive insurance markets: An essay on the economics of imperfect information', *Quarterly Journal of Economics* 90(4): 619-627.
SOS, RFV. Allmän försäkring. Socialförsäkring. Olika år.
SZW (1997) *Income benefits for early exit from the labour market in eight European countries. A comparative study*. Ministerie van Sociale Zaken en Werkgelegenheid. December 1997, No. 61.
Wadensjö, E. (1996) 'Gradual retirement in Sweden', in: Delsen/Reday-Mulvey (eds.), *Gradual retirement in the OECD countries*. Aldershot: Dartmouth.
Wadensjö, E. (1997) 'The welfare mix in pension provision in Sweden', in: Rein, M./Wadensjö, E. (1997), *Enterprise and the welfare state*. Edward Elgar.
Wadensjö, E./Palmer, E. (1996) *Curing the Dutch disease for a Swedish perspective*.

Appendix

72/07 Eligibility of older unemployed persons for disability pension when the period of unemployment benefit has expired (450 days).

74/01 Disability pension eligibility for labour market reasons in the 60-66 age groups.

76/07 Pensionable age changed from 67 to 65. Flexible pensionable age introduced: advanced and deferred withdrawal between 60 and 70 years of age. Double PTS to disability pensioners introduced. Partial pension introduced for 60-65 age group. Replacement rate 65%.

80/01 Partial pension also possible for persons working in their own business.

81/01 Replacement rate in partial pension down to 50%.

87/07 Replacement rate in partial pension 65%.

91/10 Abolishment of disability pension for labour market reasons. In a transitional phase the old rules will apply for those given notice to quit before 1990/01/01.

92/01 New law on rehabilitation. A person with reduced work capacity participating in vocational rehabilitation obtains a rehabilitation cash benefit of 100% of the insured income.

93/01 Introduction of the reduced base amount (B-2%).

93/04 Reduction of rehabilitation cash benefit to 95%.

93/07 Reduction of replacement rate at long-term sickness (more than 365 days) to 70%. Introduction of two new levels in the disability pension: 1/4 and 3/4.

94/07 Partial pension possible from the age of 61 (i.e. one year later than before). Maximum 10 hours are remunerated. Replacement rate reduced to 55%.

95/07 Basic pension part of the disability pension reduced by 6 points to 90%, with PTS increased at the same time.

95/10 The Social Insurance Board has the right to demand that the insured undergoes vocational examination or vocational training before being granted a disability pension.

97/01 Rules for granting a disability pension (as well as remuneration from sickness insurance) are made stricter. The medical reasons are further emphasized. The 'elderly rules' (less severe medical judgement in 60-64 age group) for granting disability pension are abolished.

99/01 Reformed old-age pension system initiated with the first benefits from the system being paid in year 2001.

00/01 'Dormant disability pension' introduced.

CHAPTER 13

The Particularities of Swiss Invalidity Insurance

Christopher Prinz and Bruno Nydegger Lory

1 Introduction

Until 1985, the situation in Switzerland was extremely favourable, with very high employment, unemployment rates below 1%, a high retirement age and very few people on disability benefits. The year 1985 was a turning point. While employment and retirement ages remained high, the number of people on unemployment and disability benefits started to rise. During the following decade, from 1985 to 1995, the percentage increase in the number of disability benefit recipients was greater than in most other Western European countries. Although disability prevalence is still comparatively low, the increase since 1985 has considerably raised awareness of the (working-age) disability issue and has led to extensive research efforts. And indeed, Switzerland is a particularly interesting case, as it differs from other European countries in many aspects – not only with regard to empirical trends.

In this chapter, we first describe the disability benefit system and its relationship with other, either complementary or competing, benefit schemes (section 2). We then discuss the empirical trends, with a particular focus on the 1985-1995 period (section 3). In the concluding part we first aim to identify the major causes of these trends and then summarize the main particularities of the Swiss system (section 4).

2 Invalidity insurance in context

2.1 Coverage and replacement rates

The Swiss disability benefit scheme is a two-pillar system, consisting of a public disability pension, the first pillar, and a mandatory occupational pension, the second pillar.[1] First and current legislation on public invalidity insurance (IV) dates back to 1960. Although the 1925 amendment of the 1874 constitution already mentioned that such insurance ought to be instituted, invalidity insurance in Switzerland was introduced at national level much later than in the rest of Europe.[2] The mandatory second pillar (BV) was introduced in 1985. The first pillar covers all persons domiciled in Switzerland or who are gainfully employed there. The occupational pension is mandatory for employees with annual earnings above CHF 24 120 (ceiling for the year 2000), voluntary for the self-employed, and, since 1997, also covers the unemployed.[3]

The aim of the public scheme is to provide a minimum subsistence level for everybody.[4] On the one hand, 50% of the expenses are financed through government revenues – three-quarters from the national government, and one-quarter from the regional governments (cantons). On the other hand, employers and employees finance the insurance with equal contribution rates (currently 0.7% of earnings each). Correspondingly, the self-employed have to contribute 1.4% (below annual incomes of CHF 48 300, the contribution rate varies between 0.754% [CHF 7800 income] and 1.328% [CHF 46 301 to 48 300]). Non-employed persons contribute between CHF 54 and CHF 1 400, depending on their assets. There is considerable redistribution in the system, due to the lack of a ceiling on the contribution side, but a comparatively low upper benefit limit equal to twice the minimum. As a result, the replacement rate from the first pillar alone reaches 100% for persons who receive the minimum pension (annual income of CHF 12 060). It declines to 63% for persons at the limit for mandatory second pillar insurance (CHF 24 120), and to 33% for persons earning three times this limit (CHF 72 360). This is also the level at which the maximum pension of CHF 2 010 a month is received. The combined pension of a couple (whether both are entitled to a disability benefit, or one partner has already reached retirement age and is thus entitled to an old-age pension, while the other partner is entitled to a disability benefit) is 150% of the maximum pension.

For a spouse without a disability or old-age pension, a 30% supplement is paid, plus 40% for each child under age 18 (age 25, if student), or 60% if both parents receive a pension. All benefits, including those from the second pillar, are adjusted every two years for changes in prices and wages.[5]

Disability benefits are paid from age 18 onwards. Persons who are invalid from birth, or become invalid before age 18, and other persons with less than one year of contribution to the invalidity insurance, receive a so-called 'extraordinary' benefit amounting to 133.33% of the minimum benefit. For persons with at least one contribution year but no current reference income, the benefit is calculated in relation to typical average age-specific income. If the person is not older than 25 years, the benefit is at least 133.33% of the minimum benefit. None of these groups qualify for a benefit from the second pillar, which is designed for the current labour force.

The second pillar was set up in order to secure the standard of living. Occupational pensions are financed without any government contribution. Contributions by the insured vary from 7 to 18%, depending on age and gender, and are paid on annual income between CHF 24 120 and CHF 72 360 (the contribution covers old age, widowhood and disability risks). Beyond this income, people are supposed to look for voluntary private pension arrangements. The employer's contribution to the occupational pension funds has to be at least equal to the total of the contributions of his employees (voluntary higher contributions are allowed and do often exist). Occupational pension funds are administered by registered occupational pension institutes (2 823 registered institutes in 1998). The annual benefit paid under this system in case of disability is 7.2% of the funds *that would be accumulated by retirement age* (for defined-benefit funds) or 7.2% of the funds accumulated at the time of disability (for the increasing number of defined-contribution funds).[6] The first and the second pillar taken together are designed to replace around 60% of pensionable earnings. Note, however, the subsidiary role of the occupational pension benefit. In the case of entitlements from the work injury programme (see further below for details), claims from the second pillar are not usually possible. In the case of work injuries, work accidents, occupational diseases and also non-work accidents, benefits from the work injury programme complement the benefit from the first pillar up to a certain level, thereby replacing payments from the second pillar. In other words, second pillar entitlements essentially arise from non-occupational diseases.

2.2 Definition of disability and type of benefits

Since the 1960s, the public invalidity insurance has pursued *four* aims:
(i) to integrate or reintegrate disabled persons into the labour market or their field of activity, including household work, through both medical and vocational rehabilitation measures on the principle of "integration before benefit payments",
(ii) to secure a minimum subsistence level by providing cash benefits in cases where integration or reintegration is impossible or has failed,
(iii) to subsidize institutions that support disabled people via medical and/or vocational rehabilitation programmes (both for infrastructure and operating costs), and
(iv) to offer assistance in carrying out a profession or work in the field of activity, but also in increasing mobility in general, regardless of the (residual) work capacity.

Rehabilitation

In order to achieve these aims, almost all disability-related obligations, and hence all expenditures, are concentrated in public invalidity insurance – including cash benefits, which are paid to individuals, and subsidies for medical and vocational rehabilitation, which are collectively paid to institutions. This makes for an efficient structure, avoiding unnecessary incentives to shift people between different insurance programmes or between different offices. For persons becoming disabled up to the age of 20, public invalidity insurance acts like a health care insurance regardless of work capacity. For insured persons older than 20 years, medical rehabilitation is only covered to the extent that it helps to reintegrate the person into the labour market, to keep the person in employment or to maintain the person's capacity to carry out his/her usual activity (e.g. housework). For these persons, the strictly medical treatment of the injury or disease itself is covered by the health care system.

Since the introduction of public invalidity insurance, the integration principle has been its central focus. Since mid-1999, the principle of non-discrimination of disabled persons has also been reflected in the new constitution (article 8, paragraph 2). All insured persons are entitled to suitable vocational rehabilitation measures, either in order to keep or to restore employability. There is no eligibility limit. Persons are entitled to vocational rehabilitation until successful reintegration, provided this is necessary to improve or maintain work capacity. First-time vocational education in particular often lasts three to four years. More than that, vocational rehabilitation is compulsory and ignoring a prescribed rehabilitation measure can lead to suspension or even withdrawal of the disability benefit. While enrolled in a rehabilitation programme, claimants receive a daily rehabilitation cash benefit (65% of last earnings), which usually exceeds the disability benefit. As a particular work incentive, after completion of vocational rehabilitation this daily benefit can be continued during a trial work period for up to 180 days. The main problem with vocational rehabilitation is that in practice such measures are only applied once a lasting or permanent reduction of the work capacity exists. Vocational rehabilitation during the first year of sickness is rare, which is also a consequence of the mandatory one-year waiting period before a disability benefit can be claimed.

Benefits

Entitlement to disability benefits requires a disability caused by physical or mental impairment leading to a permanent or long-lasting reduction of the work capacity. Reduction of work capacity is largely defined in economic rather than medical terms, thus referring to the earnings capacity after disablement relative to earnings before the onset of disability. With earnings capacity reduced by 40 to 49%, a claimant is entitled to a quarter benefit. With capacity reduced by 50 to 66.6%, a half benefit can be claimed, while a claimant with earnings capacity reduced by at least 66.7% qualifies for a full benefit. The adequacy and necessity of the quarter benefit has been under discussion ever since its introduction in 1988. In a referendum in mid-1999, however, 70% of the population voted against abolition of this benefit.[7] At present, though, entitlement to a benefit from the second pillar requires at least 50% earnings capacity reduction.[8]

In assessing the residual earnings capacity, only jobs commensurate to the applicant's personal situation, reintegration chances and the labour market can be considered ("Zumutbarkeit" or reasonableness). While in most countries protection of this sort has been abolished, a few countries still draw on strict (own) occupation assessment, which usually discriminates against low-skilled workers. In Switzerland, as a sort of intermediate position, the reasonableness of a job is interpreted in terms of earnings capacity rather than a specific occupation. Any job that provides an appropriate level of income would have to be accepted.[9] Furthermore, not the current labour market, that is the actual availability of jobs, but an abstract balanced labour market is used as reference. This is done with the aim of ensuring equal treatment of equal disabilities, irrespective of current economic conditions, and to distinguish between unemployment and disability policies (see also Murer, 1994). One and the same kind and extent of disablement should always lead to the same decision, i.e. entitlement or non-entitlement, be it during economic expansion or recession. In practice, however, this regulation is difficult to implement and gives rise to considerable discretion by the responsible invalidity offices.

Benefits can and are supposed to be combined with partial income up to the level of earnings before the onset of disability. Similarly, disability benefits can be combined with partial unemployment benefits. In most cases, disability benefits are de facto granted permanently, because a permanent and long-lasting reduction in earnings capacity is required. Repeated reviews of the health and disability status are not undertaken automatically, although such reviews are always possible either on request from the applicant or ex officio.

The system has one more particularity in the way in which benefit supplements for persons under age 45 are calculated. The income base for these persons is calculated by imputing an assumed career trajectory that a person would have followed had he or she not become disabled. Supplements to pensionable earnings gradually decline from 100% of annual income for a person younger than 23 years to 5% for a person between 39 and 45 years of age (Table 1). This means that persons who become disabled at a younger age are relatively better off in Switzerland than in other European countries, even if the effect is often not that large in absolute terms.[10]

With the exception of the introduction of the quarter benefit in 1988, the disability benefit scheme has remained largely unchanged since 1960. The forthcoming fourth revision of the invalidity insurance act ("4. IV Revision") continues this tendency, though it should bring in a number of cost-containment measures and various modifications. For instance, the 30% supplement for a spouse in the first pillar is going to be abolished for new benefit recipients. This is justified by the fact that today a large majority of new recipients also have entitlements from the second pillar. Furthermore, the "daily cash benefit" scheme during vocational rehabilitation will be replaced by a more transparent system.

Table 1: Supplements to pensionable earnings in per cent, by age at onset of the disability

Age at onset of disability	Supplement to pensionable earnings in %
<23	100
23	90
24	80
25	70
26	60
27	50
28-29	40
30-31	30
32-34	20
35-38	10
39-45	5
>45	0

Source: BSV.

2.3 Organizational decision structure

Swiss invalidity insurance is decentralized. Twenty-six largely autonomous cantonal invalidity offices ("IV-Stellen"), plus one office for insured persons living abroad, are responsible for the organization and implementation of the invalidity programme. The main rules for this programme are set down in the Invalidity Insurance Act, which came into force in January 1960, and a number of decrees on this matter ("Verordnungen über die Invalidenversicherung"). In addition, frequent binding directions and implementing regulations from the supervisory authority, the Federal Social Insurance Office (the BSV), regulate the work of the implementing authorities. Centralized supervision is matched by mostly centralized budgeting. The 'cantonalization' of the disability authorities was confirmed and further strengthened by law between 1992 and 1995, when a complex regional structure with several cantonal authorities was simplified through the introduction of a single office, which has to be contacted for all sorts of disability-related matters. This organizational restructuring has speeded up the decision process, and has also led to better transparency for the insured and to more harmonization between offices in different cantons (Wyss, 1999). A decentralized organizational structure means that decisions are made nearer to the people concerned and to the relevant labour markets. However, given the large discretion of the cantonal offices, it is difficult for the federal authority to exercise its supervisory responsibility.

The cantonal invalidity offices are also responsible for assessing the disability status. Until recently, and still so in many cases, medical reports by general practitioners and treating doctors form(ed) the basis for the benefit award decision. Increasingly though, invalidity offices are making use of their control function by involving additional medical experts. Such broadening of the decision basis is likely to continue, as Bachmann and Furrer (1999) discovered considerable problems in the current procedure. Treating doctors feel unable to make an appropriate decision because of the increasing relevance of psychological factors and the psycho-social environment, because of lacking knowledge of changing work requirements, and also because of unfamiliarity with the disability regulations. Also, it is expedient to use neutral medical personnel employed or authorized by the invalidity offices, since general practitioners would naturally give their patients' interests greater weight. This reduces problems resulting from knowledge deficits and from the discretion of individual doctors, but it also delays the decision process.[11]

The ultimate decision on a benefit award is made by interdisciplinary teams at the cantonal invalidity office. The teams are required to clearly justify their decision – also to make it possible for the federal authority to review cantonal decisions, which is done every third (before 2001, every fifth) year. Claimants must be given the possibility to inspect their file and to make a written or oral statement. Following an internal review in disputed cases, the final appellate jurisdiction lies with the Swiss insurance court.

The current situation is dissatisfying because decision processes not only differ between cantons, but also from case to case within the same cantonal office. A further expansion of the medical service at the invalidity offices, which was established in 1995 and which is responsible for involving additional medical experts in the case of unclear decisions or insufficient medical reports, is necessary. Because of the low prevalence of disabilities, until recently the Swiss invalidity insurance could afford a liberal interpretation of the law, but reducing the degrees of freedom is a major goal for the future.

2.4 Relationship with other social security programmes

The work injury programme

The aim of the work injury programme is to compensate the wage loss in cases of work injuries, work accidents and occupational diseases. With full invalidity, 80% of the insured wage (with a ceiling of annual earnings of CHF 106 800) is granted. This programme is operated like liability insurance and is therefore entirely funded by employers' contributions, which vary with risk (ranging from 0.04 to 17.2% of the payroll). As briefly mentioned above, in Switzerland the work injury programme has a very special position between the first and the second pillar of the invalidity programme. The work injury benefit complements the benefit from the first pillar, thereby superseding a possible benefit from the second pillar (if both benefits together exceed 90% of the insured wage, the work injury benefit will be reduced accordingly). One effect of this structure is that a certain part of the costs created by a work injury come under the social security system, because the public invalidity insurance has to provide a basic benefit if the criteria are met. While this implicitly reduces the costs of the work injury programme, the fact that this programme supersedes benefits from the second pillar is one of the three reasons explaining the high expenses of the work injury programme – which reached more than 1.5% of GDP in 1997, compared with an OECD average of 0.35%.

The second – and probably most important – explanation is that the work injury programme also includes mandatory insurance against non-work-related accidents or injuries, if the insured person works at least 8 (before 01/2000 at least 12) hours per week. For this insurance, the employee has to pay the entire contribution, although in practice employers sometimes share the costs for insurance against non-work accidents. Around one in two reported accidents and consequently almost half of the expenditure of the work injury insurance is not work-related. This unusual regulation becomes particularly complex in view of the fact that benefits from the second pillar, the occupational invalidity programme, are only paid subsidiary to benefits from the public invalidity and the work injury programme.[12]

A third reason for the unusually high work injury expenditure is the required low minimum level of disability. Between 1996 and 2001, permanent benefits could already be granted with a 1% reduction in work capacity. Since mid-2001, 10% work capacity reduction has been required, a minimum that was also informally applied until 1996. As a consequence, work injury benefits are de facto rather low on average, notwithstanding the high replacement rate in case of full disability. Three out of four of these benefits are paid to persons with a level of work incapacity below the minimum required for a benefit from the public invalidity insurance, which is 40%.

The interlocking of the work injury programme has another unusual side effect. In many cases, disability status has to be checked by both the work injury and the invalidity insurance. Using largely the same procedure and the same disability definition, albeit different minimum degrees of disability, work injury insurance providers can do their own medical assessment. Only since 2001, following an agreement between the invalidity insurance and the main semi-public work injury provider (SUVA) in 1998 and a decision of the Federal Insurance Court, must the assessment of the other authority – noting that usually the assessment from the work injury provider would come first – be taken into account.[13] Similarly, a reclassification in one insurance – following a requested or ex officio review of the disability status – has to be taken into account by the other insurance. If no objective differences exist, the two assessments should arrive at the same decision about the degree of disability.

Sickness cash benefits

Unlike most other European countries, Switzerland does not have a general mandatory sickness cash benefit programme. Minimum protection in the form of continued wage payment at a reduced rate – 80% of last wage – is guaranteed through special legislation ("Obligationenrecht"), although better solutions are found in many collective agreements. The length of this period varies with the years of service with the same employer, and can be as much as 180 days. These costs are covered by employers, who usually reinsure their risk with a private insurer. In addition, all persons between age 15 and 65 can voluntarily insure themselves against the risk of sickness with a private insurer or a recognized insurance fund.[14] For persons involved in gainful activity it is advisable to do so in particular in the first year(s) of service; during the first year, for instance, the period of continued wage payment is only three weeks. If private insurance is chosen, the amount of the daily allowance ("Taggeld") is set by agreement between the insurer and the insured person, but the replacement rate is also usually around 80% of the last wage. Unless agreed otherwise, benefits are payable after a three-day waiting period for up to 720 days within a period of 900 consecutive days.

Unfortunately, no data on the proportion of the labour force covered by such arrangements (voluntary insurance, with or without employer contribution) is available. Notwithstanding the lack of a mandatory sickness cash benefit programme, disability benefits are not awarded before a waiting period of one year after onset of the disabling condition.[15]

Unemployment insurance

The Swiss unemployment insurance scheme offers comparatively generous benefits. The replacement rate of the unemployment benefit is 80% of last earnings, if the insured person has dependent children, is disabled or earns a low income, and 70% in all other cases. Since 1995, benefits have been payable after a five-day waiting period. Since 1997, benefit duration has depended on age, with 150 days up to age 50, 250 days between ages 50 and 60, and 400 days over age 60. The duration is always 520 days – irrespective of age – for disability or work injury benefit recipients.[16] Within a period of two years ("Rahmenfrist"), the duration of the benefit can be extended with a relatively short period of earnings in between ("Zwischenverdienst"). After the two-year period, twelve insurance months within three years are required before a new entitlement can be created.

Unemployment insurance also offers partial benefits in case of partial unemployment, which can be combined with partial disability benefits. A direct transition from unemployment to disability benefit is possible after a one-year waiting period from the onset of the disability.

Early retirement

Again quite different from systems in other countries, the Swiss pension insurance does not offer a generous possibility for retirement before the statutory age, which is 65 years for men and 63 years for women (62 years before 2001, and 64 years from 2005). It is possible to retire at age 63 (men) or age 62 (women) with an actuarially reduced benefit (6.8% permanent reduction for each year), but this option is hardly used.[17] The consequence of this rigidity is a comparatively high activity rate among persons aged 55 to 64 – 81% among men and 64% among women in 1999 – and hence still a high average age at retirement.

Upon reaching retirement age, full disability benefits are transformed into old-age pensions, usually at the same level (but certainly not lower).

This must be seen in the context of the two-pillar pension scheme. Persons becoming disabled while still of working age are not able to contribute adequately (if at all) to their occupational pension. Disability benefits effectively paid beyond retirement age counteract such discrimination.

3 Empirical trends

3.1 Expenditures by the invalidity insurance

During the first 15 years after introduction of public invalidity insurance in 1960, real expenditure grew very rapidly, e.g. 12% annually between 1965 and 1975 (Table 2). After having reached a certain degree of maturity, expenditure increases slowed down to slightly above 3% annually between 1975 and 1990. Between 1990 and 1995, unexpectedly, parallel to a significant increase in the unemployment rate, annual expenditure on the public invalidity insurance again grew at a rate of more than 7% per year, or from just over four to almost seven billion francs – in nominal terms – within only five years. It was during this period that expenditure started to exceed contributions by a considerable amount. As a consequence, the invalidity insurance accumulated a deficit, which by 1997 had reached almost one-third of annual contributions – notwithstanding the fact that the rate at which expenditure increased had slowed down, although still remaining above the level for 1975 to 1990. This deficit caused concerns about the sustainability of the system and led to the setting up of an extensive research programme. By 1999, the deficit would have reached 50% of annual contributions but was reduced to 20% by means of a capital transfer from another social insurance scheme.

Table 2 also shows that public invalidity insurance covers a large range of disability-related costs. In 1999, cash benefits (disability pensions) made up only about 62% of the total costs – and this share has continuously declined over the last 30 years.[18] Expenditures for rehabilitation measures have developed in parallel with those for cash benefits; the growth rates for these two programme components have been similar during most of the period. Until 1995, there was a gradual shift from medical to vocational rehabilitation, although expenditure for medical rehabilitation still exceeds that for vocational rehabilitation. Altogether, in 1999 rehabilitation measures amounted to less than one-sixth of total costs. While cash benefits are paid only to working-age disabled persons, it should be emphasized that rehabilitation expenditure mostly benefits people below age 25 (most medical measures and all special training measures).[19] Only around one-fifth of to-

Table 2:   Expenditure by the public invalidity insurance 1965-1999

In mill. of Swiss francs (nominal)	1965	1975	1985	1990	1995	1999
Cash benefits	184	1065	1935	2606	4238	5199
Rehabilitation measures	64	319	505	702	1136	1273
of which medical	37	143	174	242	339	400
of which vocational	7	34	80	135	238	277
of which other	18	126	216	278	489	525
Subsidies to institutions	17	197	435	684	1197	1592
Administration and interest	11	50	112	141	256	261
Total	276	1631	2986	4133	6826	8362
In % of total expenditure	**1965**	**1975**	**1985**	**1990**	**1995**	**1999**
Cash benefits	66.6	65.3	64.8	63.1	62.1	62.2
Rehabilitation measures	23.3	19.6	16.9	17.0	16.6	15.2
of which medical	13.3	8.8	5.8	5.8	5.0	4.8
of which vocational	2.5	2.1	2.7	3.3	3.5	3.3
of which other	6.5	7.6	7.2	6.7	7.2	6.9
Subsidies to institutions	6.3	12.1	14.6	16.5	17.5	19.0
Administration and interest	3.8	3.1	3.7	3.4	3.7	3.1
Annual real growth in %		**1965-75**	**75-85**	**85-90**	**90-95**	**95-99**
Cash benefits		11.9	3.0	2.9	7.0	3.7
Rehabilitation measures		10.4	1.6	3.5	6.9	1.4
of which medical		8.0	-1.0	3.5	4.0	2.7
of which vocational		10.0	5.7	7.4	8.7	2.4
of which other		13.9	2.4	1.9	8.6	0.3
Subsidies to institutions		18.7	4.9	6.0	8.5	5.7
Administration and interest		9.8	5.1	1.5	9.2	-0.9
Total		12.1	3.1	3.4	7.3	3.6

Source: BSV (various years).

tal rehabilitation costs benefit people between ages 25 and 64. The third relevant expenditure category is subsidies to (private) institutions and organizations providing services to disabled people, some of which are directly linked to rehabilitation measures; these are subsidies to construction as well as to operating costs. In all periods, these costs have grown more rapidly than overall costs and accounted for 19% of the total in 1999. Again, a large proportion of these costs cannot be attributed to the working-age disabled. Although even an approximate estimate of this proportion is not possible, it is fair to conclude that cash benefits constitute at least three quarters of all expenditures targeted at disabled persons of working age.

Another aspect worth noting is the similar development of the growth rates for all expenditure categories, with generally much higher growth rates between 1990 and 1995 compared with the five years before and the two years afterwards. This would suggest that all disability-related expenditures are to be explained by the same underlying causes. It has not been just the increasing number of disability benefit recipients (see below) that has led to an explosion of public invalidity insurance expenditure.

3.2 Structure of disability benefit recipients

The number of disability benefit recipients has continuously increased from around 100 000 in 1980 to around 200 000 in 2000 (Table 3). Largely corresponding to changes in total expenditures, the increase was greatest in the 1990s. A comparison of growth rates in benefit recipients in Table 3 and in cash benefits in Table 2 sheds some light on the causes of expenditure trends. In the period 1986-90, most of the inflation-adjusted real increase in cash benefits could be explained by the increase in the number of disability benefit recipients. Between 1990 and 1995, when the number of benefit recipients grew even more rapidly than during the five years before, this increase still accounted for only two-thirds of the growth in expenditures. In this period, the benefit level per recipient must also have increased significantly. During the second half of the 1990s, there was again a strong similarity between the two growth rates, with the recipiency growth rate slightly exceeding the expenditure growth rate.

Table 3: Development of the number of disability benefit recipients, 1986-2000

	Age	Disability benefit recipients				Annual growth rate		
		1986	1990	1995	2000	1986-90	1990-95	1995-00
Women	20-34	8 450	9 541	11 020	11 991	3.0%	2.9%	1.7%
	35-44	8 974	10 284	13 265	17 985	3.4%	5.1%	6.1%
	45-54	13 841	16 431	21 554	27 421	4.3%	5.4%	4.8%
	55-59	10 503	11 708	13 824	17 698	2.7%	3.3%	4.9%
	60-61	5 202	5 407	6 156	7 343	1.0%	2.6%	3.5%
	20-61	46 970	53 371	65 819	82 438	3.2%	4.2%	4.5%
Men	20-34	9 675	11 249	13 428	14 183	3.8%	3.5%	1.1%
	35-44	8 814	10 437	14 327	20 389	4.2%	6.3%	7.1%
	45-54	14 418	16 648	22 532	29 777	3.6%	6.1%	5.6%
	55-59	13 681	14 756	17 290	21 564	1.9%	3.2%	4.4%
	60-64	23 021	23 145	26 054	27 770	0.1%	2.4%	1.3%
	20-64	69 609	76 235	93 631	113 683	2.3%	4.1%	3.9%
Total	20-61/64	116 579	129 606	159 450	196 121	2.6%	4.1%	4.1%

Source: BSV (various years). Note that these figures include only those pensions paid in Switzerland. Including pensions paid abroad would increase the total by about 20%.

Since the benefit system itself did not change significantly between 1990 and 1995, the increase in benefit levels per recipient can be explained only by two factors: (i) higher entitlements of new benefit recipients, and (ii) changes in the composition of the benefit recipient population. The gender distribution of the benefit recipient population remained constant: women constituted around 42% of all recipients over the whole period since 1980. The age distribution, on the other hand, changed. The number of recipients in the 35-54 age range increased most rapidly, and in the over-55 age group the increase was larger among the younger ones (there is little difference in this pattern between women and men). To what extent this 'rejuvenation' of the benefit recipient population could contribute to an increase in the average benefit per recipient is not so clear, though.

One factor that has strongly contributed to higher benefit averages is the increase in the proportion of full disability benefits (which require a degree of disability of at least 67%) from 71% in 1990 to 75% in 1998. Indeed, 85% of the increase in the number of benefit recipients between 1990 and

1998 was due to the increase in the number of full benefits (Table 4). Quarter benefits, with a disability degree between 40 and 49%, also increased very rapidly in relative terms (6.8% annual growth), but the absolute numbers still play a very minor role.

Table 4: Disability benefit recipients by degree of disability, 1990 and 1998

Degree of disability in %	Pattern in 1990 in %	Pattern in 1998 in %	Annual growth 1990-1998 average in %	Increase 1990-1998 absolute	Increase 1990-1998 % of total
40-49	2.8	3.4	6.8	2549	5%
50-66	26.2	21.8	1.8	5087	10%
67-100	71.0	74.8	4.8	42254	85%
Total	100.0	100.0	4.1	49890	100%

Source: BSV (various years).

Table 5: Disability benefit recipients by cause of disability, 1982-1997

Cause of disability	% distribution, women			% distribution, men		
	1982	1990	1997	1982	1990	1997
Congenital disabilities	23	21	16	16	16	13
Accidents	6	6	7	12	13	13
Diseases, of which	71	73	77	72	71	73
mental illness	20	26	32	15	21	26
rheumatic diseases	17	19	21	20	19	21
Cause of disability	Average annual growth		Increase 1982-1990		Increase 1990-1997	
	1982-90	1990-97	abs.	% of total	abs.	% of total
Total	2.5	4.6	23238	100%	49890	100%
Congenital disabilities	1.6	1.6	2842	12%	2785	6%
Accidents	3.6	5.6	3280	14%	6314	13%
Diseases, of which	2.5	5.1	17116	74%	40791	82%
mental illness	6.4	7.9	11989	52%	22094	44%
rheumatic diseases	2.9	6.1	5185	22%	13168	26%

Source: BSV (various years).

A further important structural change in the recipient population resulted from changes in the cause of disability. In the period 1982 to 1990, but more so between 1990 and 1997, the proportion of benefit recipients falling into the category "congenital disabilities" declined steadily among both women and men (Table 5, upper panel). In this group, the majority were young people with limited or even no contribution record and thus often minimum benefits. This decline was compensated by a corresponding increase in the proportion of disease-related disabilities. These were people with work records of varying length, who on average receive benefits above those of the former group, thereby raising the average benefit level.

The table shows that, indeed, 74% of the 1982-90 growth in the number of benefit recipients and even 82% of the 1990-97 growth was due to the increase in disease-related disabilities (Table 5, lower panel). Among these, mental illness grew by far most rapidly. By 1997, it already accounted for 32% of all recipients among women and 26% among men. In this category we might also expect to find a higher proportion of better-educated and also better-paid claimants with higher average entitlements.

3.3 Incidence and prevalence rates

Disability prevalence, which is the number of disability benefit recipients per 1000 people of the respective working-age group, increased slowly until 1990 and very rapidly during the 1990s (Table 6). Overall, there were 30 recipients per 1000 of the working-age population in 1986, and 45 per 1000 in 2000, roughly a 50% increase within only 14 years. Disability prevalence gradually increases with age, this increase being more pronounced among men than among women. In 2000, prevalence rates for women in the 55-59 age group, for instance, were five times higher than for women aged 20 to 34; for men they were even more than seven times higher.[20] Overall prevalence rates are still higher among men than among women, which is entirely due to the difference among those over age 55, but this difference is becoming smaller as a consequence of stabilization of rates for men at that age. Among both women and men, increases in prevalence rates were highest in the 35-44 age group, i.e. among people in their prime working age, and lowest among people over age 55. This is surprising because, in view of the general lack of generous early-retirement options in this country, stronger increases among people close to retirement ages would not have seemed unlikely.

Table 6. Disability prevalence rates by age and gender 1986-2000

	Age	Disability stock / risk population				Prevalence rates index (1986 = 100)			
		1986	1990	1995	2000	1986	1990	1995	2000
Women	20-34	11	12	14	18	100	104	127	156
	35-44	18	21	25	32	100	112	136	173
	45-54	35	38	44	54	100	110	125	155
	55-59	57	63	70	78	100	111	123	137
	60-61	74	78	83	96	100	105	112	130
	20-61	25	27	32	40	100	108	128	161
Men	20-34	13	13	16	20	100	100	128	154
	35-44	17	20	25	33	100	114	145	192
	45-54	37	38	44	57	100	104	121	155
	55-59	81	83	89	94	100	103	110	117
	60-64	152	152	151	153	100	100	99	101
	20-64	35	35	41	50	100	100	117	143
Total	20-61/64	30	31	37	45	100	103	122	151

Source: BSV (various years). Note that these figures include only those pensions paid in Switzerland.

Disability incidence rates measure the annual likelihood of becoming a benefit recipient; this is calculated from the ratio of new benefit recipients to the population potentially at risk to become benefit recipients. Such statistics on new benefit recipients are available only for 1999. In addition, estimates for the years 1985 and 1995 are available from Donini and Eschmann (1998). These estimations include all persons who were recipients in the beginning of year x + 1, but not in the beginning of year x. Overall, disability incidence grew from 4.3 per 1 000 in 1985 to 5.5 in 1995 and even 6.2 in 1999, an increase of more than 40% (Table 7). While incidence rates for men increased by only 17% from 1985 to 1995 and even declined thereafter, the rate for women increased more rapidly after 1995. By 1999, gender differences in the overall incidence rate had almost disappeared; below age 55, incidence rates are now higher among women, while the opposite holds for the population over age 55. This development is at least partly related to the increasing labour force participation of women.[21]

Table 7: Disability incidence rates by age and gender in 1999, and estimates from stock data for the years 1985 and 1995

	Age	Disability flow / risk population			Incidence rates index (1985=100)		
		1985	1995	1999	1985	1995	1999
Women	20-34			2.3			
	35-44			4.5			
	45-54			8.9			
	55-59			12.7			
	60-61			13.4			
	20-61	3.1	4.4	6.1	100	144	198
Men	20-34			2.3			
	35-44			4.0			
	45-54			7.3			
	55-59			13.0			
	60-64			17.3			
	20-64	5.5	6.4	6.2	100	117	113
Total	20-61/64	4.3	5.5	6.2	100	127	143

Sources: Donini and Eschmann 1998, BSV 2000.

3.4 Regional differences

The regional organizational structure of the public invalidity insurance programme has a number of advantages (e.g. better transparency and decisions nearer to the people concerned and to the labour markets relevant for them), and some disadvantages (need for the federal disability authority to exercise its supervisory responsibility). In any case, detailed data for each of the 26 Swiss cantons make very interesting regional analyses possible, which go beyond what can be done in most other European countries.

Table 8 shows that there is considerable variation in disability levels as well as increases in the number of disability benefit recipients between the cantons. Note that in this table the cantons are grouped into two clusters: the 19 predominately German-speaking cantons (group A), and the 7 pre-

Table 8: Disability benefit recipients per 1000 employed in 1995, and increase in the number of disability benefit recipients 1982-98, by canton

Canton	Disability benefit recipients per 1000 employed	Average annual percentage growth in the number of disability benefit recipients		
	1995	1982-1990	1990-1998	1982-1998
Zug	25	4.3%	5.5%	4.9%
Zürich	31	2.7%	4.6%	3.6%
Uri	35	-0.1%	2.1%	1.0%
Thurgau	36	3.3%	4.2%	3.8%
Nidwalden	36	3.6%	2.8%	3.2%
Graubünden	37	1.8%	2.8%	2.3%
Bern	38	0.8%	2.7%	1.7%
Schwyz	38	1.7%	3.8%	2.8%
Aargau	40	2.5%	4.3%	3.4%
Obwalden	40	1.7%	3.4%	2.5%
St. Gallen	41	2.9%	4.9%	3.9%
Schaffhausen	42	2.2%	4.8%	3.5%
Glarus	43	1.2%	3.1%	2.1%
Luzern	44	1.4%	4.1%	2.8%
Appenzell a.Rh.	45	0.8%	4.2%	2.5%
Appenzell i.Rh.	45	0.3%	0.7%	0.5%
Solothurn	46	1.0%	3.7%	2.4%
Basel-Stadt	48	3.6%	4.1%	3.8%
Basel-Landschaft	52	4.0%	5.4%	4.7%
Average group A	*40*	*2.1%*	*4.1%*	*3.1%*
Genève	43	6.2%	5.2%	5.7%
Vaud	52	3.3%	5.0%	4.2%
Valais	52	0.6%	3.3%	1.9%
Fribourg	53	1.1%	3.9%	2.5%
Neuchâtel	56	3.0%	2.7%	2.8%
Ticino	61	1.1%	4.2%	2.6%
Jura	64	3.0%	3.6%	3.3%
Average group B	*55*	*2.6%*	*4.3%*	*3.4%*
Unweighted average	**44**	**2.3%**	**4.1%**	**3.2%**

Source: BSV (various years).

dominately non-German-speaking cantons (group B). The average national disability level in 1995, in this case measured as the number of working-age disability benefit recipients per 1000 people employed, was 44 per 1000. The average in group A cantons was 10% below, the average in group B cantons almost 25% above the national average. In fact, with one exception, disability levels in the group B cantons, which also have significantly higher unemployment levels, were higher than in any of the group A cantons.

Increases in the number of benefit recipients over time also differed markedly between cantons. In this case, we do not find a systematic difference between the two clusters of cantons. Rather, we find very high increases in both groups. The three cantons with the highest percentage increases both in the 1982-90 and in the 1990-98 period were quite untypical ones: Zug, the canton with the lowest disability level in 1995; Basel-Landschaft, the canton with the highest level in cluster A; and Genève, the canton with the lowest level in cluster B.

Table 9 provides another example of regional variations. The first two columns give the ratio of the number of recipients of rehabilitation measures to the number of recipients of invalidity pensions, which is larger than one in all 26 cantons, and 2.4 on average both in 1991 and in 1997. Are there cantons that systematically offer one or the other type of measure or benefit? Since the aim of rehabilitation measures is to avoid benefit recipiency, the ratio between these two types of benefits/measures could lead to certain speculations. This question is particularly interesting because there is very little overlap in the number of benefit recipients – only a small minority of people receive both a pension and a rehabilitation measure within the same year.[22]

There are significant differences in this ratio among the 26 cantons. In all cantons, the ratio is very stable over time; with a few exceptions, the 1991 and 1997 ratios are almost identical. The recipient ratio is below the national average in all seven group B cantons – ranging from 1.3 in Genève to 2.3 in Jura, on average more than 20% below the national mean. With the exception of the very small canton Basel-Stadt, it is higher in all 19 group A cantons – ranging from 2.4 in Luzern to 3.4 in Thurgau. A plausible conclusion could be that cantons in cluster A have a higher rehabilitation measure/pension ratio (Table 9) and lower disability benefit recipiency (Table 8) because they have better labour market conditions with better work and reintegration possibilities for people with reduced working capacity. The consistency in the ratio over time would imply persistent differences in labour

Table 9: Ratio between recipients of rehabilitation measures and recipients of disability pensions 1991 and 1997, and annual percentage growth in the number of recipients of rehabilitation measures between 1991 and 1997, by canton

Cantons	Ratio of recipients of rehabilitation measures to recipients of disability pensions		Annual growth in the number of recipients of rehabilitation measures
	1991	1997	1991-97
Basel-Stadt	1.7	1.4	0.7
Luzern	2.4	2.4	5.7
Basel-Landschaft	2.4	2.4	6.6
Solothurn	2.5	2.4	4.9
Glarus	2.7	2.4	2.0
Bern	2.3	2.5	4.8
Zürich	2.6	2.5	5.4
Obwalden	2.7	2.6	3.5
Appenzell a.Rh.	2.8	2.6	3.1
St. Gallen	2.9	2.6	3.6
Zug	3.2	2.6	2.9
Graubünden	2.4	2.7	6.2
Aargau	2.6	2.7	6.7
Schwyz	2.9	2.7	3.1
Schaffhausen	2.6	2.8	7.1
Appenzell i.Rh.	2.2	2.9	8.3
Uri	3.0	3.1	3.9
Nidwalden	3.5	3.1	1.1
Thurgau	2.9	3.4	8.2
Average group A	*2.6*	*2.6*	*5.1*
Genève	1.4	1.3	5.7
Ticino	1.4	1.4	4.8
Neuchâtel	1.7	1.9	5.6
Vaud	2.1	2.1	5.7
Valois	2.1	2.1	4.2
Fribourg	2.2	2.3	6.7
Jura	2.3	2.3	5.3
Average group B	*1.9*	*1.9*	*5.5*
Unweighted average	**2.4**	**2.4**	**5.2**

Source: BSV (various years).

market conditions between the two clusters. Indeed, the high success of vocational rehabilitation found by Buri (2000) suggests that there is considerable selection for rehabilitation of cases with good integration potential – and better regional labour market conditions clearly increase this potential.

The last column in Table 9 shows that the percentage increase in the number of recipients of rehabilitation measures in the 1991-97 period was unrelated to the level of the rehabilitation measure/pension ratio. It also shows little relation to the growth in the number of disability benefit recipients during the same period (compare column 4 in Table 8).

4 Conclusions

4.1 Summary of Swiss particularities

The paper started out by claiming that the Swiss invalidity insurance and recent empirical trends are characterized by a number of aspects quite different from the situation in other countries. In conclusion, these particularities are summarized in the following.

- First of all, the *relationship between the different subsystems* providing benefits for disabled people is unusual. The two-pillar system de facto has three interacting components:
    (i) public mandatory invalidity insurance, the first pillar, a substantial part of which is government-funded, which guarantees a basic subsistence level;
    (ii) the mandatory occupational pension system (mandatory for employees covering annual earnings between CHF 24,120 and CHF 72,360), the second pillar, funded in equal shares by employers and employees, which should secure the standard of living; and
    (iii) work injury insurance, which – as far as occupational accidents, injuries and diseases are concerned – is entirely funded by the employer.

    While two-pillar disability pension schemes are still a minority in Europe, and also worldwide, reforms in some European countries seem to be moving in that direction. The peculiarity of the Swiss system is the interwoven character of the work injury programme. Work injury benefits complement the benefit from the first pillar in the case of work injuries, other injuries or occupational diseases, thereby superseding a possible benefit from the second pillar depending on the disability cause. This is even more interesting since insurance against non-work-related accidents is mandatory for employees with at least eight hours of gainful activity (in this case the insured person pays the entire contribution). Furthermore, disabled persons in need can claim means-tested supplementary benefits; this applies mainly to disabled persons with no work injury or second-pillar claim. As a result of this complex structure, which breaks the logic of a two-pillar system, various benefit combinations are possible. Persons with a disability can receive only the first (general disability of 40% or more), only the third (work injury under 40%), the first and the third (work injury over 40%), the first and the second (general disability of 50% or more), and even all three benefits (work injury plus general disability, e.g. due to non-work related accidents and mental diseases, over 50%) – combinations which very much differ in terms of benefit levels, and funding. For instance, employers finance about 25% of the first pillar, 50% of the second pillar, and 100% of the work injury programme, except for non-work accidents.

A very positive aspect, rather unusual in a European comparison, is the high concentration of disability tasks (and expenditures) in the first pillar, public invalidity insurance. Apart from securing benefits at a subsistence level for everybody, this programme is responsible for nearly all other tasks for persons with disabilities – in particular, medical and vocational rehabilitation – which eliminates inefficiencies caused by shifting responsibilities between different insurance bodies.

- Another peculiarity is the *administrative structure of the system*, which is fully decentralized in terms of organization and implementation (26 relatively autonomous cantonal invalidity offices), yet with centralized budgeting and supervisory responsibility. The 'cantonalization' of the invalidity offices, which was confirmed and further strengthened by law in 1992, is fundamental; this obviously improves transparency and permits decisions nearer to the people concerned and to the labour markets relevant for them. However, given the large discretion of the regional offices, it is difficult for the federal authority to exercise its supervisory responsibility. Standardized operational statistics for each of the cantonal offices, which are still being collected, will help to solve this structural dilemma. In this respect, uniformity in the decisions of cantonal authorities is an important issue; this was, for instance, also emphasized by the Swiss parliament, the Federal Council ("Bundesrat"), in its response to a parliamentary question (compare the Answer of the *Bundesrat* to the Interpellation Dormann 1998). The proposed introduction of regionally organized medical offices under the direct supervision of the Federal Social Insurance Office should contribute to a standardization of criteria used in everyday practice.[23] Nevertheless, detailed investigations into the organizational structures and the decision procedures in the 26 cantonal offices are indicated. Such explorations would aim at identifying *good practice*, which could then easily be taken over by other invalidity offices, thus contributing to overall efficiency and equity.

- A third particularity are the various *details in the disability recognition process*, which highlight the above-mentioned discretion for cantonal offices. Among these are the use of an economic disability definition and the comparatively low extent of central medical control. Worth mentioning are two interesting concepts, which are, however, difficult to implement with uniformity. The first is the *restricted (own) occupation assessment*. In each individual case, the proposed job must be verified for its 'reasonableness' relative to the person's remaining capacities – based on the achievable income rather than the type of job. Income assessment seems to be a reasonable compromise between a strict (own) occupation assessment and the complete abolition of such type of assessment. However, a certain amount of arbitrariness depending on the administrator in the invalidity office is probably unavoidable. The second unusual concept is the reference to a *theoretical balanced labour market*. The idea is to avoid the choice between the abstract approach (with no reference to the actual labour market at all), and the concrete one, which takes actual job vacancies into account. Rejection or award of a disability benefit should be independent of current economic conditions, be it a boom or a slump. Again, in practice it will be difficult to implement this regulation uniformly. While it seems desirable to keep these two uncommon concepts, it is of utmost importance to guarantee identical application all over Switzerland. A number of administrative federal instructions to the cantonal offices try to do so.

- The structure of the disability benefit population, notably the *age structure of disability benefit recipients* in Switzerland, is also unusual. Unlike many other European countries, disability benefits in this country are not merely used as an early-retirement instrument – which is all the more astonishing in view of the fact that basically no other early retirement benefit exists. A considerable proportion of benefit recipients are under 50 years of age. Likewise, the increase in disability incidence during the 1990s was higher among persons under 50. The good news is that, apparently, invalidity insurance does not push or pull workers out of the labour market as much as in other countries. In this context account should be taken of possible, though unknown, consequences for the invalidity insurance stemming from recently implemented changes in the old-age insurance scheme. Increased flexibility regarding the retirement age could contribute to a higher disability application rate among elderly, to the extent that invalidity insurance will offer higher benefits (i.e. without actuarial reduction). At the same time, reasons for the increasing disability incidence among the under-50s – much of it caused by mental illness – should be investigated. Until 1995, there appeared to be a correlation (though not necessarily a causal one) with the increasing unemployment rate, not least because of the discretion of regional invalidity offices. During the last few years, however, unemployment has declined while disability benefit prevalence and incidence has continued to increase, thereby possibly "hiding" higher rates of unemployment.[24] More detailed longitudinal analyses would be highly desirable.

- Finally, *disability statistics and data* are scarce and of limited quality. This is true to a certain extent for invalidity insurance because data on new benefit recipients has been available only since 1999. It is even more true, however, for the second pillar, the occupational pension scheme. For this programme, even basic data (e.g. on the stock of benefit recipients) is lacking. It is not known how many first-pillar disability benefit recipients also receive a second-pillar benefit, although the Federal Social Insurance Office estimated a figure of not more than 45% for 1998 (BSV, 2000: 15, fn. 19). For this reason, it is virtually impossible to study the effects of the relationship between the three interacting components empirically. Although setting up an adequate database is a longer-term project, the required, e.g. legal, basis should be provided as quickly as possible. Regarding the first pillar, major obstacles to the creation of a database on new benefit recipients have been removed recently (in a binding letter of recommendation, a 'Kreisschreiben', to

all cantonal invalidity offices). Regarding the second pillar, we should emphasize that the existing legal framework would have to be better exploited in terms of the needs of the first pillar, the invalidity insurance.
- Last but not least, Switzerland is quite atypical in a comparative European perspective because until today *major reforms* of the disability system *have not been enacted*, despite the rapid increase in disability prevalence since 1990. This is also true of regulations in complementary social security systems, such as the unemployment or the pension system, which could have had an impact on the disability scheme. Since the early 1980s, only two relevant changes have taken place. One is the introduction of a reduced partial benefit for persons with 40-49% work capacity in 1988 (in a referendum in 1999, the Swiss population rejected the plan to abolish this benefit). The other one is the change in the decentralized organizational structure, which started in 1992 and was completed in 1995. Apart from this, the two-pillar disability system has remained unchanged for the last two decades. Discussion on how to reduce the soaring deficit of the invalidity insurance, however, is becoming more intense. This concern has led to major research efforts into the reasons of the ongoing development, this book being one of the resulting products.
- Not only the disability benefit system but also some of the complementary, or competing, systems are very special. For instance, a generous early-retirement programme is lacking, and the sickness cash benefit system is voluntary. Such regulations might suggest an excessive use of the invalidity programme. To put it another way, a main question in the Swiss context is *why disability prevalence is still comparatively low in this country*.

4.2 Causes of recent trends

Both the answer to the question as to why disability prevalence in Switzerland is still comparatively low and the question of why disability prevalence has suddenly increased considerably since 1985 and even more so since 1990, seem to some extent be related to the development of the unemployment rate. Before 1985, Switzerland had a full employment economy with high rates of economic activity. All systems of social protection of the working-age population were characterized by low rates of utilization. After 1985, the unemployment rate started to increase from less than 1% to more than 2% in 1990 and around 4% in the 1993-1997 period. This incidence of unemployment, a hitherto unknown social problem, has – as low as the level might seem from an outside perspective – obviously revealed the impact of some of the peculiarities of Swiss invalidity insurance, such as the complexity of the system. Hence, while invalidity insurance itself has hardly changed during the last decades, the cost-driving elements of the system were not visible until the late-1980s. In other words, while an exogenous determinant, the increase in the unemployment rate, seems to have driven developments in invalidity insurance in the post-1985 period, endogenous determinants were responsible for the considerable increase in the disability prevalence rate (see also Aarts, de Jong and Prinz, 2000). A system with characteristics like the Swiss one can have very low prevalence only as long as unemployment is virtually absent – also because people with reduced work capacity are likely to be affected by rising unemployment first.[25]

Some of these determinants endogenous to the Swiss invalidity insurance that can be held responsible for the increase in disability prevalence are:

- The offering of partial disability benefits, which tends to encourage a larger group of people to apply for a benefit. Given the distribution of benefit recipients over disability groups, these partial benefits seem more relevant in Switzerland than in other European countries, even if during the 'disability boom' the proportion of partial benefits decreased. Also, the minimum percentage of disability required (40%, confirmed by a recent referendum) is relatively low in international comparison. Such 'disadvantages' of a partial benefit scheme must be weighed against the incentive to work part-time.
- The exceptional way in which benefit supplements for persons under age 45 are calculated, by which persons becoming disabled when they are young are relatively better off than older persons (a betterment which is unknown to systems in other European countries) – although such regulation seems justified for various reasons (seniority in wages, lacking or low second-pillar capital).
- The granting of benefits to people who have never been employed (e.g. housewives), or who have not contributed to the system (people invalid at birth or having become invalid before working age). Such systems automatically result in a larger benefit recipient population, but also provide more (minimum) security for the non-employed.

- The inherent complexity of the system, which is enhanced by two regulations. First, the degree of disability is determined by the residual earnings capacity relative to the earnings before the onset of disability (medical-economic definition of disability). Second, in assessing residual capacity only jobs that are commensurate with the applicant's personal situation, reintegration chances and the labour market can be considered. As to the latter, not the current labour market situation but an abstract balanced labour market is used as reference.
- This complexity and the still prevailing, though declining, responsibility of the general practitioner in determining the disability status give rise to a large degree of freedom on the side of the programme's gatekeepers at the cantonal invalidity offices. To the extent that general practitioners give their patients' interests greater weight than that of the programme, this poses a serious risk.

Similarly to most Western European countries, Swiss unemployment rates have declined in the last few years, reaching 3% by 1999 and less than 2% by the end of 2000. Disability incidence (only among women) and disability prevalence, on the contrary, have continued to increase. This does not necessarily conflict with the decisive role of unemployment developments in explaining disability benefit recipiency trends. The relationship between unemployment and disability is notoriously asymmetric: while increasing structural or cyclical unemployment is likely to drive disability prevalence upwards, a corresponding decline in unemployment will not automatically imply a decline in the number of disability benefit recipients. The latter figure is much less susceptible to economic fluctuations or cycles,[26] and much of the disability benefits are de facto permanent, even if procedures to review the benefit status exist. For this reason, any disability insurance should always try to attract as few unemployment cases as possible – which is unlikely to be achieved with a system with considerable discretion.

Apart from unemployment, the ageing of the working age population, increasing employment and activity rates of women and the changing approach to illness are, or seem to be, exogenous explanations for the increase in disability prevalence – in Switzerland as well as elsewhere. The ageing of the working age population accounted for some 25% of the increase in disability benefit recipiency during the 1990s for men and for some 15% of the increase for women. Increasing economic activity of women also had a certain effect, because full-time employment is de facto more likely to lead to benefit award than part-time or non-employment. The impact of the changing approach to illness is difficult to quantify. Several factors could explain the persistent increase in mental ill-health. Today, mental ill-health is less stigmatizing than it used to be. The observation of a steeply growing number of psychiatrists and psychotherapists may point to a new industry that has an interest in making their patients' mental health claims socially acceptable. Gatekeepers involved in adjudicating invalidity insurance claims may find it more difficult to assess the vocational consequences of mental ill-health than of other complaints. The traditional medical model, which underlies assessment procedures in invalidity insurance, may be less adequate as regards mental ill-health.

Some of the forces driving disability benefit recipiency, such as population ageing, are inescapable. Other problems may be reduced by reforms to some of the system's components, such as replacing the reduced earnings capacity by a reduced work capacity level (which could be successful only in combination with abolition of own occupation assessment). Clearly, several of the peculiarities of the Swiss invalidity insurance – such as total population coverage – have very positive effects in terms of adequacy and equity of benefit entitlements. To the extent that the particularities of the Swiss system are desirable elements that should not necessarily be removed, the higher disability benefit prevalence would have to be accepted as the disability recipiency level characteristic for a country in these socio-economic circumstances. Following this logic, the main reform need arises from reducing gatekeepers' discretion in the benefit claims and awards process.

Notes

1. In fact, the system consists of three interacting components, because the work injury insurance – which was introduced 40 years before invalidity insurance – is effectively embedded between these two pillars, and also because the work injury programme covers non-work accidents as well. This is explained in more detail further below, in particular in section 2.4.
2. In most countries, schemes to cover invalidity risks were instituted before 1940 and often even before 1914 (see Dixon and Hyde, 2000).
3. To be more precise: it is mandatory for earnings between CHF 24,120 and CHF 72,360 per year (this range is called "coordinated earnings"), while insurance beyond this earnings level is voluntary.
4. Benefit recipients in need who receive at least half of a disability benefit from the public scheme are entitled to supplementary benefits to the first pillar ("Ergänzungsleistung"). These supplementary benefits, which are not social insurance benefits, are financed by tax revenue. They are means-tested and granted on demand, making up the difference between income and expenditure (for rent, sickness insurance, nursing or other care and

other essential needs). Supplementary benefits to the first pillar are based on a federal law, but their enforcement is the responsibility of the cantons. The federal government contributes between 10 and 35% of the total expenditure, depending on the financial capabilities of the canton.

5   In the current discussion around the fourth revision, it is aimed to make an adjustment every three years.
6   In the current discussion around the fourth revision, the insurers demand a – mainly demographically caused – reduction of around 6.9%.
7   In the current discussion around the fourth revision, even the implementation of a three-quarter benefit – for degrees of invalidity of 60 to 69% – is more or less decided.
8   Currently, a revision is under review, according to which a quarter benefit from the second pillar will be introduced when earning capacity is reduced by 40 to 49%.
9   The unemployment insurance also uses the term reasonableness. In contrast to invalidity insurance, this is explicitly defined; all jobs paying 70% of previous earnings would have to be accepted.
10 These supplements are also meant to compensate for low cumulated capital in the second pillar.
11 Since 2001, four pilot projects with regional medical services (RMS) under the supervision of the Federal Social Insurance Office exist, where several cantons participate in each service. The main goals to be achieved with RMS are a more equal "unité de doctrine" and an acceleration of the medical assessments. The possibility to examine the insured person is an important element; until now, the medical staff of the cantonal invalidity office had to decide on the basis of medical reports.
12 In practice, complexity arises from the fact that the assessment needs to elucidate to what extent a disability is caused by an accident (which is covered by work injury insurance) and a disease (which is covered by occupational pension insurance).
13 The determined degree of disability can differ because the work injury programme covers work accidents, non-work accidents and occupational diseases but not general diseases such as mental illness. Until the final decision of the invalidity insurance, a temporary work injury benefit is granted.
14 Such private insurance is usually, though not necessarily, taken out together with equally private – but in this case mandatory – basic (and perhaps complementary) health insurance.
15 For a work injury claim, however, there is no mandatory waiting period.
16 Before 1997, the duration of the benefit used to be dependent on the length of insurance rather than age.
17 In the second pillar, the mandatory occupational scheme, retirement is possible at age 60/62, depending on the pension fund regulations.
18 Entitlements from the second pillar and from the work injury programme are not included in this table.
19 Note that people younger than 20 years are entitled to various medical and vocational and educational measures irrespective of their integration possibilities.
20 Note that, because of different legal retirement ages, the group of women over age 60 comprises only ages 60 to 61 rather than 60 to 64 among men.
21 It may seem surprising that in a system with full population coverage increasing activity rates have an impact on disability rates. To a certain extent this is explained by a higher likelihood of full-time employed workers to get awarded benefits (or, in other words, earnings capacity assessed to be reduced by at least 40%) as compared to inactive and in particular part-time employed persons – which are primarily women (see Baumann and Lauterburg, 2001).

22 Note, though, that only 45% of the recipients of rehabilitation measures were of working age.
23 Since January 2001, four pilot regional medical service projects have been in operation in several cantons. In these services, for the first time physicians from the disability authority are allowed to examine the benefit claimant. The forthcoming revision of the Invalidity Insurance Act will provide for definite implementation of these new services throughout the country.
24 In many countries, though not in Switzerland until now, a considerable part of disability benefit recipiency was identified as hidden unemployment – most notably in the Netherlands.
25 The fact that long-term unemployment spells do not automatically lead to disability (see Eschmann and Donini, 1995) does not refute this hypothesis.
26 The Netherlands, where a considerable decline in unemployment in the 1990s has led to surprisingly little change in disability prevalence, again are the best example of this asymmetric relationship.

References

Aarts, L./de Jong, Ph./Prinz, Ch. (2000) *Determinanten der Inanspruchnahme einer Invalidenrente*. Eine Literaturstudie. Forschungsbericht Nr. 10/00. Bern: BSV.

Bachmann, R./Furrer, C. (1999) *Die ärztliche Beurteilung und ihre Bedeutung im Entscheidverfahren über einen Rentenanspruch in der Eidg. Invalidenversicherung*. Forschungsbericht Nr. 6/99. Bern: BSV.

Baumann, K./Lauterburg, M. (2001) 'Gleichstellungsdefizite in der IV', *Soziale Sicherheit* (CHSS) 5/2001: 275-277.

Breitenmooser, B./Foffa, D./Guggisberg, K./Roullier, C./Donini, F./Nydegger Lory, B. (1999) '"Eingliederung vor Rente" – realisierbares Ziel oder bloss wohltönender Slogan?', *Soziale Sicherheit* (CHSS) 6/99: 1-11.

BSV (various years) *Invaliditätsstatistik*. Bern: Bundesamt für Sozialversicherung.

Buri, M. (2000) 'Wirksamkeit beruflicher Massnahmen der Invalidenversicherung', *Soziale Sicherheit* (CHSS) 6/2000: 327-330.

Dixon, J./Hyde, M. (2000) 'A Global Perspective on Social Security Programmes for Disabled People', *Disability and Society* 15 (5): 709-730.

Donini, F./Eschmann N. (1998) 'Anstieg der IV-Rentenbezüger: Erklärungsansätze', *Soziale Sicherheit* (CHSS) 4/1998: 202-207.

Dormann (1998) Zunahme der Rentenzusprachen in der Invalidenversicherung. *Interpellation* 98.3639 am 17.12.1998 und Antwort des Schweizer Bundesrates.

Eschmann, N./Donini F. (1995) 'Führt Arbeitslosigkeit zu Invalidität? Betrachtungen anhand statistischer Erhebungen', *Soziale Sicherheit* (CHSS) 6/1995: 321-324.

Murer, E. (1994) 'Arbeitslosigkeit – Invalidität: eine Abgrenzung', *Zeitschrift des Bernischen Juristenvereins* (ZBJV) Band 130: 185-214.

Prinz, Ch. (1999) *Invalidenversicherung: Europäische Entwicklungstendenzen zur Invalidität im Erwerbsalter*. Band 1 (Vergleichende Synthese). Forschungsbericht Nr. 7/99. Bern: BSV.

Wyss, F. (1999) Invalidenversicherung. Gesamtschau und Organisation. Mimeo. Bern: BSV.

List of Contributors

Leo Aarts, is Partner in Aarts, De Jong, Wilms & Goudriaan Public Economics (A.P.E. bv), a research and consultancy firm, The Hague

Emanuele Baldacci, Senior Statistician at the National Accounts Directorate of the Italian Statistical Office, Rome

Svenn-Åge Dahl, Researcher at the Foundation for Research in Economics and Business Administration (SNF), Bergen

Stanislawa Golinowska, Professor of Economics at the Jagiellonian University of Cracow and the Institute of Labour and Social Studies in Warsaw; Senior Researcher at CASE (Centre for Social and Economic Research), Warsaw

Raija Gould, Researcher in Social Policy at the Central Pension Security Institute, Helsinki

Hans-Tore Hansen, Associate Professor at the Department of Sociology, University of Bergen

Per H. Jensen, Associate Professor in Comparative Welfare State Studies at Aalborg University

Philip R. de Jong, is De Kruyff Professor of Economics and Social Security at the University of Amsterdam, and Partner in Aarts, De Jong, Wilms & Goudriaan Public Economics (A.P.E. bv), a research and consultancy firm, The Hague

Agneta Kruse, Senior Lecturer at the Department of Economics of the University of Lund

Bernd Marin, Executive Director of the European Centre for Social Welfare Policy and Research, Vienna

Bruno Nydegger Lory, Scientific Assistant at the Economics, Concepts and Research Unit of the Swiss Federal Social Insurance Office, Berne

Katarzyna Pietka, Economist at CASE (Centre for Social and Economic Research), Warsaw

Christopher Prinz, Project Co-ordinator at the OECD Social Policy Division, Paris, Research Associate at the European Centre for Social Welfare Policy and Research, Vienna

Gustavo De Santis, Professor of Demography at the Faculty of Political Science of the University of Messina

Tine Stanovnik, Associate Professor of Economics at the Faculty of Economics, and Senior Research Fellow at the Institute for Economic Research, Ljubljana

Cveto Ursic, Director of the Vocational Rehabilitation Centre, Institute for Rehabilitation, Ljubljana

Holger Viebrok, Research Fellow at the Department of Economics of the Centre for Social Policy Research, Bremen

Karl Wörister, Researcher in Social Policy at the Chamber of Labour, Vienna

Wohlfahrtspolitik und Sozialforschung
Herausgegeben vom Europäischen Zentrum Wien mit dem Campus Verlag, Frankfurt am Main/New York

Band 1: DE SWAAN, A. (1993)
Der sorgende Staat. Wohlfahrt, Gesundheit und Bildung in Europa und den USA der Neuzeit
345 Seiten, *vergriffen*

Band 2: KENIS, P., SCHNEIDER, V. (Hg.) (1996)
Organisation und Netzwerk.
Institutionelle Steuerung in Wirtschaft und Politik
566 Seiten, *vergriffen*

Band 3: FRIEDBERG, E. (1995)
Ordnung und Macht.
Dynamiken organisierten Handelns
419 Seiten, EUR 45,-

Band 4: CATTACIN, S. (1994)
Stadtentwicklungspolitik zwischen Demokratie und Komplexität.
Zur politischen Organisation der Stadtentwicklung: Florenz, Wien und Zürich im Vergleich
237 Seiten, EUR 34,90

Band 5: KRÄNZL-NAGL, R., RIEPL, B., WINTERSBERGER, H. (Hg.) (1998)
Kindheit in Gesellschaft und Politik.
Eine multidisziplinäre Analyse am Beispiel Österreichs
536 Seiten, EUR 51,-

Band 6: FEHÉR, F., HELLER, A. (1995)
Biopolitik
110 Seiten, EUR 29,90

Band 7: HELLER, A. (1995)
Ist die Moderne lebensfähig?
229 Seiten, EUR 24,90

Band 8: PRINZ, CH., MARIN, B. (1999)
Pensionsreformen.
Nachhaltiger Sozialumbau am Beispiel Österreichs
500 Seiten, EUR 45,-

Für Bestellungen: Campus Verlag, Postfach 90 02 63, D-60442 Frankfurt am Main.
Tel: (069) 97 65 16-0; Fax: (069) 97 65 16-
Internet: www@campus.de, info@campus.de, vertrieb@campus.de

Wohlfahrtspolitik und Sozialforschung
Herausgegeben vom Europäischen Zentrum Wien
mit dem Campus Verlag, Frankfurt am Main/New York

Band 9.1: DAVY, U. (Hg.) (2001)
Die Integration von Einwanderern.
Rechtliche Regelungen im europäischen Vergleich
1056 Seiten, EUR 69,-

Band 9.2: WALDRAUCH, H. (2001)
Die Integration von Einwanderern.
Ein Index der rechtlichen Diskriminierung
582 Seiten, EUR 51,-

Band 10: MARIN, B. (2000)
Antisemitismus ohne Antisemiten.
Autoritäre Vorurteile und Feindbilder
880 Seiten, EUR 51,-

Für Bestellungen: Campus Verlag, Postfach 90 02 63, D-60442 Frankfurt am Main.
Tel: (069) 97 65 16-0; Fax: (069) 97 65 16-
Internet: www@campus.de, info@campus.de, vertrieb@campus.de

Public Policy and Social Welfare
A Series Edited by the European Centre Vienna

vols. 1-10 with Campus Verlag/Westview Press, Frankfurt am Main/Boulder, Co.

Vol. 1:	EVERS, A., WINTERSBERGER, H. (Eds.) (1990; 2nd ed.) **Shifts in the Welfare Mix.** Their Impact on Work, Social Services and Welfare Policies pp. 412, *out-of-stock*
Vol. 2:	EVERS, A., FARRANT, W., TROJAN, A. (Eds.) (1990) **Healthy Public Policy at the Local Level** pp. 242, EUR 22,-
Vol. 3:	NOWOTNY, H. (1990) **In Search of Usable Knowledge.** Utilization Contexts and the Application of Knowledge pp. 166, EUR 22,-
Vol. 4:	MARIN, B. (Ed.) (1990) **Generalized Political Exchange.** Antagonistic Cooperation and Integrated Policy Circuits pp. 284, EUR 29,-
Vol. 5:	MARIN, B. (Ed.) (1990) **Governance and Generalized Exchange.** Self-Organizing Policy Networks in Action pp. 386, EUR 29,-
Vol. 6:	KRAAN, R. et al. (1991) **Care for the Elderly.** Significant Innovations in Three European Countries pp. 248, EUR 22,-
Vol. 7:	PESTOFF, V.A. (1991) **Between Markets and Politics.** Co-operatives in Sweden, pp. 244, EUR 22,-
Vol. 8:	KENIS, P. (1992) **The Social Construction of an Industry.** A World of Chemical Fibres, pp. 240, EUR 22,-
Vol. 9:	MARIN, B., MAYNTZ, R. (Eds.) (1991) **Policy Networks.** Empirical Evidence and Theoretical Considerations pp. 336, *to be ordered from Campus Verlag only*
Vol. 10:	FERGE, Z., KOLBERG, J. (Eds.) (1992) **Social Policy in a Changing Europe** pp. 316, EUR 29,-

Public Policy and Social Welfare Vols. 1–10
Orders: Publications Officer, European Centre, Berggasse 17, A-1090 Wien
Tel: (01) 319 45 05-27; Fax: (01) 319 45 05-19; Email: stamatiou@euro.centre.org

Public Policy and Social Welfare
A Series Edited by the European Centre Vienna

Vol. 11: *Child, J., Crozier, M., Mayntz, R. et al.* (1993) **Societal Change Between Market and Organization**, pp. 228, £27.50

Vol. 12: *Kriesi, H.* (1993) **Political Mobilization and Social Change**. The Dutch Case in Comparative Perspective, pp. 294, £27.50

Vol. 13: *Evers, A., Svetlik, I.* (Eds.) (1993) **Balancing Pluralism**. New Welfare Mixes in Care for the Elderly, pp. 316, £27.50

Vol. 14: *Qvortrup, J., Bardy, M., Sgritta, G., Wintersberger, H.* (Eds.) (1994) **Childhood Matters**. Social Theory, Practice and Politics, pp. 396, £29.50

Vol. 15: *Fehér, F., Heller, A.* (1994) **Biopolitics**, pp. 106, £23.50

Vol. 16: *Evers, A., Pijl, M., Ungerson, C.* (1994) **Payments for Care**. A Comparative Overview, pp. 350, £27.50

Vol. 17: *Bauböck, R.* (1994) **From Aliens to Citizens**. Redefining the Status of Immigrants in Europe, pp. 250, £27.50

Vol. 18: *Kenis, P., Marin, B.* (Eds.) (1997) **Managing AIDS**. Organizational Responses in Six European Countries, pp. 384, £30.50

Vol. 19: *Heller, A., Puntscher Riekmann, S.* (Eds.) (1995) **Biopolitics. The Politics of the Body, Race and Nature**, pp. 179, £27.50

Vol. 20: *Phillips, D., Berman, Y.* (1995) **Human Services in the Age of New Technology**. Harmonising Social Work and Computerization, pp. 151, £27.50

Vol. 21: *Bauböck, R., Heller, A., Zolberg, A.* (Eds.) (1996) **The Challenge of Diversity**. Integration and Pluralism in Societies of Immigration, pp. 280, £26.50

Vol. 22: *Evers, A., Haverinen, R., Leichsenring, K., Wistow, G.* (Eds.) (1997) **Developing Quality in Personal Social Services**. Concepts, Cases and Comments, pp. 312, £25.00

Vol. 23: *Bauböck, R., Rundell, J.* (Eds.) (1998) **Blurred Boundaries: Migration, Ethnicity, Citizenship**, pp. 356, £28.50

Vol. 24: *Marin, B., Meulders, D., Snower, D. J.* (Eds.) (2000) **Innovative Employment Initiatives**, pp. 558, £28.50

Vol. 25: *Stanovnik, T., Stropnik, N., Prinz, Ch.* (Eds.) (2000) **Economic Well-being for the Elderly**. A Comparison across Five European Countries, pp. 272, £26.00

Vol. 26: *Prinz, Ch.* (Ed.) (2003) **European Disability Pension Policies**. 11 Country Trends 1970-2002, pp. 430, £25.00

Vol. 27: *Kenis, P., Maas, F., Sobiech, R.* (Eds.) (2001) **Institutional Responses to Drug Demand in Central Europe**. An Analysis of Institutional Developments in the Czech Republic, Hungary, Poland and Slovenia, pp. 412, £27.50

For orders: www.ashgate.com